Communism, Anticommunism, and the CIO

Communism, Anticommunism, and the CIO

Harvey A. Levenstein

Contributions in American History, Number 91

GREENWOOD PRESS
Westport, Connecticut • London England

Library of Congress Cataloging in Publication Data

Levenstein, Harvey A   1938-
       Communism, anti-Communism, and the CIO.
       (Contributions in American history ; no. 91
ISSN 0084-9219)
       Bibliography: p.
       Includes index.
       1. Trade-unions and communism—United States—
History. 2. Congress of Industrial Organizations.
3. Socialism in the United States—History. I. Title.
HX544.L45   335.43′0973   80-787
ISBN 0-313-22072-7 (lib. bdg.)

Library of Congress Catalog Card Number: 80-787
ISBN: 0-313-22072-7
ISSN: 0084-9219

First published in 1981

Greenwood Press
A division of Congressional Information Service, Inc.
88 Post Road West, Westport, Connecticut 06881

Printed in the United States of America

10 9 8 7 6 5 4 3 2 1

For Lisa and Monica

CONTENTS

PREFACE

My study of this topic stemmed initially from my interest in the old question: "Why no socialism in the United States?" The labor movement and its relationship to socialism are clearly central to this question. Moreover, my research on American labor's foreign policy convinced me that one of the major reasons American unionists were able to embark on their dubious adventures abroad after World War II was because the left-wing opposition within the union movement lacked the strength to curb their anti-Communist excesses. Thus I wanted to explore the reasons for the absence of, if not a full-blown socialist labor movement, at least a left-wing ginger group alongside the more centrist unions.

Originally, my tendency was to search for answers to the question "Why no socialism?" among the deep-rooted forces in American history and society: such things as the divisive effects of immigration, race, and ethnicity, problems that Marxists have often blamed for impeding the development of class consciousness among American workers. I considered the Commons-Perlman emphasis on American workers' job consciousness, as opposed to class and political consciousness, and the Hartzian stress on the absence of a feudal stage in American history and the resulting consensus regarding Lockeian liberalism, and so on. But most models, even the most anti-Marxist, seem to accept a Marxist precept that may well be wrong: that in most advanced industrial societies, the natural condition of the working class will be one of growing class and socialist consciousness and that this will be reflected in the nature of the labor unions. This precept has formed the basis, it is assumed, for the socialist union movements and political parties that are so notable in Europe and so absent in the United States. The major emphasis has been on the deep-rooted factors that make the United States so unique, the theory that Communists labelled "American exceptionalism."[1]

I think that the postwar history of varied leftist unions and political parties in the advanced industrial world seriously undermines this approach. It is becoming apparent that union politics in various nations may directly reflect neither the level of working class consciousness nor the workers' inherent attraction to or repulsion from leftist ideas. Rather, more mundane political forces seem to have played major roles in determining the politics of labor movements across much of the world. Many of these forces are the product of a host of variables, of which the level of class and socialist consciousness of the working classes are only two. Often more important are such factors as the nature and structure of political systems and (from the point of view of most of these theories) *dei ex machina* such as the effects of war and foreign occupation. A recent study comparing American unionists' perceptions of unions with those of unionists in more radical and "political" unions in Argentina, Italy, and India seems to bear this out. The author found little difference in the members in terms of "job-consciousness" *versus* "political" consciousness. Adherence to *all* the unions, with their varying political stances, was based overwhelmingly on job-related issues.[2] I have become convinced that the absence of a major Socialist or Communist component in the American labor movement has less to do with the nature of the American working class than it does with historical accident. Had it not been for the events, many of them accidental, leading to the Bolshevik assumption of power in Russia in 1917, the leading left-wing socialist organization able to exploit the new labor organizing possibilities of the 1930s would not have been likely to be Leninist. Yet this fact played a major role in determining the fate of the left-wing of the American labor movement. The Leninist organizational form, as well as the Communists' connections with the Soviet Union, both of which were of dubious value to Communists in the labor movement, were important factors in dooming communism in that movement, especially when the cold war (itself not inevitable) made the Moscow connection a liability. There is little evidence that the presence or absence of high levels of class conscious-

1. A useful encyclopedic synopsis of most of the answers that have been given to this question may be found in Seymour Martin Lipset, "Why No Socialism in the United States?" in *Sources of Contemporary Radicalism*, ed. Seweryn Bialer and Sophia Sluzar (New York: Westview Press, 1977), pp. 31-149.

2. William H. Form, "Job Unionism vs. Industrial Unionism in Four Countries," in *The American Working Class in the 1980's*, ed. Irving Louis Horowitz, et al. (New Brunswick: Transaction Books, 1979).

ness, political alienation, or deep-rooted pro- or anti-socialist beliefs played dominant roles in determining the fate of the Communists.

Theories that emphasize deep-rooted explanations stumble upon a major block in explaining the politics of the labor movement: ultimately, they view the overall political stance of labor organizations as reflections of the political beliefs of the membership. Presumably "job consciousness" and an emphasis on bread-and-butter gains indicate support for capitalism and opposition or indifference to socialism. Yet the substantial body of evidence that union leaders have relatively little effect on the political behavior of their members would indicate that most union members make a bifurcation between their attitudes toward their own unions and unions in general. Indeed, recent polls indicate that even in Britain, which supposedly has the most class conscious and "bloody-minded" working class of all, close to half of the union members think that British unions wield too much power. The key role these unions played in supporting the "moderate," if not conservative policies of the Labour party in the 1970s also raises doubts about theories which link high levels of class consciousness with political radicalism.

However, if one considers that the absence of a leftist union movement is not inevitable in the United States, neither can one delude oneself into thinking that its presence would have indicated a working class attracted to socialism. The major political effect would have been not a massive outpouring of working class support for the kind of socialist party the American political system makes almost inconceivable, but a substantial leftward shift in the center of gravity of American politics, as leftist unions added their financial and manpower support to the American political equation.

Much of the research for this study was financed by the Canada Council and its successor agency, the Social Sciences and Humanities Research Council of Canada. McMaster University's Arts Research Board also helped defray research travel expenses and the McMaster Faculty of Humanities helped meet the cost of typing. My thanks to all of them. Two years at the Centre for the Study of Social History of the University of Warwick, first as a visiting lecturer and then as a visiting fellow, during which much of the writing and rewriting of the manuscript took place, exposed me to much that significantly altered my ideas, not just about this book, but about labor and social history in general. This is not to say, however, that Royden Harrison or anyone else there is at all to blame for what follows. Neither is David Shannon of the University of Virginia, who provided encouragement when it was most needed. So did many colleague-friends at McMaster, especially those who bought me drinks at the Faculty Club bar when *they* were most needed. I cannot begin to list the things I would like to thank Mona for, so, as usual, I will not even try.

Permission to use oral history memoirs from the Columbia University Oral History Collection, the oral history collections of the Wayne State University Archives of Labor History and Urban Affairs and the Pennsylvania State University Archives of Labor History is gratefully acknowledged. The following memoirs from the Columbia collection, all copyrighted by the Trustees of Columbia University in the City of New York, and each carrying the date of its copyright, have been used: John Brophy, 1972, Earl Browder, 1975, James Carey, 1975, Julius Emspak, 1972, John P. Frey, 1975, Edwin A. Lahey, 1972, Frances Perkins, 1976, Jacob Potofsky, 1975, and Lee Pressman, 1975.

Hamilton, Ontario, Canada and Warwick, England, 1979

Communism, Anticommunism, and the CIO

1 THE COMMUNIST PARTY AND AMERICAN LABOR, 1919-1935

The news from Moscow in the autumn of 1935 was not unexpected. The Communist International was recognizing what the Great Depression had wrought in the world. Rather than Communist revolution, it had brought an upsurge of fascism. The very existence of socialism as an example for the rest of the world was now endangered by the emergence of an aggressive, fanatically anti-Soviet government in Germany and the rise of governments and movements sympathetic to it throughout the world. At an international congress of the world's Communist parties in Moscow, the Communist International therefore announced a change in the party "line." Consequently, Communists would concentrate their energies on heading off the Fascist threat. They would cooperate with all sincere anti-Fascists, including liberals and social democrats, to create "people's fronts," broad political coalitions to head off fascism. In order to create these coalitions the Communists would have to abandon their struggle for the immediate overthrow of every capitalist government. Instead, where necessary, the dream of a Communist-led dictatorship of the proletariat would be put on the back burner. Communists would support programs of democratic reform more congenial to their nonrevolutionary partners.

For Communist trade unionists, especially in North America, the change in line did not involve a totally new pattern of action, at least for those few comparative old-timers who had been in the movement for over six years. In fact, in the unions, it amounted to the abandonment of the relatively recent course inaugurated during the so-called "Third Period," the extremely sectarian radical phase begun in 1928 and 1929 in reponse to the Communist International's conviction that the collapse of international capitalism was imminent. Then, Communist unionists were ordered to prepare for the takeover of power by creating Communist unions, organized along Bolshevik lines, to serve as the vanguard of the proletariat when the revolutionary moment arrived. In the United States this meant the creation of unions that would compete directly with those of the American Federation of Labor (AFL).

But the "Third Period" itself had meant a return to the original stance of American Communists, for the Communist party of the United States had been created by leftists of varying tendencies attracted by the hope that the Bolsheviks had somehow found a shortcut to revolution. The older Socialist party of America, already riven by American entry into World War I, and reeling from government persecution for its anti-interventionist stance, had supplied many of the initial supporters of the new revolutionary movement. The syndicalist Industrial Workers of the World, virtually driven into oblivion by government repression, but still a haven for impatient souls attracted by its espousal of "direct action," had produced its share of recruits, as had the remnants of Daniel De Leon's Socialist Labor party, perhaps the most authentically Marxist of the American leftist organizations. So had various other leftist sects, especially in the New York and Chicago areas.

When the Communist International was formed in 1919, two American Communist parties, comprised of defectors from the Socialist Party of America, responded to its call. The adherents of the sect that first appropriated the Communist party (CP) label were overwhelmingly foreign-born. A rival Communist Labor party, formed within days of the CP in September 1919, was dominated by American-born radicals, including that idol of the American Left, John Reed.[1]

There were a number of differences between the two groups, but on the trade union question, both pursued similar policies. Both inherited from the left wing of the Socialist party an aversion to working within the conservative AFL, and favored the creation of authentic left-wing unions rather than the takeover of AFL unions from within. The two differed mainly on the question of the Industrial Workers of the World (IWW). The CP was generally more critical of it than the Communist Labor party, which tried to woo it into the fold.[2]

But, as often happens with small sectarian groups, the labor policies of both parties were more fantasy than fact. As the Communist leader Charles Ruthenberg later stated, "It would have been difficult to gather a half-dozen delegates who knew anything about the trade union movement" at the founding conventions of both parties.[3]

The great wave of strikes and labor agitation in 1919 passed by with both parties playing minimal roles. No unions or strikes were radical enough to warrant their support. Instead, they exhorted striking workers to abandon their trade unionist goals and to convert their economic strikes into political efforts directed at the overthrow of the bourgeois state.[4]

The Comintern could abide two feuding little sects in the world's greatest capitalist power for only so long. In May 1921, it forced the two to merge, and the Communist Party of America was formed. The merger was consummated at a time when the international Communist line was on the verge of changing. The expected wave of Communist takeovers in the advanced capitalist countries had not materialized. The Soviets, plagued by civil war and economic dislocation at home, could no longer look abroad, to Germany especially, for aid from friendly socialist governments. In the United States, the party had been driven underground by the Palmer raids and a wave of government terror. Its influence in the most crucial sector, among the working class, was almost nil. Lenin's condemnation of leftist sectarianism in his pamphlet *Left-wing Communism: An Infantile Disorder*, published in late 1920, struck a responsive chord among many ex-Socialists in both parties, who were fearful of treading the IWW path into oblivion.[5] At its founding convention in Woodstock, New York, the new party decided to abandon its sectarian trade union line. While reaffirming that the party itself would remain underground, illegal, and committed to the armed overthrow of the capitalist state, it backed off from the excesses of dual unionism. Revolutionary elements were to stay within their existing unions and not desert them for new unions. They should fight expulsions and not encourage splits because of "some remote revolutionary aim."[6]

This major departure was reinforced the next month at the meeting of the Third Congress of the Communist International in Moscow, which ordered all Communist parties to go even further along this path. Communist unionists were urged to abandon the sectarian dream of forming small, tightly-knit revolutionary unions in favor of a policy of gradually winning the great mass of workers to their side by working within existing trade unions and labor federations. For American Communists, it meant the end of their ambivalent courtship of the IWW and the beginning of an affair with the detested AFL.[7]

The rejection of dual unionism was confirmed at the first congress of the Red International of Trade Unions, held as the Comintern congress was winding down. The new "Profintern," as it was called after its Russian name, specifically ordered that "revolutionary cells and groups" be created within the AFL. "There is no other way by which one can gain the working mass in America than to lead a systematic struggle within the unions," it said.[8]

Many years of left-wing Socialist hostility to the AFL and two years of futile underground bickering and government persecution gave the party few roots to cultivate in the AFL. So desperate were they for anyone who knew anything about AFL unionism that they made Earl Browder, a Kansas City ex-Populist, ex-Socialist, ex-syndicalist who while working as an accountant in 1912 had become active in the AFL office workers union, an honorary charter member mainly because he had served on the Kansas City AFL council and was a delegate to the 1916 AFL convention. In large part because of his AFL experience and connections, Browder was elevated to the second rank of the party leadership almost immediately. He organized the AFL union segment of the American delegation to the first Profintern Congress and functioned as a kind of unofficial leader of the delegation.[9]

However, the big catch was not hooked until that congress. William Z. Foster was one of the most famous labor leaders in America. A tough, up-from-the-working-classes descendant of poor English and Irish from New England, he had made a name for himself as a syndicalist who had rejected the IWW for the AFL. Convinced that the road to Socialist revolution lay through the organization of increasing numbers of workers into trade unions, he had led a brilliant successful strike of Chicago packinghouse workers in 1917. So great was the instant legend that developed about him that Samuel Gompers was persuaded to swallow his suspicions of Foster's radicalism and appoint him to head the massive organizing campaign that led to the Great Steel Strike of 1919-1920, the largest industrial action in American labor history up to that time. Foster, still the reluctant bride, had agreed to attend the Profintern Congress as an "observer." Impressed by what he saw, he joined the Communist party upon his return.

Foster had organized a band of his followers into the Trade Union Educational League, whose mission it was to stimulate militant, radical, industrial unionism within existing unions. As part of the bait in recruiting him, the Profintern agreed to make the TUEL the labor section of the Communist party. Foster's membership in the party was kept secret until 1923 but, in an unusual arrangement, Communist trade union activity was run by him, almost independently, from TUEL headquarters in Chicago. Browder, the other trade union expert, was assigned to Foster's command post but, after difficulties arose between New York, the political headquarters, and Chicago, the labor headquarters, he functioned as a liaison between the two.[10] His party membership still secret, Foster was appointed secretary of the Red International Committee, which functioned as the American branch of what was now called the Red International of Labor Unions (RILU), comprising various small independent unions.[11]

Foster was not parachuted into Communist labor leadership without controversy. Some small Communist union locals among food, metal, and public service workers, already affiliated with RILU through the United Labor Council of America, a New York-centered organization whose membership also included representatives from Communist minorities in some AFL unions in the New York area, protested to the Profintern Foster's claims to dominance of Communist labor unionism. Moscow responded by ordering that the activities of both groups, the IWW (which was still being wooed) and the Communists in other independent unions be coordinated through a joint Council of Action.[12] But when, after some delay, the Council of Action was finally formed in June 1923, Foster's opponents were again confounded, for Foster was named chairman. The Council, changing its name to the Red International Committee, served as another vehicle for extending Foster's influence over Communist trade unionism.[13]

Nonetheless, Foster's heart remained with his baby, the TUEL. As banner carrier for the new Communist line of working within the existing trade union movement, the TUEL proclaimed itself the enemy of "obsolete craft unionism" and the "pitiful conservatism" of Samuel Gompers and the conservative clique who ran the AFL. It lamented that the other industrial giants, England and Germany, were much more highly unionized than the United States and demanded massive campaigns to organize the unorganized into huge industry-based unions. Part of the reason for the "vigor elsewhere; stagnation here," said its opening manifesto in 1922, was that "for fully thirty years" radicals had "systematically deserted and neglected the trade unions. Afflicted with chronic secessionism, they have attracted the overwhelming mass of the liveliest spirits among the workers to the futile project of building up all sorts of dual unions based upon ideal principles." Now, said the TUEL, they must "rid themselves of the dual union secessionist tendency that has negated their efforts for so long" and "organize themselves within the trade unions" to radicalize them. The TUEL, "a virile educational league, operating within and in support of the trade unions, and by no means in opposition to or competition with them," would be their instrument.[14]

These attitudes, essentially Foster's, shaped much of the Communist labor union work until 1929 and after 1935. They represented a complete reversal of the sectarian stance from 1919 to 1921. Rather than standing outside the labor movement, berating its leadership and exhorting the workers in speeches and pamphlets to direct themselves to revolution, Foster emphasized the necessity for Communists to abandon speechifying and become "good union men." The respect Communists gained through working hard at the "day-to-day detail work" of running unions, he argued, would propel them into leadership positions. "If the militants get control of the unions they can put across their radical philosophy very easily," he observed in 1922, for American workers were "ripe for radical ideas."[15]

Although Foster's plan required bureaucratic slogging, the very antithesis of what people joined the romantic Party of the 1920s for, his prescription provided a smoother way than the sectarian policy for radicals to gain at least some power and influence. Militants could postpone revolutionary action until they were in control of their unions. Once in control, the militants could play a conventional trade union role while convincing themselves that this was helping to "put across" their radical philosophy.

Foster and TUEL had a tough row to hoe in the 1920s. The party itself, rent by factionalism, had declined to a small band of about 10,000-12,000 by 1923. Although a high proportion, from two-thirds to three-quarters, were "proletarian" in occupation, only 35 percent of them belonged to unions. Moreover, the vast majority of the party's working class members were foreign-born, useful, perhaps, in the short run, but a barrier to the long run conversion of the American-born working class to socialism.[16] Nevertheless, surprising progress was made during those first two years. Browder, working with Foster in the TUEL, was astounded at the number of radicals still hiding in the AFL woodwork. The response by AFL unions and city centrals in favor of the two pillars of the TUEL campaign, amalgamation of existing craft unions into larger, industrial unions and the formation of a labor party, surpassed their wildest expectations.[17] In the coal mining industry, the Communists supported Alexander Howat of Kansas, a popular opponent of John L. Lewis' control of the United Mine Workers union, and became an important part of the anti-Lewis coalition.[18]

Their most important base, however, was in the Chicago labor movement. There, they gained control of one-fifth of the seats on the AFL's Chicago Federation of Labor. Working closely with Foster's friend and admirer, John Fitzpatrick, its dominant personality, the TUEL exercised considerable influence in that important body. As long as it did so, Gompers and the AFL conservatives were reluctant to attack the TUEL openly.

In mid-1923, however, the Communists blundered terribly. Swept up in the Byzantine factionalism that wracked the party, Foster, in order to protect his left flank, participated in the Communist "capture" of the new Farmer-Labor party from Fitzpatrick and, against Fitzpatrick's wishes, helped launch it into independent political action prematurely. Embittered, Fitzpatrick turned the Chicago Federation of Labor against the TUEL and the TUEL lost its main base, the Chicago labor movement.[19] Foster the adept trade unionist had stepped aside for his alter ego, Foster the party politico, with disastrous results. It would not be the last time that the successes of Communist trade union leaders were undermined by the intervention of their top leaders. Perhaps it was fitting that Foster, wearing two hats, perpetrated the first such major intervention against himself.

Fortified by many progressives alienated by the Farmer-Labor party fiasco, Gompers and the conservatives counterattacked. The AFL condemned the TUEL as a Communist conspiracy. It called for the expulsion of TUEL adherents and many of its constituent unions complied. With the roof falling in on the TUEL, Foster tried to defend his strategy to inner party doubters. The recent conventions of the AFL, the Illinois Federation of Labor, and the Molders Union had all given "striking illustrations of the growing power of the revolutionary labor movement," he told the Red International Committee in October 1923. But his opponents from the United Labor Committee of America grumbled that, in concentrating on the AFL, the TUEL was not only ignoring important independent unions but the great mass of the unorganized as well.[20]

Foster's opponents soon had a turn at the trough. In 1925, the Comintern intervened in the notorious civil war sweeping the American party and divided the leadership of the party between the two main contending factions. Foster's faction was deprived of control of the political apparatus of the party, which was handed to the faction led by Charles Ruthenberg, but Foster remained trade union secretary and head of the TUEL. Ruthenberg's supporters were able to show their mettle as labor organizers free of Foster's tutelage, because the Comintern recommended the organizing of the unorganized into new Communist unions. They began to rework old IWW territory in the textile industry and led a spectacular strike of thousands of immigrant workers in the Passaic textile mills in 1926.[21]

Despite the AFL offensive, the TUEL pressed on. In 1926, it could smell success in the United Mine Workers union, where, as partners in the "Save the Union" campaign supporting John Brophy's bid to replace John L. Lewis as president, Communists seemed on the verge of sharing power in that important union. But with the union's paid bureaucracy fanning out over the country to line up support for the incumbent machine, Lewis mounted a vicious Red-baiting campaign against Brophy, climaxed by a speech at the AFL annual convention where, pointing his finger at William Z. Foster sitting in the gallery, he called Brophy the creature of that "arch-priest of communism in the United States" who made annual visits to Moscow for orders. When

some of Brophy's followers deserted, Lewis won handily and immediately mounted a full-scale purge.[22] By January 1927, Foster was
lamenting that in all the important coal districts left-wingers had been
removed from elective office and were being threatened with expulsion by the central organization under Lewis.[23] So effective was the
purge that few of Lewis' opponents attended the UMW convention
that month, which dutifully centralized union power even more and
barred Communists from membership.[24]

Yet the Communists doggedly pressed on, following Foster's strategy.
"Every member of the Party an active member of a trade union" was
made an "internal Party slogan" in 1927.[25] When the Lewis-led bitum-
inous coal miners struck that year, the Communists did all in their
power to aid the strike, trying to demonstrate that hostility to Lewis did
not mean abandoning the UMW. Whenever men under their leadership
struck, the Communists were specifically enjoined to cooperate immediately with the Lewis leadership.[26] Even after Brophy's defeat
seemed to demonstrate the virtual impossibility of ousting Lewis
democratically, the Communist leadership persisted along that path.
They offered to help set up a new miners' newspaper, edited by
Brophy, which would lead a campaign to have the "corrupt" election
investigated by an impartial committee.[27]

Although the newspaper did not pan out, the Communists were
accepted as a major component of the progressive Save-our-Union
Committee, which, trying to pry Lewis from his grip on the fading
UMW, rallied around Brophy. By April 1928, Lewis' election frauds
and expulsions had become drearily commonplace, and the union,
recently whipped by employers in a disastrous strike, seemed on the
verge of collapse. Yet, when a powerful movement calling for secession
from the UMW and the creation of a new union arose in the Committee, the Communists were instrumental in defeating the proposition.[28]

The Communists displayed a revulsion for dual unionism in the
needle trades as well. There, too, they found themselves fighting for
honest elections and democratic rights against anti-Communists who
relied on purges, control of the electoral machinery and dispropor-
tional representation to retain union power. Only in the fur workers
union were they able to overcome such a machine. Their forces in the
Amalgamated Clothing Workers were beaten back with relative ease by
the coalition supporting Sidney Hillman, a Socialist. In the International Ladies Garment Workers Union, however, the anti-Communist
machine, also dominated by Socialists, had a much more difficult time.

Despite a ban on TUEL members as dual unionists and repeated
suspension of leftists, the Communists had built up impressive support
in the ladies garment workers industry, wracked as it was by techno-

logical and organizational changes that had severely weakened the union's bargaining strength, a weakness that was easily associated in the minds of members with a flabby, often corrupt leadership. By 1925, the Communists and their allies controlled the three major ILGWU locals, all in New York City; this meant that they had the support of a large majority of the union membership.[29] When the Socialist-dominated General Executive Board ordered the suspension of the leaders and executive boards of the three ILGWU locals on the pretext that they allowed an outsider, a Communist, to speak at their May Day rally, 40,000 dress and cloak workers massed at Yankee Stadium in an impressive display of support for the Communists. They voted overwhelmingly to stage a symbolic work stoppage to demonstrate their opposition to the GEB. The stoppage, at the height of the garment "season," was a huge success, with tens of thousands of workers attending rallies denouncing the union's leadership and demanding reinstatement of the leftists. The Joint Action Committee, standing firmly for union democracy, had clearly rallied a large majority of ladies garment workers behind it. It began collecting dues that would normally have gone to the GEB.[30] Clearly, the moral, financial, and power-political basis for a new dual union was rapidly being formed.

But the Communists had little tactical flexibility in this struggle for power. Afraid of being condemned as dual unionists by inner party rivals, they had no alternative to pressing for reinstatement. When ILGWU President Morris Sigman, pressed on all sides to save the union, finally conceded their reinstatement, it was primarily on his terms. The basis of the Sigman machine, the "rotten borough" system of representation at union conventions which gave each local, no matter how small or phantasmic, equal representation, was retained. All the Communists received was Sigman's verbal assurance that a referendum on proportional representation, their demand, would be drawn up at a special convention and put to the membership.[31]

At the convention, the Communists were double-crossed. Sigman's canny aide, David Dubinsky, chairing the marathon convention, ruled that there had not been a pledge to have a referendum, but merely a promise to support one. Anything Sigman had said could not tie the hands of the delegates, who were free to vote as they wished. Enraged, Louis Hyman, the head of the JAC, leaped to his feet and shouted, "Let's march out!" whereupon the entire leftist delegation, representing a clear majority of the union's membership, left the hall.

Now, at last, the time to form a rival union had come. The delegates were there, the issues were there. All that was necessary was to hire another hall (preferably, in the time-honored fashion, just down the road). But the party's political leadership would not abide dual union-ism on any account. Bill Dunne and Ben Gitlow, the party representa-tives at the convention, rushed up to Hyman in a rage and ordered him back into the hall. When Hyman, although not a party member but totally dependent on party support for his position, demurred, Dunne is reputed to have said, "Then you'll crawl back on your belly!"[32] Again, a compromise which failed to recognize the real power and support garnered by the Communist trade unionists was forced upon them by the one-dimensional, inflexible political leadership. It gave the Left somewhat more representation in the union convention but overall control of the ILGWU remained in the hands of the Right.

Still, rank-and-file support for the leftists continued to grow. But intraparty factionalism was approaching a frenetic peak, with all the top leaders looking frantically over one shoulder at American rivals and the other for supporters in Moscow. Left and Right had become so confused that decisions of almost any kind were liable to be attacked from either side. Thus, when rank-and-file strike sentiment built up in May and June 1926, all the party factions felt compelled to jump on that bandwagon, despite the doubts of Hyman and Charles Zimmer-man, the leaders of the JAC, regarding the outcome.[33]

Hyman and Zimmerman were concerned primarily about the ability of the workers to hold out long enough to force their employers to compromise. They should have been more concerned about the ability of the party political leaders to do so. The strike garnered surprisingly solid support. In its eighth week, it seemed that an acceptable agree-ment had been worked out with the employers. The leaders of the Communist Needle Trades Committee met with William Weinstone, Ben Gitlow, and Joseph Zack, three party political leaders assigned to the strike, and all agreed that the settlement should be accepted. However, when they took their decision to the leading Communist "fraction" in the ILGWU, cold feet began to set in. Some were wary because Foster had just condemned right-wing deviationism at the TUEL convention, pointing specifically at the ILGWU. When one party unionist casually suggested that perhaps it was possible to extract a little more from the employers, Weinstone panicked and shouted, "Let's make another attempt." The others, fearful of being thrust into right field, were soon stampeded into voting to hold out.[34]

Again, excessive concern over hewing to the strategic line led the union's Communists into frittering away their chance at power. The GEB now stepped in and accepted the settlement, effectively splitting the union and undermining the strike. The Communist locals, strug-gling to keep the strike going, were expelled, and rightist rivals were created.

Even under these circumstances, though, with dual unionism practically forced upon them, the party's political leaders would not hear of deviation from the official Profintern line. In April 1927, with their position as well as that of the rightist-led remnant of the union crumbling, the party's Needle Trades Committee followed Foster's lead and voted against forming a new union. Rather, they decided, they would continue the fight for reinstatement.[35] Even when the Communists as well as two non-Communist groups opposed to the expulsions were denied admission to the ILGWU convention in 1928, an act that practically forced them to try to form a new union, the party stuck to its line. Although the Political Committee agreed that Communists in the industry should build up shop committees and present economic demands with an eye to calling a national convention to form a new union, that final step was put off. Instead, they "tried to maintain an independent organization that fell short of being a full-fledged new union."[36]

The leadership's propensity to apply the party line mechanically and inflexibly, manifested in excessive fear of dual unionism, was not the only soft spot in the united front line. Another was the growing weakness of the main object of Communist attentions, the AFL. What was the use of expending so much effort to capture a union movement that represented only ten percent of the country's workers, many of them the "aristocracy of labor" rather than the downtrodden masses among whom socialism was expected to flourish? These criticisms had been raised by Foster's opponents in 1923 and brushed aside by the party leadership and the Profintern. Now, in 1928, the Profintern, the Comintern, and the Communist party began to ponder them seriously. Moreover, boring from within had succeeded in propelling Communists to power in only one union, the small fur workers union. In the other needle trades unions, in mining, in the International Association of Machinists, and in various other AFL bodies, it had merely led to expulsions.

Also, in Moscow, titanic power struggles were impelling a reappraisal of the line. Stalin had just taken a major step towards consolidating his power by eliminating the threat from the Left posed by Trotsky and his supporters. Now, he was beginning to move against his ally on the Right, Bukharin. In the Comintern, one of the first places in which the new attack on the Right was manifested was in mounting criticism of the excesses of the united front line in the trade union sphere.

Foster was lucky, for although he was perhaps the foremost proponent of boring from within, the offensive against its excesses was led by his *patrón* in Moscow, Arnold Lozofsky, the head of the Profintern. Lozofsky had been an admirer of Foster and TUEL since Foster's first days in the party. He had ensured that control of trade union work stayed substantially in Foster's hands even as the opposing group led by Jay Lovestone rose to a majority position and power in the party. Foster initially defended the party's trade union policies against Lozofsky's mounting attacks, allying briefly with Lovestone, his despised rival, to do so.

When it became clear that Lozofsky was speaking with the authority of Stalin behind him and that the international trade union line was about to change as part of a broader swing to the Left by the entire Comintern, Foster fell into line.[37] At its Sixth World Congress in July and August 1928, the Comintern followed Stalin's lead and mounted an onslaught against Bukharin and the Right. The collapse of capitalism was imminent, the Congress decided, and Communist parties must prepare themselves for the assault on power. For Communist unionists, this meant the abandonment of their efforts to achieve a "united front" by working "from above," that is, by effecting coalitions with social democrats and reformists to gain control of mass organizations. Now, the watchword was "united front from below." In effect, this meant no united front at all. Communists were to build up their own unions, gathering the masses together in Communist unions which would help in the final assault on political power. Dual unionism was no longer anathema. It was now policy.

American Communists were slow to respond. Foster, while a leader of the leftist minority, was even more repelled by dual unionism than Lovestone and the Right. In January 1929, seeing the writing on the wall, he formally withdrew his opposition to the formation of new unions, and declared that they were to be the party's "major task." However, hanging onto a shred of his former predilections, he said that this did not mean that activities in the old unions should be abandoned.[38]

The leaders of the "majority" faction of the party, Jay Lovestone, Ben Gitlow, and Bertram Wolfe, were not quite so adept as Foster at trimming their sails to get on the new course. Armed with an overwhelming majority at the American party's last convention, they had tried to challenge some aspects of the Comintern's latest directives. They succeeded in convincing Stalin that they were incorrigible sectarians, extremely clever in inner-party struggles for power but unable to create a mass-based Communist party. When, in Moscow, they refused to submit abjectly to the new line but insisted on a few minor variations, they were totally repudiated. Control of the party was handed over to the opposing faction, of which Foster was still a leader.[39]

Most of Lovestone's followers deserted him in a flash. Those who did not were swiftly deposed and later expelled. Bert Miller, the organizational secretary whom Lovestone left in charge in New York while he went off to Moscow, was sacked by the newly anti-Lovestone party secretariat. For those who remained, the lesson was a striking one. It had nothing to do with which was the best or worst line for the party to follow. Rather, it was a striking demonstration of who really decided the party's general political line. In the midst of the carnage, Jack Johnstone, Foster's longtime aide, working with Browder at that time in the TUEL, summed up the lessons he had learned in a rambling private letter to another member of the Foster faction. There had been little real difference in policy between the two factions, he confessed. The main difference was that "our line was not an anti C.I. line." They must now obey the Comintern's orders and eliminate factionalism from the party. "The drastic and quick act against Miller is indicative of what will happen to anybody who tried to fight the C.I. and the C.I. requires no groupings in the Party to help it. The Party will carry out the C.I. line with the assistance of the C.I. and under the direction of the C.E.C. and its subcommittees."[40]

It is easy to conclude from the upheaval of 1928-1929 and the evidence provided by letters such as Johnstone's and stories about Foster[41] that from then on the party simply marched to Moscow's far-off tune with all its members straining their ears for changes in cadence. On the highest level of policymaking this was certainly true. There is little denying that the left and right turns of the following years were coordinated from Moscow. Yet fear of disobeying the Kremlin played a relatively minor role in keeping most American Communists in line. Rather, the knowledge that they were part of a vast international movement, already in power in the then second largest country in the world, gave Communists in the United States, remote from power and facing overwhelming odds, the courage to carry on. Somehow or other, by carrying out the same policies that comrades in many other countries were pursuing, they would reinforce each other and facilitate the inevitable triumph of socialism on an international scale.[42]

Another great attraction of Bolshevism was linked to the belief in the absolute necessity of a common, coordinated policy on the national as well as the international level. The Leninist way of achieving this was through the creation of a party in which discipline was all-important. Once the line was decided upon, the small "vanguard" of the proletariat would apply it zealously and wholeheartedly, no matter what their previous objections to it. As Theodore Draper pointed out, "The great lure of the Bolshevik Revolution was that it took a problem that had plagued the whole Socialist movement for decades and, in a matter of a few months, seemed to present a ready-made solution that was irresistibly quick and simple. One thing could not be argued away: the success of the Russian Bolsheviks. In May 1917, there were only 11,000 members of the Bolshevik party in all Russia. Yet five months later the Bolsheviks seized power. Somehow they had found a short-cut."[43] Central to that "short-cut" was the discipline of the Leninist party. The Mensheviks and the Social Revolutionaries had been too busy arguing among themselves, too debilitated by internal squabbling to get on with the job of seizing the leadership of the working classes and, with it, power. The same would happen, American Communists thought, to the Socialists and other splinter groups on the American Left. Thus, the party crisis of the late 1920s reaffirmed to most Communists, as it did to Johnstone, that internal party discipline was all-important. The crisis had been brought on, not by Lovestone's faulty line, although that had something to do with it, but by his excessive sectarianism.

But all of this affected the minds and souls of the party leaders closest to the top of the hierarchy: those who devoted themselves to party work. Over the next few years, with the change of line, an increasing number of party members became full-time unionists as well. They devoted most of their time to organizing and running unions. They had little time or inclination to spare for internal party squabbling. As the party mounted a serious and partially successful effort to go out and organize new unions for the first time, a bifurcation began to take place. There gradually emerged a substantial number of Communists, most of them card-carriers, some not, who, rather than arguing about how to seize the leadership of the masses in New York cafeterias, were going out in the field and doing it. They would gradually build up a different kind of relationship to the party, the Comintern, and communism than that of the party's political leadership. Eventually, the recurring domination of the former by the latter would play a major role in destroying the possibility of a Communist labor movement emerging from the United States in the 1930s and 1940s.

Although Foster was able to hold his nose and shift over to de facto dual unionism, he was still closely identified with the debilitating factionalism which the Comintern was determined to expunge from the American party. He was therefore passed over in the search for a new leader. The prized post was given to Earl Browder. Although an aide of Foster's, Browder had managed to distance himself enough in the last crucial years of the factional wars to be considered the kind of independent healer who could patch up the party's torn corpus.

On that score the Comintern proved to be substantially correct. Whether it was the demeanor of ex-accountant Browder, the departure of arch-factionalist Lovestone, or simply the onset of the kind of economic crisis that gave Communists the feeling that their day had finally come, the party became more united than it had ever been. Debilitating factional strife did not return until after World War II when Foster replaced Browder at the helm.

One of the party's first tasks after the excision of the Lovestone faction was to apply the new trade union line seriously and enthusiastically. A start had been made in the formation of new unions, but it had been a hesitant one. The party's own people in the needle trades had balked at dual unionism. In coal mining, the Communists, forced to break with the anti-Lewis insurgent movement, were reduced to a small dispirited band, sprinkled unevenly over some of the major mining areas, by no means the basis for a new union.[44] Nevertheless, the needle trades, mining, and the textile industry were the areas in which the party achieved its greatest influence. Therefore, to demonstrate that it was indeed going along with the new Profintern line, during the last months of the Lovestone ascendancy, the party had its adherents create three new unions, the National Miners Union and the National Textile Workers Union, founded in September 1928, and the Needle Trades Workers Industrial Union, born on January 1, 1929. The miners claimed a membership of 15,000, the textile workers 5,000, and the needle trades union, which united garment and fur workers in one union, set their membership at 22,000. Later, Foster admitted that even these modest claims were rather dubious.[45] Whatever they really were, the numbers were deemed substantial enough for the next major step to be taken. In September 1929, the TUEL transformed itself into a new trade union central, the Trade Union Unity League. The TUUL declared it would comprise three different types of organization: first, national industrial unions, such as the three already formed. Second, in industries where its strength did not warrant full-blown unions, local unions and shop committees would be grouped together in national industrial leagues, "industrial unions in embryo." Finally, in a bow to Foster's secret passion, leftist minorities in conservative unions would also be represented.

Party leaders took pains to ensure that its third function would not seem out of step with the new Third Period thrust. In October, they declared that the AFL had now "completed its transformation into an organ to suppress and disorganize the masses, and to further capitalist rationalization. It is a strike break organization. It is therefore wrong to recruit the unorganized workers into the AFL unions." But a crack in the AFL door was left open. The unorganized could be enlisted in the AFL only if they were recruited "directly into the left wing for struggle to overthrow the reformist bureaucracy."[46] Less than two months later, TUUL was already under attack within the party for not being leftist enough. Its program was a "mere relic of Lovestoneism," charged the "American-Canadian Group on the Internal Situation of the CPUSA," the product of its commitment to the "theory of *MILITANT REFORMISM*," a heresy embodied in its call for the founding of a revolutionary labor party.[47] Because of the constant fear of such leftist attacks, Foster and the TUUL were never able to capitalize on the approximately one-third of Communist trade unionists who remained within AFL unions. Rather than a vanguard, they constituted a kind of embarrassing appendix, going their own way with hardly a role in the party's trade union plans, which centered on the new dual unions.

The creation of the TUUL and new Communist unions complicated even further an already densely tangled internal organizational web. Relations between the party's political leaders and its trade union activists had always been a problem. The possibilities that the latter might use their relatively independent power base to pursue policies different from those of the former were always there. Moreover, there was always the danger that if totally immersed in internal union affairs, Communist unionists would lose sight of the larger political goals, becoming no different from AFL-style business unionists. Thus, especially for Leninists who believed in the all-importance of discipline and a single, unified line, it was necessary to coordinate continually the activities of Communists in different unions.

As a result, Communist unionists were organized on two different levels. In theory at least, since the mid-1920s the "shop nucleus," a group of Communists working on the floor of the same factory, formed the basis of Communist organization in industry. On the levels above them, in the union local and industrial union, lay the party "fractions." Yet often there were too few Communists in a shop to constitute a stable nucleus. Communists active in the same union usually simply organized themselves into fractions. Moreover, Communist leaders active in city central labor bodies such as the Chicago AFL would often call themselves a fraction. Furthermore, party members would also belong to party "units," so-called "cells" which comprised people in a city block, neighborhood, or town. Although the secular counterparts of shop nuclei, these would often also comprise people in the same shop or union. In addition, each district of the party had its trade union committee of the District Executive Committee, responsible for coordinating trade union nuclei and "local fractions" in that district. The latter, of course, were also subject to the guidance of their "national fractions," and both were responsible to the Trade Union Committee of the party's Central Executive Committee.[48] So hopelessly jumbled did the lines of responsibility become that in 1927 the party's Fraction Secretary despaired of being able to issue an accurate report on the results of a campaign to organize more fractions. Not only did many of the party's District Organizers seem not to take the task seriously, not bothering to report on the fractions in their districts, but there was confusion over exactly what constituted a fraction. In the mining industry, for example, shop nuclei were reported as trade union fractions. As a result, it was impossible to make even an informed estimate as to how many authentic fractions actually existed.[49]

The creation of the TUUL and a number of Communist unions and industrial leagues served to heighten the confusion. Shop nuclei and their hazy role seemed to form a large part of the problem. They sounded fine in theory: the organizations that would bring the party directly in contact with the masses on the shop floor, the members handing out leaflets, publishing "shop papers," selling the *Daily Worker*, and interpreting the meaning of the party's program to the workers in a myriad of ways. They were often the darlings of the most left-wing of the party's bureaucrats, those whose exhortations emphasized the necessity to carry out the mandate "to place in the center of the Party the daily needs of the American working class." One of the recurring battle cries of the Third Period was to "activize the shop nuclei." When, in 1930, new recruits began to flock to the party, the Comintern tried to ensure that they were directed into shop nuclei. In a cable to the party, it warned that unless the new recruits were directed into "factory and street nuclei" to be trained in short courses with the most capable being brought to party schools, they would soon withdraw and "compromise the Party in the eyes of the working mass."[50]

The party tried valiantly to heed the directive. In 1930, those few nuclei that existed were barely functioning. In March 1934, on the other hand, the party reported 328 of them active, 188 of which had been formed in the eight months since the party leadership issued an open letter criticizing the party for not recruiting a high enough proportion of industrial workers and for inadequate "shop work."[51] Yet, the role of shop nuclei themselves remained a problem. They demanded time that could perhaps be more fruitfully devoted to organizing unions. Workers' interest in attending their meetings would often flag. Invariably, recalled Browder, the burgeoning nuclei recorded in the impressive statistics "would just disappear in our fingers."[52]

As for the labor unions, in 1930 the new "revolutionary unions" comprised less than 20,000 members. By early 1934, they claimed a membership of 125,000.[53] But it had by no means been all onwards and upwards for the TUUL. The union on which many of its initial hopes rode, the National Miners Union, garnered considerable support (a larger following than Lewis had) in the seething mines of western Pennsylvania, eastern Kentucky and Ohio in 1931, but the fierce strikes it led were crushed by the mine owners, primarily because of the inability of the impoverished union to provide enough relief for the starving strikers. Later, still bereft of resources, the NMU tried to lead a strike in Harlan County, Kentucky, after the UMW had given up on the bitter, Bible-thumping, violent hill country. Here again they were crushed by their lack of resources as well as by the growing awareness of the religious hill people that NMU leadership represented a social philosophy that was the antithesis of all they believed.[54]

Despite the setback among miners, which siphoned off many of their organizational and financial resources, the Communists managed to set up ten industrial unions from 1931 to 1933. Most of them were quite miniscule, their membership calculated in hundreds, rather than thousands, but some provided footholds and organizational experience for Communist unionists who would play a major role in the future when the atmosphere for union organization was more congenial. The Lumber Workers Industrial Union, for example, although claiming a membership of only 3,000 in 1933, provided some of the militants who would later form the core of Communist support in the left-wing International Woodworkers Association. The Furniture Workers Industrial Union, although tiny, still provided a basis for the United Furniture Workers, a small but real CIO union. The Marine Transport Workers Industrial Union, organized in New York City in March 1933, provided a number of the cadres who later came to dominate the National Maritime Union.[55]

Although Communists had been unable to take over or create any viable unions in the auto industry in the 1920s, their cadre, which numbered about 400 in 1930, had garnered a reputation in the industry as militant partisans of workers' rights and industrial unionism. They had also come to control the only union in the industry that favored industrial unionism, the Auto Workers Union, which competed, with little success, against the few AFL craft unions with contracts in the industry. Already engaged in "dual unionism," Communists were able to create a TUUL auto industry union by simply affiliating with the TUUL in 1930.[56] But the depression, which hit auto sales particularly hard, decimated, rather than increased, the number of members working in auto factories, and led the auto industry Communists to expend much of their energy organizing Communist Unemployed Councils for their ex-workmates.

Although the AWU did manage to bounce back somewhat in 1933, recruiting 4,000 members during a massive inconclusive strike against the Briggs Company as well as during some smaller, mainly unsuccessful strikes, it was no match for the giants of the auto industry. The desperation of the depression, company spies, picket-line smashing police, hostile local authorities and media—all helped batter the union back from any small footholds it had managed to carve out.[57] However, through the AWU, Communists reinforced their reputation as militant industrial unionists, willing and able to organize and sacrifice for strike action in a way their AFL rivals were not. This reputation helped them recruit many of the leaders who would soon make them such a powerful component of the United Auto Workers.[58]

The most successful of the TUUL unions in conventional terms was the Needle Trades Workers Industrial Union, mainly because the fur workers union, now converted into its Fur Section, remained the dominant union in the industry. Among both ladies' and men's garment workers, despite a considerable number of Communist supporters among the Jewish operators, cutters, and tailors, the NTWIU was unable to keep up with the rival ILGWU, Alalgamated, or Cap, Hat, and Millinery Workers. Its membership, including fur workers, never exceeded 30,000.[59]

The Textile Workers Union had less success, despite immense sacrifices in Gastonia, North Carolina, the terror-ridden southern mill town where it concentrated most of its initial efforts. The depressed textile mills of the Northeast were only slightly more fertile for Communist organizing. The Communists could console themselves only with the thought that the AFL union had done no better.[60]

The Cannery and Agricultural Workers Industrial Union exemplified the problems involved in organizing the virtually unorganizable fields the Communists staked out in depression-ridden America and the sacrifices Communist organizers were willing to make for their ideals. Since its founding as an "industrial league" in 1930, it had displayed an intense commitment to a noteworthy feature of Communist unionism at that time, racial equality. Moreover, it promised that a special effort would be made to recruit Mexican workers. Mexican immigrant labor now comprised the vast majority of the labor force in the agro-industry that had boomed in the Southwest and yet had been ignored by unionists. AFL unionists regarded Mexicans as enemies at worst, unorganizable at best. Working against enormous odds in the lonely terror-ridden atmosphere of vast rural areas dominated by growers who had state and local police and judicial authorities in their service, the tiny band of CAWIU organizers, hounded by night-riding vigilante groups, managed to organize a few strikes among the impoverished migrants working in California's large "factory farms."[61] But in April 1930, just as the union seemed on the threshold of some success in California, the California authorities administered a crushing blow. Over 100 union leaders and supporters were arrested, many to be tried under California's law against "criminal syndicalism," apparently destroying the union.[62]

But the party bounced back. In 1931, a small group of determined organizers was sent back into the fields to help direct a series of mainly futile spontaneous strikes in California, Colorado and New Mexico.[63] However, after leading a successful strike of fruit workers in the summer of 1932, the union found itself riding a great wave of harvest-time strikes, many of which wrested substantial gains from employers. These culminated in the CAWIU-organized strike of cotton pickers in California's San Joaquin Valley in the fall of 1933. Between 12,000 and 18,000 workers struck over 100,000 acres of cotton fields at harvest time in the greatest agricultural strike in American history.[64] Significantly, three-fourths of the strikers were Mexicans, graphic proof that, contrary to conventional American wisdom, Mexicans would engage in organized industrial action even under the most adverse conditions. The strikers withstood armed attacks by growers and their vigilantes which left three of their number dead and managed to wrest a substantial wage increase from their resentful employers.[65]

Ironically, it was not the CAWIU's success among Mexicans that most heartened Browder, but quite the reverse. He was pleased by the CAWIU's success among Americans because, along with the Lumber Workers Industrial Union, it had displaced the IWW as the foremost union in its field, demonstrating that the party had now "fully taken over and absorbed all of the specifically American traditions and forces on the West Coast" and was well on the road to fulfilling its post-1929 task of "Americanizing" itself.[66] The organized agricultural workers were especially important, said Browder, because they would link the urban working class to "the poor and middle farmers" to create the basis for a farmer-labor struggle against capitalism.[67]

The chance to test this flight of fancy never came, for the union soon paid the price for organizing migrants. Once the cotton harvest was over, the workers dispersed to gather other crops in other places, most of which never saw a union organizer. With no formal recognition of the local as a bargaining unit by the growers, the union disappeared from the San Joaquin Valley cotton fields.[68]

For those workers who moved to southern California's Imperial Valley, Communist organizing efforts bore some additional fruit, albeit bitter. There the CAWIU mounted its second and last major strike, one that was crushed through violent repression. In Irving Bernstein's words, "it was less a labor dispute than a proto-Fascist offensive by the grower-shippers and the corrupt local officials they dominated to suppress civil liberties in order to destroy unionism."[69] Local and state police used tear gas and mass arrests to break up picket lines and turned their backs as American Legion and grower vigilante gangs raided strike meetings and kidnapped and beat strike leaders. The half-starved strikers caved in and the CAWIU was reeling. Soon after, in July 1934, the entire leadership of the CAWIU in California was arrested and seventeen of them were charged with criminal syndicalism. Eight were convicted and sentenced to long prison terms. The arrests and trial, coinciding as they did with the party's abandonment of the TUUL, gave the *coup de grâce* to the CAWIU.[70]

In the fields of the West, the union left little for its eventual successor, the Cannery and Agricultural Workers of America, to work with, including its brief success among Mexican migrants. The depression, by creating a huge influx of Okies from the bankrupt farms of the midwestern "dust bowl" to the West and Southwest and tremendous pressure for the repatriation of Mexicans to Mexico, decisively reversed the ethnic balance among western agricultural laborers; Mexicans became a small minority of the farm labor force.[71] But the Communists had at least earned themselves a reputation for bravery on the West Coast. This was recognized, in a perverse way, by the secretary of the AFL's California State Federation of Labor who commented on the trial of the CAWIU leadership: "Only fanatics are willing to live in shacks or tents and get their heads broken in the interest of migratory laborers."[72]

Although driven from the huge farms of the West, the CAWIU did manage to make some gains in the East. Led by Donald Henderson, an economist fired from the faculty of Columbia University for allegedly neglecting his teaching duties in favor of party activities, it wrested a contract from giant Seabrook Farms in New Jersey in 1934 and was granted proportional representation with the company union by Campbell's Soups in its Trenton, New Jersey, cannery.[73] These later became important locals of the Communist Food and Tobacco Workers Alliance—CIO.

By 1934, however, the Communists' trade union line was changing once again, retreating from the excesses of the Third Period. The Nazi rise to power in Germany crushed the largest Communist party outside the Soviet Union—a party upon which so many international Communist hopes had ridden—and posed a new threat to the Soviet Union. Responding to a Comintern directive of March 1933, Communist parties began again to search out alliances with the Socialists whom they had attacked earlier as betrayers of the working class. Unity in the face of fascism, the common danger, became the most pressing need, and throughout the world Communists tried to form united fronts with other leftists to meet this threat. Communist trade unionists began to back off from the more extreme forms of dual unionism and show a new propensity to seek out alliances and mergers with non-Communist unionists.

In America, the trend was reinforced by local conditions. Despite increasing membership rolls, the TUUL showed no signs of seriously rivalling, let alone supplanting, the AFL. In 1933-1934 the apparent governmental support for labor unionism embodied in the National Industrial Recovery Act had led to a nationwide burst of union organizing from which the TUUL had benefited substantially. But as Browder ruefully admitted in April 1934, the AFL had benefited even more. Whereas the TUUL claimed to have added 100,000 members in 1933, bringing its total membership to 125,000, the AFL had likely added 500,000 new members to its rolls, giving it over 2.5 million members.[74] By early 1934, the party's Politburo was seeing signs of change in the AFL. The bourgeoisie was trying to transform it into a mass organization, it said, and Communists should give *"the most serious attention to"* their work in the AFL's "mass unions."[75]

While uncertainty about policy towards the AFL was permeating party headquarters, on the local level many Communists had already been tempted to abandon the TUUL for the AFL. In the auto industry, Communists had been abandoning the AWU to work in burgeoning AFL locals since the fall of 1933.[76] In the steel industry, a series of defeats in local strikes led SMWIU leaders to try to convince the party leadership that dual unionism was suicidal and that some sort of accommodation with AFL unionism must be reached.[77] Reeling from crushing defeats, Communists in the coal industry were abandoning the National Miners Union and joining the Progressive Miners of America by early 1934.[78] Even before the TUUL line changed they were trying to propel the PMA back into the AFL.[79]

Meanwhile, with party approval, many Communists had been working in non-Communist unions all along. Despite the TUUL's attempts to be comprehesive, in many industries its unions simply did not exist. Communists in those fields had therefore joined whatever labor organizations existed at the time, whether affiliated with the AFL, "independent," or company-dominated employee representation groups.

Moreover, in some cases, the weakness of the AFL locals or unions made it more tempting for Communist workers to take them over than to create new TUUL unions. For example, in San Francisco in 1932, Communists helped organize dockworkers into a strong local of the AFL International Longshoreman's Association led by Harry Bridges at the same time that they were still recruiting West Coast seamen into the TUUL's Marine Workers Industrial Union. By April 1934, before the TUUL was scuttled and the return to boring from within began in earnest, fully 30 percent of the party's union members, 1,431 of them, were active in 117 fractions in AFL locals.[80]

When, in 1934, the official labor line did change, the TUUL followed the RILU book and, in September 1934, offered to negotiate a "merger" with the AFL. The weakness of the TUUL in comparison with the AFL, as well as the obsessive anticommunism of William Green, Matthew Woll, John P. Frey, and the "old guard" clique which dominated the AFL, made the offer laughable. The Communists had hoped to negotiate from a somewhat stronger position by merging first with some of the independent unions, whose membership was estimated at 400,000; these independents had emerged during the 1933-1934 strike wave and had not affiliated with the AFL, but the TUUL call for the formation of such a new federation in spring 1934 brought no response.[81] Its offer to the AFL in September brought nothing but vituperation.

But, in Foster's words, the TUUL had "no illusions as to the responsiveness of the AFL labor moguls . . . [and] went ahead with its policy of amalgamation from the bottom."[82] The AFL responded with a letter from Green to all AFL unions warning of the Communists' infiltration and calling for their expulsion. The Communists were not deterred. Union after union was disbanded, their memberships trying to slip into the AFL as unobtrusively as possible. Only the Fur Workers were able to name their terms. Much stronger than their AFL rival, they entered the weak AFL fur workers union with control of the powerful New York Joint Board, the committee of locals which was by far the strongest unit in the union.

The attempts of the AFL old guard to drive the uninvited guests from its household were shrugged off by the Communists. When the 1935 AFL Convention passed a resolution barring Communists from holding union office, the party's Central Committee pooh-poohed it as a face-saving device, toothless because of its dependence upon local and state AFL councils, "a majority of whom in the basic industries" were opposed to it. "The old, conservative leadership of the AFL is tottering," the Central Committe told its district leaders.

Altho reelected for another year its power to sabotage the leftward swing of organized labor has been paralyzed. Henceforth organized labor is definitely on the road towards bitter and gigantic class battles—becoming consciously aware of its increasing revolutionary role.

The party must grasp this new opportunity by wooing over to its program and tactics "all the best elements in the AFL, including State officials," said the Central Committee directive. While the fractions set about their main task, the winning over of the rank and file to the "United Front from below, the District leaders must forge working United Fronts with all progressive officials—and those officials who for whatever reason show leftward and (or) progressive tendencies— regardless of their past record," on the issues of formation of a Labor party and support for industrial unionism. Thus, the drive for a "United Front from below" would be complemented by one for a "United Front from above."[83]

By April 1936, just as the AFL was being split by the formation of the Committee for Industrial Organization, the Communists had completed their return to the fold. From the point of view of party membership figures, the shift had brought substantial benefits. Thanks to a recruitment campaign that concentrated on union members, the party could now begin to call itself a party with substantial roots in the organized labor movement. Thirty-six percent of its members were now in AFL unions. However, the Party's union members were concentrated in light industry and in New York because of its relative success in the needle trades. It was only there that "shop units" were functioning in their intended fashion. In the "basic industries," the party was still relatively weak with only 7.2 percent of its members employed in the large factories associated with heavy industry.[84]

It is easy to exaggerate the importance of the TUUL as a factor in creating the basis for subsequent Communist strength in the AFL and CIO. It is also tempting to speculate that had the party clung to it in the post-Wagner Act period when union organizing was easier, the TUUL might have developed into a strong left-wing labor federation. Yet this is to ignore the basic weakness of the TUUL as well as its exposed position in the face of government repression and employer hostility. It also ignores what the Communists themselves recognized during the 1934 wave of unionization: the workers whom they coveted most, those in the "basic industries," naturally gravitated toward the well-known AFL. The TUUL was simply too weak to woo them. As party leaders recognized in 1934, the workers who flocked to AFL unions were not necessarily enamored of conservative AFL unionism with its commitment to craft unionism and its bias against the unskilled. Yet, although the TUUL represented industrial unionism and a commitment to the unskilled, it simply lacked the resources to present itself as a credible opponent to the giant corporations in the mass production industries as the AFL.[85]

By conventional trade union standards then the TUUL was hardly an outstanding success. It was even less successful as an agent of the revolution. Communist unions are supposed to act as the economic arms of the party and to provide recruits for the party from among the working class. In its latter role the TUUL was a rather dismal failure. Of the 125,000 members it claimed in 1934, only 3,567 were party members.[86] Assuming that a substantial number of them went from the party into the union, rather than vice versa, and that an inordinate proportion were New Yorkers in the fur and needle trades, means that in the depths of the worst economic crisis in American history the party was unable to recruit more than about 2,000 members from the tens of thousands who passed through its "revolutionary" unions.

The relatively low party membership totals were the result of a tremendous turnover in membership. From early 1931 to February 1934, the party's dues-paying membership increased from 8,526 to 22,344. Yet 34,251 members, almost one-and-one-half times the membership, had been recruited and left.[87] The overwhelming majority of these new recruits (85 percent in one recruiting drive which netted 6,000 members in 1931)[88] appear to have been industrial workers.

There had been no great change of line during this period to inspire massive defections. Franklin D. Roosevelt and the New Deal had not yet inspired enough confidence to wean away many of those disgusted enough by capitalism to join the Communist party in the first place. A large part of the party's problem among industrial workers likely originated, not in its general line, but in its unique form of organization and in the very conditions of party life. It demanded a life-style that most Americans, especially those in the working class, found distinctly uncongenial, to say the least. Supposedly a party rooted in the working classes, success in the party depended very heavily on mastering middle class skills. From the time of initial recruitment, party members were subjected to endless hours in quasi-classrooms, listening to lectures. They were given turgid readings to do at home and asked to write reports. "The ORG-DEPT deems it imperative that detailed reports on the manner in which the above directives are being carried out should be sent weekly to the Center," read a typical 1935 directive ordering a concentrated effort to swing the AFL to the Left.[89] This meant that each shop unit, each fraction, and each section would have to write weekly reports for the district organizers to comb through, summarize, and in turn write up. Rarely have revolutionary movements demanded a devotion to bureaucracy of this order from their members.

In the 1920s, after the party's foreign language federations were abolished, many of the party's immigrant members were left swimming in strange bureaucratic waters and dropped out. Those that stayed were severely disadvantaged by their language difficulties. In the auto industry where the main task of the shop nuclei, turning out "shop papers," was perhaps most successful, all except one of the shop papers were written, initially at least, by a party functionary. An analysis of one of these nuclei in 1928 pointed out that half the members spoke English with difficulty, the other half not at all.[90] Although the proportion of American-born workers in the party increased, they were hampered by their working class education and culture. Later, even immensely literate Jessica Mitford found the paperwork daunting. "The CP was a great believer in forms and charts," she wrote. "There were forms for new members seeking data on Class Origin, Age, Extent of Marxist Reading, Activity in Mass (meaning non-Party) Organizations; there were forms for dues payments and Monthly Sustainers; there were even forms for requesting temporary withdrawal from activity. Eventually the information on these forms would be collated, charted in triplicate, and forwarded to the national, state and county offices."[91] Not only were the lessons, the debates, the reports, the readings, and the meetings run by middle class rules, but mastery of them was made even more difficult by the peculiar argot that American Communists developed, the apparent product of inept attempts to sound proletarian and over-immersion in documents poorly translated from German and Russian.

Moreover, Communist party membership demanded sacrifices of a kind that few American workers would make. Most important were its immense demands on their precious leisure time. Had the time been spent organizing strikes, manning picket lines, or in other forms of energetic action, its sacrifice would have been tolerable, but most of the party's demands were for more meetings, more reading, more talking, more reports. The more active one was in the party and the higher one rose, the more crushing the bureaucratic burden became. Thus, the very thing that Communists regarded as one of the major strengths of Leninism, its emphasis on a highly conscious, well-organized party elite, impeded it from recruiting party members from its chosen constituency.

Similarly, the Leninist emphasis on discipline discouraged working class recruitment. In practice, the American party was never so well-disciplined as it hoped or pretended to be, especially in its relationship to unionists developing their own power bases. Even during the heyday of the "Bolshevized" party, the Third Period, Communist unionists in the auto industry, for example, ignored party directives that they found inappropriate to local conditions "with a frequency that Party leaders found disconcerting."[92] Moreover, in practice friendly persuasion was the norm when those on the higher rungs of the organizational ladder told those below what to do. Nevertheless, members were continually reminded that an ability to take and carry out orders, even if one did not agree with them, was a *sine qua non* of good Leninism. Yet this very quality is widely despised in America, especially among workers who chafe at taking orders all day from foremen and other supervisors. American males who were raised to pride themselves on their ability to "think for themselves" and "take orders from nobody" (the very qualities which might predispose one to seek radical solutions to the depression) were asked to perform an about-face upon joining the party.

Thus in its attempts to recruit working class members, the Communist party seemed on the other side of the radical coin from the Industrial Workers of the World. The Wobblies' loose form of organization, weak disciplinary demands, and emphasis on action appealed to a very native, American kind of working class rebelliousness. Yet these very factors weakened the IWW's effectiveness, made it gravely unstable, and ultimately laid it open to the repression that crushed it. The Communists during the Great Depression, on the other hand, found that their superior organization and stiffer internal discipline produced the very atmosphere that turned off many rebellious spirits. Feisty young revolutionaries would join the party, expecting to rush to the barricades to battle the forces of reaction, only to find themselves dozing off at endless orientation sessions. Hoping to overthrow a system dominated by those who pushed them around, they found themselves having at least to pay lip service to a discipline as severe as that on the factory floor.

Despite the high turnover in new members, party leaders were unable to question the bureaucratic forms to which they were wedded; that would have meant questioning the essential nature of a Leninist party as they conceived it. They dimly recognized that part of the problem might be the sheer tedium of much of party life, but their solutions almost invariably threw even more coals on the fire. The party's projected solution to the turnover problem in 1934 was typical: more frequent nuclei meetings, daily tasks for everyone, more direction, more checkups on members' activities, "sharp political criticism of all opportunistic errors and deviations," and on and on.[93] Nowhere was an attempt made to adapt the Bolshevik form of organization to the needs and personalities of rebellious American industrial workers. Unless this were done, there was little chance of the party converting itself into a political party with a mass working class membership.

But while they fretted about slim membership and toiled heroically to recruit working class members, they hoped to succeed in gaining power not by recruiting millions of workers into the party but by amassing millions of followers. A "mass-based" party did not require massive membership. Indeed, as Theodore Draper said, this was one of the central appeals of Bolshevism. What was crucial was for party members to take the lead in mass-based organizations, leading the working classes to communism, performing, thereby, their role as a "vanguard." In this process, of course, labor unions, the most massive of the mass-based organizations, the gathering places of the working class, became crucial. The fact that only a small minority of American workers was attracted to membership in the Communist party did not mean that they could not be attracted to Communist union leadership. The struggles of the 1920s and early 1930s had demonstrated that these were two different matters.

In this reasoning, the Communists were substantially correct. American workers, especially during hard times, were not particularly anti-Communist. Despite the high proportion of Catholics among the work force, the American working class was not infused with the kind of brooding anticommunism that characterizes much of Latin America's Roman Catholic peasantry. Even those who shared this kind of anti-Communist heritage, such as the Mexican-Americans of the Southwest and the fundamentalist Protestants of Harlan County, were often able to compartmentalize their religious and other objections and follow Communist leadership in union matters.

In fact, to most American workers, unions were simply not so important. To the Communists, unions were crucial in the struggle to capture political power. To most workers they remained one of a number of organizations, associations, and loyalties in their lives, ranging from churches to their neighborhood bars and the St. Louis Cardinals. Unions were agencies that protected them from employers' whims and helped them get a better deal on the factory floor and in their pay envelopes. If Communist leaders could achieve these objectives as well or better than others, they would support them. In ensuing years, when Communists demonstrated that ability, millions of American workers did follow their lead, at least in union matters.

Although Communist tactics did bring great rewards, party unionists were often deprived of enjoying the fruits of their labors by another consequence of the Leninist form of organization: there could be no open opposition tendency in a Communist party. There could be debate over proposals for major changes in policy, but once the party line was defined, members were forced to support it or face expulsion. As a result, Communists dealt with the outside world with a unity, discipline, and maximized effectiveness that more internally democratic parties could not hope to achieve. However, "democratic centralism" had untoward effects its proponents never recognized. When changes in line occurred, no new group of leaders identified with the new line were poised to take the helm and direct the party down a course to which they were openly committed previously. The old leadership invariably scrambled to remain in control, steering the party on a new course, which they had most likely attacked bitterly only shortly before. In the United States, the expulsion of the Lovestone group set the party unalterably on this course. Whether sincerely committed to current policies or not, few party leaders survived into the mid-1930s who had not at some time earlier denounced whatever strategies they were now pursuing. The eternal necessity for each member to demonstrate to friend and foe alike within the party that he had indeed "mastered" the line resulted in an inherent tendency for party leaders to apply it overzealously, mechanically, and inflexibly. In short, "democratic centralism" meant that the wrong people were often trying to lead Communists down what might have been the right path.

This weakness was particularly apparent with Browder and the other battle-scarred veterans of the 1920s who directed the CPUSA through the rightward shift of the Popular Fronts and wartime years. In their zeal to prove their commitment to the new Right turn they took it to extremes that even its frightened originators in Moscow had not envisaged. The secret doubts that must have plagued these professional revolutionaries who enlisted in the American Communist cause when it was a conspiracy demanding immediate revolution must have spurred them into even greater excesses as they careened down the rightward path. At least so it seems from the vantage point of the labor movement. As the next chapters will show, the strategic decision to reenter the main stream of the American labor movement was probably the wisest one American Communists ever made. Their participation in the CIO was the only thing American Communists did that brought them close to the reins of real power. The many hundreds of CP members who worked to build the CIO achieved remarkable power in the labor movement by demonstrating their effectiveness as good union men, essentially the mandate that Foster had given the old TUEL. Most often, they functioned almost independently of party direction, adapting the general party line to local circumstances with considerable flexibility. On this basis Communist power in the union movement mushroomed. Yet much of that power was dissipated through the intervention of the party political leadership, at crucial times, forcing Communist unionists into postures that ultimately proved to be their undoing.

NOTES

1. James Weinstein, *The Decline of Socialism in America* (New York: Monthly Review Press, 1967), ch. 4; Theodore Draper, *The Roots of American Communism* (New York:

Viking, 1957), chs. 9, 10, 11; Robert Rosenstone, *Romantic Revolutionary: A Biography of John Reed* (New York: Knopf, 1975), 339-57.

2. Draper, *Roots*, 186.

3. *The Liberator*, February 1923, cited in Draper, 198.

4. Ibid., 198-99.

5. Weinstein, *Decline*, 248-51.

6. Draper, *Roots*, 274.

7. Ibid., 274-78.

8. Ibid., 318.

9. "Biographical Data," Earl Browder, Papers, George Arents Research Library, Syracuse University, Syracuse, N.Y. (hereafter cited as Browder Papers), Series 2, Box 2, "Earl Browder" Folder; Earl Browder, Oral History Interview, Oral History Collection of Columbia University, New York, N.Y. (hereafter cited as COHC), 116-18, 123-38; Draper, *Roots*, 307-10.

10. Draper, *Roots*, 311-22.

11. Minutes of Meeting of Red International Committee, New York, N.Y., February 11, 1922, Browder Papers, Series 2, Box 19, "TUEL" Folder.

12. Ibid.

13. Charles Ruthenberg to V. Kolaroff, May 16, 1923, Ibid.; Minutes of Conference to Form Committee of Action, New York, June 5, 1923, Browder Papers, Series 2, Box 15, "Red International" Folder; "The Red International Committee," *Labor Herald*, August 1923.

14. "The Principles and Program of the Trade Union Educational League," *Labor Herald*, March 1922.

15. *The Worker*, April 22, 1922, also cited in Draper, *Roots*, 350-51.

16. The estimates are from Draper, *Roots*, 393.

17. Browder, COHC, 120.

18. Melvin Dubofsky and Warren Van Tine, *John L. Lewis: A Biography* (New York: Quadrangle, 1977) 122-25.

19. Browder, COHC, 151-58; Theodore Draper, *American Communism and Soviet Russia* (New York: Viking, Compass ed. 1963), 49.

20. Minutes of the Meeting of Red International Committee, New York, N.Y., October 20, 1923, Browder Papers, Series 2, Box 15, "Red International" Folder.

21. Vera Buch Weisbord, *A Radical Life* (Bloomington: Indiana University Press, 1977), ch. 5. They also led the New York City fur workers strike of the same year. In this case, they successfully "bored from within" an AFL union with only nominal TUEL participation. Draper, *American Communism*, ch. 9; Bert Cochran, *Labor and Communism* (Princeton, N.J.: Princeton University Press, 1977), 30-34.

22. Dubofsky and Van Tine, *Lewis*, 127-28.

23. Minutes of TUEL National Committee Meeting, January 17, 1927; Browder Papers, Series 2, Box 19, "TUEL" Folder.

24. Dubofsky and Van Tine, *Lewis*, 128.

25. "Organizational Results of Trade Union Fraction Campaign" (1927), Browder Papers, Series 2, Box 19, "Trade Union Committee of Central Executive Committee" Folder.

26. Minutes of the TUEL National Committee Meeting, January 17, 1927; Minutes of Meeting of Trade Union Committee of Central Executive Committee, April 12, 1927, Browder Papers, Series 2, Box 19, "Trade Union Committee of Central Executive Committee" Folder.

27. Ibid., Minutes of CEC Mining Sub-Committee, May 25, 1927.

28. William Z. Foster, *From Bryan to Stalin* (New York: International Publishers, 1937), 212.

29. This is conceded even by the strongly anti-Communist Melech Epstein, *Jewish Labor in U.S.A., An Industrial, Political and Cultural History of the Jewish Labor Movement,* vol. 2, 2nd ed. (New York: Ktav Publishing, 1969), 133-39.

30. Ibid., 138-39; James Prickett, "Communists and the Communist Issue in the American Labor Movement, 1920-1950" (Ph.D. diss., University of California at Los Angeles, 1975), 60-108.

31. Epstein, *Jewish Labor,* 141.

32. Ibid., 142.

33. Irving Howe, *The Immigrant Jews of New York* (London: Routledge Kegan and Paul, 1976), 335.

34. Epstein, *Jewish Labor,* 145-46.

35. Minutes of Trade Union Committee of Central Executive Committee Meeting, April 12, 1927.

36. Prickett, "Communism and the Communist Issue," 100.

37. Draper, *American Communism,* 282-85.

38. William Z. Foster, "The Decline of the American Federation of Labor," *Communist,* January 1929, 56-58.

39. Draper, *American Communism,* 286-88.

40. Jack Johnstone to Morris [Childs?], May 21, 1929, Browder Papers, Series 1, Box 5, Folder "I."

41. The best of these, recounted in Saul Alinsky's biography of John L. Lewis and repeated in various other works has Powers Hapgood, a leader in the rebellion against Lewis, expressing his astonishment to Foster at the party's sudden abandonment of the "Save Our Union" movement in favor of setting up a new miners union. Foster had just written a fine book, exposing the bankruptcy of the American labor movement, in which he also denounced dual unionism, said Hapgood. How could he now desert that position? "Foster looked off in the distance for a moment or two and then, turning back to me, said quietly, 'Powers, the Communist Party decided that policy. As a good Communist I just have to go along.' " Saul Alinsky, *John L. Lewis* (New York: Knopf, Vintage Books, 1970), 58.

42. Joseph Starobin, *American Communism in Crisis, 1943-1957* (Cambridge: Harvard University Press, 1972), 44-45, made this point well.

43. Draper, *Roots,* 101-2.

44. Dubofsky and Van Tine, *John L. Lewis,* 164-67.

45. Foster, *From Bryan to Stalin,* 216.

46. October 1929 Plenum, Central Committee, "Resolution on Trade Union Work," Browder Papers, Series 11, Box 4, "CP Resolutions" Folders.

47. "Statement of American-Canadian Group Disassociating Itself from Comrade Clark's Attitude toward the Party as Expressed in November issue of 'Communist International,' " n.d. [November 1929?], Browder Papers, Series 11, Box 7, "Foreign Parties" Folder.

48. "Organization of the Party Trade Union Work," Browder Papers, Series 22, Box 19, "Trade Union Committee, of CEC" File.

49. "Organizational Results of Trade Union Fraction Campaign," Browder Papers, Series 2, Box 19, "Trade Union Committee of CEC" Folder.

50. "Draft Resolution for Keeping New Members," Browder Papers, Series 11, Box 4, "CPUSA Reports" Folder.

51. "Organizational Status of the Party, 1934," Chart in Browder Papers, Series 11, Box 3, "Charts-CP" Folder.

52. Browder, COHC, 272.

53. Draft report, "Where Our Party Stood at the Seventh Convention and Where It Stands Now," Browder Papers, Series 2, Box 4, "CPUSA-8th Convention" Folder.

54. Dubofsky and Van Tine, *John L. Lewis*, 172; Theodore Draper, "Communists and Miners, 1928-1933," *Dissent*, Vol. 19 (spring 1971): 376-77, 380-87; Tony Bubka, "The Harlan County Strike of 1931," *Labor History*, Vol. 11 (winter 1970): 41-57; Cochran, *Labor and Communism*, 53-57.

55. Foster, *Bryan to Stalin*, 240.

56. Roger Keeran, "Communists and Auto Workers: The Struggle for a Union, 1919-1941" (Ph.D. diss., University of Wisconsin, 1974), 12-50, 61-62.

57. Ibid., 86-103; James Prickett, "Communists and the Communist Issue," 109-26; Sidney Fine, *The Automobile under the Blue Eagle* (Ann Arbor: University of Michigan Press, 1963), 21-39.

58. Keeran, "Communists and Auto Workers," 115-76, 185; Wyndham Mortimer, *Organize! My Life as a Union Man* (Boston: Beacon Press, 1971), 54-59.

59. Foster, *Bryan to Stalin*, 238.

60. Weisbord, *A Radical Life*, ch. 9-12; Cochran, *Labor and Communism*, 34-36; Foster, *Bryan to Stalin*, 236.

61. Mark Reisler, *By the Sweat of Their Brow: Mexican Immigrant Labor in the United States, 1910-1940* (Westport: Greenwood, 1976), 238, 247.

62. Carey McWilliams, *Factories in the Fields* (Philadelphia: Lippincott, 1939), 213-14.

63. Ibid., 215; Foster, *Bryan to Stalin*, 242.

64. McWilliams, *Factories in the Fields*, 222; Reisler, *Sweat of Their Brow*, 239.

65. Irving Bernstein, *Turbulent Years: A History of the American Worker, 1933-1941* (Boston: Houghton Mifflin, 1970), 156-60; Reisler, *Sweat of Their Brow*, 239.

66. Earl Browder, "Draft Report to the Eighth Convention," Browder Papers, Series 2, Box 4, "CPUSA-8th Convention" Folder. Even with regard to the sectarian battle, this was not strictly true, for despite some support in the West, the IWW's Agricultural Workers Industrial Union, which had achieved some success in the years just before and during World War I, had been based primarily upon native-born and European migrants, and its strength had been concentrated primarily in the Midwest.

67. Ibid.

68. Reisler, *Sweat of Their Brow*, 240.

69. Bernstein, *Turbulent Years*, 160.

70. McWilliams, *Factories in the Fields*, 224-28; Bernstein, *Turbulent Years*, 160-70.

71. Reisler, *Sweat of Their Brow*, 247.

72. *New York Times* (hereafter *NYT*), January 20, 1935, cited in Reisler, 237.

73. Donald H. Grubbs, *Cry from the Cotton* (Chapel Hill: University of North Carolina Press, 1971), 82; Bernstein, *Turbulent Years*, 151.

74. Browder, "Draft Report to the Eighth Convention."

75. CPUSA, Political Bureau, "Directives on Work within the AFL and Independent Trade Unions," *Communist*, vol. 13, no. 1 (January 1934): 113-15.

76. Mortimer, *Organize!*, 60; Keeran, "Communists and Auto Workers," 183.

77. Staughton Lynd, "The Possibilities of Radicalism in the Early 1930's: The Case of Steel," *Radical America*, vol. 6, no. 6 (November-December, 1972): 46.

78. Foster, *Bryan to Stalin*, 260.

79. They still kept battling the PMA leadership, though, as well as Lewis and his machine. Ralph [?] to Bill Gebert, March 18, 1934, Henry Corbishley to Gebert, March 19, 1934, Browder Papers, Series 1, Box 4, Folder "G"; Foster, *Bryan to Stalin*, 256-57; Draper, "Communists and Miners," 391.

80. "Organizational Status of the Party, 1934," Browder Papers.

81. Foster, *Bryan to Stalin*, 272-73.

82. Ibid.

83. Central Committee of the Communist party, "Directive on the AFL," November 16, 1935, copy in John P. Frey, Papers, Library of Congress, Washington, D.C., Box 5, Folder 7.

84. F. Brown, "New Forms of Party Organization Help Us to Win the Masses," *Party Organizer* (July-August, 1936), 8-9.

85. Jack Stachel, "Some Problems in Our Trade Union Work," *Communist,* vol. 13, no. 6 (June 1934): 527; John Williamson, "Lessons of the Toledo Strike," *Communist*, 13, 6 (June 1934), 639-54.

86. "Organizational Status of the Party, 1934," Browder Papers.

87. "Party Growth-Fluctuation," chart in Browder Papers, Series 2, Box 3, "Charts-CP" Folder.

88. "Draft Resolution on Keeping New Members, 1934," Browder Papers.

89. Central Committee of the Communist Party, "Directive on the AFL," November 16, 1935, copy in Frey Papers, Box 5, Folder 7.

90. Vera Buch, "The Functioning of a Detroit Shop Nucleus," *Party Organizer* (July-August 1928), cited in Keeran, "Communists and Auto Workers," 26-27.

91. Jessica Mitford, *A Fine Old Conflict* (London: Michael Joseph, 1977), 70.

92. Keeran, "Communists and Auto Workers," 106.

93. "Draft Resolution on Keeping New Members, 1934," Browder Papers.

2 COMMUNISTS AND THE CREATION OF THE CIO, 1935-1939

"Who gets the bird—the hunter or the dog?" was John L. Lewis' oft-quoted reply to those who complained of the large number of Communists among the CIO's new organizers. Many have found the answer unconvincing. Indeed, for years the idea persisted that the CIO itself was somehow the creation of the Communist party. As late as 1949, Saul Alinsky, who wrote a biography of Lewis, felt compelled to ask Lee Pressman, his Communist former aide, whether the Communists had "engineered" the CIO.[1] During the 1950s, on the other hand, CIO anti-Communists minimized the role of the CP, calling it slow to grasp the significance of the formulation of the CIO and late in climbing aboard John L. Lewis' boat.[2] Neither of these views was substantially correct. Members of the CP did play a major role in organizing many of the unions that came to dominate the CIO. They also exercised substantial influence in national CIO affairs, through members' occupying important positions on Lewis' staff and through their representatives on the CIO's Executive Board. Nevertheless, CP power in the CIO was often overestimated because of the assumption that all Communists in unions acted in concert and followed the same policies. At least until American entry into World War II, there is little indication that, in essentials, this was the case. Most of the images of a small, well-disciplined, Moscow-directed army, marching in step with well-coordinated left turns, right turns, and about-faces, are based on the Communists' stands on foreign policy issues, which few American workers cared about and which affected their pocketbooks hardly at all until at least late 1941.

The CP did not "engineer" the breakaway of the CIO from the AFL; indeed, at first, it opposed the break. Having only recently adjusted to their own abandonment of dual unionism, the party leaders were leery of falling back into that cauldron. As the conservative-dominated AFL Executive Council prepared to suspend the recalcitrant unions of the CIO in mid-1936, the party called for furious activity on the part of its adherents to protest and prevent the suspensions.[3] When the suspensions came, the party still refused to support secession. At the November 1936 AFL Convention it tried to steer a middle course between those it said proclaimed "unity at any cost" (and were therefore prepared to sell industrial unionism down the river) and those who supported the creation of a new federation. It supported the CIO within the AFL, but opposed a new, dual federation.[4]

Despite the efforts of the Communists to preserve the unity of the AFL, the majority of the AFL Executive Council remained intransigent. Led by John L. Lewis, the CIO unions walked out, turning the Committee for Industrial Organization into the basis for a new confederation. Still, the small Communist-dominated unions in the AFL did not leave the AFL, en masse, with Lewis. Most remained in the AFL until well into 1937. True, the fledgling United Electrical Workers Union, strongly influenced by Communists at its top, followed Lewis, to whom it was heavily indebted because his intervention had been decisive in its survival. Communists in the United Auto Workers, in a strong but still minority position, simply went along with the union majority who swept it into the CIO in late 1936. But it was not until the UAW's remarkable victory over giant General Motors in early 1937 and the surprise cave-in of United States Steel to the newly-formed Steel Workers Organizing Committee in April 1937, that a pronounced shift of Communist unions into the CIO took place. In April, the Communist-led Transportation Workers Union abandoned the AFL for the CIO. In the same month, a Communist-led segment of the International Association of Machinists abandoned that union for the United Electrical Workers. During the next few months, most other Communist-led or Communist-influenced unions followed suit, including the National Maritime Union, the Fur Workers, the Maritime Federation of the Pacific, the International Woodworkers Association, and the International Union of Bookkeepers and Stenographers, which became the nucleus for the United Office and Professional Workers Association.

Some went enthusiastically, others with some reluctance. Harry Bridges' Communist-dominated West Coast longshoremen's union displayed no over-zealous kowtowing to the new party line. His union did not switch until after the rest, and when it did, his mistrust of Lewis was evident. Negotiating with CIO Director of Organization John Brophy, he was openly dubious about Lewis' offers of financial and organizational aid and tried to pin Brophy down into reaffirming these promises.[5] Brophy, in turn, as yet harbored few fears of a massive CP invasion of the CIO. He opposed Lewis' overture to Bridges, but on the grounds that Bridges was "too AFL-minded."[6]

Not all Communists left the AFL. One Communist-led union, the Hotel and Restaurant Workers Union, never did. Many other individual Communists remained in their AFL unions. In April 1937, while many New York area unionists, Communist and non-Communist, were deserting the AFL for the CIO, a New York Communist AFL representative was exhorting a meeting of fellow AFL Communists to stay with the organization and take the wind out of the CIO's sails by organizing the unorganized.[7]

Party leaders remained apprehensive about the CIO until well into 1937, and with good reason. William Z. Foster, recovering from a heart attack that had laid him low in 1932, brooded in the background, ready to pounce on the missteps of those who had shunted him aside. Lewis was still Lewis, he warned the party's Central Committee in mid-1937, and only the exigencies of the moment held him back from purging the Reds in the CIO as he had done in the UMW. Lewis must be supported now, said the wily party infighter, but there was no guarantee that he would not turn on them again.[8] Shortly thereafter, when Browder and other party leaders encouraged the Communist-led segment of the Machinists Union to leave the AFL for the UE, Foster, still suspicious of the CIO, opposed the move.[9]

Aside from Lewis' past, there was considerable evidence to support Foster's fears. In the spring of 1937, some party leaders saw "reactionary possibilities" in the Wagner Act, recently upheld by the Supreme Court. They suspected (correctly, it turned out) that the government's direct intervention in the machinery of labor relations would allow it to join with their opponents within the union movement to purge them. Reports were coming in from places such as St. Louis of actual or threatened purges of Communists in local CIO unions, allegedly inspired by Lewis, Sidney Hillman, Charles Howard, and the CIO national leadership. Homer Martin, president of the UAW, was already engaged in an offensive against the Communist faction in that union. Some Communists feared that this might be the harbinger of future purges, to be accompanied by a Lewis-Hillman-Roosevelt declaration that the main job of organizing the unorganized had already been accomplished and the time to consolidate the CIO's gains had arrived.[10]

In May 1937, suspicion that Communist CIO organizers had already been deliberately purged (exacerbated by rumors that thirty more party members in the CIO were slated to "walk the plank") ran so high that a special meeting of party representatives from all over the nation was called to help devise a defensive strategy. Some members of the

Politburo of the Central Committee, especially those who sided with Foster, argued that more should be done to differentiate the CP and its position from the CIO so that, in the event of a break, the CP could snatch the banner of leadership from the Lewis-Hillman-Howard group.[11]

But the events of 1937 did not bear out Foster's forebodings. Rather, they played into the hands of his rival, Earl Browder. The usefulness of the Wagner Act in aiding union organization began to be recognized. Rather than firing Reds, Lewis was hiring them. Not only did the organization of the unorganized into the CIO not grind to a halt, but it seemed to be accelerating. The CP's embrace of the CIO picked up momentum accordingly. Publicly, even Foster waxed lyrical over the CIO as "the means to unite all the present scattered struggles of the workers, farmers, middle class, Negroes, youth, etc., into one mighty progressive mass movement; into a great American People's Front against fascism and wars," if only its leaders would see the light.[12]

The *Daily Worker* threw its weight decisively behind the new organization. In private, Foster began complaining that the *Daily Worker* was beginning to read like a CIO publication. There was nothing distinctively Communist about its line in labor struggles.[13] Clarence Hathaway, the pro-Browder editor of the *Daily Worker*, could defend himself only feebly, for, essentially, Foster's charge was true. Under Browder, the CP line was becoming almost indistinguishable from that of liberal Democrats; the *Daily Worker* reflected this.[14] The CIO was becoming the focus of Browder's Popular Front strategy. In the short run, it would provide working class support for the broad anti-Fascist coalition he was creating. In the long run, it would be the foundation of the Farmer-Labor party around which the progressive forces dissatisfied with the two old parties would rally.[15]

Communist hopes for joining with the Socialist party and other radical groups in forming the Farmer-Labor party had foundered in 1936, in part, Browder admitted, on the rocks of Roosevelt's popularity among labor unionists. Yet, although agreeing with many of the things Roosevelt and his supporters stood for, said Browder in May, "we Communists cannot take responsibility for supporting Roosevelt or his party."[16] It was not a particularly satisfying stance, and it was made even more uncomfortable by the necessity to run a Communist sacrificial lamb in the 1936 presidential election because of the failure to work out a common platform with the SP.

When the Farmer-Labor party failed to materialize in 1937, Communists were encouraged to work for "progressives" in both major political parties in the 1938 congressional elections, a tactic that left much to be desired by those who had joined the Communists in the

hope of working for socialism. As the party leaders sank deeper into
the mire of the New Deal politics, it became ever more necessary to
cling to the dream of the Farmer-Labor party. The CIO thus became
even more important to the top Communist strategists than it might
otherwise have been.

But the party leaders lived in a world of self-delusion with regard to
labor. Their grand directives had little effect on the day-to-day activities of the party's adherents in the unions. For the most part, they were
simply giving their cachet to and providing some rationalizations for
what was taking place in a spontaneous and undirected fashion. Young
party militants and sympathizers, eager to do something practical to
help the working class, naturally were attracted into a union movement
that was firing the imaginations and galvanizing the energies of a
whole generation of young radicals. It is likely that, had the party tried
to prevent this, it rather than the new CIO unions would have been the
major loser. Furthermore, there is no indication that the party leadership played a major role in deciding which unions became heavily
Communist in orientation and which did not.

During the crucial organizational periods, in the turmoil of directing strikes and fighting other factions for control, the directives of the
party leadership were often simply ignored. When midwestern party
leaders active in CIO organization were called to Cleveland for a
supposedly crucial strategy session with Browder, they complained
such meetings interfered with valuable CIO organizational activities.
Indeed, so swept up did party members become with union affairs that
it was difficult for them to perform any party functions at all.[17]

This had been a problem even before the formation of the CIO. In
mid-1936, the party had tried to reorganize its units (the so-called
"cells") to combat this tendency. When different trades such as sailors
and longshoremen belonged to separate units, complained a Section
Organizer, they functioned "not as Party units but rather as fractions,
to take up trade union matters only." In his opinion, the only way to get
the members to abandon their one-track obsession with unionization
and force them to work on the rest of the party's political program was
to put members of four or five different unions in one unit.[18]

Although they continued to disappoint the party's political hierarchy with their lack of attention to party affairs, the CP unionists soon
acquired for themselves a well-deserved reputation as the best organizers in the CIO. In later years, opponents would emphasize their
mastery of parliamentary procedure and their well-organized, disciplined caucuses to explain their rise to power in so many unions,[19] but
it is now clear that much more important was the fact that, in most
unions that they came to control, they were simply the hardest-working

and most effective organizers. In the recollections of the early days of organizing, especially those of anti-Communists, there runs the theme that the upsurge of union organization in the middle and late 1930s was usually the work of a determined few, with Communists or people allied with them playing a role out of all proportion to their numbers.

Most of the CIO unions were organized by nuclei of five or six people in a shop, sometimes the remnants of previous unsuccessful unions or participants in employee representation plans. They were most often young, with less to lose than the majority of family-bound, middle-aged workers. At a UAW dinner honoring retiring members who were middle-aged in the 1930s, a younger UAW officer remarked to Harvey Swados:

> They try to remind me of the good old days when we fought together to build the union. The fact is that most of these guys who are retiring now, and were middle-aged then, never lifted a finger to help us when we were young and reckless and had nothing to lose. Our union was built by young men. The middle-aged climbed aboard when it looked safe, but now that they're getting old they like to think that they participated in the early growth of the union.[20]

The small core of unionists were usually recruited by local or travelling organizers who had made discreet inquiries to find those with previous or apparent interest in unionism. The nucleus would begin the arduous task of signing up an indifferent, fearful, or skeptical work force, would pretend that they had more support than they actually had, and would call a strike for recognition while hoping that the large majority of their co-workers would not cross the picket lines.[21] In union after union, non-Communists have testified to the persistence, energy, and courage of the Communists who played key roles at this stage. "They make damn good organizers," said one of their lifelong opponents in the UE.[22] They were "the key people in organizing the organized," said a man who led the attack on them in a UAW local.[23] "They were on the front lines doing the organizing," said a self-described UAW "right-winger." "After they did the dirty work, so to speak, in came those who were going to do the negotiation."[24]

Even the most fervid anti-Communists had to admit their effectiveness. "I admired the CP, their ability to get things done, to publicize situations, etc., and when ever it came to getting help in our difficulty, we were always pleased to have anyone's aid," wrote Southern Tenant Farmers Union leader, H. L. Mitchell, to a friend in 1936, explaining why he had leaned towards it, rather than the SP, in 1935.[25] Father Charles Owen Rice, who made a career out of leading the Catholic attacks on them, later admitted that he was "quite impressed by them"

in the 1930s.[26] John P. Frey, the obsessively anti-Communist head of
the AFL Metal Trades Department, said that John L. Lewis used them
as organizers, despite his personal anticommunism, because they were
clearly the best. Frey ascribed their success as organizers to training
schools to which he thought they were sent. There, he said, they were
taught picketing, sabotage, striking, and the like, and the women were
taught by a Communist photographer how to be photographed to their
best advantage while being beaten up by the police. They repeated
their lessons over and over again, he claimed, and were as carefully
trained as actors.[27]

But it was not just zeal and training that gave the Communists an
influence out of all proportion to their numbers in the new industrial
unions. The greatest industrial depression the nation had ever undergone inhibited most workers from risking unemployment by taking
the lead in union organization. When strikes broke out, they joined,
and they often did so militantly and en masse, but there was little
indigenous organization, ideology, or leadership for them to turn to
within the plants. As David Brody has suggested, the kinds of circumstances that produced the militant shop-steward-led, rank-and-file
shop floor movements in early twentieth century Britain were generally absent in the mass production industries of Great Depression
America.[28] Large segments of the American working class were therefore ripe to follow outside leaders, at least in union matters.

Despite their reputation for tactical expertise, during the 1930s the
Communists continued to commit one of their major tactical errors.
Despite the fact that their political affiliations were often either obvious or highly suspect, they continued the tactic of confessing their
adherence to the party only under extraordinary circumstances. Although the party leadership was now above ground, and Browder and
his associates participated in local and national politics about as openly
as any Democratic or Republican party regional bosses, Communist
unionists were discouraged from disclosing their allegiance. When
young Julius Emspak was being considered for the post of secretary of
the newly formed United Electrical, Radio, and Machine Workers
union and someone in the meeting asked whether he was a Communist, he adopted a standard response to the question. Years later, he
recalled it with approval: "I didn't open my mouth," he said. "It was
handled by a half-dozen different delegates. . . . It was settled, fast, on
the basis . . . that it was nobody's business what anybody was, he was a
member of the union, and that was that."[29] When Wyndham Mortimer
was called a "ComMUNEist" by a conservative AFL Metal Trades
Department leader in 1935, he gave another standard response: "I will
not dignify the wild charges made against me . . . by either denying or

admitting them. Redbaiting is, and always has been, the employers' most potent weapon against those of us who believe in and fight for industrial unionism."[30] When Mortimer and a committee of auto workers asked the AFL Executive Council for a national charter, David Dubinsky of the International Ladies Garment Workers Union asked him how many of his committee were Communists. "I don't know and I don't care a damn . . .," replied Mortimer. "Such a question is irrelevant and out of order."[31] To the very end, as long as they retained their ties to the party, neither Emspak, Mortimer, nor most of the other lesser union leaders would admit to any direct connection with the party.

The policy of denying membership in the party had been adopted in the 1920s as a defense against the clauses inserted in many AFL union constitutions denying office or even membership to party members. After considerable soul-searching the Party reluctantly agreed that members might deny party membership in order to avoid expulsion from a union. A 1925 directive ordered those whose party membership could be proven to claim to have left the party.[32] The policy was reaffirmed in May 1926, when, faced with an order by John L. Lewis expelling TUEL members and Communists from the UMW, the party ordered its adherents to stay in the union, intensify their work in it, and, if threatened with expulsion, to deny membership in the party, TUEL, or any other persecuted organization.[33]

But, as happens in organizations of all kinds, the policy that was created to meet extraordinary circumstances was soon adopted in all sorts of situations where it was less relevant, mainly because it was more convenient. Thus, beginning in the mid-1920s, Communists in American unions routinely denied their party affiliation, often citing not the threat of expulsion but the anticommunism of the American working class as their reason. Declarations of party affiliation impeded gaining the confidence of workers, it was argued, and were best put off until later.

Nevertheless, to work openly as Communists within the unions and to elevate the reputation of the party among the workers remained the ideal. It was a goal constantly aspired to at all levels,[34] but only the abandonment of "boring from within" in 1928 and 1929 and the creation of openly left-wing unions allowed this goal to be pursued on a widespread scale. Even then, the temptation to hide party membership was sometimes irresistible. The party leaders in New York were greatly dismayed by the Communists who played a leading role in the great Briggs strike of 1934 for concealing or downplaying their affiliations. In their fear of alienating their non-Communist allies and scaring off strike supporters, they had forfeited a golden opportunity to gain recruits and prestige for the party.[35] After the line changed again, many party militants almost automatically lapsed back to the easier way, hiding their party membership not just in the union movement but in the whole series of "Front" groups that emerged during the late 1930s.

The fear of a Lewis-led purge had provided some justification for evasiveness in the early days of the CIO, but, when this threat evaporated, the main impetus was the fear that workers would not follow Communists. Even in unions such as the UE, where most of the membership came to know that the bureaucracy and leadership were top-heavy with Communists, party members were reluctant to be identified for fear of alienating the members. The rank and file, recalled a UE Communist years later, "would support individual Communists because they found them to be good leaders or because they liked them personally, but they tolerated party membership rather than accepting it and regarding it as something good. They thought it was a handicap."[36] After 1939 and 1940, when clauses barring Communists from holding office were written into a number of union constitutions, there were additional excuses for secrecy.

Top union leaders, often called "notables," were especially secretive about their Communist connections. Their CP membership cards were hidden from the regular party bureaucracy and they were assigned code names that were used in many party meetings. The only union president who ever openly admitted party membership while in office was Ben Gold, of the small Fur and Leather Workers Union. Admission of party membership was somewhat more common as one went down the union hierarchies, but still relatively rare. When M. Hedley Stone, a rising young Communist in the National Maritime Union who joined the party in late 1937, decided that he was proud of his membership and wanted to make it public, party waterfront chief Roy Hudson stopped him from carrying out this rash idea. When the zealous Stone took the idea to Jack Stachel, a party *guru*, Stachel just laughed and said, "You certainly won't be helping the cause if you do that. We will tell you when we are ready to have you come out in the open as a communist." Hudson also convinced the new recruit to use another standard Communist evasion: it was he who persuaded the Jewish sailor that he would be more successful as a labor organizer if he changed his name from Morris Stein to M. Hedley Stone.[37]

Circumlocution worked against the party in a number of ways. Most obviously, as the leadership sensed in 1934, it prevented the party from taking full credit for its contributions (which were meant to change workers' attitudes toward communism). Furthermore, secretiveness fed distrust. Lying and evasiveness are generally frowned upon in America. Whereas in other cultures many things are valued more highly than openness and frankness, Americans are raised to admire someone who "stands up for what he believes" and "doesn't mince words." When, in 1938, a close union associate asked him to join the party, Ralph Rasmussen, a left-leaning Mine, Mill, and Smelter Workers union vice-president, replied that he "did not want to become part of any secret organization that was ashamed of itself."[38] Among people raised to believe that "honesty is the best policy," and to "never tell a lie," there are few labels worse than that of "sneak."

Yet few Communists seem to have been concerned about this. When called away from an explosive situation in Michigan in 1937 to attend a party meeting in Cleveland, Wyndham Mortimer complained that absences by party leaders for any length of time aroused suspicion. His remedy for this was revealing: "it was therefore even more necessary to keep the time and place of CP meetings secret." In many instances, to avert suspicion, Mortimer's Michigan Communists found themselves forced to hold meetings after midnight.[39] No one at the Cleveland meeting seems to have questioned the policy of deception itself, even to the extent of balancing the benefits of secrecy against those of a good night's sleep.

Secrecy also made the task which the Communists were most interested in, that of radicalizing the American working classes, doubly difficult. Their reluctance to reveal their true political colors combined with the essentially reformist tack to inhibit them from even raising the question of socialism among the workers they organized. Recalling the struggles of the 1930s, a Communist Packinghouse organizer said:

About socialism, you didn't talk socialism per se. You talked about issues and saw how people reacted. You talked about how people could attain these things . . . If you are an honest leader, recognized and supported by the workers, you could raise and talk about issues. You couldn't talk about socialism and what it meant in an abstract sense. You had to talk about it in terms of what it would mean for that person. We learned that you can't manipulate people but that you really had to be concerned with the interests and needs of the people. However, you also had to have a platform—a projection of where you were going.[40]

Fearful of alienating new recruits to the union, the Communists all too frequently kept their "platform," their projection of where they were going, to themselves.

They did so because of repeated disappointments in converting the leaders of the small nuclei of newly organized unions away from a narrow bread-and-butter conception of union action to a broader struggle for socialism. Almost invariably, recalled a Communist organizer for the Steel Workers Organizing Committee in the 1930s, when he would persuade the leaders of the little nuclei to call together potential converts to communism to secret get-togethers, the leaders themselves would back down, leaving him holding the radical bag. They were unprepared, he thought, to "make the jump" from "status quo politics" to "a more progessive kind of politics."[41]

Most party recruitment was done privately, on a one-to-one basis. Days, weeks, and months would often be spent sizing up, courting, then popping the question to a potential recruit, only to be turned down. It was often not because the workers were unsympathetic to the party. Many followed and admired the Communists, but had no desire to devote all of their meager spare time to the drudgery that membership in the party held out to them: the endless round of shop nucleus and fraction meetings, regular party unit meetings, and union meetings, as well as the special conferences and rallies of various "front" organizations.

For most Communist unionists it was really much simpler to organize unions than to recruit party members. Someday, somehow, under Communist leadership, they would help to create the Revolution. Whatever the current trade union line, Communist unionists were always succumbing to the temptation to sacrifice party obligations in favor of trade union activities. By 1933, stinging criticism of Communist unionists by party leaders was commonplace. Massive Communist participation in the rise of the CIO accentuated the problem and weakened the ties between the leadership and the unionists.[42] In late 1936, a middle-level party official in a midwestern mill town lamented this tendency. The local party section, as well as the few party members inside the mill, had been very successful in helping a local union drive, he wrote, recruiting almost 300 workers into the union despite the spying and terrorism which made public meetings and recruitment almost impossible. "Almost all of these recruits were spoken to personally by the comrades," he reported. Yet, out of all those recruits to the union, only two were persuaded to join the Party. "What do our comrades say to this?" "Let us build the union first, and then we can start building the Party."[43]

The reticence of Communist unionists about party affiliation proved of considerable benefit to John L. Lewis and his successor as president of the CIO, Philip Murray. They could avoid defending the right of Communists to dominate unions by claiming ignorance of the extent of Communist power in the CIO while enjoying the benefits of having superb Communist organizers and talented Communists on the CIO staff, most especially the man often reputed to be the eminence grise, Lee Pressman.

The role of Pressman, whom Lewis appointed as general counsel of the fledgling Steel Workers Organizing Committee and the CIO, has been surrounded by controversy. Pressman later admitted having been a party member in 1935-1936 when he belonged to the (later-famous) Communist fraction in the Agriculture Department. He dropped his party membership in 1936 mainly to avoid its possible revelation, which might be used to oust him from the important position he was assuming under Lewis.[44] He remained committed to the party and often functioned as an intermediary between the party leadership and the CIO's non-Communist leaders. A brilliant lawyer, smooth, articulate, and natty, ("Look, a coal miner from New York!" someone exclaimed when Pressman, in a blue pin-striped suit, showed up to represent Lewis at an early CIO meeting.), he was often credited by witch-hunting congressmen in the early cold war years with having wielded great influence on both Lewis and Murray. Pressman always denied this even after he was forced out of the CIO and broke with the party. The CIO was run by Lewis, Murray, and Hillman, he said, and the CP went along with them, rather than they with it.[45]

It is difficult to challenge Pressman's assessment. In the cases of all three men, when policy divergences arose between them and the Communists, they went their own way. Furthermore, both Lewis and Murray expected to crush the Communists once they had served their purpose. When Secretary of Labor Frances Perkins warned Lewis that she had heard rumors that his new general counsel was a Communist, Lewis assured her that he had heard the same reports. "He may be a Communist," she said he told her, "or he may think he is. You can never tell with these young men. But I want to assure you that John L. Lewis knows how to use him. I can use him. I assure you that when I'm through with him I will shake him out if I don't want him any more. John L. Lewis knows how to do that kind of thing."[46]

Although Pressman outlasted Lewis in the CIO, it is difficult to find any important situation where his influence on Lewis or Murray substantially helped the Communists in the CIO, except in a negative sense. Communists were obviously better off with him in the post of general counsel than they would have been with someone who was anti-Communist. His role was mainly one of smoothing relations between Lewis, Murray, and the Communists and helping to head off conflicts.[47]

The other Communist to hold an influential position in the national CIO bureaucracy was Len De Caux, a post-World War I immigrant from England. An upper-middle class graduate of exclusive Harrow and the not-so-exclusive enlisted ranks of the British army, De Caux had dropped out of Oxford and migrated to America in the hopes of

joining and helping the working class. He had ambled through the
IWW, joined the Communist party of Great Britain during a stint in
England during the mid-1920s, and entered the CPUSA after his
return to the United States. During this time, he carved out a career for
himself as a labor press journalist. On John Brophy's recommendation, Lewis hired him as publicity director of the CIO in late 1935,
despite a curriculum vitae that included positions with some of Lewis'
most vituperative opponents. According to De Caux, Lewis was interested only in whether someone supported "what we're trying to do."
So accustomed was he becoming to hiring ex-UMW-opponents (such as
Brophy himself) that he hired De Caux in an almost offhand manner.[48]

When the *CIO News* was started in 1937, De Caux was appointed
editor. From this position, he was able to exert considerable, if un-
measurable, influence. The *CIO News* was a newspaper in its own right
and also formed the central pages containing the national news around
which a number of union papers were wrapped. At one stage, its
circulation was close to one million. In addition to the influence he
wielded through this medium, De Caux helped many other leftists with
journalistic ambitions to find jobs and developed an extensive network
of contacts in the labor press.[49]

The appointments of both Pressman and De Caux were rather fortuitous, the result of Lewis' search for competent men to staff his
headquarters rather than a conscious policy of hiring Communists. On
the lower levels, however, among the hundreds of organizers who
flocked onto the SWOC and CIO payrolls, Lewis deliberately hired
many Communists.

Lewis' motives for hiring Communists were clearly opportunistic
and rather cynical. His own staff at the United Mine Workers was
rather limited in quality as well as numbers. He had made his peace
with his most talented rival, John Brophy, and brought other of his
UMW aides, such as Philip Murray and Allan Haywood, into the CIO
national office. A number of his other Socialist ex-opponents in the
UMW, notably Adolph Germer and Powers Hapgood, were also added
to the CIO payroll. But for the massive job of organizing the unorganized, he had to fall back on outsiders. The Communists were the most
obvious alternative. When an increasingly apprehensive Brophy would
warn him of their growing strength in the CIO, Lewis would reassure
him that he would work with them only as long as necessary and then,
"when it gets too difficult, we'll get rid of them."[50]

Lewis also made certain to keep his home base, the UMW, firmly
under control. Although Brophy and the other Socialists who had
fought him in the UMW were welcomed back into the fold, the Communists were not. Indeed, the clause in the union constitution barring

them from holding office continued in force. The Communist political leadership, in turn, now gave coal mining, previously one of their prime areas of concentration, a wide berth, obviously fearful of arousing Lewis' ire with even the faintest interest in a renewed struggle for control of the UMW. To them, Lewis now had assumed a political importance that far outshadowed that of the miners: the man whom Browder was to call "this Samson of Labor"[51] was creating, in the CIO, the organization that would become the keystone of the People's Front in America. Narrow-visioned people in the field could not be allowed to sabotage the correct application of the line through ultra-leftist sectarian bids to undermine his power. Thus, meticulously hewing to the letter of their grand strategy, the party leadership held Communists back from renewing their efforts in a field in which they had long-standing experience, residual contacts, and a considerable amount of sympathy, a field in which they had scored some of their few successes of the 1920s.

It is no accident that ultimately the Communists of the 1930s were least successful in gaining power in the union towards which the party leadership directed most of its attention and probably intervened in most directly, the Steel Workers Organizing Committee.

Lewis thought the steel industry crucial because as long as it remained unorganized, the coal miners union would always be vulnerable. The party leaders thought it of paramount importance because it was the steel industry—the largest employer in the country and, as everyone since the nineteenth century including Joseph Stalin had thought, the most basic of the basic industries. It was also of special interest to William Z. Foster, whose national reputation still rested, in large part, on his leadership of the AFL's Great Steel Strike of 1919-1920.[52] Browder could not ignore steel without giving his rival a potential weapon against him. Furthermore, SWOC was the major employer of new organizers in 1937 and 1938.

The party's Steel and Metal Workers Industrial Union had disbanded in the fall of 1934, and the Communists in steel had joined the decrepit AFL Amalgamated Iron and Steel Workers, given a brief deathbed reprieve by the National Industrial Recovery Act (NIRA). They spent much of their time fighting expulsion by the old-line conservative leadership and discouraging their non-Communist allies in the rank-and-file movement from calling what seemed like a premature national strike.[53] When Lewis came along with his hundreds of thousands of dollars, and the Amalgamated was transformed into SWOC, political leaders in New York and the Midwest leaped to muster support for it. As soon as the SWOC campaign began, the CP set up a special Steel

Organizing Committee led by Foster, and ordered all party members to aid SWOC in every possible way. Special steel and auto sections of the *Daily Worker* were issued.[54] Working in the SWOC campaign became the top priority item for Communists in steel-making areas. In Ohio, the entire staff of the party and the Young Communist League in the steel areas were ordered into SWOC.[55] Foster claimed that, in 1937, sixty of SWOC's 200 organizers were Communists.[56]

Although they did not openly identify themselves, the Communists' entry into SWOC was by no means surreptitious. All involved in union affairs knew more or less who they were. Lewis and his aides desperately needed them and were determined to use and control them. When, at SWOC's first conference, there was a demand that Communists be excluded from the organization, the Lewis-dominated leadership refused to support it.[57]

Within SWOC, the CP was especially strong in Ohio, the Allegheny Valley, and the Chicago area. So strong was their influence in the midwestern SWOC that there was probably considerable truth in opponents' charges that they were the true leaders of the disastrous "Little Steel" strike of 1937.[58] At one stage, Van Bittner, head of the SWOC drive in the Chicago area, asked for Lewis' help in heading off the upsurge of Communist influence there. According to John Frey's account, unsubstantiated elsewhere, Lewis authorized him to fire a number of Communist organizers but backed down after some delegates from the CP's National Committee talked to him.[59] So great were some anti-Communists' fears of Communist control of the Chicago area SWOC that Frank Rosenblum of the Amalgamated Clothing Workers, who was coordinator of CIO unions in the Chicago area in 1939, refused to support the organizational efforts of SWOC and the leftist Packinghouse Workers Organizing Committee because he thought they were Communist-controlled.[60]

But, although well-grounded in terms of the number of SWOC and Packinghouse organizers in the Chicago area who were Communists, the fears were essentially unfounded, for they were based on the assumption that the Communists were out to grab power in those organizations. In fact, the party's top political leaders were working hard to prevent just such an occurrence. Determined to show Lewis and the liberals that they were sincere about creating a Popular Front and were willing to work as junior partners in liberal-led coalitions, they restrained their members from making bids for power. They never made a move against Ralph Helstein and the non-Communist leftists in control of Packinghouse, nor against the decidedly centrist leadership of SWOC. Indeed, when an important SWOC conference was called for December 1937, the party leadership in New York ordered SWOC Communists *not* to pack the convention. There was to be no more than 40 percent Communist representation from any one local, they told their followers.[61]

The structure of SWOC also helped Lewis' anti-Communists remain in firm control. It was built from the top down, with power firmly concentrated at the top. Indeed, despite its enormous growth, it retained its organizing committee format until 1942, giving the union's top officers total administrative power.[62] SWOC organizers were all hired, paid, and fired by the head office. When they organized a local, they would be moved on to another area. Thus, Communist organizers could not stay behind to entice leaders of the locals they organized into the party camp. If, by chance, they had managed to find some old leftists to run the local, they would leave behind a leftist local. If, as was more likely, the years of blacklists and anti-unionism since the Great Steel Strike of 1919 had taken their toll among steelworkers, they would leave non-Communist locals that would naturally drift under the influence of Lewis, Murray, Van Bittner, and the others who ran SWOC. Thus, a Communist who had helped to organize twenty-five SWOC locals lamented that despite a few successes, Communists "weren't too successful" in wooing the leaders of the locals they helped to organize to a leftist position.[63]

Communist prospects in steel also received a setback with the surprise capitulation of the industry's giant, United States Steel, to SWOC in mid-1937. Although they welcomed it joyously, the absence of a long, bitter assault on that bastion meant there was less opportunity for them to prove their mettle and gain control over crucial locals. Instead, there and elsewhere, the more conservative men who had staffed the employee representation plans became the nuclei around whom the new locals were constructed.[64] Communists remained important in SWOC as long as "Little Steel," the other violently anti-union steel concerns, held out. Communist activists played an important role in that four-year battle, but when the struggle was over, they were quietly fired by SWOC head Philip Murray.

From 1938, when the weeding out process began, to 1942, when Murray privately declared it substantially completed[65] and SWOC was ready to become a normal, albeit still highly-centralized union, there is no indication that the Communist leadership ever challenged the purges or sought to increase Communist power by calling for the democratization of SWOC. To do so would have meant applying the Popular Front and wartime lines with a flexibility they either did not have or dared not use. One could not alienate liberal allies such as Lewis and then Murray with bald challenges to their power in their own bailiwicks. Instead, the Communists continued to offer up the skulls of their self-sacrificing activists in the creation of an empire from which they would be excluded.

The Communists were much more successful in the next largest CIO union, the United Auto Workers. In the long run, their position in the entire CIO revolved around their success or failure in that union. As long as they remained a force in it, their enemies in the CIO were hampered in mounting a full-scale onslaught against them. When control of the UAW slipped into the hands of their enemies after World War II, their position in the CIO quickly eroded.

Many of the factors which hampered Communist growth in the USW were absent in the UAW. The major auto companies were dogged in their opposition to unionization. General Motors was not United States Steel. It caved in only after a violent struggle, the kind of tenacious battle which allowed Communist organizers to show their mettle in spectacular strikes such as the sit-in at Flint. Ford, with its private army of union-busting goons, was as stubborn an opponent as were the "Little Steel" corporations. Like them, it gave in to unionization only after the rearmament-inspired boom in government contracts in the early 1940s made it economically suicidal to put up with disruptive labor relations. As a result, the Communists in the auto industry gained for themselves a reputation as superb organizers, hard-working unionists who could lead strikes. Moreover, the employee representation plans which had helped conservative unionists assume leadership roles in many SWOC locals were not widespread in the auto industry. Ironically, the major leader produced by an auto industry's ERP was Wyndham Mortimer, the dogged Communist organizer whose followers took over the ERP at the White Motor Corporation in Cleveland in 1934.

It was in auto unionism that the importance of leadership was demonstrated on a grand scale. During the 1920s and even in the early years of the depression, work in the auto plants had been high paying and relatively easy. As a result, it attracted a number of college dropouts or graduates, frequently political, often socialist in their proclivities.[66]

Exacerbating the job insecurity and economic deprivation of the depression were the speed-ups of assembly lines that were the auto industry's usual response to an economic pinch. The result was an explosion of wildcat strikes, often led by relatively well-educated workers with left-wing political convictions.

Communists in the auto industry had begun to abandon their TUUL union relatively early (in late 1933) to begin working in the AFL federal unions which proliferated as auto workers, like so many others, flocked to the AFL unions to which the NIRA had seemed to give such a massive shot in the arm. The failure of AFL unionism to extract concessions from the companies in 1934 and the disillusionment this bred with its conservative leadership strengthened the hand of the Communists and other leftists within the industry; they represented what seemed absolutely necessary if unionism were to survive in the auto industry, the creation of a single industrial union which included the skilled and unskilled. The AFL leadership fought a rearguard action against this, first clinging to the federal unions which would allow the eventual apportionment of the skilled auto workers into the appropriate craft unions and then conceding an industrial union charter designed to keep control of the union in their sympathizers' hands. By 1935 the Communists were playing the leading role in the growing anti-old guard "Progressive" coalition. Mortimer (one of the few activists over 35) had established a union-wide reputation for canny leadership from his Ohio base and other talented Communists were building followings in Michigan as well. Many non-Communists had shown themselves impervious to the red-baiting tactics of William Green and the man he chose as the union's provisional president, Francis Dillon. As in so many other industries, non-Communist unionists were enough impressed by their organizational ability, honesty, and commitment to industrial unionism and union democracy that the redbaiting Jeremiads of the AFL leadership fell on generally deaf ears.[67]

When the delegates assembled at the first United Auto Workers convention in South Bend in May 1936, the UAW Communists displayed the same kind of caution regarding the seizure of power that was to characterize their SWOC counterparts the next year. The new union had few major outposts in Michigan. Its strong Ohio base and Mortimer's reputation gave the Communists a solid foundation for a bid for control. There was a widespread belief that, should he choose to run for president, Mortimer would easily attract three-fourths of the delegate votes. But some delegates argued that, although he was clearly the most able, Mortimer's CP connections would be used to smear the new union.[68] Communist delegates went to John Williamson, the CP's Ohio organizer, and William Weinstone, the Michigan organizer, for advice. Both men, the representatives of the party's political leadership at the convention, said that preserving a united front with non-Communists was of the utmost importance in combatting the hostility of Green and the AFL leadership. Mortimer's candidacy was thereupon abandoned, and the CP helped elect Homer Martin, an unemployed liberal preacher from Kansas City with a gift for tent meeting oratory, as the UAW's first president.[69] Mortimer had to settle for the post of first vice-president, but the Communists were gratified that the convention had approved their entire program and their Progressive caucus now dominated the executive board.

Mortimer was sent to Michigan, where he and Robert Travis, another Communist from Ohio, were instrumental in organizing the Flint local whose 1937 "sit-down" strike, in conjunction with one in Mortimer's old bailiwick in Cleveland, was crucial in forcing General Motors to yield to the union. Despite the reluctance of the Communists who played leading roles in the sit-downs to expose their party connections, the wave of organization that followed led to expanded Communist power in the Michigan UAW and made them by 1938 the single most powerful organized political force in the UAW. Their influence in the new union was owed almost exclusively, not to any conspiratorial prowess, but to their consistent commitment to industrial unionism and their demonstrated ability to work long, hard, and successfully for it.[70]

Because, like UE, it had been organized to a great extent from the bottom up, power in the early UAW was quite diffused. This, combined with the unusually large number of workers willing and able to battle for union office, soon led to a virtual explosion of factionalism. Despite their opponents' feeling that the Communists were the most authentically working class in origin,[71] there were many college-educated people in all factions, from Homer Martin, the Reuther brothers, Richard Frankensteen, Richard Leonard, John Anderson, and George Woodcock to Carl Haessler, a Rhodes Scholar and Ph.D. from the University of Wisconsin who edited a number of Communist UAW newspapers. Although, overall, the Communists seem to have had relatively fewer college-educated leaders than the Socialists and Reuther-followers, they did have their share of people from backgrounds atypical among auto workers. A number, such as Nat Ganley (né Kaplan), William Weinstone, and Maurice Sugar (the influential general counsel of the UAW for a number of years) were from Jewish radical backgrounds. If there was a common characteristic which this rising generation of politicized union leaders often shared, it would seem to be radical parents, usually militant prewar unionists and Socialist Party of America supporters. John W. Anderson, a UAW Trotskyist, recalled:

The people who organized the CIO and UAW were not pure and simple trade unionists. They were members of the Socialist Party, the Communist Party, the IWW, the Proletarian Party, and people who saw and were looking forward to a new society. And the sacrifices they were willing to make were not those for a nickel an hour, but for something far greater.[72]

Despite the highly ideological nature of so many of the UAW's early activists, or perhaps because of it, from the outset UAW factions revolved around their leaders. The best exploiter of personal power turned out to be the ultimate victor, Walter Reuther. From the earliest days, Reuther cultivated *liderismo* and a cult of his own personality. On the picket lines members of his personal power base, the Detroit West Side local, would sing not "Solidarity Forever," the UAW and CIO song, but "Reuther Is Our Leader."[73] When John W. Anderson complained that Reuther was not giving the rank and file enough voice in running his local, Reuther responded to the term "rank and file" by saying, "It is the leadership that is important, it is not the rank and file. It is the leadership that is important!"[74]

Reuther had sensed an important truth about American unionism. The CP was strong in the UAW mainly because a few leaders such as Mortimer and Travis happened to be in the right place at the right time, creating a following for themselves and their factions through their determined leadership under fire. Reuther, who cooperated with the Communists until 1938, gained strength for similar reasons. There was little difference in their respective power bases: for example, both the "Red" Flint local and Reuther's Detroit West Side local bargained with GM and comprised generally the same kind of workers doing similar jobs.

CP strength in the UAW depended not on John L. Lewis or the CIO, but on the efforts of Communists within the auto industry, aided by some, such as Ganley, Weinstone, Sugar, and John Williamson, who had been seconded to them by the national CP. If anything, Lewis inherited a union with strong CP influence and worked, subsequently, to weaken that influence. Similarly, there is more accident than pattern in CP strength in the other budding young CIO unions. The one consistent theme is that it was strongest in the newest unions, and weakest in the older, established unions and their directly-controlled offshoots, such as SWOC, the creature of the UMW, and the Textile Workers Organizing Committee, controlled by Sidney Hillman's Amalgamated Clothing Workers.

Perhaps the most striking example of the influence of personality, accident, and leadership came along the waterfronts. On the East Coast, longshoremen joined the right-wing, racketeer-infested International Longshoremen's Association, run by Joseph Ryan, a tough anti-Communist later jailed for stealing union funds. On the West Coast, they followed dynamic Harry Bridges out of the ILA into his new International Longshoremen's and Warehousemen's Union, a name that would soon become synonymous with Communist unionism. As if to guard against generalizations ascribing West Coast longshore radicalism primarily to the long tradition of labor radicalism on the West Coast, the situation was reversed among sailors. It was East Coast sailors who were the pillars of the left-wing National Maritime Union, whereas their West Coast counterparts stayed in the right-wing International Seamen's Union.

Bridges built up a considerable following in 1934 when he distinguished himself as a clever tactician in the violent series of confrontations that led to the San Francisco general strike. After he led his San Francisco local out of the ILA, most of the union's other West Coast locals, weaker ones led by admirers of his, went along too. Similarly, Joseph Curran, a tough, ham-handed sailor with a face and bearing like a professional boxer, emerged from the lower decks as a natural leader. East Coast sailors followed him first into the arms of the Communists, and then, after the war, out of their embrace.

Although both Bridges and Curran had the requisite reputation for "toughness" in the face of employers, their attraction sprang from different images. Whereas Bridges had built up a reputation for himself as "brainy" and canny, Curran was renowned for the axe he had taken between his shoulder blades. While Curran would boast to reporters about having been expelled from school in seventh grade "for not attending regular,"[75] Bridges would let it be known that he spent his spare time reading the classics on economics and socialism. When a reporter acquaintance showed him a list of books on the economics of socialism that Paul Sweezy had recommended to his class in economics at Harvard, Bridges said that he had read them all.[76] Bridges, the Australian immigrant from a well-off Catholic family, had fallen in love with adventure, the sea, Jack London, and radicalism. He affected a rough-and-ready exterior and cultivated his pugnacious-sounding Australian accent. But Bridges' leadership rested ultimately on his brains. "Hell, he knew more about what to do than the rest of us combined," recalled a Communist associate from the early 1930s.[77]

Curran's attraction sprang, ultimately, from his machismo. In his union, it was the Communists who provided the brains. In 1937, a *Fortune* reporter found National Maritime Union members well satisfied with the Communists in that regard. They differentiated between the "smart" Communists who dominated NMU headquarters, he wrote, and what they regarded as "the screwy Union Square crowd." As translated by *Fortune* into the Luce empire's version of fo'c'sle lingo, the sailors were saying of the Communists: "Smart boys. They're going where we want them to go right now—democratic unions with a firm tie-up to shore workers. The Coms, they say, are fighters: they've got ideas on strategy and they keep their noses clean on money."[78]

Curran had turned to the Communists for help when, unprepared, he had been thrust into the leadership of the rebellion against the old, corrupt International Seamen's Union. The ISU was a famous union, founded by leathery Andrew Furuseth before World War I, but it had been buffeted, torn, and virtually swamped by the great open shop drive of 1919-1921. Its growing corruption had weakened it further and the depression seemed to deliver it a coup de grâce. Curran was an unknown sailor on the S. S. *Californian* in 1936 when a voyage to the West Coast provoked a movement among the crew for pay equal to that of the West Coast-based sailors. A strike at sea would have been mutiny, severely punishable, and a mere picket line would have been ineffective, so, led by Curran, the crew sat in, refusing to move the ship from the harbor at San Pedro, California.

The intervention of Secretary of Labor Frances Perkins to end the sit-in and the subsequent firing of the crew members when they reached home port thrust Curran into the national limelight. An instant celebrity, he easily assumed the leadership of a movement to replace the ISU with a dynamic new sailors' union. Although long on fame, Curran was short on organized support, and he turned to the many Communists in the New York City area who were itching to get involved in organizing seamen. A generation raised on Jack London stories jumped at the chance to work with the nuclei of ex-IWWs and rugged militants who still infested that hard-living trade.

Curran worked closely with the Communists, filling the NMU staff with party members and going along with the party's line on foreign policy. However, he never took out a party card and pirouetted away whenever the pressure mounted to do so. He came to party meetings only when lured there under false pretenses, such as an invitation to stop off at someone's house on the way to a baseball game.[79] He also kept his fences mended among anti-Communists by giving them the impression that his alliance with the Communists was purely one of convenience rather than conviction. Philip Murray, for one, was convinced that Curran was basically anti-Communist and would some day desert.[80] Years later, an unsympathetic Len De Caux wrote that after a conference on the subject with Curran in 1937, Sidney Hillman emerged saying to his friends, "Joe is a good boy, a real good boy. He has to act red in his setup. But he's all right. We can handle Joe."[81]

But the party needed Curran and his ilk as much as he needed them. As the SWOC situation proved, hard work and dedicated organizers were not enough to create left-wing unions. The charismatic leaders, the Currans and the Bridges, were often indispensable. As if to prove the point, many of the same Communists who had been so successful in bringing the West Coast dockers into the ILWU and the East Coast sailors into the NMU fell flat on their faces when they tried to lure East Coast waterfront workers from the AFL's International Longshoremen's Association. Supported by Lewis, Bridges, and the national CIO office, they mounted a massive drive in late 1937 and early 1938. According to ex-party member Hedley Stone of the NMU, "ninety percent of the people who went to work as organizers were members of the Communist Party, attended unit meetings and were given directives; and they made a colossal failure of the drive."[82] The zeal of the organizers could not compensate for their lack of a Curran or Bridges, especially in the face of Joe Ryan of the ILA who had Curranesque qualities himself and gangster support to boot.

Another union in which leadership proved to be crucial in allowing the CP first entry and then exit was the Transport Workers Union, led by Michael Quill. The TWU was always a relatively small union in terms of membership, but, like a professional sports team, its New York City base gave it exposure in the New York-headquartered national media out of all proportion to its real importance. Furthermore, in an age marking the final arrival of the Irish not only into the upper reaches of political and economic power, but also into the hearts of America (Hollywood was embarking on a veritable cult of the Irish), the heavily Irish TWU, and especially its super-Irish president, "Irish" Mike Quill, made colorful media copy. With a gift for what made good newspaper copy, Quill was able to manipulate members into thinking of the TWU as "his" union, while keeping the Communist party hierarchy, to which he belonged, thinking it was theirs as well.

The party hierarchy had good reason to think that the TWU was theirs. It was one of the few unions created from scratch entirely by Communists. In 1933, a recent Hungarian immigrant party member named Desiderio Hammer had been assigned by the party to organize taxi, bus, trolley and subway workers in New York City. He soon recruited two Irish workers, Quill and Pat O'Shea, to head the new union. They and the rest of the seven founding members of the union soon joined the party. With the colorful and personable Quill and O'Shea out front, working among the predominantly Irish transit workers, Hammer, his name now changed to John Santo, and the CP provided the initial basis for union organization: the money; the lawyers; the nuts-and-bolts knowledge of how to set up a newspaper, issue pamphlets, and run an office. Within a few years, they had managed to win contracts for most New York City transit workers, were rapidly expanding their organization in other major cities, and were casting covetous eyes on the growing number of airline employees. John L. Lewis took a shine to Quill and helped the fledgling AFL union. When Lewis walked out of the AFL, the TWU accompanied him into the CIO with no hesitation.[83]

Committed to Irish nationalism as well as communism, Quill was no business unionist with his eye only on the next contract and the size of his office staff. From the beginning, he wanted to act on the widest stage possible. In 1936, he ran successfully for councilman in New York City on the Communist-supported American Labor party ticket and became a fixture in local politics. But his political life, his influence, his fame, and his power were all dependent upon his TWU base. In a crunch, he would sacrifice his politics in order to retain it.

Although the party political leadership concentrated on steel and auto, and the media on the colorful longshoremen's, sailors' and transit workers' unions, it was in the electrical industry that Communists made their most substantial gains. Here again, a crucial factor in their success was that previous unionization drives, including that of TUUL, had failed, leaving the scattered Communists in the industry without an established union hierarchy to fend off. Meanwhile, the tough anti-unionism of the major corporations in the field, General Electric, Westinghouse, RCA, and Ford's subsidiary, Philco, gave leftist unionists the opportunity to prove their mettle in strike after strike. There was no United States Steel to cave in early and easily in the electrical industry, and neither was there a SWOC, firmly controlled from above and beyond.

The UE was the outgrowth of the amalgamation of a number of independently organized unions in the radio and electrical appliance industry. Although many of the local leaders were skilled workers, and many of the unions had AFL federal charters and were theoretically to await their apportionment among the appropriate AFL craft unions, the previous failures of the AFL craft unions in the industry had converted most of the membership to industrial unionism. Moreover, many of the men who were most active in the early days were politically radical and committed ideologically to industrial unionism. It was a common belief in the industrial form of organization that united Communists and non-Communists in an effort to form a new national union. As it emerged, the United Electrical, Radio and Machine Workers of America embraced three major groups: an AFL radio workers' union, some Communist-led electrical workers' unions, centered primarily in Schenectady, New York, and Lynn, Massachusetts, and Communist-led East Coast machinists, refugees from the SMIU who had found a temporary home in the AFL International Association of Machinists.

The radio workers were led by James B. Carey, a cocky and ambitious young Irish-American who in 1933 had managed the first successful major strike in the industry against Philco in Philadelphia. His union thereupon received an AFL federal union charter, allowing it to operate relatively independently until such time as the AFL

Executive Council decided how it was to be divided up. Only twenty-one at the time, Carey found the limelight to his liking and set about encouraging other budding radio and electrical workers' locals. Soon, he had created a federation of Radio and Allied Trade Workers unions within the AFL, and tried, unsuccessfully, to wrest a charter as a separate industrial union from a largely unwilling AFL Executive Council. John L. Lewis had taken up the federation's cudgels in his conflict over industrial unionism within the Executive Council,[84] and Carey and his union became early supporters of Lewis' Committee for Industrial Organization. When the Executive Council spurned their pleas and ordered the radio workers to submerge themselves in the craft-oriented International Brotherhood of Electrical Workers as Class "B" (i.e., second-class) members, Carey allied with the Communists instead.

Carey and the Communists had opposed each other in Philadelphia in 1933,[85] but the Communist change of line drew them together. In 1934 and 1935, Carey had flirted with a number of non-AFL locals controlled by Communists, many of them remnants of TUUL, but had drawn back from formal affiliation with them for fear that it would doom his chances of getting an AFL charter. Once the hopes were dashed, however, and the new CIO path opened up, the way was cleared for a mutually beneficial formal alliance, giving his union a numerical and organizational shot in the arm and the Communists another point of reentry into the mainstream of the labor movement. In March 1936, at a convention in Buffalo, Carey's band united with a larger group of Communists and their fellow travellers, as well as with some other independent electrical locals, to form the United Electrical and Radio Workers of America.[86] Any misgivings the ambitious young Carey might have harbored were assuaged by giving him the post of president of the new union. Not only was this in line with the new tendency for Communists to abjure grabs for total power in the union movement, but it was especially effective with Carey, whose swelling ego was easily massaged by high-sounding titles. Surrounding him in authority, though, were some very heavy pieces of Communist artillery.

Communist strength was centered in two large General Electric locals at Lynn, Massachusetts, and Schenectady, New York. It was from the latter that the secretary-treasurer of the UE, Julius Emspak, came. A protégé of John Turnbull, the English-born leftist founder and leader of the local, Emspak was associated from the beginning with the left-wing of the UE. Raised in a Socialist household, he had followed the rest of his family into the General Electric plant and was working as a tool and die maker when he received a Gerard Swope scholarship, courtesy of GE, to study at Union College in Schenectady. He did well enough there to take up a graduate fellowship in history from Brown University. Life in the Ivy League during the depression left him dissatisfied, and before completing his master's degree he returned to work at GE. It is likely that by that time his background, his undergraduate training, and the depression had turned him toward the CP. Whether he was actually a member of the party when he returned is not known. In 1949, in order to comply with the Taft-Hartley Act, he announced that he had resigned from the party, but there was no indication when he had joined.[87] An ex-Communist from his local claimed later to have signed up his brother Frank in 1935.[88] In any casy, by 1942 Emspak was allegedly firmly established as one of the party's most important secret "notables."[89]

Although Communist party members did not have a majority on the first executive board of the UE, they did have enough influence among others such as Turnbull to hold their own.[90] The Left was soon strengthened by the adherence of an important AFL federal union in Westinghouse's large plant in South Philadelphia, a local whose IWW-oriented leadership had managed to extract recognition from the company.[91]

The final triumph of the Communists and their allies in the UE was ensured in 1937 when James Matles brought into the union a band of ex-Steel and Metal Workers Industrial Union locals. Matles, who emigrated from Rumania in 1929 at age 19, had apparently joined the party soon after his arrival. By 1930 he had already organized a TUUL local among the machine tool workers of Brooklyn.[92] Hardworking and able, he soon made his way up the party and union hierarchy. He became the head of the New York section of SMWIU and then, in late 1933, was allegedly made the head of all party work in the metal trades.[93] With the abandonment of dual unionism in 1935, the steel section of the SMWIU tried to find a home in the AFL's Amalgamated Iron and Steel Workers Union, while the Matles-led Metal Workers Industrial Union negotiated entry into the AFL's International Association of Machinists. In the process, Matles began to play down his Communist affiliations. Whereas in 1933 he had signed a public statement, published in the *Daily Worker*, in support of the Communist party's program, as the change of line approached in 1934 he became cautious about exposing his connections.[94] The delicate negotiations over entry into the anti-Communist IAM made him even more hesitant to appear a wild-eyed Red.[95] In any event, Matles was not wild-eyed and was generally regarded, by friends and most foes alike, as a top-grade union man, smart, dedicated, efficient, honest, and honorable.

The birth of the UE allowed Matles and his locals to abandon their delicate position in the IAM and jump to a more radical union, joining

UE as a group in 1937. Matles was made UE's director of organization. Two of the three top full-time officers of the UE were now either bona fide members of the party or members in all but name. In addition, the majority of its membership was now led by people who responded to the party rather than to Carey.

The AFL had played into the Communists' hands by refusing to charter Carey's industrial union, forsaking the chance to head off Communists in the electrical industry by creating a strong, anti-Communist equivalent of SWOC. Now, Carey, having been driven into alliance with the Communists, helped assure their increasing strength. As Carey basked in media attention and hobnobbed with the celebrities of the liberal and labor world, he began to disdain the dull slogging, the endless meetings with the not-so-glamorous and the not-so-bright that constitute the nuts and bolts of running a union. Matles and Emspak, meanwhile, let Carey take the limelight while they hired and ran the staff. As director of organization, Matles took on a slew of Communist organizers. Emspak did the same with office personnel. So common was the assumption that CP membership was prerequisite for jobs in the UE that hopeful applicants would arrive at interviews with Emspak with their party cards sticking ostentatiously from their pockets.[96] Carey, meanwhile, allowed himself to be recruited as vice-president of the Communist-led American Youth Congress and was active in the League against War and Fascism and other Communist "front" organizations.[97]

The fact that the Communists were well established in the electrical unions before the CIO was even created made them particularly invulnerable to outside intervention. During its formative years the UE received little in the form of aid from Lewis and the CIO, giving Lewis, Hillman, and other non-Communist CIO leaders little leverage within the organization.[98] Furthermore, unlike SWOC, the UE had been formed from the bottom up. Because it was essentially a coalition of independently-organized unions, the UE had a relatively democratic constitution with many features ensuring local autonomy and decentralization of power. The districts into which UE was organized were exceptionally powerful, paying the salaries of their own elected officers. With much of the support for the Communists resting at the local level, it was difficult to conceive of an anti-Communist coup from above. The task of overthrowing its leadership would have to involve arduous battles for local after local, for district after district.

Overall, then, the Communists owed their strength in UE to the survival of radical nuclei in the industry, the flotsam and jetsam of years of sinking radical dreams. Whether they were Schenectady Socialists, New York City Jewish Communists, English class-conscious militant Socialist unionists, or "all-American" IWWs, with few exceptions they managed to take the lead in organizing local unions. They soon coalesced under the leadership of the movement that seemed to come closest to satisfying the radical aspirations of the mid-1930s, the Communist party.[99]

As for the role of the party political leadership, aside from encouraging Matles to pull his group out of the IAM and join the UE, it is likely that they welcomed rather than planned the Communist rise to power in the UE. Matles would allegedly report regularly to the party political leadership and party members within the union would meet regularly to coordinate policy, but there is little indication that the party political leadership played a significant role in deciding the strategy of the UE leftists with regard to union affairs.[100]

Thus, while the party's top leaders were transfixed by steel, auto, waterfront and transport, Emspak, Matles and Carey were busily organizing what became the third largest CIO union and the largest in which Communists held sway. Living together in cheap Manhattan apartments, while working out of a tiny New York office, the executives of the new union managed to direct a massive strike against RCA's giant Camden, New Jersey, plant which forced the company to concede, first, an NLRB election and finally, in 1937, recognition of the UE and reinstatement of fired strikers with full pay. Meanwhile, by the end of 1936, Turnbull and his cohorts at GE in Schenectady had managed to rustle up enough signed cards (an inordinate number of which were apparently signed by themselves) to force an NLRB-supervised election, which they won.[101] Shortly thereafter, in April 1937, Westinghouse's large East Pittsburgh works voted to be represented by UE. With the central fortresses of the two giants, GE and Westinghouse, having fallen, and with key divisions of Philco and RCA in hand, the UE became a credible union. When the Supreme Court upheld the constitutionality of the Wagner Act in 1937, organizing became somewhat easier, and union membership rose rapidly thereafter. Many of the new locals that now entered were Communist-led, their path smoothed by the growing number of Communists in the union's New York City head office.

Yet many locals remained anti- or non-Communist, including Carey's Philco local in Philadelphia. The large Bridgeport, Connecticut, local was a focal point of opposition to Communists almost from the start. Giant Westinghouse Local 601 in Pittsburgh was a battleground between Left and Right, a favorite target of anti-Communist insurgents after the Communists gained the upper hand in 1940. Again, there are few generalizations one can make about why some locals and areas went Communist and others did not. What does stand out is the key role of individual radicals: of the Communists, Socialists, and IWWs who had been passed over and seemingly crushed by the prosperity and anti-unionism of the 1920s now given a new lease on life by the cataclysmic depression. The biographies of many of the UE left-wing leaders, like those of many other leftists in other unions, point to the survival through the 1920s of the American radical tradition. As in the case of UAW Communists, the one characteristic almost all seem to share was left-wing, socially-conscious parents, or at least exposure to radical ideas at a young age. Throughout the 1920s and early 1930s they had been inculcating their children with their ideas and values or, like Turnbull in Schenectady, preaching the Gospel to younger workers whom they took under their wings. It was this younger generation who led the new unions and unionists down the leftist path.

Perhaps the most obvious examples of the persistence of an indigenous radical tradition lay in the International Union of Mine, Mill, and Smelter Workers and the International Woodworkers of America. Both unions were the products of "Wobblie" country, based in part on the transient workers who filled the open-pit mining towns and lumber camps of the Midwest and West. Indeed, Mine, Mill was the direct descendant of the Western Federation of Miners, the most successful of the IWW unions. The IWW had also been strong in the lumber camps of the Midwest and West before and during World War I. Although its influence had been snuffed out by wartime and postwar repression, memories of it and the old time radicalism were still nurtured in many a loggers' camp.

In Mine, Mill, the Communists rose to predominance relatively slowly, but the radical heritage of the miners provided a solid basis of support among the general membership. The old WFM, which had changed its name to the International Union of Mine, Mill, and Smelter Workers of America and joined the AFL in 1916, had almost withered away by the early 1920s, the victim of employer counterattacks and internal dissension. But memories of it lingered on into the 1930s, perpetuated by old-timers in the mining camps and the young men, often their own sons, who sat and listened to their tales of confrontation with the bosses. In an industry where bitterness and conflict have generally been the hallmarks of labor relations, these tales were a potent radical brew. The WFM heritage also left Mine, Mill with a tradition of militant rank-and-file participation in the union. The motto of the resurgent union became the old IWW and WFM slogan: "An injury to one is an injury to all."[102] Although communism itself had few roots among the miners, their heritage was one which made them practically immune to fear of radical labels.

Communists were active almost from the beginning of the revival of Mine, Mill, but as one of a number of militant groups. From its rebirth in 1934, the more conservative groups who guided the union kept them under surveillance and tried to suppress them.[103] Indeed, they likely would have been able to keep the Communists down, even after the growth of CP support and influence on the local level during the next few years, had leadership not played a crucial role in helping the CP vault into power.

The question of leadership cut both ways in Mine, Mill. In essence, the Left was aided by it and the Right did not have it. Crucial to the rise to power of the Communists was the shift of President Reid Robinson to their position in 1937-1938. Robinson was from a militant Socialist unionist background. His father, a Socialist, had been a member of the WFM and IWW in British Columbia and had helped revive Mine, Mill after the passage of NIRA. When, in 1936, the revival faltered and the union's conservative leadership was discredited, the middle-of-the-roaders turned to Robinson, only twenty-six but groomed for leadership by two years as a local union leader, as the man to head off the more left-wing candidate, who was supported by the CP, among others.[104] But the change in leaders did little to improve the union's flagging fortunes. Its organizing efforts were crippled by the continuing depression in the copper industry, which was hard hit by the recession of 1938 and did not reach the high road to recovery until 1940. Young Robinson, though, blamed failure on the lackadaisical attitude of his moderate and conservative supporters. The Communists, on the other hand, were good organizers, and he gradually came to rely on them.[105] When anti-Communists in the all-important Butte mining district organized a potent movement to oust Robinson, Robinson committed himself completely to the Communists, who helped him forge miners' locals in the rest of the country into a "machine."[106]

As president of the union, Robinson controlled organizing efforts, and it was here that Communists and their supporters poured in. He imported Ben Riskin, from UE, to work as research director and a chief adviser. Other appointments of "outsiders" with connections with left-wing unions soon had tongues wagging about Robinson's "new friends".[107] Yet Robinson was able to circumvent his conservative-dominated Executive Board and, with Communist help, assume the initiative in new organizing. While the Right remained programless, leaderless, and aimless, Robinson and his "new friends" were able to establish for themselves the reputation for vigorous unionism that eventually led, during the war, to their complete domination of the union. When, in 1940, the union's anti-Communist vice-president, whom Robinson thought of as a nice old man, but a lazy do-nothing,[108] objected to the Communists' increasing presence in the union, Robinson is reputed to have said, "Look, the Party organized this union. Some of you fellows just got in the way."[109]

There was opposition from the start to the move leftward. The Connecticut district, for example, was a major anti-Robinson center. But its leader, John Driscoll, who was to lead the anti-Communist, anti-Robinson battle for years, was hampered by the fact that, try as he might, he was no Walter Reuther. It was not simply that his power base was not so strong. For years, until the war, the anti-Communists controlled a larger portion of the Executive Board than did the Left,[110] but the right-wing leaders were repeatedly outmaneuvered by the Left.[111]

In Mine, Mill, then, the Left was able to secure a stronghold through a combination of circumstances. The birth of a virtually new union required the organizing sacrifices that Communists were prepared to make, as well as the bureaucractic expertise that they had to offer. The industry had a radical heritage which at most made workers receptive to Communist ideas and at least made them relatively immune to "red-baiting."[112] Finally, leadership again played a decisive role. It is unlikely that the Communists would have been able to achieve the strength they did in the union had Robinson not turned to them for help.

In the International Woodworkers of America, leadership worked against the Communists. Loggers were known as surly and militant, and had produced many IWWs. But nothing of the scope of the WFM had existed in the industry, and unionism was virtually nonexistent among woodworkers after World War I. The CP had formed a lumber workers' union in 1929, but gained little ground. The NIRA had stimulated the formation of some AFL federal union locals in 1933, which became the National Council of Sawmill and Timber Workers in 1933, but the Council was taken over by William Hutcheson's Carpenters Union, and one of Hutcheson's conservative cronies, A. W. Muir, was sent out to run it. The CP, meanwhile, had abandoned its unions and its followers had made their way into the Council. One of them, Harold Pritchett, a British Columbian who had been an organizer for the Workers' Unity League, the Canadian counterpart of TUUL, led the battles against Muir.

The failure of a Muir-led strike in 1935 swelled the rebels' ranks, and they managed to survive his subsequent maneuverings and the union's reorganization. Although the insurgents were willing to stay in the AFL, Hutcheson and his supporters on the AFL Executive Council virtually drove them into the CIO by labelling them crypto-CIO supporters and refusing to deal with them. They took with them around two-thirds of the organized lumber workers. In July 1937, after receiving promises from Lewis and Brophy that the CIO would contribute $50,000 to their organizing fund, the large majority of them voted to form the IWA and join the CIO.[113]

Pritchett and his group emerged in control of the Executive Board of the new union, but their grip on the union was not very secure. They had a solid base in British Columbia, but anti-Communists had considerable support in the Columbia River valley. From the outset, then, the new union was weakened by intense struggles: with the Carpenters Union, whose AFL supporters imposed a crushing boycott on handling all IWA-produced materials and between leftists and rightists within the IWA. The bitter conflicts made new organizing virtually impossible, and this in turn fed the charges of the opposition that Pritchett and his group were mismanaging the union's finances and falling down on the crucial job of organizing, accusations that severely weakened the leftist grip on the union.[114]

Communists did succeed in gaining and retaining the upper hand in a number of less important CIO unions. In 1937, within two years of abandoning TUUL for the skeletal AFL furriers' union, Communists swamped the old leadership and swept into control of the International. With Ben Gold, the Communist head of the New York Joint Council as newly-elected president, they announced their departure from the AFL to join the CIO.[115]

Gold, Irving Potash, and their Communist cohorts soon turned the union into a secure stronghold. Without rival unionism to exploit, the racketeers who had plagued the industry's labor relations were eliminated, and employers were generally more relieved to be dealing with Communists than with the likes of Louis Lepke. After it negotiated some advantageous contracts, the Communist leadership established a solid reputation among the membership as honest, progressive unionists who could deliver the goods on bread and butter issues. This, along with the fact that many of the members shared the leadership's political beliefs, made it relatively easy for Gold to admit openly CP membership.[116]

Communist struggles to organize agricultural workers continued into the Popular Front era but with changing strategy. In 1935, using a Communist-led union of black sharecroppers in Alabama as a springboard, they made unity overtures to the Southern Tenant Farmers Union, which had considerable Socialist and liberal support. While H. L. Mitchell, the STFU leader, held his union back, Donald Henderson rallied sharecroppers and the surviving TUUL agricultural activists into the National Committee for Unity of Agricultural and Rural Workers, which enlisted a scattering of Communist and non-Communist agricultural unionists (a number of whom were now in AFL federal locals) in an unsuccessful drive to secure an AFL charter for a new national agricultural workers union. A breakthrough occurred when, in the euphoria following the great auto and steel victories of early 1937, Harry Bridges convinced Lewis that the CIO could steal a further march on the AFL (and collect an additional $3,600 a month in per capita dues to boot) by organizing agricultural and cannery workers into the same union.[117] At a meeting with Henderson arranged by Bridges and Pressman, Lewis promised Henderson that if he could create a credible national cannery and agricultural workers union it would get a CIO charter and financial aid.[118] Henderson duly gathered together a motley collection of impoverished cannery, agricultural workers, and sharecroppers unions in Denver, Colorado, in July 1937 and founded the United Canning, Agricultural, Packing and Allied Workers of America.

After some hesitation, the STFU joined as an "autonomous" branch of the union, but Mitchell's suspicion of the Communists soon intensified. He interpreted the national union's attempt to collect dues as a Communist bid to take over the STFU and suspected, correctly, that some of his subordinates were now more loyal to the Communists than to him. Relations between Mitchell and Henderson deteriorated until, in early 1939, Mitchell and his followers pulled the STFU, or what remained of it, out of the Cannery Workers. All suffered as a result. So consumed had he become with the intra-union struggle, Mitchell admitted later, that the hard work of organizing sharecroppers had been neglected. Thereafter, neither the STFU nor the UCAPAWA was able to gain significant support among southern farm labor and the STFU faded away.

Lewis was of little help to the struggling union. In January 1938, barely six months after its foundation, he cut off CIO aid to UCAPAWA, leaving twenty-six of its twenty-eight organizers without financing, and began pressuring the impoverished union to increase its contribution to the CIO.[119] Whether Communist leadership or its failure to produce dues was the major factor in sapping Lewis' interest is a moot point. The union thereafter puttered along, gaining some contracts among East and West Coast canners and among North Carolina tobacco workers, but never became a force in the fields.

The CP achieved more in the United Farm Equipment Workers Union, organized with the help of Communists from the auto industry whose organizational problems were similar. Thanks to their control of the Farm Equipment Organizing Committee, formed in 1938 in Chicago, where Communist power was second only to New York City, and a successful organizing strike against giant International Harvester, they managed to gain a CIO charter in 1942 despite UAW claims that it was operating in its jurisdiction.[120]

The United Retail and Wholesale Employees of America, formed by Communist-led secessionists from the AFL Retail Clerks International Protective Association, was granted a CIO charter in May 1937. It had some success in organizing department store personnel, especially in New York City, and by 1939 probably had almost 75,000 members.[121]

The United Office and Professional Workers of America, formed out of some AFL federal locals in May 1939, was less successful in organizing white-collar workers; its 1939 membership was 25,000-30,000.[122] It became most notable in later years when, as bargaining agent for the burgeoning office staff of most CIO unions, it placed union leaders in some rather uncomfortable positions.

Although Harry Bridges was unsuccessful in his attempts to displace ex-IWW Harry Lundeberg's AFL Sailors Union of the Pacific, he assisted Communists in making some headway in the West Coast maritime industry through their control of the CIO's National Union of Marine Cooks and Stewards as well as the Allied Fishermen's Union. Always dependent on the ILWU for assistance, they were generally regarded as minor outposts of Bridges' empire.

The American Communications Association was formed in 1937 under Communist leadership on the basis of the American Radio Telegraphists Association. Its first president, Mervyn Rathbone, was widely regarded as a party member or fellow traveller.[123] His successor, Joseph Selly, had been active in the TUUL and was even more closely identified with the party. The union's main successes came in organizing telegraphers, especially in the New York City area.

Communists also played a major role in the Packinghouse Workers Organizing Committee, formed in 1937. Again, the remnants of earlier packinghouse TUUL unions played a major role, especially in the crucial Chicago area. Other radicals were active as well. (The Trotskyists and syndicalists had dominated the important Austin, Texas, local since its founding in 1933.)[124] However, the Communists never challenged the union's non-Communist but "progressive" leadership, which, under Ralph Helstein, tended to follow their line on foreign policy, at least until the cold war years, and was particularly tolerant of their activities.

Perhaps the most celebrated unions where Communists exerted great influence were those where their actual numbers were fewest: the Hollywood unions. The dominant union among the studio technicians was the AFL-affiliated International Association of Theater and Studio Employees (IATSE). The CIO's competing union, the Confederation of Studio Unions, was led by Herbert Sorrell, a fellow traveller. Although it made inroads in some areas, the CSU never came close to IATSE in size and power. The CIO did manage to organize those in more visible positions into various "talent guilds" for which the Communists achieved some minor fame. Although they never came close to dominating it, they did achieve considerable influence in the Screen Actors' Guild, mainly because they were active, noisy, and exerted some influence over liberal allies such as Ronald Reagan. Nevertheless, under the stern anti-Communist leadership of conservative actors such as Robert Montgomery and George Murphy, they never became more than a vocal minority in that union.[125] Among the directors (presumably the most individualistic, authoritarian, and least egalitarian of crafts), the Communists were practically nonexistent. Only seven of the approximately 500 members of the Directors' Guild were party members in the late 1930s.[126]

The writers were a different story. Communists played a major role in founding the Screen Writers' Guild in 1933 and they and their fellow travellers controlled a majority on its executive board. Led by John Howard Lawson, Dalton Trumbo, and Ring Lardner, Jr., the party-oriented group formed a vocal, articulate, and effective forum for Communist views in Hollywood, helping to rally many liberals in the Hollywood community to Communist-supported causes.

Overall, then, there is little evidence of pattern or grand design in the mosaic of Communist unions. Opponents often charged that grand schemes for wartime sabotage formed a pattern. Bridges' longshoremen's union, embroiled in controversy from the start, was often accused of being a key part of some overall plan. So, of course, was the NMU and, increasingly, the UE. Even the TWU was often included. By the postwar era, many of these charges were graced with academic respectability. Vernon Jensen, for example, introduced his 1954 monograph on Mine, Mill by speculating:

It is not easy to prove, but it is not unlikely, that the strategic importance of the nonferrous metals industry to our economy was, along with other considerations, a paramount reason for Communist attempts to control unionism in the nonferrous metals industry. A better way of crippling a defense or war economy in the United States than to cut off or obstruct the production of nonferrous metals could hardly be devised.[127]

Yet, as Jensen's book itself confirms, there is no indication that CP strength in Mine, Mill was the result of any master plan drawn up in Moscow and New York. Rather, it was to a large extent the result of an anti-Communist, Reid Robinson, unexpectedly turning coat and inviting in the Communists.

As for overall patterns, it is difficult to think of the amount of time and effort Communists expended throughout the 1920s and 1930s on the textile and needle trades, hardly of crucial strategic importance, to realize that like everyone else they tried to take power wherever the opportunities were most readily available to them, rather than in conformity with some rigid design for sabotage. They did have predilections, such as their well-justified conviction that the steel industry was of crucial importance in unionizing American workers, but often their egalitarian impulse led them to expend inordinate energy on organizing those least powerful and least strategically placed: tragic cases such as the migrant workers, "losers" such as southern textile workers, the infinitely replaceable Macy's salesclerks, or hospital workers. These people lay at the very bottom of the union ladder.

As for patterns in the response to Communist overtures among American workers, the most striking feature is the lack of apparent pattern. In part, this is merely the result of the previous entrenchment of conservative unionism in a whole series of industries, plus the successful efforts of anti-Communists, such as those who controlled the UMW and SWOC, to get in first and keep the CP out. Most conservative unionists were able to remain entrenched in most industries for basically the same reasons that the Communists were able to gain control of many unions: the importance of leadership in American unions and the generally low levels of rank-and-file participation in their affairs. Unions, even in the emotion-charged 1930s, were simply not a major outlet for the activities, social or political, of most American workers. The new CIO unions did provide a field upon which a new generation of leaders, themselves often nurtured in the American radical tradition, could operate, but their political radicalism was rarely a reflection of rank-and-file views.

So crucial are the advantages for those in power in an American union, in terms of patronage, control over large bureaucracies comprising their supporters, and power to eject or crush dissidents, that successful rank-and-file rebellions are rare. Successful union rebellions need a combination of extraordinary circumstances, ranging from splits in the power structure verging on civil war to substantial external aid from other unions and/or government. It is no wonder that the most successful way of changing unionism in American industry has generally not been rebellion from within but competition from outside. This is one of the reasons dual unionism has always been so dreaded. The CP made great inroads in the union movement of the 1930s in large part because the creation of the CIO created an opportunity for successful dual unionism. It is rather ironic that, in this sense, the tactic that they officially abandoned, along with TUUL, in 1935, proved soon thereafter to be so advantageous to them.

NOTES

1. "NO!" retorted Pressman, who went on to minimize the influence of the party on the organization and maximize the role of Lewis himself. Saul Alinsky, *John L. Lewis* (N.Y.: Knopf, Vintage Books, 1970), 153.

2. E.g., Max Kampelman, *The Communist Party vs. the CIO* (New York: Praeger, 1957), 14.

3. *Daily Worker*, June 26, 1963.

4. Jack Stachel, "Problems Before the 56th Annual Convention of the A.F. of L.," *The Communist*, vol. 15, no. 11 (November 1936), 1046-53.

5. John Brophy, *A Miner's Life* (Madison: University of Wisconsin Press, 1964), 274.

6. Len De Caux, *Labor Radical* (Boston: Beacon Press, 1970), 234.

7. Jay Lovestone to John Brophy, April 6, 1937, John Brophy, Papers, Catholic University of America Library, Washington, D.C., Box A5-6.

8. "Communist Meeting, New York, June 24, 1937," intelligence report on plenary session of Central Committee, CPUSA, June 18-20, 1937, John P. Frey, Papers, Library of Congress, Washington, D.C., Box 5, Folder 9.

9. Earl Browder, Oral History Interview, Oral History Collection of Columbia University, N.Y., N.Y. (hereafter COHC), 349.

10. "Communist Meeting, New York, April 23, 1937," report on meeting of Politburo of the Central Committee of the CPUSA, Cleveland, April 17, 1937, Frey Papers, Box 5, Folder 9.

11. "CIO-Communist Notes," mimeographed newsletter, in Frey Papers, Box 5, Folder 9.

12. William Z. Foster, *From Bryan to Stalin* (N.Y.: International Publishers, 1937), 336.

13. "Communist Meeting, New York, June 24, 1937," Frey Papers.

14. Ibid.; Harvey Levenstein, "The Daily Worker," in *The American Radical Press*, ed. Joseph Conlin (Westport: Greenwood Publishing, 1973), 1, 224-43.

15. "Communist Meeting, New York, June 24, 1937," Frey Papers.

16. *DW*, May 10, 1936.

17. "Communist Meeting, April 23, 1937," Frey Papers.

18. "B," Section Organizer, "Functioning and Problems of the Waterfront Units," *Party Organizer*, vol. 9, no. 4 (April 1936), 18.

19. E.g., James Carey, Oral History Interview, COHC, 252.

20. Harvey Swados, *Radical at Large* (London: Rupert Hart-Davis, 1968), 69.

21. E.g., see Mario Manzado's recollections of CP tactics in organizing close to twenty-five SWOC locals in the Chicago area in Staughton and Alice Lynd, eds., *Rank and File* (Boston: Beacon Press, 1973), 140, as well as Wyndham Mortimer, *Organize! My Life as a Union Man* (Boston: Beacon Press, 1971), ch. 8 and 9; John W. Anderson, Oral History Interview, Wayne State University Archives of Urban History and Labor Affairs, 166-71; and Julius Emspak, Oral History Interview, COHC, 69. Emspak said that of the 9,000-odd workers at the Schenectady General Electric plant, only ten or twelve were really active in setting up the union that came to represent them. The House Un-American Activities Committee, making a different point, agreed. U.S. Congress, House, Committee on Un-American Activities, *Hearings on Communist Infiltration of Labor Unions*, 81st Cong., 1st sess. (1949), 651.

22. Harry Block, Oral History Interview, 1967, Pennsylvania State University Archives of Labor History, State College, Pa. (hereafter PSUA), 15.

23. Russel Leach, Oral History Interview, Wayne State University Archives of Labor History and Urban Affairs (hereafter WSUA), 19.

24. Al Leggat, Oral History Interview, WSUA, 17.

25. H. L. Mitchell to Gardner Jackson, September 3, 1936, Southern Tenant Farmers Union, Papers, cited in Donald Grubbs, *Cry from the Cotton* (Chapel Hill: University of North Carolina Press, 1971), 81.

26. The Reverend Charles Owen Rice, Oral History Interview 1, PSUA, 13.

27. John P. Frey, Oral History Interview, COHC, 645.

28. David Brody, "Radical Labor History and Rank-and-File-Militancy," *Labor History*, vol. 16, no. 1 (Winter 1975), 117-26. Brody also points out, quite aptly, that the Lynds' *Rank and File*, which was intended to underline the importance of rank-and-file militancy in organizing American labor, does not quite achieve this with regard to the 1930s. The interviewees from this period were largely CP militants sent in to organize factories, rather than people percolating up from the shop floor.

29. Julius Emspak, Oral History Interview, COHC, 88.

30. Wyndham Mortimer, *Organize!*, 82-83.

31. Ibid., 88-89. Even in his eighties, Mortimer could not abandon the habits of a lifetime. His otherwise lively autobiography is marred mainly by his evasiveness about his relationship to the party.

32. Central Executive Committee, CPUSA, "Resolution on the Fight Against Expulsions in the Machinists Union," undated [1925?] copy in Daniel Bell Collection, Tamiment Institute Library, New York University, New York, N.Y., Box 6.

33. Draft of Plan for Work in Miners Union and Agenda for National Miners Conference, Chicago, May 8-9, 1926, Earl Browder, George Arents Research Library, Syracuse University, Syracuse, N.Y., Papers, Series 11, Box 19, "Trade Union Committee of CEC" Folder.

34. E.g., William Z. Foster, "The Situation in the Machinists Union and the Immediate Tasks of the Left Wing," supplement to "TUEL General Metal Trades Program Now in Effect," undated [1926?], cited in (?) Goldsmith, untitled, unpublished, undated [1956?] ms. in Bell Collection, Box 6, "Goldsmith Mss." Folder.

35. Roger Keeran, "Communists and Auto Workers: The Struggle for a Union, 1919-1941" (Ph.D. diss., University of Wisconsin, 1974), 90-107.

36. Frank Emspak, Interview with Tom Wright, November 1969, cited in Frank Emspak, "The Break-Up of the Congress of Industrial Organizations (CIO), 1945-1950" (Ph.D. diss., University of Wisconsin, 1972), 49.

37. CIO, Transcript of the Hearings before the Committee to Investigate Charges against the International Longshoremen's and Warehousemen's Union, Washington, D.C., June 1950 (hereafter referred to as CIO, "ILWU Hearings"), copy in CIO, Papers, Office of the Secretary-Treasurer, Wayne State University Archives of Labor History and Urban Affairs, Detroit, Mich. (hereafter Carey Papers), Box 110, 610-12.

38. U.S. Congress, Senate, Comittee on the Judiciary, Subcommittee on Internal Security, *Hearings on Communist Domination of Union Officials in Vital Defense Industry—International Union of Mine, Mill, and Smelter Workers of America*, 82nd Cong., 2nd sess. (1952), 147.

39. Report, "Communist Meeting, New York, April 23, 1937," Frey Papers, Box 5, Folder 9.

40. Staughton and Alice Lynd, eds., *Rank and File*, 85.

41. Ibid.

42. Keeran, "Communists and Auto Workers," 104-5.

43. L. J. Braverman, "Some Good Union Organizers Poor Builders of the Party," *Party Organizer*, vol. 10, no. 1 (January 1937), 28.

44. U.S. Congress, House, Committee on Un-American Activities, *Hearings Regarding Communism in the United States Government*, part 2, 81st Cong., 2nd sess. (1950), 2850-2900.

45. Daniel Bell, interview with Clint Golden, October 26, 1955, Bell Collection, Box 3; Lee Pressman, Oral History Interview, COHC, 163-74.

46. Frances Perkins, Oral History Interview, COHC, vol. 6, 240.

47. John Brophy, Oral History Interview, COHC, 671.

48. Len De Caux, *Labor Radical*, 219-21.

49. Ibid., 269.

50. Brophy, COHC, 671.

51. James Wechsler, *Labor Baron: A Portrait of John L. Lewis* (New York: Morrow, 1944), 124.

52. For example, when the SWOC campaign began, Foster supplemented his previous pamphlet on steel organizing with seventeen pages of instructions on tactics to the CP organizers. It was all practical advice of the kind that would apply to organizers of any ideology, except, perhaps, for the Stakhanovist recommendation that "Principles of Socialist competition should be introduced to stimulate the work of organizers, to create friendly organizing rivalry between workers and workers, department and department, mill and mill, town and town." William Z. Foster, "Outline of Organizing Methods in the Steel Campaign," in Frey Papers, Box 5, Folder 9.

53. Staughton Lynd, "The Possibilities of Radicalism in the Early 1930's: The Case of Steel," *Radical America*, vol. 6, no. 6 (November-December 1972), 52-53.

54. Memorandum, March 1, 1937, Frey Papers, Box 5, Folder 9.

55. John Williamson, *Dangerous Scot* (New York: International Publishers, 1969), 125.

56. Foster, *From Bryan to Stalin*, 374.

57. Walter Galenson, *The CIO Challenge to the AFL* (Cambridge: Harvard University Press, 1960), 111.

58. Rice, OH-1, PSUA, 13; Report, "Communist Meeting, New York, June 24, 1937," Frey Papers.

59. Frey, COHC, 650.

60. Gus Scholle to Adolph Germer, June 23, 1939, Adolph Germer, Papers, State Historical Society of Wisconsin, Madison, Wisc.

61. Report, "Communist Meeting, Gary, Indiana, October 14, 1937," Frey Papers, Box 5, Folder 9.

62. Galenson, *CIO Challenge*, 112.

63. Lynd, *Rank and File*, 142.

64. Rice, OH-1, PSUA, 14.

65. Rice, OH-1, PSUA, 13; "Steel Workers and Communists," Interview with Clint Golden, October 26, 1955, Bell Collection, Box 3.

66. It also drew on a large stream of relatively uneducated migrants from Appalachia and the rural South, who proved to be surprisingly class-conscious and militant unionists. See John C. Legget, "Sources and Consequences of Working-Class Consciousness," in Arthur Shostak and William Gomberg, eds. *Blue-Collar World* (Englewood Cliffs, N.J.: Prentice-Hall, 1964), 235-47.

67. Keeran, "Communists and Auto Workers," 115-214; Mortimer, *Organize!*, 60-68; Williamson, *Dangerous Scot*, 101-3.

68. Keeran, "Communists and Auto Workers," 214-15; Mortimer, *Organize!*, 60-68; Williamson, *Dangerous Scot*, 101-3.

69. Williamson, *Dangerous Scot*, 102-3.

70. Ibid.; Sidney Fine, *Sit-Down* (Ann Arbor: University of Michigan Press, 1969), 220-23; Keeran, "Communists and Auto Workers," 226-85.

71. John W. Anderson, Oral History Interview, WSUA, 36.

72. Ibid., 29.

73. Ibid., 62.

74. Ibid., 63.

75. "The Maritime Unions," *Fortune*, vol. 16, no. 5 (September 1937), 134.

76. Edwin Lahey, Oral History Interview, COHC, 67.

77. Charles P. Larrowe, *Harry Bridges: The Rise and Fall of Radical Labor in the United States* (New York: Lawrence Hill, 1972), 16; Dalton Trumbo, *Harry Bridges* (Hollywood: League of American Writers, 1941); "The Maritime Unions," *Fortune*, vol. 16, no. 3 (July 1937), 132-34.

78. "The Maritime Unions," *Fortune*, vol. 16, no. 5 (September 1937), 137.

79. Testimony of Hedley Stone, CIO,"ILWU Hearings," 594.

80. James Carey, OH, COHC, 341.

81. De Caux, *Labor Radical*, 235.

82. CIO, "ILWU Hearings," 394.

83. L. H. Whittemore, *The Man Who Ran the Subway: The Story of Mike Quill* (New York: Holt, Rinehart and Winston, 1968), 19-24; U.S., Congress, House, Committee on Un-American Activities, *A Communist in a "Workers' Paradise." John Santo's Own Story*, 99th Cong., 1st sess., 1963 (Washington, D.C.: U.S. Government Printing Office, 1963).

84. Minutes of the AFL Executive Council Meeting, January 9 and February 14, 1935, 150-55, cited in "Goldsmith Ms.," Bell Collection, Box 6.

85. Irving Bernstein, *Turbulent Years: A History of the American Worker, 1933-1941* (Boston: Houghton Mifflin, 1970), 104.

86. "Goldsmith Ms.," 30-46; James Matles and James B. Higgins, *Them and Us* (New York: Prentice-Hall, 1974), 22-53.

87. *New York Times*, October 22, 1949.

88. U.S. Congress, House, Committee on Un-American Activities, *Hearings Regarding Communism in Labor Unions*, 80th Cong., 1st sess. (1947), 217.

89. Louis Budenz, former labor editor of the *Daily Worker*, claimed that Emspak's code name was "Comrade Juniper" and Bridges' was "Comrade Rossi." U.S. Congress, House, Committee on Education and Labor, *Investigation of Communist Infiltration of UERMWA*, 80th Cong., 2nd sess. (1948), 353-56.

90. "Goldsmith Ms.," 46.

91. Matles and Higgins, *Them and Us*, 54.

92. James Matles, Oral History Interview, PSUA, 1-14.

93. Affidavit of Sidney Mason, former UE staff member, Brooklyn, N.Y., undated [1956?], Bell Collection, Box 6.

94. *Daily Worker*, November 6, 1933.

95. Sidney Mason, Affidavit, Bell Collection.

96. Julius Emspak, Oral History Interview, COHC, 239. Emspak told this story in order to deny the charges. According to him, he would lean forward and push the cards back in, hiring on objective criteria alone. In any event, an extraordinary number of party members and fellow travellers did end up on the UE payroll, including, as the final straw for Carey, Carey's own private secretary, whom he suspected of spying on him for Emspak.

97. His opponent, Albert Fitzgerald, later made the point that despite Carey's subsequent denials, he was well aware at the time of their true nature (Albert Fitzgerald, Oral History Interview, PSUA, 30). It would be doing Carey a disservice to conclude that he was one of the few men in public life who did *not* know.

98. Julius Emspak, OH, COHC, 125-28.

99. Even their original opponents within the union, the group surrounding Harry Block in the large Westinghouse local in Pittsburgh, were from Socialist backgrounds. The Reverend Charles Owen Rice, Oral History Interview 2, PSUA, 15.

100. U.S. Congress, House, Committee on Un-American Activities, *Hearings Regarding Communism in Labor Unions*, 80th Cong., 2nd sess., 1947, 217-21; House Committee

on Education and Labor, *Investigation of UERMWA*, 212-16; U.S. Congress, House, Committee on Un-American Activities, *Hearings on Communist Infiltration of Labor Unions*, 81st Cong., 1st sess., 1949, 651-55; Sidney Mason, Affidavit, Bell Collection. Twenty years after leaving the party, Earl Browder was as cryptic as ever regarding the intricate relationship between the party and the UE; "The Party people were in close rapport with the central leadership," he said, "and they were at the same time the chief leaders of the union." Browder, OH, COHC, 391-92.

101. House, Committee on Education and Labor, *Investigation of UERMWA*, 212-17.

102. Vernon Jensen, *Nonferrous Metals Industry Unionism, 1932-1954: A Story of Leadership Controversy* (Ithaca: Cornell University Press, 1954), 2-5, 12; See Vernon Jensen, *Heritage of Conflict* (Ithaca: Cornell University Press, 1950), for the bitter background of labor relations in the field.

103. Jensen, *Nonferrous Metals*, 11.

104. Reid Robinson, Oral History Interview, PSUA, 1-21; Jensen, *Nonferrous Metals Industry Unionism*, 30-35.

105. Robinson, OH, PSUA, 24.

106. Testimony of Alex Cashin, Transcript of Meeting of CIO Committee and Provisional Mineworkers Committee Re: IUMMSW, March 25-26, 1947, in Carey Papers, Box 111.

107. Jensen, *Nonferrous Metals*, 52-53.

108. Robinson, OH, PSUA, 24.

109. This story was told by ex-Communist Maurice Travis, who had been the top party member in the union. U.S. Senate, Committee on the Judiciary, Internal Security Subcommittee, 82nd Cong., 2nd sess., 1952, *Hearings on Communist Domination of Union Officials in Vital Defense Industry—International Union of Mine, Mill, and Smelter Workers*, 138.

110. Even by 1941, only three out of nine Executive Board members were acceptable to Robinson and the Left, and one of them was dying. Jensen, *Nonferrous Metals*, 73-75.

111. Ibid., 78.

112. It had been used for so long and so often by company spokesmen against union sympathizers of all stripes that even the right-wing in the union shied away from it. Ibid., 47.

113. Irving Abella, *Nationalism, Communism, and Canadian Labour* (Toronto: University of Toronto Press, 1973), 112-13; Verson Jensen, *Lumber and Labor* (New York: Rinehart, 1945), 122-55; Bernstein, *Turbulent Years*, 624-30.

114. Abella, *Nationalism, Communism, and Canadian Labour*, 113; Lorin Cary, "Adolph Germer: From Labor Agitator to Labor Professional" (Ph.D. diss., University of Wisconsin, 1968), 130-44; Jensen, *Lumber and Labor*, 213-36.

115. Philip S. Foner, *The Fur and Leather Workers Union* (Newark: Nordan Press, 1950), 25-44; Robert D. Leiter, "The Fur Workers' Union," *Industrial and Labor Relations Review*, June 1950, 163-80.

116. Leiter, "Fur Workers' Union," 180-85.

117. Grubbs, *Cry from the Cotton*, 71-87, 162-66; Carey McWilliams, *Factories in the Fields* (Philadelphia: Lippincott, 1939), 268-73; Bernstein, *Turbulent Years*, 150-51.

118. John Brophy, "Twenty Years with CIO," unpublished ms., John Brophy, Papers, Catholic University of America Library, Washington, D.C., Box A5-41, chap. 11, 4-7.

119. Grubbs, *Cry from the Cotton*, 167-88; Louis Cantor, *A Prologue to the Protest Movement* (Durham: Duke University Press, 1969), 95-120.

120. See chap. 10 for the political complexities of that dispute.

121. Walter Galenson, *Rival Unionism in the United States* (New York: Russel and Russel, 1940), 22.

122. Ibid.

123. Kampelman, *Communist Party vs. the CIO*, 196.

124. David Brody, *The Butcher Workmen* (Cambridge: Harvard University Press, 1964), 223.

125. David Saposs, *Communism in American Unions* (New York: McGraw-Hill, 1959), 62.

126. Ibid.

127. Jensen, *Nonferrous Metals*, xiii.

3 THE RISE OF ANTICOMMUNISM IN THE CIO, 1938-1940

To the party leadership in New York City, 1938 and 1939 brought a feeling of burgeoning power over the labor movement. Although the CIO as a whole was losing momentum, leftist unions were gaining remarkable strength. The Communist leadership nursed the hope that, with the Communist and "progressive" forces in labor swelling in number, the conservative leadership of the AFL would be repudiated by AFL liberals enamored of the New Deal, who would thus lay the groundwork for the reunification of the labor movement.[1] The formal links between the party's political leadership and its union leaders were improved and strengthened. Regular meetings to coordinate the activities of party trade unionists and party militants on the district level were expanded.[2] Representatives of the party's political arm became fixtures at union conventions, coordinating and directing the strategy of the increasingly visible leftist caucuses.

But, except for their intervention at union conventions, there is little to indicate that the party's political leadership played a significant role in directing the work of the Communists within the unions. The new district meetings, for example, functioned mainly as morale-boosting rallies. There, party militants would be encouraged to help one or another CIO union in its drive to organize workers in the area.[3] Instances of party leadership overruling the trade union leadership on bread-and-butter issues and imposing their will on reluctant unionists are rare, albeit noteworthy and important, as will be seen.

Indeed, if anything, the party's tethers on Communist unionists were loosening. As part of Browder's overall campaign to prove that communism was simply "Twentieth Century Americanism," the party had been moving towards a new, more open, and seemingly more "democratic" posture. It was announced that fractions had been abolished in the unions. No longer would Communist union members be obliged to attend fraction meetings to receive, discuss, and coordinate the implementation of "the line."[4] "Shop papers," published by nuclei and fractions in various plants, were also abandoned, and party militants were thereby encouraged to play a less distinctive role in the broad coalitions they were to help build. The party leadership also tried to allay the suspicions of non-Communists by being more open about what its line actually was. Roy Hudson, its labor coordinator, declared himself proud that at the UAW convention in August 1939, Browder had publicly proclaimed the Communist party position.[5]

The reins could be loosened a bit because, for the most part, there was little maneuvering to be done. The line of the party was virtually indistinguishable from the line of the CIO. Indeed, for most Communists in the CIO, the overall "line" was simply the party's mandate to build the CIO.

When it came to questions of foreign policy, a peculiar convergence of interests took place between Communist and pro-Communist union leaders and the party's political leadership. This was a sphere of all-consuming interest to the political leadership and of relatively less importance to the union leadership. Rare was the union leader, on the Left or Right, who did not accept the maxim that the mass of the membership cared little for foreign policy issues and would be moved into rebellion only by bread-and-butter issues. Thus, the leftist union leaders could pay their party dues, as it were, by having their union conventions and their newspapers trumpet the foreign policy line. It seemed to cost little in terms of control of the unions, yet it proved their orthodoxy.

Besides, they generally believed in it. Some, such as Reid Robinson, the Mine, Mill leader, felt limited by a lack of education and background in the area. For them, it seemed natural to follow the lead of sophisticates in foreign policy such as Pressman.[6] It is no accident that when, after the war, massive amounts of evidence were culled from the union press and the testimony of defectors in multifarious attempts to prove that the left-wing unions were "slavish" followers of Stalin and his minions, the overwhelming bulk of it concerned the leftists' support of the "twists and turns" of the line in foreign policy. Indeed, the paucity of evidence regarding ways in which the CP line and the intervention of the political leadership affected the members of a union on pocketbook issues forced anti-Communists to inflate the significance of isolated events such as the strike of the UAW at North American Aviation in June 1941 out of all proportion. On the other hand, differences among the left-wing unions, such as their various attitudes towards the beginnings of Sidney Hillman's push for labor participation in government agencies in 1939, were ignored.[7]

The CP and its adherents in the CIO earned a reputation for functioning as a well-oiled coordinated machine within the CIO because they did so most effectively in the most visible place: at the annual CIO conventions. There, with the eyes of non-Communist unionists and the national press on their every move, they caucused secretly and generally voted as a bloc. From 1937 on, according to Michael Quill, they would meet with a representative of the CPUSA and receive instructions on how to vote on various issues.[8] It was here that Pressman would often play an important role, coordinating strategy and smoothing communications between the party's political representatives and leftist union leaders.[9]

The party's Politburo would also meet before the regular meetings of the CIO's Executive Board, in time to inform those to whom Eugene Dennis referred as "our union friends" of the party's wishes regarding such major issues as proposals for reunifying the AFL and CIO and international trade union collaboration.[10]

For the most part, the party's political leadership was primarily concerned about the CIO's stand on national political and foreign policy issues, and there was little reluctance among its members and followers in the CIO to go along with it on these issues. After all, by mid-1939, there was little in Browder's public political position with which Roosevelt himself would likely have disagreed privately. Even Foster was totally swept up by the new line by early 1939. He wrote Browder confidentially in February 1939 that the CIO leftists should encourage compromise and unity with the AFL in order to strengthen the liberal camp and provide support for Roosevelt's "peace policy."[11] But the party leadership's willingness to compromise to promote unity in the face of domestic and foreign reaction was not shared by most CIO unionists, including John L. Lewis, who was becoming increasingly dubious of Roosevelt's policies and discomfited by the Communist role in the CIO.[12] Moreover, in mid-1939, a growing obsession with unity at all costs led Browder to force a compromise on UAW leftists that many regarded as a needless surrender of power in an all-important union.

The key figure in turning back the Communists in the UAW was Sydney Hillman, the president of the Amalgamated Clothing Workers of America. A growing power within the CIO and in national politics, Hillman was intensely committed to both the CIO and reformist politics. The Jewish leader of a largely Jewish union, he also harbored a deep concern over the rise of fascism in Europe. Until 1939, he had downplayed the danger of the Communists in the CIO. When his New York-based associate, David Dubinsky, pulled his International Ladies Garment Workers Union out of the CIO and returned to the AFL in

1938, in part because of his fear of growing Communist influence in the CIO,[13] Hillman refused to go along. Within the American Labor Party, the New York state political party used as a vehicle for channelling left-wing support to Roosevelt, Hillman had tried to live with the Communists rather than oust them as Dubinsky had.

During the 1920s Hillman, like Dubinsky, had fought bitter battles with Communists trying to "bore from within" his union. Although he had been somewhat less hysterical about the battle than Dubinsky, Hillman still carried the scars of those conflicts. The main difference between them was that he, like Lewis, thought the Communists could be controlled and directed towards useful ends, such as organizing the CIO. When, in 1936, Frances Perkins warned him that she thought Lee Pressman was a Communist, Hillman assured her that this was not true.[14] Although, in early 1937, along with others, Hillman did note that Pressman seemed to be the only one in the CIO leadership who seemed to be able to get through to the GM sit-down strike leaders, Hillman ascribed it to Pressman's youth, and the youth of the sit-down leaders, rather than, as Perkins and others suspected, common fealty to the party.[15] Hillman was also able to turn a blind eye to the apparent party connections and sympathies of his own senior lawyer, John Abt, preferring not to acknowledge what almost everyone else assumed.

Nevertheless, like Lewis, Hillman always thought that one could let the Communists go just so far before running the danger of changing from the user to the used. When they threatened to become the dominant force in a union, he was ready to step in to stop them. He reached this point regarding the Communists in the CIO during the spring of 1939, at about the same time that Lewis, with whom he fought increasingly, had the same thought.[16]

Hillman's determination to limit CP influence in the CIO surfaced in spectacular fashion in March 1939, when he intervened dramatically in the UAW convention in Cleveland to help head off what might have been a Communist victory.

Almost from the moment he assumed the UAW presidency, Homer Martin had been alienating a growing number of auto unionists, especially the Socialists and Communists, whom he tried to weaken by centralizing union power. Yet, to the dismay of many UAW Communists, the party leadership urged a policy of restraint and submission in the face of Martin's increasingly serious depredations. When Martin demoted Robert Travis, the top Communist UAW organizer, in early 1938, the Communists, in the words of a disgusted Socialist ally, assumed "an almost Christ-like" position for the sake of "unity at almost any cost."[17] Only the mid-1938 attempt by Martin (acting on the advice of Communist expellee and arch-factionalist Jay Lovestone) to purge the leadership of all his opponents forced the party politicos to drop their opposition to spirited resistance. Even here, Browder felt compelled to justify the resistance in convoluted Popular Front terms and to restrain the Communists from bids to gain control of the union. Martin's attempted coup, he told UAW Communists, was really an attack on the New Deal, for its "immediate incentive" was an attempt to defeat the reelection bid of Frank Murphy, the liberal Democratic governor of Michigan who was close to Roosevelt. To head this off, Lewis must be convinced to help the anti-Martin coalition. "So far as concessions and compromises are concerned," Browder wrote, "we can accept almost anything that is acceptable to Lewis himself." There would be no Communist bid for power.[18]

Thanks in part to Lewis, Martin was forced out of the UAW-CIO into the rival AFL where, with Lovestone and a little band of followers, he set up a competing auto workers union. When, in March 1939, the UAW-CIO gathered in Cleveland to elect a new president and executive, the Communists were in the forefront of the triumphant coalition that had driven him out. By now they had developed broad support within the union. Although Wyndham Mortimer still had an excellent chance at winning the union presidency, the Communists had an even more attractive candidate, George Addes.

Addes had all the qualifications for union leadership. Honest and intelligent, he was also down-to-earth and well-liked. (Indeed so likeable that he taught others how to win friends and influence people at a Dale Carnegie School.)[19] He also displayed a willingness to go along with the Communists on almost all important issues, something that characterized him for his remaining years in union leadership. When the UAW Communists rallied behind Addes, only the ambitious Socialist Walter Reuther was left as a serious rival for the presidency, and even he did not think he had much of a chance against the man from Dale Carnegie. A few days before the convention, he secretly offered to support Addes.[20]

At the convention, Mortimer and Addes were clearly the most popular leaders. The mere mention of Addes' name provoked spontaneous chants of "We Want Addes" and the singing of "Addes Is Our Leader, We Shall Not Be Moved."[21] Mortimer estimated that the Communists and their allies controlled 85 percent of the delegate vote while Addes felt there was no question that he would be elected by an overwhelming majority.[22] But the victory within their grasp was snatched from their hands by visitors from the East. Sidney Hillman and Phillip Murray, the two powerful CIO union presidents who had helped nullify the Martin coup, arrived at the convention determined to head off a Communist victory. Although publicly denying any interest in influencing the union's elections,[23] they lobbied forcefully for eliminating the UAW vice-presidencies, currently Communist strongholds, and for the selection of R. J. Thomas, an ineffectual man who had only recently defected from Martin's camp, as president. Indeed, they had the convention move into closed session where they urged moderation on the union, and Murray, carried away, delivered an angry denunciation of communism and Communists.[24] Despite their obvious anti-Communist biases, Murray and Hillman came armed with a major trump card. Although the relationship of their mission to the wishes of John L. Lewis was and remains unclear, they carried the endorsement of none other than Earl Browder. Browder was convinced that, were Addes and his Communist supporters to roll into power in the UAW, anti-Communists would be driven into Martin's UAW-AFL, exposing the Communists to the charge of having "wrecked" the union. This would be proof that, contrary to their professions of the fealty to the Popular Front, they were indeed the same old sectarian dual unionists of the Third Period. It would lead inevitably, it seemed, to the disintegration of the carefully constructed alliance with Lewis and the other liberals in the CIO which was the centerpiece of Communist political strategy. When Mortimer and other UAW Communists still balked at supporting Thomas, Browder himself, surrounded by a phalanx of party leaders, arrived in Cleveland. The overriding concern of these cautious men was not to maximize Communist influence in the UAW-CIO, but to ensure that the Communists could not be accused of sectarianism. Thomas was their man, they argued, because he would be able to woo back most of the 17,000 members who had followed Martin into the UAW-AFL, helping that most essential element of the Popular Front, "labor unity."[25]

As a result, most of the UAW Communists and their followers shifted their support to Thomas, forcing Addes to drop his candidacy and settle for the post of secretary-treasurer. In this instance, wrote an anti-Communist labor reporter, their opportunism made the Communists "so self-effacing" that they were no longer a threat in the union.[26] After Thomas' election, drunken left-wing delegates marched through downtown Cleveland, singing "Addes Is Our Leader, Thomas Gets Our Votes."[27]

Had they known what lay in the future, they would have become too drunk to sing. The Communists, who had gone along with the abolition of the vice-presidencies their men occupied, had in fact just passed the high water-mark of their formal power in the CIO. While Thomas tried to avoid committing himself to the leftist coalition, Walter Reuther, a masterful union politician, built up a powerful machine that he soon turned on Thomas, the Communists, and their allies. Reuther's election to the union presidency in 1946 owed much to Thomas' inability to counteract the assault on power that Reuther was organizing under his very nose. In turn, the triumph of Reuther proved crucial in shifting the internal balance of power in the CIO against the Communists, paving the way for a massive anti-Communist purge that could hardly have been contemplated had the UAW been controlled by Communists and their sympathizers. If any single event could be said to have contributed most to this crucial defeat of the Communists in postwar America, it was Browder's intervention.[28]

The CPUSA political leadership saw their role as that of relating and adjusting CP tactics within unions to the overall policies of the party, in the same way as the Comintern had coordinated and rationalized the policies of various Communist parties on an international level, but like repeated occupants of the seats of power in Moscow, they thus inevitably forced subordinates into actions which made sense from far away but not on the scene. In the interests of a coordinated overall strategy, the political leadership had promoted a tactical retreat in the UAW. Unfortunately for them, in later years, that tactical retreat contributed to a strategic rout.

In general, the Communists in the CIO were almost always better off the more remote they were from the control of Browder and his theorists, who were obsessive in applying "the line." They often confused the claim of Marxism to explain everything with the idea that the line of the only authentic Marxist party, if correct, must apply uniformly to everything. Furthermore, like Stalin, they interpreted the Bolshevik emphasis on the necessity for centralized leadership to mean the leaders were ultimately more competent to make decisions than underlings, no matter how remote they were from the field. The history of Communists within unions until that point should have showed them the folly of their position. As the previous chapter indicates, Communist strength owed little to either the grand strategy or the tactical advice of Browder, Foster, Hudson, and the general staff on 12th Street. Its weakness owed much.

The change in line that followed the signing of the Soviet-German Non-Aggression Treaty in August 1939 did nothing to deflate the growing hubris of Browder and the leadership. Abruptly, the party, which had been applauding any and every attempt to halt the spread of fascism, including the hesitant attempts of the Roosevelt administration to involve itself more deeply in European and Asian affairs, now became a bulwark of anti-interventionism. The war that broke out in Europe was labelled an imperialist war. The Roosevelt administration's accelerated rearmament efforts were soon attacked as the policies of a government following the line of the "warmongering Wall Street and imperialist bourgeoisie."[29]

In contrast to its quite devastating effects among the party's intellectual, middle class, and Jewish following, the change of line caused hardly a ripple among the party union membership. Indeed, Browder later maintained that, if anything, it strengthened the party's base in the unions by moving it closer to the position of John L. Lewis.[30] Probably more apt was Robert Ozanne's observation that "the switches in foreign policy by and large did not conflict with [workers'] economic interests. . . . Probably the majority of workers did not attend enough meetings nor read the union newspapers regularly enough to even be aware of this significant foreign policy shift."[31]

If the mass of the membership was little affected by the change in line, it was of decisive importance in alientating Hillman and a growing number of CIO liberal internationalist leaders. It solidified their residual feeling that the Communists were merely Moscow agents, ready to sacrifice millions of people to fascism at the behest of Stalin. Even in 1939-1940, when most CIO unions had not become quite as bureaucratized and resistant to rank-and-file pressure as they would later, the opinions of these leaders were highly important, for the mass of the membership counted little in deciding the unions' political path.

Now, in the ALP, Hillman's forces joined with Dubinsky's in a fierce struggle against the Communist-backed cohorts led by Congressman Vito Marcantonio and blocked the renomination of City Councilman Michael Quill on the ALP ticket. When Quill refused to sign their anti-Communist pledge, he was forced to run as an "independent" and, because of New York's peculiar proportional representation system, lost the City Council seat he would have retained had he received the same number of votes and ALP endorsement.[32]

It was Hillman's interventionism regarding the war, rather than his anticommunism, that brought him into conflict with John L. Lewis during this time. Lewis had been carving out for himself a curious position regarding foreign affairs. During 1937-1938, he had emerged as an eloquent opponent of the rise of fascism in the world. He had called for united fronts to oppose fascism in a wide variety of forums, from mass meetings at Madison Square Garden and union conventions to congressional committees. In September 1938, he had even travelled to Mexico City to deliver a militant speech to an international anti-Fascist congress sponsored by the CTM, the Confederation of Mexican Workers, whose leader, Vicente Lombardo Toledano, was widely regarded as Latin America's foremost Stalinist and fellow-traveller.[33]

But there were lacunae and anomalies in Lewis' antifascism. He had remained silent on the civil war in Spain, for example.[34] In Mexico City he urged President Lázaro Cárdenas to approve a scheme devised by William Rhodes Davis, an independent American oilman, to exchange

Mexican oil for Italian ships. Subsequently, he became involved in a complex network that included others who were uncomfortably close to the Fascist cause.[35] Although he vehemently denounced Nazi terror in Germany in 1938-1939, his recommendations for combatting fascism involved Western Hemisphere isolation rather than any efforts to curb the spread of fascism in Europe and Asia.[36] By Labor Day in 1939, this tendency had blossomed into something closely approximating the "isolationist" line of the growing America First movement. His nation-wide radio address proclaimed that "Labor in America wants no war nor any part of war. . . . Countries of the Western Hemisphere are self-contained and have no need to participate in the festering intrigues and ancient quarrels of Europe." This, combined with the absence of his usual denunciation of Nazism, aroused great disquiet among pro-Roosevelt liberals and Socialists in the national CIO. They were angered because he had ignored the previous CIO convention's firm condemnation of the spread of Nazism. His single-handed proclamation of an essentially "isolationist" policy for the CIO seemed an act of exceptional arrogance, even for Lewis.[37] But if unease with Lewis' tack was growing in Communist ranks, it did not have time to develop, for, as Browder pointed out, the Soviet-German pact seemed to set them both on the same path of non-intervention.

At first, it was not clear that Communist support for non-intervention would lead to the severing of the relationship with New Deal liberals, which seemingly had paid off so handsomely. Shortly after the outbreak of war, Communists in the labor movement were advised to continue their support for New Deal aims while opposing America's involvement in the "imperialist war" that had broken out in Europe.[38] Before the Roosevelt administration embarked on its policy of all-out support short of war for the Allies, it seemed that Communist anti-interventionism could remain compatible with continued support for the New Deal, and Communist unionists were advised to do both. In 1939 and early 1940, few union leaders (primarily the small minority who were Jewish and some committed "internationalists," such as Carey and John Brophy) were alienated by the Communists' new tack. But as American involvement in the Allied cause deepened in early 1940, CP attacks on it intensified, while liberal support for it grew. Although in mid-1940 the Communist leadership claimed to be gratified by a "spreading opposition among the masses to imperialist war, to involvement in the war and preparations for war," its opposition to Roosevelt's foreign policy represented a minority view within the CIO. The party called the commitment of the majority of the CIO Executive Council in June 1940, to cooperate fully with the Administration's defense effort "very unsatisfactory."[39]

Labor should take the lead in opposing the war and the Administration's policies, said the party. But how? Nowhere was there a call for a wave of strikes. Rather, members were exhorted to "Explain, explain, explain."[40] Thus, party members and followers of the line were most conspicuous in their public denunciations of the war. Communist unionists organized and attended innumerable antiwar rallies, demonstrations, and meetings. The union newspapers they controlled, from the *UE News* to the *Timberworker*, duly trumpeted the "Yanks are not coming" line. But there were no clearcut instances of strikes intended primarily to damage the defense effort.

Initially, the mutual interest in opposing Roosevelt's interventionist policies seemed to thrust the CP and Lewis more closely together. As Hillman and other liberals became first disturbed and then distraught over Lewis' foreign policy and his attacks on Roosevelt, the Communists became Lewis' most notable supporters in the high echelons of the CIO. The apotheosizing of the "Samson of Labor" in the *Daily Worker* and the leftist press knew few bounds. Yet Lewis would not really play their game. In the end, he proved more willing to help destroy their power (and along with it his) than commit himself to an alliance with them. As Foster had always suspected, Lewis was still Lewis, no one's man but his own and, deep down, still a cynical anti-Communist.

Just before the Stalin-Hitler Pact, when John Brophy, the director of the CIO, had expressed concern over growing CP strength in the CIO, Lewis had reassured him with his usual response: They would work with them only as long as necessary and, "when it gets difficult," said Lewis, "we'll get rid of them."[41] Ironically, then, one of his first steps in the attempt to limit CP power in the post-Stalin-Hitler Pact era was to dump Brophy as part of a general reorganization of the CIO staff that substantially weakened the CP.

Despite his antipathy towards communism and his fear of CP influence in the CIO, Brophy was not an avid hounder of Reds. He had often been blamed by anti-Communists outside the CIO for encouraging the rise of the Communists.[42] Thus, when Lewis abolished Brophy's post and demoted him in mid-October 1939, much of the press interpreted the blow as a move to limit Communist influence in the CIO.[43] Although Lewis' demotion of Brophy probably resulted from disagreement over foreign policy, the abolition of the post of national director of the CIO and the reorganization of its top administration were attempts to limit CP power in the CIO, especially that of Harry Bridges, who found his position as West Coast director of the CIO also abolished. Furthermore, the person Lewis chose to inherit much of Brophy's power, Allan Haywood, the new director of organization, was a much more aggressive anti-Communist than Brophy, who shied away from purges. Indeed, an order was given to take no more Communists onto the CIO staff.[44]

Lewis, of course, denied that the reorganization had anything to do with communism. Bridges' position was abolished, he said, because putting him in charge of the entire West Coast had spread him "too thin."[45] However, Haywood soon began to oversee a counterattack against Communist influence in the very place where Bridges had been shunted aside: in the Pacific Northwest.

The International Woodworkers Association had been wracked by dissension almost from the day it was founded in 1937. Opposition to its president, Harold Pritchett, and the leftists who controlled it centered in the well-organized Columbia River Valley area. When, in early 1940, the union executive board called for a special per capita assessment to finance a new organizing drive, these anti-leftist locals refused to pay it.

Pritchett and his supporters then made a major mistake. They turned to the national CIO for aid. Emulating the steel industry, they signed an agreement, similar to that which created SWOC, to provide half the funds for the organizing drive if the CIO provided the other half and to turn over the direction of the campaign to the CIO.

Adolph Germer, the man whom Lewis chose to head the drive, could not have been more antithetical to the IWA leftists. A German-born Socialist, he was one of a number of Lewis' UMW opponents who had made peace with him after the formation of the CIO. Germer was not only an anti-Communist but also an ardent interventionist. Uncertain about his ability to shake up the IWA leadership itself, he was confident he could at least neutralize the IWA leftists' influence in foreign policy.[46]

Germer's campaign began almost as soon as he arrived in his new Seattle headquarters, attacking the "peace movement" propaganda in IWA publications. Finding "some lack of concentration on the organizing campaign," Germer warned IWA organizers to give exclusive attention to organizing tasks. Those who devoted "any time or have interests other than organizational work" would be fired.[47]

In early August 1940, when the IWA lost an important election to its arch-rival, the AFL's Pulp and Sulphite Workers' Union, Germer ascribed the loss to the AFL's effective exploitation of the Red issue. Convinced that the Communist leadership was gravely damaging to the IWA.[48] Thus, he became the unofficial leader of the IWA opposition. Initially discreet, for fear of alienating Bridges and the ILWU who were making substantial contributions of men and money to the IWA organizing drive,[49] Germer soon busily tried to undermine the leftists, intervening with the youthful editor of the union newspaper to

have him tone down its "peace" line, refusing to hire organizers recommended by IWA Executive Board members, pressing the Board to
condemn the CP, and making speeches claiming that the leftists controlled the union through "paper locals."[50] He found himself playing a
leading role in acrimonious public confrontations in September 1940
at the Washington State CIO convention, where he helped the right-
wing challenge the control of the Bridges group, leaving the convention to end in an inconclusive uproar, and in October at the IWA
convention. There again, turmoil resulted from a Germer-supported
resolution condemning Communist interference in the IWA, one
which was coupled with praise for Germer and his efforts.[51]

Leftist protests over Germer's activities to Lewis and Haywood
received evasive replies, but Haywood assured Germer that he had the
full confidence of the head office.[52] Finally, the left-wing majority of
the union's Executive Board formally demanded Germer's removal
and the termination of the organizing agreement.[53] A showdown was
temporarily averted only through newly elected CIO president Philip
Murray's mediation in a secret meeting of the antagonists at the
Atlantic City CIO convention in November 1940.[54]

Thus, Lewis had initiated what was to become the first successful
attempt to oust Communists from control of an important CIO union.
His motives, as usual, were obscure. After all, the IWA leftists were
widely regarded as incompetents whose inability to run the IWA and
compromise with their intra-union opponents would ultimately destroy the union and weaken the CIO. Still, the demotion of Brophy and
his replacement by the more aggressively anti-Communist Haywood,
the reorganization of the CIO directorships to cut into Bridges' power
on the West Coast, the choice of the anti-Communist Germer as the
man to go to Seattle, and the support given to Germer's attempts to
undermine and oust the leftists indicate that at the very least Lewis was
ready to weaken the Communists in the CIO when the chance presented itself, even though they were the major supporters of his controversial domestic and foreign political views.

Hillman's anticommunism by then knew few bounds. From 1940
until June 1941, he marched from union convention to convention,
calling for anticommunist purges. His most notable success came in the
UAW. The "Unity Caucus," which had overthrown Martin, had been
falling apart over the spoils of power almost since the day of its victory,
and Communist support for "isolationism" and attacks on Roosevelt's
foreign policy had heightened the venom that the Reuthers, who felt
strongly about the Nazi threat, felt towards the Communists.[55] With
Hillman's support, the Reuthers administered a crushing blow to the
Communists by having the June 1941 convention endorse Roosevelt

for reelection overwhelmingly and bar members of organizations declared illegal by the United States government from holding union office. It also approved a resolution condemning "the brutal dictatorship and wars of aggression" of Germany, Italy, the Soviet Union, and Japan.[56]

The repeated attacks on Roosevelt by Lewis and the Communists forced CIO liberals such as Hillman, Murray, and James Carey to rethink or refine their ideas on the relationship between government and labor. In essence, they were forced to choose between the perils of carving out domestic and foreign policies independent of the government and of reinforcing the fruitful relationship they had established with the New Deal, the White House, and large segments of the Democratic party, especially since the passage of the Wagner Act. In the end, despite the fear and awe with which he was regarded in the CIO, Lewis' attempt to lead the CIO down an independent path caused him to lose the CIO leadership. As a result, the hands of such leaders as Murray, Hillman, and Carey, who were coming to regard the CIO's interests as best served by close collaboration with the government, were strengthened.

At first, issues such as labor's "independence" from government control, long-term issues, were obscured by the foreign policy grounds upon which the conflict took place. Indeed, only Lewis, at heart more of a Gompersian regarding government and labor than Samuel Gompers, was one of the few who saw the issue clearly. However, despite the fog surrounding its origins and implications, the relationship established with the government between 1939 and 1941 ultimately paid off handsomely for the CIO liberals when, after the war, the federal government stepped in to help them crush the Communists.

The setting for the establishment of the collaborative relationship was the outbreak of war in Europe and the growing crisis in Asia. The Roosevelt administration had abandoned hope for further New Deal reform in the face of a conservative-dominated Congress and concentrated instead on whittling away at the Neutrality Laws to send increasing arms aid to the Allies. It also began a massive mobilization of American military might in anticipation of future participation in the war. As a result, hundreds of millions of dollars worth of new contracts were soon flowing from Washington, washing away many of the problems of the Great Depression. With employment soaring, the main concern of the government now became full production rather than full employment. To ensure that halts in production due to strikes were kept to a minimum, the government invited union participation in some of the new groups supervising the mobilization.

The idea of union participation in the planning and direction of the economy was not a new one even for conservative American unionists.

Samuel Gompers himself had jumped at the chance to be a member of President Woodrow Wilson's Council of National Defense and spent much of World War I lobbying for as great a role for the AFL in executive branch decision-making as possible, despite his theoretical opposition to "political" unionism and his hoary admonitions to keep unions independent of politics and political parties. He saw that from executive branch positions "labor" representatives could help the AFL solidify and expand its power.[57] The new mobilization after 1939 prompted the revival of this idea in the CIO; its most prominent standard bearers were two men closely associated with the "new" industrial unionism, Sidney Hillman and James Carey.

Hillman was smart, competent, and ambitious. He longed to make waves in a larger pond than his relatively small Amalgamated and was active in liberal politics. He had an early taste of federal power and influence when he served on one of the NRA labor boards and, as Lewis' ambition, ego, and foreign policy came into increasing conflict with Roosevelt's, FDR began to use Hillman as his main pipeline to and from the CIO. In June 1940, when the fall of France to the Germans gave defense mobilization a tremendous impetus, Hillman was appointed to head the Labor Division of the newly-created National Defense Advisory Commission, a body that was to play a key role in mobilization. This enraged Lewis. Not only was Hillman obviously being groomed as a counterweight to him within the CIO but FDR had not even gone through the motions of clearing the appointment with him, Hillman's putative boss.[58]

In October 1940, the conflict between Lewis and Roosevelt exploded in dramatic fashion when Lewis made a national radio speech vilifying FDR and exhorting unionists to support his Republican opponent, Wendell L. Willkie, in the upcoming presidential election. Hillman, meanwhile, had emerged as Lewis' most vocal opponent within the CIO, attacking his "isolationism" and defending Roosevelt.

Most CIO members found themselves torn between the two: Lewis, the giant who had single-handedly created the CIO, and Roosevelt (whose Wagner Act had also been instrumental in its creation), the patrician who by 1940 had convinced most workingmen that he too was committed to their interests. Few of those who were unconvinced of FDR's affection for the workingman thought that the Republicans could provide a candidate who cared more. Yet, Lewis plunged on, staking his job on the outcome of the election. If Roosevelt were reelected, he vowed he would step down as president of the CIO.

CIO liberal anti-Communists such as James Carey and Philip Murray were put squarely on the spot, forced publicly to choose between their two leaders,[59] but the Communists were not much better off. For a while, in mid-1940, they had nursed the hope that Lewis would use his wealthy political machine, Labor's Non-Partisan League, as the basis for a new third party. These possibilities had been dashed, they lamented, by "the Hillmans,"[60] and the Communist party was forced to put up its own national ticket. While the Communists were realistic enough not to expect Lewis to come out in support of their sacrificial lambs for president and vice-president, they had been hoping that he would at least plump for some kind of third force. Indeed, from their point of view, anyone and almost anything was preferable to Wall Street lawyer Willkie, already labelled in the public eye as a friend of the despised private utility corporations. Yet, Lewis plunged on and went all the way with Willkie.

CIO leftists were mortified, especially when it became apparent that Lewis was insisting that his CIO allies follow him into the Willkie camp. They avoided him like the plague, ducking into washrooms or around corners when they saw him coming. According to Pressman, "the most difficult period in their lives was this period. . . . They played leap-frog, they played somersaults, they issued double-talking statements. . . . They were going batty."[61] Although some of the leftist unions praised his anti-Roosevelt speech,[62] the only major leftist leader Lewis was able to catch up with and extract a pro-Willkie commitment from was Mike Quill, who owed him a tremendous debt for his help in organizing the TWU. Even then, Quill was terrified that his predominantly Irish Democratic membership would find out. No sooner would Willkie campaign literature arrive at TWU headquarters for distribution than Quill's aides would truck it to an incinerator.[63]

Why did Lewis take a stand that made his friends and supporters so uncomfortable? Why not at least attack both major parties and come out for some form of neutrality? Most observers ascribed Lewis' behavior to varying degrees of power-hunger (the desire to show that he was a king-maker, that he, the man who had supposedly rejected overtures to be FDR's vice-presidential candidate, was more revered by unionists than FDR) and/or sheer hatred of Roosevelt. Melvin Dubosky and Warren Van Tine make a good case for the centrality of Lewis' substantive policy differences with Roosevelt and his calculation that Willkie was worth a gamble.[64] Saul Alinsky had another explanation, one whose credibility is reinforced by Lewis' rather two-faced relationship with the left-wing in the CIO. He pointed out:

If Lewis came out with a condemnation of both the Republican and Democratic parties, he would be supporting the left wing's position on the election, thereby greatly enhancing their prestige and consolidating the position of all the left-wing leaders in the CIO. They would turn to their people and say, "Look, even our great John L. Lewis agrees with us!"[65]

If it was an attempt to put some distance between himself and his Communist supporters, Lewis' endorsement failed, for the Lewis issue and the Communist issue had become inextricably linked in the CIO.

"John L. Lewis is through—this is really the end for him!" Sidney Hillman had exclaimed upon hearing his endorsement of Willkie.[66] By the time the CIO annual convention assembled in Atlantic City two weeks later, after Roosevelt's successful bid for a third term, Hillman and the other pro-administration unionists had rounded up enough support, centered in the Amalgamated, UAW, SWOC, and United Rubber Workers, not only to ensure that Lewis kept his promise to quit but to force through some kind of repudiation of Communists as well. The blanket condemnation of Communists and Communist participation in the CIO which they came to the convention demanding was widely regarded as a blow to Lewis as well, for he was still considered their protector in the CIO.

In the middle was Philip Murray, the man Lewis had selected to succeed him as CIO president. Murray was a Scottish immigrant who had risen in the UMW as part of Lewis' machine. He had distinguished himself mainly by his intense loyalty to Lewis, his administrative ability, his fervent Catholicism, and his sincere feeling for the men at the mill gates. He always claimed that he was never happier than when he was with the real people, the miners and steelworkers he represented. He had faithfully, and a bit reluctantly, allowed Lewis to move him out of his beloved mineworkers union and make him the head of SWOC. Now, he was stepping in to save the equally beloved CIO from disintegration. He had no desire, therefore, to go along with Hillman (for whom he had little affection anyway) and purge the Communists from the CIO. Although in SWOC he had made a name for himself as a quiet but ruthless anti-Communist, weeding them out wherever possible, he began his tenure as CIO president with somewhat different intentions. He wanted to halt the growth of communism in the CIO, the drift leftward, but thought that a purge would be suicidal. What concerned him was the public's linking the CIO with communism. He insisted, as a condition of assuming the presidency, that the convention approve some kind of condemnation of communism.[67] Yet he seemed willing to allow Communists to retain the bailiwicks they had carved out for themselves in the CIO. Although he refused to accept Harry Bridges as a vice-president of the CIO, he did so on the grounds of the "unfavorable publicity" this would generate. He allowed Bridges to select an alternative to himself, who turned out to be Curran.[68]

The Communists harbored grave doubts about Murray. His SWOC purges and reputation for being a priest-ridden tool of the anti-Communist Catholic clergy did not bode well for them. Still, with Lewis adamantly rejecting their pleas to run again, they had no alternative but to accept his own nominee. They could only hope that he would continue to be what so many people, including Lewis, assumed he was, Lewis' puppet. Reluctantly, in a series of back room meetings on the eve of the convention they agreed not only to support Murray, but also to accept a compromise anti-Communist resolution that would avoid a divisive floor fight on the issue and a possible ban on Communists in the CIO. Pushed through with no debate or opposition (and introduced, ironically, by Pressman, as secretary of the resolutions committee), the resolution stated that the CIO rejected consideration of "any policies emanating from totalitarianism, dictatorships and foreign ideologies such as Nazism, Communism and Fascism." It condemned "the dictatorships of Nazism, Communism and Fascism as inimical to the welfare of labor, and destructive of our form of government" and warned that the CIO "must not be diverted by strange, foreign doctrines opposed to our concept of industrial and political democracy."[69]

Communist acceptance of the resolution was a severe propaganda defeat, for, in accepting the lumping together of nazism, fascism, and communism in the same category, in preference even to a condemnation of communism per se, they fed what would later become one of the most effective features of the liberal attack on them: the idea that communism was simply another kind of "totalitarianism," and that there was little to choose between Hitler, Mussolini, and Stalin. Communism, one of whose major attractions during the 1930s was that it was thought of as the opposite pole of fascism and nazism, was now becoming identified with the two movements that were to become the United States' enemies in war, and the Communists themselves went along with this view.

The Communists accepted the resolution because the anti-Communists seemed prepared to break up the CIO and join the AFL were it not passed. This would leave them isolated, even from Lewis who had helped shape the compromise,[70] and vulnerable to the hoary charges of having "wrecked" a labor organization. It would also expose them to the power of a federal government which backed their labor enemies.

The deal did not succeed in driving political division from the convention floor where each side flayed the other. Hillman, whose government post had kept him in Washington while the convention opened, rushed to Atlantic City when he heard that Lewis had charged that he was preparing to follow David Dubinsky and Max Zaritsky back into the AFL. He was especially embittered because in his speech Lewis had reportedly said, "Dubinsky, Zaritsky, and so forth," in a particularly anti-Semitic way. He thought that this was part of a campaign by Lewis to label the unions opposing him as "Jewish-controlled."[71]

More effective were Lewis- and Communist-mounted attacks on Hillman's role in government. They argued that the defense mobilization program amounted to a huge sellout to big business. Its major contracts all went to the largest corporations, many still defying the Wagner Act, and their administrators came from the same firms. The program was bloating corporate profits in the name of national defense while demanding labor restraint on the same patriotic grounds.

Hillman could only feebly defend the administration's record. He lamented the weakness of his Advisory Commission and pleaded that it be given time. Although it had no power to enforce either its policies or the labor relations law, he had met with the head of Bethlehem Steel and hoped to meet shortly with Henry Ford to convince them to change their labor policies. He then lapsed into an emotional attack on the "elements who cannot participate in the democratic process because they don't think; they take orders. Their loyalty is to an organization outside of this organization." The UMW had a clause in its constitution barring them from membership, he pointed out, and what was good enough for them was good enough for the CIO.[72]

Murray tried to carve out a compromise position on the CIO's relationship to the government. On the one hand, he agreed with Lewis that the present defense mobilization system was not working in labor's best interests. The granting of $1.2 million in contracts to non-union Bethlehem Steel especially rankled the head of SWOC. However, he refused to follow Lewis into the anti-Roosevelt camp. Instead, he proposed that defense mobilization be restructured and overseen by industry councils. In each of the major defense industries, representatives of government, labor, business, and consumers would join in boards that would monitor the defense program. They would ensure that "true collective bargaining" took place, would watch for corruption, and try to settle labor disputes. Those disputes that they could not resolve would be sent up to another board of review and, if settlement was not reached there, to a final board, of which the president of the United States might be a member. On all levels, labor would have major representation on the boards.[73]

Murray's plan clearly derived at least in part from ideas that had been in the air since the onset of the Great Depression, ideas that had been embodied in the Swopes Plan and the National Industrial Recovery Act. But they also reflected the considerable influence which Catholic social philosophy exerted on him, especially in the idea that cooperation, rather than conflict, should characterize relations between the classes. This approach to labor relations represented the very antithesis of what the Communists stood for. But Murray shied away from facing its anti-Communist implications. Above all, he was a union man and was desperate to preserve the CIO's unity. For the moment he did not entertain the kind of ideas with which Hillman had begun to toy, ideas that led inexorably to a purge of Communists in the CIO. Yet the pressures that eventually would lead him to change were there already, not only inside the CIO, but in the confluence of forces that were developing outside the labor movement, to some of which he and other CIO non-Communists were extremely sensitive.

NOTES

1. Roy Hudson, "The Path of Labor's United Action," *Communist*, vol. 18, no. 10 (October 1939), 927-38.

2. Testimony of Louis Budenz, U.S., Congress, House, Committee on Education and Labor, *Investigation of Communist Infiltration of UERMWA*, Hearings before a Special Subcommittee, 80th Cong., 2nd sess., 1948, 350-51.

3. Ibid. Their aid was not always welcomed by anti-Communist CIO organizers. See the complaints about Communists showing up in isolated logging towns to press their services on rightist organizers in Adolph Germer to Allan Haywood, September 30, 1940, Adolph Germer, Papers, State Historical Society of Wisconsin, Madison, Wisconsin.

4. The intention was to give party members more leeway in exercising their own judgment, yet the party leadership still feared that the new independence might lead to lack of coordination of policy and, worst of all, a breakdown of party discipline. There were, therefore, limits to independence. Roy Hudson, the party's labor secretary, answered criticism of the new freedom by pointing out that "the Party cannot and will not undertake to decide what its members will do in unions, but it will always reserve the right to decide who is worthy of membership in the Communist Party." Roy Hudson, "The Path of Labor's United Action," 936.

5. Ibid., 935.

6. Reid Robinson, Oral History Interview, Pennsylvania State University Archives of Labor History, State College, Pa. (hereafter PSUA), 36.

7. Julius Emspak, Oral History Interview, Oral History Collection of Columbia University (COHC), 253. Most of the leftist unions supported him, but the UE, for example, did not.

8. See p.244 for what I think is full listing for Carey Papers. CIO, "Transcript of Hearings before the Committee to Investigate Charges against the International Longshoremen's and Warehousemen's Union," Washington, D.C., June 1950 (hereafter referred to as CIO, "ILWU Hearings"), copy in CIO Papers, Office of the Secretary-Treasurer, Wayne State University Archives of Labor and Urban Affairs, Detroit, Mich. (hereafter WSUA), Box 110, 158-69.

9. E.g., see Daniel Bell, interview with James B. Carey, 1955, Daniel Bell, Collection of Material on Socialism and Communism in the U.S.A., Tamiment Institute Library, New York University, New York, N.Y. Box 6, "CPUSA" Folder, wherein Carey claimed he had Pressman's hotel room "bugged" at the 1943 convention and listened with great interest while Roy Hudson, the party's labor expert, berated Pressman for not doing a good enough job at this.

10. Dennis to Browder, n.d. ("Sunday," early 1939?), Earl Browder, Papers, George Arents Research Library, Syracuse University, Syracuse, N.Y., Series 1, Box 3, "Dennis" Folder.

11. William Z. Foster to Browder, February 21, 1939, in Browder Papers, Series 1, Box 4, Folder "I."

12. Melvin Dubofsky and Warren Van Tine, *John L. Lewis: A Biography* (New York: Quadrangle, 1977), 320-21.

13. Benjamin Stolberg, *Tailor's Progress* (Garden City: Doubleday, 1944,) 270.

14. Perkins, COHC, vol. 2, 238.

15. Ibid., vol. 2, 242.

16. Dubofsky and Van Tine, *John L. Lewis*, 319-20.

17. Joe Brown to Edward Lieck, February 2, 1938, cited in Roger Keeran, "Communists and Auto Workers: The Struggle for a Union, 1919-1941," (Ph.D. diss., University of Wisconsin, 1974), 298.

18. Browder to Jack [Johnstone?], July 12, 1938, Browder Papers, Series 1, Box 5, "J" Folder.

19. George Addes, Oral History Interview, WSUA, 1.

20. Ibid., 27.

21. United Automobile Workers of America, *Proceedings of the Special Convention, 1939*, 44, 600-601, also cited in Keeran, "Auto Workers and Communists," 310.

22. Wyndham Mortimer, *Organize! My Life as a Union Man* (Boston: Beacon Press, 1971), 162.

23. UAW, *Proceedings of the Special Convention, 1939*, 535.

24. At one stage in his off-the-record speech to the closed session of the convention, Murray, flushed with anger, turned to Wyndham Mortimer and shouted, "And now this Red Shylock is demanding its pound of flesh!" Mortimer, *Organize!*, 132; Addes, OH, WSUA, 29.

25. Nat Ganley, Oral History Interview, 19-23; Carl Haessler, Oral History Interview, 40; John Anderson, Oral History Interview, 85, all in WSUA; Al Richmond, *A Long View from the Left* (Boston: Houghton Mifflin, 1973,) 238-43; John Williamson, *Dangerous Scot* (New York: International Publishers, 1969,) 104; Len De Caux, *Labor Radical* (Boston: Beacon Press, 1970), 317; Mortimer, *Organize!* 163-64; Keeran, "Communists and Auto Workers," 309-11.

26. Edward Levinson, *Labor on the March* (New York, 1939), 282; also cited in Prickett, "Communists and the Communist Issue," 219.

27. Leo Fenster, introduction to Mortimer, *Organize!*, xiii.

28. Soon after it occurred, Irving Howe and B. J. Widick correctly saw Reuther's 1946 victory as "the decisive event" in the destruction of Communist power in the CIO as a whole. Irving Howe and B. J. Widick, *The UAW and Walter Reuther* (New York: Random House, 1949), 150. Bert Cochran disagrees with the considerable number of regretful Communists and ex-Communists who thought in 1939 or subsequently that Browder's intervention in the convention was disastrous and unnecessary, calling this "day-dreaming." Bert Cochran, *Labor and Communism* (Princeton: Princeton University Press, 1977), 141. However, Cochran's judgment seems to rest on two unsubstantiated bits of reverie of his own: first, he asserts that Addes and his ally Frankensteen "would not have consented to defy Murray and Hillman, even had the Communists been disposed to do so, nor would many delegates." (Ibid.) Yet nowhere in Addes' recollections nor in the other oral histories of the time is this mentioned as a factor. On the contrary, there is widespread evidence in the autobiographies and oral histories, as well as in the dissertations by Keeran and Prickett (see bibliography), that Addes and most delegates would indeed have disregarded the advice of Hillman and Murray, especially since they did not come with a clear mandate from Lewis. Second, he asserts that, had Addes become president, "he would no longer have been dependent on his alliance with the Communists" and "given the pressures of the times, the nature of the man and his outlook, and the thinking of most of the so-called left-wing caucus, the probability was

that instead of being crushed by Reuther during the cold war, the Communists would have been crushed by Addes." (Ibid.) Although Cochran, who was active in UAW's factional struggles during this period, might know something about Addes' personality that is not privy to the rest of us, neither does he provide evidence to support this assertion. Certainly, by the time of the postwar struggle for control of the UAW any ideological difference between leaders and factions had become totally obscured by the intense job-hunger, opportunism, and double-crossing that seemed to permeate all sides. Yet, in the end, Addes was one of the few non-Communist leaders who resisted Reuther's blandishments and stuck with the Communist-supported coalition's sinking ship. In 1947, he rejected Reuther's secret offer to allow him to stay as secretary-treasurer if he would desert the Communists. (Addes, OH, 39.) Instead, he went down to defeat by the Reuther machine and was soon out of the union business entirely, and running a bar/night club in Detroit.

29. "A.B.," "Review of the Month," *Communist*, vol. 19, no. 7 (July 1940), 592.

30. Browder, COHC, 376.

31. Robert Ozanne, "The Effects of Communist Leadership on American Trade Unions" (Ph.D. diss., University of Wisconsin, 1954).

32. Quill to Father Charles Owen Rice, January 12, 1940, the Reverend Charles Owen Rice Papers, PSUA (hereafter referred to as Rice Papers), Rolls A-B.

33. Harvey Levenstein, *Labor Organizations in the United States and Mexico: A History of Their Relations* (Westport: Greenwood Press, 1971), chap. 10.

34. He later claimed that this was due to pressure from Philip Murray, who in turn was influenced by the pro-Franco position of the Catholic church (John Brophy, "Autobiography," chap. 17, 1, Brophy, Papers, Catholic University of America Library, Washington, D.C., A5-41; Saul Alinsky, *John L. Lewis* [N.Y.: Knopf, Vintage Books, 1970], 200) but in asking Gardner Jackson to cut his links with the Loyalists when he went to work for the CIO he cited the possible pro-Franco sympathies of the many second-line CIO leaders who were Catholic. (Dubofsky and Van Tine, *John L. Lewis*, 289.)

35. See Levenstein, *Labor Organizations*, ch.10; Hugh Ross, "John L. Lewis and the Election of 1940," *Labor History*, vol. 17, no. 2 (Spring 1976), 150-89. Dubofsky and Van Tine point out that the evidence does not, however, support the contention of Ross (and Ladislaw Farrago in the bestseller *Game of the Foxes*) that Lewis was either sympathetic to or duped by the Nazis. (Dubofsky and Van Tine, *John L. Lewis*, 345.) However, like President Cárdenas, a sincere anti-Fascist who backed up his words with deeds, Lewis likely found other considerations, mainly a desire to keep the United States out of war, overriding any reluctance to deal with the Fascists.

36. See Levenstein, *Labor Organizations*, Chap. 10.

37. John Brophy, "Autobiography," Chap. 17, 4-5.

38. Roy Hudson, "The Path of Labor's United Action," 927-38.

39. "A.B.," "Review of the Month," *Communist*, vol. 19, no. 7 (July 1940), 592.

40. Ibid., 593-94.

41. Brophy, COHC, 672.

42. E.g., see the extensive correspondence surrounding the charge by *Our Sunday Visitor*, circulated nationally in Catholic churches, that Brophy was a lapsed Catholic who had gone over to the Communist side (various letters, March 31 to May 25, 1937, John Brophy, Papers, Catholic University of America, Washington, D.C., Box A5-5), and the conflict over similar charges in August 1938, by the *Pittsburgh Catholic* and in September 1938, in *America*, the national Jesuit weekly. Brophy to the editor of the *Pittsburgh Catholic*, August 27, 1938; Brophy to Francis Talbot, S.J., Editor, *America*, September 24, 1938, October 8, 1938; Talbot to Brophy, October 8, 1938, October 11, 1938, Brophy Papers, Box A5-5. The hounding continued even after September 1939,

when Brophy's anticommunism became more manifest. Then, a Brophy statement to the *New York Times* was misquoted to make it appear pro-Communist and circulated among Catholics. The Reverend Thomas Darby to Brophy, November 24, 1939. Brophy to Darby, November 29, 1924, Brophy Papers, Box A5-7.

43. Sister M. Camilla Mullay, "John Brophy, Militant Labor Leader and Reformer: The CIO Years" (Ph.D. diss., Catholic University of America, 1966), 169.

44. Dubofsky and Van Tine, *John L. Lewis*, 320-23.

45. *The New York Times*, October 16, 1939.

46. Germer to Alan Haywood, July 13, 15, 22, 1940; Haywood to Germer, July 22, 1940; Germer to John Gibson, July 13, 1940, Germer Papers. See Lorin Cary, "Adolph Germer, From Labor Agitator to Labor Professional" (Ph.D. diss., University of Wisconsin, 1968), 130-44.

47. Germer to Alan Haywood, June 23, 1940, Germer Papers.

48. Germer to Haywood, August 8, 1940, Germer Papers.

49. Germer to Michael Widman, August 9, 1940, Germer Papers.

50. Cary, "Adolph Germer," 140-44; Germer to Haywood, September 4, 1940, Memoradum, September 9, 1940, Germer to Haywood, September 9, 1940, Germer Papers.

51. "Statement of Continuations Committee for an Autonomous and Democratic Washington State Industrial Union Council," March 11, 1941; Germer to Haywood, October 10, 1940, October 13, 1940; Germer to John L. Lewis, October 15, 1940, Germer Papers.

52. O. M. Orton to John L. Lewis, October 11, 1940, Lewis to Orton, October 14, 1940, Haywood to Germer, October 11, 1940, Germer Papers.

53. Robert Williams to John L. Lewis, November 15, 1940, Worth Lowery to John L. Lewis, November 18, 1940, Germer Papers.

54. Haywood to Orton, December 10, 1940, E. L. Bentley to William Dalrymple, December 6, 1940, Dalrymple to Haywood, December 11, 1940. Haywood to McCarty, December 31, 1940, Germer Papers.

55. As Victor Reuther wrote, to ascribe the Reuther attack on the Communists to sheer opportunism is to ignore the sincere, at times heartrending involvement of the Reuther brothers with European anti-Nazis and anti-Fascists, strengthened by their contacts with the anti-Nazi underground and refugees from Germany, Austria and Italy during their trip to and stay in the Soviet Union (Victor Reuther, *The Brothers Reuther* (Boston: Houghton Mifflin, 1976), 70-111, 221-22.

56. Haessler, OH, WSUA, 67; Keeran, "Communists and Auto Workers," 329-31. Lewis attended the 1940 convention as well, but did not openly side with Reuther. Indeed, the Communists were pleased by Lewis' purported snub of Reuther at the train station reception. (Haessler, OH, 67.) However, the lack of support for the Reuther forces did not indicate distaste for Reuther's by-then strident anticommunism. Rather, Hillman and Lewis opposed his foreign and domestic political stance and, like many old-line unionists, neither man liked Reuther personally.

57. E.g., see Levenstein, *Labor Organizations*, chap. 6

58. Alinksy, *Lewis*, 182-83.

59. These two chose Roosevelt.

60. Gene Dennis, "Labor and the Elections," *Communist*, vol. 19, no. 9 (September 1940), 820-25.

61. Lee Pressman, COHC, 389-90.

62. These were the NMU, Mine, Mill, TWU, Office and Professional Workers, State, County, and Municipal Workers, and Cannery and Agricultural Workers. Walter Galenson, *The CIO Challenge to the AFL* (Cambridge: Harvard University Press, 1960), 60.

63. Pressman, COHC, 239.

64. Dubofsky and Van Tine, *John L. Lewis*, 357-59; Hugh Ross seems to see it as the result of the evaporation of Lewis' hopes for a CIO-supported third party as well as his hostility to Roosevelt. Ross, "John L. Lewis and the Election of 1940," 160-75.

65. Alinsky, *Lewis*, 174.

66. Bernstein, *Turbulent Years*, 720.

67. Ibid., 726.

68. J. Edgar Hoover to FDR, December 12, 1940, FDR Papers, Franklin D. Roosevelt Library, Hyde Park, N.Y., OF 10-B, Box 24.

69. CIO, *Daily Proceedings of the Constitutional Convention*, 1940, 1.

70. Pressman, CHOC, 391-94.

71. CIO, *Proceedings*, 1940, 159, 183; Louis Breier, B'nai B'rith Anti-Defamation League, "Memorandum re interview with J.B.S. Hardman and Sidney Hillman," December 11, 1940, copy in Earl Browder, Papers, Series 11, Box 10, "Labor Salaries" Folder.

72. CIO, *Proceedings*, 1940, 185-88, 191.

73. CIO, *Proceedings*, 1940, 131-33.

4 THE OUTSIDE FORCES MUSTER: THE RISE OF ANTICOMMUNISM OUTSIDE THE CIO, 1935-1941

Anticommunism has a longer history in the American labor movement than communism. In colonial times, artisans who tried to organize had to face charges by employers that they were not merely out to improve working conditions but were, in fact, out to expropriate the property of the employers. Since then, the old "Red herring," the charge that unionists stood for anarchy, communism, free love, or whatever else was uppermost among the fears of the middle classes at any given time, has become one of the most common devices used to rally public opinion against strikes and unionism.

American unionists, therefore, had developed a certain degree of immunity to the charges by the 1930s, especially when they came from their traditional source, anti-union employers. Most of the unions whose membership surged upwards in the 1930s, from the most conservative AFL craft unions to authentically Communist unions, did so in the face of employer-sponsored charges that they were in fact Communists.

The militant tactics of some CIO unions and the astounding numbers of workers they organized in the mass production industries made them an especially tempting target for employer anticommunism. Thus, a General Motors paper pounded away at the men sitting in its factories in the massive sit-down strike of late 1936 with the message that they were dupes of the Communists, using the tactics of Russian and Italian Communists and "acting in the best interests of a vast conspiracy to destroy all for which life is worth living."[1] The National Association of Manufacturers greeted the rise of the CIO with a pamphlet entitled *Join the CIO and Help Build a Soviet America*, over two million copies of which were distributed by employers.[2] When the La Follette committee investigated employer abuse of civil liberties in the late 1930s, the most frequent justification it heard for employer anti-union activities was anticommunism. It "was used to justify everything from the confiscation of union literature to the killing of the Memorial Day marchers."[3]

Most charges were groundless. The AFL was their target almost as frequently as the CIO. Within the CIO, SWOC was often the main center of attention. During the Little Steel strike of 1939, President Tom Girdler of Republic Steel told his employees that the only issue was "Must Republic and its men submit to the communistic dictates and terrorism of the CIO?" Explaining why he spied on union organizers, a company police sergeant said, "Well I, being a family man, with nine children—I didn't want to see anything turn communistic in Youngstown."[4]

In part because of the manifest absurdity of most charges levelled by business leaders, it was not too difficult to persuade most workers that employer anticommunism had ulterior motives and should be ignored. This is not to say that the charges were invariably groundless or cynical. Years later, recalling the West Coast waterfront strike of 1934 that marked the emergence of Harry Bridges, Roger Lapham, a leading shipowner, said: "I was convinced myself, though I don't think the public was at the time, that this was a move that went beyond the aims of the usual accepted labor leadership. It was to get power. To get control, on the part of the Communist Party . . . control of the waterfront, control of transportation."[5] Unfortunately for people like Lapham, the close association between the Girdleresque charges of their fellow employers and vicious strikebreaking helped link the two together in the minds of even the most conservative unionists. Bridges himself later recalled:

It was all very well to use strikebreakers and a lot of publicity on us, and the old Red scare, but when they started to put strikebreakers in the place of the teamsters union, which was an old established and conservative union, and started to call the teamsters a bunch of Reds, it just didn't work.

So, we got then the full cooperation of the teamsters.[6]

By the mid-1930s, not only had employer anticommunism become linked in workers' minds with anti-unionism, but many anti-Communist union leaders had become so accustomed to being charged with communism themselves that they distrusted all anticommunism and attacked "Red-baiting" as vigorously as the Communists. Until the late 1930s, for example, Walter Reuther (later a master of the art) would repeatedly warn unionists not to be taken in by "Red-baiting," for it inevitably played into the hands of anti-union employers. "George," he would warn George Addes, "don't play the bosses' game. Don't ever become a Red-baiter."[7]

Employer anti-Communist propaganda, then, had little effect on workers themselves. Rather, it was the indirect ramifications of employer anticommunism that were most important; their ability to influence the media, middle class public opinion, and the government. Because of the many newspapers, magazines, and radio stations which were generally sympathetic to employers, the CIO was easily tainted, in the public eye, with at least a very pink hue. Even William Allen White, the epitome of the most tolerant stream of midwestern progressive Republicanism, called the employer drive to oust "Communists and their sympathizers" from the leadership of unions "one red-baiting campaign [which] has our complete approval." While they did have the right to "rant politically" and "rant about industry," said White in a widely reprinted editorial, Communists should be barred from union leadership because their aims were not those of the 95 percent of unionists who were "decent, law-abiding, and self-respecting" and wanted only better wages and working conditions. These things did not matter to the Communists, wrote White.

> What the Communist labor leader wants is trouble and the right to make wide-spread trouble—trouble that breaks down industry, trouble that shakes the industrial fabric and threatens revolution. So the Communist labor leader will strike for meanness. He will picket viciously. He will back up labor racketeers who shake down employers. The Communist is a bad lot as a labor leader. He should be fired out on his tin ear and that right summarily if the labor movement in America is to get anywhere.[8]

Employer anticommunism also made its mark in another crucial area: state and local government. Local police and judicial authorities often cooperated with employers in labelling unionists as Communists. The San Francisco police department, for example, abetted by the state government of California, began the investigations into Harry Bridges' political affilations, the first of a long series designed to force his deportation. The La Follette committee's hearings are full of examples of harassment, arbitrary arrest, beatings, and occasional murders perpetrated by local and state police forces on union organizers of all kinds in the name of anticommunism.[9]

By 1941, however, there were signs that at least some local police departments were beginning to make sharp distinctions among CIO unionists, differentiating between Murray, Hillman, and Carey and their Communist opponents. For example, when Adolph Germer was in the midst of the battle for control of the IWA, the Portland police called in his ally, William Dalrymple, the CIO regional director, and showed him an undercover agent's warning that the Communists were planning an attack to drive Germer and him from the West Coast.[10]

State and local governments also learned to differentiate between AFL conservatives and CIO radicals, helping the former versus the latter. In April 1941, two locals of the AFL's International Association of Machinists struck shipbuilders in the San Francisco Bay area in defiance of John P. Frey, the conservative head of the AFL Metal Trades Department, who had just negotiated a master shipbuilding agreement covering them and the rest of the West Coast, and announced that they were joining the CIO. Frey rushed back to San Francisco and enlisted the aid of the San Francisco police department's subversive activities squad, which opened its files to him. The information that the locals' leaders had spoken at Communist-organized meetings helped Frey enlist the aid of the San Francisco and Oakland municipal governments and police departments in breaking the strike.[11]

The AFL itself provided another important source of anticommunism, but was hampered by the same factors that hampered the business community: first, it had an obvious axe to grind, one that had nothing to do with communism. Second, because most AFL anti-Communist broadsides were as scattered and almost as all-embracing as those of employers, lumping CIO anti-Communists together with Communists, they too generally backfired within the CIO and served primarily to help keep "Red-baiting" in disrepute.

The immediate origins of AFL anticommunism lay in the continuing battle between the followers of the Socialist Party of America and those of Samuel Gompers for control of the AFL before World War I. The Socialists had been labelled as "political" unionists, out to turn the AFL into the arm of a political party, while Gompers' followers styled themselves "economic" unionists who would improve workers' lives through the use of economic pressure and eschewed permanent alliances with political parties. Still, it was Gompers' alliance with President Woodrow Wilson and support of the war effort that helped destroy his Socialist opponents along with the rival Industrial Workers of the World.

In the postwar era, the newly-organized Communists became the "political" enemy to watch and extirpate. Gompers' wartime love affair with government was cut short by peace and the Republican victory of 1920. Although it continued to try to establish close relations with those in Washington who might help, the AFL leadership reverted to the essentially laissez-faire economic philosophy that seemed best to justify the kind of unionism they represented, a libertarian philosophy which emphasized freedom and the right of men to organize for their mutual benefit. From this point of view, the best thing that government could do regarding labor was not to intervene, especially in its attempts to organize.

In the new offensive against the Communists who tried to divert labor onto the "political" path, the old-line AFL conservative leadership found allies among the remnants of Socialist power in the AFL, unionists whose socialism was rapidly giving way to a de facto commitment to the Gompers path. For example, when, following the lead of some Communists and left-wing Socialists, the 1936 UAW Convention refused to endorse Roosevelt for reelection, Adolph Germer, Gompers' old Socialist opponent, fumed: "Communists and Socialists have taken over the Convention and are voting not as auto workers but according to their political views," a Gompersian distinction that Germer would hardly have made twenty years earlier.[12]

Even as the split that led to the formation of the CIO was still in its infancy, William Green and the group who dominated the AFL Executive Council were concerned about quashing communism in the new unions. Green himself warned the first convention of the fledgling UAW to have nothing to do with Communists, and the convention dutifully passed a resolution condemning foreign Communist meddling in the internal affairs of other countries.[13] At the AFL Convention in 1937, John P. Frey charged, justifiably, that the CIO was infested with Communists. But in the fashion so typical of employer and AFL attacks, he then weakened his case by going too far. John L. Lewis, he charged, was a frequent guest at the Soviet Embassy, and photographs of Lewis and embassy officials were being circulated in the Soviet Union.[14]

Often, AFL rivals of newly-founded CIO unions would pick up the employers' charges of communism and broadcast them for their own purposes. A good example of their dissemination through a whole range of interest groups, with the AFL in the middle, was the campaign against Harry Bridges. Employer charges of communism, unsubstantiated and based primarily on the fact that he was a militant unionist, were given some credence by the San Francisco police department, which, at the shipowners' behest, did its utmost to prove the charges. Independently, Joseph Ryan, from whose International Longshoremen's Association Bridges was splitting, began to call Bridges' group a "bunch of Communists," a generic term Ryan used, along with "crooks" and "gangsters," to label any dissidents in his corruption-ridden union. Meanwhile, the American Legion's Committee on Americanism had begun broadcasting the charges nationwide, closely followed by other superpatriots. Finally, bureaucrats in the Immigration Department began leaking damaging anti-Bridges evidence to the press and to the House Committee on Un-American Activities, whose chairman, Martin Dies, was soon threatening to impeach Secretary of Labor Perkins for not deporting Bridges.[15]

When David Dubinsky took his ILGWU out of the CIO and back into the AFL in 1938, in part because of Communist power in the CIO, his union and the *New Leader* magazine, which it subsidized, quickly emerged in the forefront of AFL anticommunism, attacking Communists in the CIO. Yet again, the attacks backfired within the CIO, alienating the very anti-Communists who were encouraged to purge the Reds. Indeed, at one stage, while in the midst of directing the anti-Communist offensive in the IWA, Adolph Germer found himself labelled a Red in the *New Leader*. No sooner had he finished a battle with Vice-President Joe Orton over the IWA newspaper's support for a Communist-front "Peace Conference" in Chicago, making it clear that the CIO leadership disapproved of the conference and arguing that the union newspaper had no business supporting it, then Victor Riesel wrote an article in the *New Leader* labelling it a CIO-backed conference, further proof that the CIO was Communist-dominated. Germer wrote Riesel an enraged letter, beginning with "For months I have been reading your silly drivel concerning the CIO, but you reached the depths of moral perfidy . . . ," and calling Riesel "an unconscionable scoundrel," and a "liar" with a "dwarfed and polluted mind."[16]

Vituperation and outrage were ineffective defenses, however. Shortly thereafter, the rival AFL in the Northwest was distributing a leaflet emblazoned with a red hammer and sickle containing the following ditties:

> The Commies are coming, the Commies are here,
> Germer our new Savior said.
> And tho' he pretended he was white as could be
> Around the ears he was RED.
>
> Director Dalrymple thought us all so simple
> And said he was a Commie no more.
> He lied and he lied and did his damndest to hide
> The hammer and sickle he bore.[17]

Such tactics, of only marginal effectiveness in luring workers from the CIO to the AFL, helped prevent the formation of a common anti-Communist front within the prewar union movement. Germer and other CIO anti-Communists were caught repeatedly between the leftists who charged that to "Red-bait" was to play the employers' and

AFL's game, and the employers and AFL unionists, who were "Red-baiting" *them* as well. The very absurdity of much AFL propaganda seemed to confirm the leftist assertion that the AFL was merely using the Communist issue to destroy the entire CIO.

On the other hand, the AFL charges were having some effect at the very top. Dubinsky's defection in 1938 had been accompanied by a growing number of liberal journalists who joined in Red-baiting the CIO. Louis Stark, the influential labor reporter of *The New York Times*, an admirer of both Dubinsky and the CIO, began to criticize Communist penetration of it. Benjamin Stolberg, a freelance journalist whose series of articles on the CIO in *The Nation* had positively glowed over the organization, now produced a book, *The Story of the CIO*, which described a well-intentioned organization subverted by Stalinists.[18] This growing wave of liberal anticommunism apparently made Lewis even more wary of becoming regarded as a Communist tool. It helped persuade him to try to limit Communist influence in the CIO in October 1939 and may also have played a role in his offer to resign the CIO presidency in 1939.[19]

On occasion the AFL collaborated with employers to head off radical unionism. In 1939, recalling his union's role in crushing the first Curran-led strike on the East Coast in 1936, Joe Ryan, head of the AFL International Longshoremen's Association, said,

We got some money from the shipowners. . . . We said "Give us money; we are going to fight them." We got the money and drove them back with baseball bats where they belonged. Then they called the strike off.[20]

Later that year, the NMU struck for three months in a successful bid for recognition despite the beatings by "AFL professionals who hunted them like rabbits around the piers."[21]

Their attacks on communism in the CIO put AFL conservatives such as John Frey in the same bed with some unlikely people. Perhaps the strangest were the remnants of various groups who had defected from or were expelled from the CP after the late 1920s, together with some segments of the Socialist Party of America.

By far the most notable of the defectors was Jay Lovestone, who was later to head the AFL's international affairs department. After he and his followers were ousted from the CP in 1929, he had formed the "CPUSA-Opposition," which struggled in the morass of sectarian politics until 1937 when he surfaced as a top aide to Homer Martin in the UAW. "A formidable hater,"[22] Lovestone had a positive gift for making enemies. He stacked the UAW headquarters staff with his own men and women, but his group lacked a real power base within the union.[23] Using tactics that often parodied those of which Communists were accused, he persuaded Martin to embark on a wholesale purge of his opponents in the union. Not only were Communists such as Mortimer fired, but so were such anti-Communists as the Reuthers, all labelled as Communists or their "tools." Before long, Lovestone and Martin had almost single-handedly forced together the grand coalition that walked out on them in 1938 and reconstituted the union, driving Lovestone, Martin, and their few faithful adherents into the AFL where they worked in vain for a number of years to keep their UAW-AFL afloat.

As for the Socialist Party of America, the Great Depression and the comings and goings of the sects who had fled or been driven from the CPUSA in the late 1920s deprived it of any real unity of purpose or policy towards the CP. In some areas, such as within the UAW and the PWOC, Socialists tended to cooperate with Communists rather than battle them, often despite Socialist party directives to the contrary.[24] Some Socialist party members or sympathizers in the national CIO, such as John Brophy, cooperated with Communists, albeit rather grudgingly, repressing their reservations about the CP's ultimate place in the CIO. Others, such as Powers Hapgood, whom Browder described as "a sort of sympathizer of the Communist Party,"[25] went further in their friendship.

On the other hand, the group of Socialists and ex-Socialists surrounding David Dubinsky in New York were among the most vicious of the anti-Communists. Battle-hardened from the garment industry wars of the 1920s, their hatred for the Communists knew few bounds. Fueling this bitterness was the fact that the Communists, including most Jewish ones, were vocal opponents of Zionism, something dear to the hearts of Dubinsky and many other garment union Jewish Socialists who formed the backbone of the Labor Zionist movement in America.

Furthermore, while Dubinsky and the garment union Socialists were supporting socialism and kibbutzim in Palestine, they were rapidly drifting away from it within the United States. They found FDR and the New Deal much more congenial to their purposes than the old Socialist party, wracked by division. In their view it was leaning too far left and, perhaps worse, appeared doomed to wander in the political wilderness. The political dividends of playing the major party game were clearly greater than those of sectarian politics and the SP.

The Stalin-Hitler Pact heightened the tension further, pushing more Jewish Socialists into the Dubinsky camp, especially as Communist attacks on Roosevelt's foreign policy grew louder. By spring 1940, the *New Leader,* which was in the forefront warning about the new

"Nazi-Communist" menace in the CIO, had received subsidies not only from the ILGWU and its satellite, the Cap and Millinery Workers, but from Hillman's Amalgamated and some locals of the Butchers and Bakers unions as well.[26]

Yet, much of this anticommunism was localized. The influence of Dubinsky and his group did not stretch far beyond the banks of the Hudson. Their alarm over Nazi anti-Semitism was not shared by most Americans, especially non-Jewish unionists. Their unions, although influential in national politics through campaign contributions and because of New York's importance in presidential elections, were not particularly powerful within the trade union movement because of their small size.

A more important force from another part of the politico-religious spectrum was the Catholic church. The Great Depression created problems for many institutions in the world, not the least of which was the church. In 1931, the Pope issued a special encyclical on labor relations, called *Quadragisimo Anno* (Fortieth Year), because it was issued on the fortieth anniversary of Pope Leo XIII's famous encyclical *Rerum Novarum* of 1891. Leo XIII tried to confront late nineteenth-century liberalism and socialism by encouraging Catholics to support certain kinds of welfare state activities to ameliorate industrial evils, thereby seeming to soften the bellicose opposition of the church to most aspects of the nineteenth-century liberal state. But Leo XIII's instructions were generally interpreted as opposing Catholics joining secular trade unions. In 1931, the church tried to accommodate itself to the upsurge of worldwide interest in unionism by encouraging Catholics to join unions of predominantly Catholic workers maintaining formal ties with the church. This instruction was obviously aimed at Europe, Latin America, and Quebec, where Roman Catholics formed the bulk of the labor force. But what about countries such as the United States, where unions based on religion would be regarded as extremely divisive and would face immense obstacles in securing working class support? Moreover, the formation of Catholic unions would likely feed exactly the kind of anti-Catholic hysteria that the American Catholic hierarchy had historically feared. The encyclical seemed to provide only an admonition that Catholics who did join non-Catholic unions be given continual moral and religious training by the church.

The church in the United States therefore avoided the issue during the early 1930s, which were characterized by repeated failures on the part of most unionists to organize. Furthermore, the AFL had many Catholic members, and the church hierarchy was clearly reluctant to alienate AFL Catholics by promoting a new form of dual unionism.

The split in the AFL and the rise of the CIO put matters in a different perspective. The CIO was a new union movement, apparently more radical than the AFL both in ideology and leadership. It was very secular, very "materialistic," and seemed to take many cues from the mortal enemies of Catholics, the Communists. Many parish priests warned parishioners that it was a dangerous organization.

Yet the CIO experienced its major successes and derived most of its support from industries in which Catholics were most prominent among the labor force. The steel, auto, rubber, longshore, and electrical industries were populated by heavily Catholic ethnic groups: Irish, Poles, Slovaks, and other Central and Southern Europeans.

Some priests, such as the famed Father Charles Coughlin, kept up the battle against the CIO into the late 1930s, but others, led by influential figures in the hierarchy, began to follow their members into the CIO. Rather than opposing it, they sought to redirect it, to steer it away from socialism and communism where it seemed to be heading, and lead it toward goals more compatible to those of the church.

The response of "liberal" churchmen to the rise of industrial unionism in the mid-1930s became a twofold one. First, they encouraged a "labor priest" movement such as had begun in Europe. Priests in some dioceses were detailed to specialize in working with unions and unionists, at times becoming chaplains of union locals. More often, they simply made themselves the pastors and advisors of Catholics in large locals. Second, they created a number of "labor schools" or "workers' schools," in which Catholic unionists were instructed in the church's teachings regarding labor and were trained to be both good unionists and good Catholics.[27] The second response began to arouse controversy when Catholic bishops, priests, and laymen formed organizations to ensure that Cathoic unionists in secular organizations hewed to the church's precepts. A number of groups soon coalesced into the highly controversial Association of Catholic Trade Unionists (ACTU).

The various lines of this broad Catholic movement paralleled each other, meshed, and, as frequently, clashed with each other. The priests who worked as "labor priests," teaching in the workers' schools and working with ACTU, spanned much of the political spectrum and often disagreed on tactics and goals. Often charged with being the Catholic equivalent of the Communist party, ACTU itself was composed of two major warring factions, who disagreed on a whole range of issues.

Nevertheless, the dominant voices in most of these groups tended to be the "liberal" Catholics. One of their most articulate spokesmen was the Most Reverend Edward Mooney, Bishop of Rochester during the mid-1930s. Appointed to the crucial Archbishopric of Detroit in 1937, Mooney preached a mélange of Leo XIII and Pius XI. Like Leo XIII, he condemned the evils of unbridled laissez-faire capitalism and its rapacious exploitation of workers. Like Pius XI, he condemned the rise of monopoly and the concentration of wealth and power in a few hands. To remedy these ills, Mooney preached a philosophy that ultimately influenced a number of Catholic leaders in the CIO, especially Philip Murray. The solution, said Mooney, lay in the Catholic concept of cooperation, rather than competition. All classes in society must cooperate with each other to work out ways in which Christian ethics, the elements of Christian justice, could be applied to the economy.[28]

Mooney's line was echoed differently in various quarters, but many of its implications were widely shared. First, it was an injunction to work towards some kind of a corporate state where industrial and economic conflicts would ultimately be settled, not by strikes, violence, or exploitation, but by mutual agreement among representatives of all the interest groups in an industry or sector.[29] Second, to avert the danger that "cooperation" might become the sham it was in Fascist Italy, workers should be represented by real unions, unions that were honest and independent of employer, government, or any other "outside" control. Hopefully, the rising CIO would fit that bill. Indeed, its militancy in organizing the unorganized held out the hope that soon the vast majority of American workers would be represented by unions.

Finally, the Catholics involved in various aspects of this new "Catholic worker" movement[30] tended to believe that their major enemy was the Communists. This was not simply because the Communists had developed strongholds in the CIO, but also because the Communists were the only other group who had what the Catholics had so much faith in: an ideology. Infusing the thought of the liberal Catholic anti-Communists in and around the CIO was the idea that, ultimately, the moderate, wobbly, political center would be pulled either in the direction of the Catholics or the Communists. Catholic activists believed that, with no higher ideals of their own, with no appeal beyond self-interest and self-aggrandizement to hold their factions together, people such as the Reuthers would ultimately have to move in one direction or the other. Thus the job of Catholics in the labor movement was to ensure that they would move in the right direction.

Many priests, "labor" and otherwise, found themselves in the difficult position of defending the CIO against charges that it was a Communist organization while attacking Communists within the CIO. Father Raymond Clancy, one of Detroit's most active "labor priests," provided a good illustration of the convolutions this type of defense and attack involved. In a 1939 article he admitted that "there have been and still are subversive forces at work in certain unions," but said that their power had been exaggerated. Yet, to demonstrate the necessity for vigilant anticommunism, he cited approvingly a SWOC official who told him that "if the Communist Party can't rule, it will ruin. It tries to use the union for its own interests." The interests of Communists and unionists were diametrically opposed, said the SWOC man, according to Father Clancy: "Where the unionist strives to better wages and working conditions and to encourage harmonious relations with the employer, the Communist endeavors to disrupt all harmony and engender class hatred through the intensification of injustice."[31]

Clancy preached something that was to become part of the gospel of liberal anti-Communists, both secular and clerical, in the postwar period: anti-Communists, he warned, must not make the mistake of attacking everyone who works for social justice as "Red," for often their efforts to improve living standards, if successful, would "erect a strong bulwark against these same Reds." Clancy and his fellow pro-CIO liberal Catholics did have grounds for complaint on this score. They often felt that they spent more time defending themselves against right-wing attacks on their support for the "Communist" CIO than against the attacks of their most dangerous enemies: the Communists. When, in October 1940, leftists were attacking Murray and Hillman as "Red-baiters," Clancy wrote to one of Murray's aides that although he had been called a "Red" by "some of our Catholic industrialists, et al.," he had yet to be labelled a "Red-baiter."[32]

This is surprising, for Clancy's active membership in ACTU certainly opened him up to attack as a "Red-baiter." Its first chapter had been founded in mid-1937 by John Cort, a young liberal Harvard graduate living in the Catholic Worker House in New York City. Cort gathered around him a group of Catholic trade unionists and liberal activists who he hoped could rally Catholic workers to the trade union cause. Taking his cue from the *Quadragisimo Anno*, Cort asserted that ACTU would become the kind of organization that the Pope had in mind when he said that among the precautions to be taken when allowing Catholic workers to join secular, non-Catholic unions, "the first and most important is that, side by side with these trade unions there must always be associations which aim at giving their members a thorough moral and religious training. . . ."[33] Cort and his band were followed by another group in Detroit, which formed a chapter of the organization in July 1938, and then by others in Pittsburgh, Chicago, and various other cities. From the beginning, the New York and Detroit chapters were by far the most important.[34]

ACTU aroused considerable opposition and disquiet within the church. Not only were conservatives upset by its pro-CIO line, but liberals also saw a number of dangers in it. Because it was an organization of laymen claiming to act for the church, it could embarrass the

church. Yet the church had little direct control over it, for the hierarchy could not control laymen the way it could clergy. In many areas,
therefore, diocesan authorities either prevented or discouraged the
founding of ACTU chapters.

Furthermore, there was always the danger that ACTU would appear
to unionists as a kind of "dual union." This was especially true in its
most visible (and important) activity, its attempts to rid unions of
Communists. What would ACTU's policy be toward unions in which
the Communists were too well-entrenched to be ejected? Would it
support the formation of rival unions? If so, would the church not be
embarrassed by inevitable charges that it was supporting "dual unionism" and trying to impose Catholic unions on Protestant workers? Most
Catholic clergymen, including many liberals, thought that Catholic
activity in support of *Quadragisimo Anno* should stop at training
workers in Catholic Labor schools. Even Archbishop Mooney, later a
fervent ACTU supporter, had initial reservations about ACTU on
these grounds.[35]

Cort and the New York group thought they avoided this problem by
having ACTU function as a kind of pressure group. Others, such as
Father Charles Owen Rice in Pittsburgh, always warned that Actists
should never support breakaways and dual unions, even in unions
such as the UE where the Communists seemed to have a hammerlock
on union headquarters. However, the Detroit chapter had fewer compunctions along these lines and, through its actions and statements,
helped to lend credibility to the widespread fear, both within and
outside of the church, that ACTU was really some kind of Catholic
counterpart to the Communist party, intent on "infiltrating" and
taking over unions and placing them under the direction of a "foreign
power." Many Catholics, especially in the hierarchy of the church,
therefore feared that ACTU would backfire and spark the kind of
anti-Catholicism that had flourished during the 1920s.

The parallel that many saw between ACTU and the Communist
party were not figments of their imagination. Neither were they accidental. From the beginning, Actists, especially those in Detroit, saw
fighting fire with fire as a useful strategy. Impressed by the ability of
small Communist groups to gain control of vast organizations, they
ascribed much of the Communist success to their organization and
tactics and tried to imitate them. The Detroit chapter organized itself
into "cells" and unsuccessfully urged New York to do the same.[36]
Actists in "cells" in Detroit union locals would meet by themselves to
decide on a common policy. Their meetings would be divided into
three parts, a "spiritual period" for prayer and reading from the
Gospel, an "educational period," in which topics such as parliamentary

procedure and the "Actist Catechism" would be studied, and a "practical period," a secret session at which they would deal with their stance on the politics of the union local.[37]

Once they had decided on a common political path within the unions, the Detroit Actists would search for the equivalent of the Communists' "fellow travellers." They would arrange meetings that included sympathetic non-Catholics, trying not to frighten them off by acting as a visibly coordinated group. They would scatter themselves around a meeting hall and act as if they were uncoordinated individuals speaking only for themselves. Yet, as the president of the chapter said, because the Actists agreed on fundamentals and had previously thrashed out their differences, they could be depended upon "to act as spearhead of the rank-and-file movement," keeping the movement "on a sound path." This would be accomplished at the general meeting by "the rank and file group, with ACTU members acting as its spearhead, but with non-Catholics prominent and vocal. . . ."[38]

This conscious aping of the strategy and tactics that supposedly had led to Communist success echoed in other spheres as well, especially in Detroit. On its founding in 1938, the Detroit chapter proclaimed that it intended to lead the labor movement towards "the establishment of a Christian Social Order as set forth in the Papal Encyclicals."[39] To ACTU-Detroit, the Pope's advocacy of Catholic organizations side by side with secular unions meant "something far transcending a mere defensive alliance of Catholics to preserve their Faith uncorrupted in the midst of unions composed of heretics and unbelievers. . . . The OBJECT, of the 'side by side associations,' " said an internal ACTU-Detroit memorandum, "is clearly defined as the INFILTRATION AND INFLUENCING of the Unions."[40] It justified its twenty-five cents a month dues on the grounds that "The Communists dig deep in their pockets to further their godless apostolate. CAN WE BE LESS GENEROUS?"[41]

In his widely distributed pamphlet, "How to De-Control Your Union of Communists," Pittsburgh Actist the Reverend Charles Owen Rice also advocated imitation of what he regarded as typical Communist tactics. "Remember," he wrote, "if you push for something and the union gets it, then you claim credit and claim that you pushed the opposition into going after it. If the union does not get it, yell sell out, double cross, ineffective, stumble bum, etc!" Form caucuses, he advised, and use "points of information" to make speeches outlining how you will vote. Stay until the bitter end of the meeting, of course, and run candidates in slates. To make things even easier, Rice included some suggested anti-Communist resolutions that could be introduced to harass Red unionists.[42]

Some non-Catholic, liberal anti-Communists saw other similarities between ACTU and the Communists. In early 1941, liberal journalist Richard Rovere found ACTU's fealty to Rome, although somewhat "less absolute" than the Communists' ties to Moscow, disturbing. Rome, he wrote, like Moscow, had its own interests, and "it is always difficult to tell which way it plans to jump, particularly in a world crisis. Moreover," continued Rovere,

the approach of both Catholics and Communists to the labor movement is millenial. . . . Catholics and Communists look to goals far in the distance, and the ends of both are so grandiose that almost any means seem justified for their attainment. Communist maneuvers in the labor movement are well known, but the fact is that the ACTU has on occasion made alliances no less cynical, sometimes with the Communists themselves.

As an example of the latter, he cited New York Actists double-crossing anti-Communist non-Catholics in the New York Newspaper Guild to forge an alliance with pro-Communist Catholics.[43]

ACTU-Detroit provided more than enough fodder for critics' fears. Most of its energies were devoted to conflicts within the UAW, which since its founding had been a contentious issue in Detroit Catholic circles. Father Coughlin had denounced the UAW initially, and when the union split into pro- and anti-Martin factions, he had backed Martin, attacking the anti-Martin forces as Communists. He had been tacitly supported in this by Archbishop Gallagher of Detroit, who refused to intervene to muzzle the attacks.[44]

A crucial shift in the church's orientation began in the summer of 1937 when Gallagher was replaced as archbishop by Edward Mooney, now also chairman of the National Catholic Welfare Conference. Like Gallagher, Mooney exhorted priests to join in "the present struggle between Americanism and Communism for the control of labor";[45] yet after Martin led his faction into the AFL Mooney still saw the UAW-CIO as something to be wooed rather than attacked. When Father Raymond Clancy, the labor priest, gave the invocation at the founding convention of the UAW-AFL in late 1939 he was careful to preface it with a formal statement decrying the cleavage and denying that he was taking sides.[46] Meanwhile, Mooney had lost his earlier compunctions about ACTU and by mid-1939 was proclaiming that it was the duty of Catholic trade unionists to join it, something that ACTU used in its recruiting drives.[47]

In factional quarrels dividing the UAW-CIO, the ACTU, with Mooney's support, played a major role in lining up support for the anti-Communists who coalesced around Walter Reuther. According to

Al Leggat, a prominent non-Catholic member of that caucus, ACTU's main contribution was to train and encourage Catholics who would not normally have thought of running for union office to do so and become active union leaders. This was especially the case at the Ford Motor Company where most of the Catholics in the union leadership were ACTU members. After the war, they became the nucleus of the group that eventually ousted the Communists from control over that crucial sector.[48]

ACTU-Detroit became a nationally visible force at the UAW conventions in 1940 and 1941, lining up with the Reuther forces to take advantage of Communist opposition to Roosevelt and to isolate the Communists. In both cases, the leftists saw the lineup of forces against them as revolving around a new Reuther-ACTU axis, a coalition which had only anticommunism in common and was willing, therefore, to ride it to the hilt. Each part of the coalition, the leftists thought, was using the other for its own purposes and would discard the other when the right time came,[49] but the time never came. Mooney remained a firm supporter, rebutting the charges of George Addes, a Catholic, that ACTU did not represent Catholicism with a statement saying, "The ACTU represents its members, and definitely represents Catholic doctrine on labor unions."[50]

Although they supported Reuther in the UAW like their counterparts in other parts of the country, Philip Murray was the real apple of the Detroit Actists' eyes. Richard Deverall, who functioned as an ACTU spy of sorts within the UAW, would report on the latest Red maneuvers to Father Clancy, who would send the information on to Vincent Sweeney, Murray's aide, making sure to include tidbits such as the Communists' calling Murray and Hillman "Roosevelt stooges" (Murray was called a "Hillman stooge" and a "Red-baiter" as well).[51] When the Communists defied Murray in the North American strike of June 1941, Paul Weber, the head of ACTU-Detroit, wired him ACTU's "unqualified support" and urged him to purge the Communists. "The time has come," he wired, "to excise the cancer of communism and the rank and file labor movement is ready for the operation." Murray thanked him for his "loyalty" and "splendid union attitude,"[52] but the Germans invaded Russia before he could take up the offer. The Reverend Charles Owen Rice of Pittsburgh, the most famous of the ACTU priests, was much closer to Murray and ultimately more influential with him. Almost single-handedly, Rice organized the anti-Communist movement within the UE in the crucial Pittsburgh area. Through his articles in the national Catholic press and interviews on the radio, he also become synonymous with ACTU and liberal Catholic anticommunism throughout the nation. Within the CIO, his influence extended far beyond Pittsburgh and the UE, reaching to New York and Washington to the top echelons of the CIO.

Rice was a relative latecomer to ACTU. He did not get around to founding the Pittsburgh chapter until December 1940. During the late 1930s he became convinced that American society "had so disintegrated during the depression it was up for grabs." Everyone, it seemed, was going along with the CP and few realized the threat it represented. An admirer of Dorothy Day and the *Catholic Worker* group, Rice thought of himself as politically to the left of the Popular Front CPUSA.[53] Armed with the belief that only Catholicism could provide the kind of ideology that could combat communism, Rice had set about trying to organize Catholics to rid the labor movement of Communists.

The first object of Rice's attention was the huge Communist-dominated Local 601 of the UE, centered in Westinghouse's Pittsburgh plants. There, in December 1940, he organized a Catholic challenge to leftist control that erupted into a dingdong battle that lasted for years, subsiding only briefly during the war and erupting again in the postwar years. Although Rice tried to give the impression that the battle was led by ACTU, in fact it was nearly a one-man show. ACTU-Pittsburgh consisted mainly of Rice, who found some Catholic anti-Communists in Local 601, organized a labor school for them, encouraged them to organize an opposition movement, helped them find an issue, and advised them on strategy and tactics. In his weekly column in the *Pittsburgh Catholic* he would give the impression that ACTU was a mushrooming movement, but this was a gross exaggeration.[54] In fact, more Actists were involved in the struggle against UE in New York.[55]

Rice's main contribution to the anti-Communist cause came from his articles and speeches. He was a facile writer with a fine journalistic touch, and a charming, eloquent speaker. His *Pittsburgh Catholic* anti-Communist articles were soon supplemented by articles in nationally circulated Catholic magazines and speaking engagements at a wide variety of Catholic organizations. Years later, after his opposition to American policy in Vietnam had caused him to repent his anti-Communist crusade, he recalled that he would write exposés of Communists everywhere, including "where they weren't," for "that lousy . . . right-wing McCarthyite—before McCarthy's day . . . the *Sunday Visitor*."[56]

Ironically, one of Rice's more notable achievements before the war was helping to save the neck of Michael Quill, to whom Rice had taken a shine early in his career. The TWU was heavily Irish Catholic and ridding it of its Communist leadership had been one of the main objectives of New York ACTU. It was also a prime objective of another anti-Communist group, the priests and laymen in the Xavier Labor

School, loosely attached to Fordham University. Despite being Jesuits who were rather hostile to Cort and his ACTU laymen, they were frequently called "ACTU" by supporters and opponents and it was often difficult to separate their actions from that of the real ACTU. When writing to Rice, Quill always carefully blamed the excesses of his anti-Communist opponents either on the Xavier School people, who he said were anti-Semitic supporters of Father Coughlin, or on "a small clique" in the leadership of ACTU-New York who were "successful in working their way in to the extent of being able to drag the good name of A.C.T.U. in the mud a dozen times."[57]

Actually, soon after its founding, ACTU-New York had supported Quill and the TWU, calling it, in 1938, "one of the great CIO unions" and complaining that the "constant Communist propaganda regarding the union" was "decidedly ill-timed."[58] Yet in 1939 it turned against Quill and joined the many other Catholic groups that had denounced Quill and his Communist supporters since 1934.[59]

The close personal relationship that Quill had developed with Rice, the famous Commie-hounder, paid off then. Ignoring the pleas of New York clergymen and Actists, Rice spoke on Quill's behalf at the 1939 TWU convention, helping to defuse a Catholic-led rebellion against the Communist union leadership. In a careful speech, Rice attacked communism but defended Quill. "If there be any comment on the leadership of the union," he said, "it is that there are too damned many Catholics, not too many Communists."[60] Rice spoke for Quill at every TWU convention thereafter.[61]

Rice's greatest coup, however, was not his relationship with Quill, where, if anything, he was being deceived. (After all, Quill was steadfastly lying to Rice, as well as to the rest of the outside world, denying that he was a member of the CPUSA when he really was.)[62] Rather, it was the close relationship he developed with Murray that ultimately was of greater importance. Not only did it reinforce Murray's visceral anticommunism, but it also illustrated Murray's two-faced nature. While Pressman and others remained convinced to the end that Murray was trying to steer a middle course between the Communists and anti-Communists, Murray was not only secretly egging Rice on, but covertly subsidizing him as well.[63]

Murray's close relationship with priests aroused disquiet among many CIO members, including Lewis. At the 1940 Atlantic City convention at which he succeeded Lewis, Lewis was greatly disturbed to see Murray surrounded by four "outside" advisers, including a priest, wherever he went. To Lewis, it seemed that Murray would not make a move without consulting his spiritual advisers.[64] Leftists at the convention thought they were facing some kind of invasion of the priesthood.[65]

Nevertheless, there is little indication that Rice, Father George Higgins, or any other individual Catholic priest had an overwhelming influence on Murray. (Indeed, at times, he found the excessive attention the priesthood devoted to him offensive and embarrassing.)[66] Clerical badgering of Murray was important as part of a larger, more generalized trend: the constant pressure churchmen placed on Catholic CIO leaders to purge the Communists from the organization.

Part of the pressure was personal: letters came to Catholic CIO leaders from priest friends casually mentioning that they were sure that one of these days Phil Murray would do the right thing and get rid of those people who were giving the CIO, which had done so much for the workingman, a bad name. Little remarks in the same vein would be passed at Communion breakfasts, christenings, and weddings. This kind of pressure was abetted by the barrage of hysterical articles in the Catholic press that warned of Communist infiltration of the CIO, alarums that increased in number and intensity in 1939 and 1940 as information from sources such as the Dies committee and John P. Frey became widely disseminated.[67] Although not particularly effective during the prewar years, this propaganda barrage acted as a kind of mental time bomb, causing the sort of residual suspicions of Communist leadership among some Catholic unionists that could be exploited in the more congenial atmosphere of the postwar years.

The influence of the prewar Catholic anti-Communist movement was therefore mainly a long-run one. In the short run, its strength and importance were often overestimated. ACTU, of course, helped inflate its own importance. By the end of 1940, although ACTU claimed only 10,000 members from among approximately 4 million Catholic members of the AFL and CIO (and that claim was likely inflated), Actists liked to give the impression that, as with the Communists, their influence could not be judged by membership figures. Like the Communists, they influenced important leaders: Murray, Brophy, Van Bittner, David McDonald, R. J. Thomas, and George Addes, it was alleged.[68] Yet, in fact, by 1941 the organization was sagging. ACTU-Detroit began to slip in membership, zeal, and power in mid-1940. Local union conferences were flagging and disintegrating. The circulation of the *Labor Leader* plummeted from a high of 5,000 to 2,800 and priests called in asking that their supply of newspapers be cut by one-half to three-quarters.[69] By May 1941, ACTU-New York was admitting defeat in its struggle against Quill and the Communists. "It is unfortunate, though sadly true," said the *Labor Leader*, "that so many Catholic transit workers still blithely follow the undoubtedly Communistic Quill and even invite him to sit in on their Communion breakfasts."[70]

After the Nazi invasion of the Soviet Union snuffed out the hope that Murray himself would lead an anti-Communist purge, ACTU withered in strength and influence. Its convention in August 1941 was a rather lugubrious affair, devoted mainly to gloomy reports from the few surviving chapters (only four of the twelve chapters managed to send representatives), the usual conflict between New York and Detroit over tactics, and desultory attempts to analyze what went wrong.[71]

Few of the attempts at self-criticism and self-analysis, which concentrated on organizational deficiencies, came to the heart of the matter, which was that ACTU was working on a faulty premise. ACTU and many of the labor schools had been founded on the assumption that members of Communist-led unions were attracted to the ideology of their union leaders. All that was necessary, therefore, was for Catholics to counter their cruel, divisive, atheistic ideology with the superior Catholic faith, and the majority of union members would see the error of their ways and elect men with sound training in Catholic principles as leaders. Only gradually did Actists and others in the movement come to realize that this premise was wrong, that the basis for Communist strength was their reputation as good, honest, hardworking unionists. Conversely, they failed to realize the significance of the rise and fall of enthusiasm for ACTU and the church in the UAW. The great surge of support for ACTU came as a direct result of Mooney's support for the UAW in the Chrysler strike of 1939. Enthusiasm waned when ACTU became merely another apparently self-serving faction in the UAW.

In summary, the failure of the prewar ACTU to rally more support to its crusade was a striking demonstration of the willingness of Catholic American workers to accept Communist union leadership. ACTU's efforts succeeded at least in informing all but the most naive members of their leaders' Communist affiliations and leanings. The lackluster response to ACTU's exhortations to throw the rascals out showed that anticommunism per se was a weak force among American workers, even among those, such as American Catholics, ideologically predisposed to it.

NOTES

1. Sidney Fine, *Sit-Down* (Ann Arbor: University of Michigan Press, 1969), 191.

2. Richard O. Boyer and Herbert M. Morais, *Labor's Untold Story*, 3rd ed. (New York: United Electrical Workers, 1973), 317.

3. Jerold Auerbach, *Labor and Liberty: The La Follette Committee and the New Deal*, (Indianapolis: Bobbs-Merrill Co., 1966), 140.

4. Cited in ibid., 140.

5. Roger Lapham, Oral History Interview, University of California at Berkeley, quoted in Charles Larrowe, *Harry Bridges: The Rise and Fall of Radical Labor in the United States* (N.Y.: Lawrence Hill, 1971), 33.

6. Quoted in Larrowe, *Harry Bridges*, 62-63.

7. UAW, "Minutes of Executive Board Meeting, September 22-27, 1947, Part 2," Walter P. Reuther, Papers, Wayne State University Archives of Labor History and Urban Affairs, Detroit, Michigan (hereafter WSUA).

8. Editorial, *Emporia Gazette*, n.d., reprinted in Kansas City *Kansan*, September 6, 1938.

9. U.S., Congress, Senate, Committee on Education and Labor, *Violations of Free Speech and the Rights of Labor* (report pursuant to S.Res. 266), 76th Cong. (Washington, D.C., USGPO, 1942).

10. Dalrymple to Murray, February 7, 1941, Adolph Germer, Papers, State Historical Society of Wisconsin, Madison, Wisconsin. The informer's report was actually quite bizarre. Purporting to discuss the anti-Germer plans of an "Alex Jamie," the leader of the so-called "Secret Six," a group of free-lance investigators, it dwelt, for the most part, on the "loose morals" of one of "Jamie's" female assistants, charging her with promiscuity, with having married a Negro, and with bearing his two children. At the same time, she was also charged with being "a queer." Another assistant was described as "a mouse colored Jew," and so on. Throughout the report there is no apparent basis for Dalrymple's hysteria. Rather, it would appear that the "Secret Six" were more intent on doing what they were famous for, investigating corruption in the Portland police department. Dalrymple, though, was quite frantic over the report, writing that it showed "just how far this Communistic element will go to either rule or ruin." The projected "attack" never materialized.

11. Ultimately, though, it was federal help, in the form of navy trucks to transport strikebreakers through the picket lines, that made the crucial difference. John P. Frey, Oral History Interview, Oral History Collection of Columbia University (COHC hereafter), New York, N.Y., 688-98.

12. *Detroit News*, May 3, 1936, cited in Irving Howe and B. J. Widick, *The UAW and Walter Reuther* (New York: Random House, 1949), 53.

13. Walter Galenson, *The CIO Challenge to the AFL* (Cambridge: Harvard University Press, 1960), 127.

14. American Federation of Labor, *Proceedings of the Annual Convention*, 1937, 383.

15. In her oral history Perkins gives a good description of the surrealistic blending together of influences, the gradual build-up of pressure from diverse origins that ultimately made its weight so strongly felt in Washington. Perkins, COHC, vol. 2, 410-77.

16. Germer to Victor Riesel, September 12, 1940, Germer Papers.

17. "October, 1940," File, Germer Papers.

18. Benjamin Stolberg, *The Story of the CIO* (New York: Viking, 1938); Melvin Dubofsky and Warren Van Tine, *John L. Lewis* (N.Y.: Quadrangle, 1977): 320. Stolberg repeated this theme in his 1944 hagiography of Dubinsky, *Tailor's Progress* (Garden City: Doubleday, 1944).

19. Dubofsky and Van Tine, *John L. Lewis*, 320-23.

20. Murray Kempton, *Part of Our Time*, (New York: Simon and Schuster, 1955), 95.

21. Ibid., 96.

22. Irving Bernstein, *Turbulent Years: A History of the American Worker, 1933-1941* (Boston: Houghton Mifflin, 1970), 556.

23. Galenson, *CIO Challenge*, 151.

24. Memo by Frank Winn, March 28, 1958, cited in Galenson, *CIO Challenge*, 151.

25. Browder, COHC, 215.

26. James Oneal to Germer, April 24, 1940, Germer Papers.

27. The labor priest movement in the United States at times ran into the same kind of problem that plagued its postwar counterparts in France and Italy: priests who were sent out to save the workers from communism ran the grave risk of becoming convinced by their mortal enemies. In the mid-1930s, the archbishop of San Francisco told Frances Perkins that a young, Fordham-educated labor priest who, full of ideas about social justice, was sent to work on the San Francisco waterfront, had become a fan of Harry Bridges. At that point, the priest coped with his admiration by assuring himself that Bridges would return to the church into which he was born. Indeed, he had bet the archbishop that he would be able to bring Bridges back into the church and had convinced the archbishop that he was right. "You'll see Bridges back in the Church before he dies," the archbishop told Perkins. Perkins, COHC, vol. 2, 385. As of this writing, the young priest had still not won his bet.

28. The Most Reverend Edward Mooney, "Industry's Great Need—Cooperation *NOT* Competition," *Catholic Action* (January 1937).

29. This idea was echoed in Philip Murray's proposals in 1940 and 1941 for "industry councils" to settle labor disputes. Murray remained wedded to the idea for the rest of his life, as did John Brophy and other CIO Catholics.

30. Including Dorothy Day and the small but influential group of left-wingers in New York who called their newspaper and movement the *Catholic Worker*.

31. Raymond S. Clancy, "Detroit ALI," *Christian Social Action*, vol. 4, no. 10 (December 1939), 212.

32. "So you are one up on me," he concluded. Clancy to Vincent Sweeney, October 15, 1940, Father Raymond S. Clancy Papers, Wayne State University Archives of Labor History and Urban Affairs, Box 2, Folder 8.

33. Unsigned memo [Paul Weber?], undated [1938?], Association of Catholic Trade Unionists Papers, Detroit Chapter, Wayne State University Archives of Labor History and Urban Affairs, Box 1; Frank Emspak, "The Association of Catholic Trade Unionists and the United Automobile Workers" (master's thesis, University of Wisconsin, 1968), chap. 1; Michael Harrington, "Catholics in the Labor Movement: A Case History," *Labor History*, vol. 1, no. 2, (fall 1960), 234-35; *Actist Bulletin*, vol. 1, no. 1 (August 25, 1938).

34. Until its demise in 1957, much of the history of the national organization involved a prolonged struggle between these two chapters for dominance of the national body. Detroit was the center of resistance to the New York chapter's recurring drives to make the decisions of ACTU's conventions binding on the membership, usually arguing that this would conflict with dioscesan autonomy and responsibility. Detroiters also resented New York's imperialist tendencies, disguised, they thought, in the feeling that as the "mother" chapter it deserved precedence. See ACTU-Detroit Executive Board, Minutes, May 12, 1939; Report of the Detroit Chapter, to the National ACTU Convention, June 30–July 1, 1956, ACTU Papers, Series 1, Box 1; ACTU, *Proceedings of the National ACTU Convention*, 1956, 7.

35. Unsigned memo [Paul Weber?], undated [1938?], ACTU Papers, Box 1.

36. Paul Weber, "Memorandum to ACTU-NY re Intra-Union Organization" [1939?], ACTU Papers, Series 1, Box 2.

37. Ibid.; *Michigan Catholic*, August 24, 1939.

38. Paul Weber, "Memorandum to ACTU-NY re Intra-Union Organization," [1939?], ACTU Papers, Series 1, Box 2.

39. "Constitution of ACTU-Detroit," ACTU Papers, Series 1, Box 1.

40. Unsigned memo [Paul Weber?], undated [1939?], ACTU Papers, Series 1, Box 1.

41. *Actist Bulletin*, vol. 1, no. 1 (August 25, 1938).

42. The Reverend Charles Owen Rice, *How to De-Control Your Union of Communists*, n.p., 1948.

43. Richard Rovere, "Labor's Catholic Bloc," *The Nation*, vol. 152, no. 1 (January 4, 1941).

44. *New York Times*, June 2, August 5, 1937.

45. Clancy, "Detroit ALI," 231.

46. Father Raymond S. Clancy, typescript "Statement" and "Invocation" for UAW-AFL Convention, 1939, Clancy Papers, WSUA, Box 2, Folder 22.

47. *Michigan Catholic*, July 20, 1939.

48. Al Leggat, OH, WSUA, 62.

49. Haessler, OH, WSUA 67-100.

50. *Labor Leader*, August 15, 1941, also cited in Philip Taft, "The Association of Catholic Trade Unionists," *Industrial and Labor Relations Review*, January 1949.

51. Clancy to Vincent Sweeney, October 15, 1940, Clancy Papers, Box 2, Folder 8.

52. Michigan *Labor Leader*, June 20, 1941, cited in Emspak, "ACTU," 54.

53. The Reverend Charles Owen Rice, Oral History 2, Pennsylvania State University Archives of Labor History, State College, Pennsylvania (hereafter PSUA), 15-16.

54. Rice to ACTU-New York, May 29, 1943, cited in Harrington, "Catholics in the Labor Movement," 239.

55. Ibid., 239-40.

56. Rice, OH 2, 22.

57. Quill to Rice, March 3, 1939; Rice to Quill, March 10, 1939; Quill to Rice, January 10, 1940; Rice Papers, PSUA, Reels C-D.

58. *Labor Leader*, n.d., cited in Whittemore, *The Man Who Ran the Subways: The Story of Mike Quill* (N.Y.: Holt, Rinehart and Winston, 1960), 102.

59. Ibid., 34.

60. Rice, OH 2, 18; Whittemore, 81.

61. Rice, OH 2, 18.

62. Quill to Rice, January 12, 1940, Rice Papers, Reels, C-D.

63. Rice, OH 2, 22.

64. Alinsky, *Lewis*, 221.

65. *Daily Compass* (New York), November 11, 1949.

66. Lee Pressman, COHC, 179.

67. One need only glance at the long lists of them in *Communism in the United States—A Bibliography*, ed. Joel Seidman (Ithaca: Cornell University Press, 1969), to get an idea of the immensity of this propaganda surge.

68. Rovere, "Labor's Catholic Bloc."

69. ACTU, "Secretary's Report of April 18 (1940)"; Paul Weber to Executive Board, undated [summer 1940?] Executive Board Minutes, ACTU Papers, Box 3.

70. Quoted in Whittemore, *Man Who Ran the Subways*, 103-4.

71. Minutes of the Second National Convention of ACTU, August 30-September 1, 1941, Hotel Roosevelt, Pittsburgh, Pa., typescript copy in Rice Papers, Reel B.

5 WASHINGTON MOVES IN

Ultimately, the federal government, with its various branches and agencies, proved to be a much more important source of anticommunism than the church, the AFL, the business community, and the state and local governments. Of course, the federal government responded also to church and business pressure, especially in Congress, and was affected at all levels by the business-dominated media. Yet, during the 1930s the executive branch of the government reacted only fitfully to the rise of communism in the CIO, often divided within itself and frequently fearful of alienating the CIO that supported it so munificently. Only the Stalin-Hitler Pact, the alignment of the United States on the side of Britain in the war, and the "Red-Fascist" scare caused the Roosevelt administration to embark on what would likely have turned into a full-scale onslaught against Communists in the labor movement had not the German invasion of the Soviet Union fortuitously snuffed out these plans.

Understandably, most of the administration's attempts to head off communism in the labor movement were confined to the period before 1936 and after 1940. Before 1936, the administration, or rather some people in it, participated fitfully in various attempts to prevent Communists from gaining ground in the labor movement. In 1933, for example, after a series of strikes in the New York City area, more than twenty of the Communist leaders of the Fur Workers union were indicted by the federal prosecutor's office, charged with violating the antitrust laws. Significantly, the charges were left hanging over the leaders' heads and were not revived until 1940. Then, with the CP attacking FDR as a "warmonger," the charges were resuscitated. The men were tried, and most of them, including Ben Gold, the union president, were convicted and sentenced to prison terms.[1]

More notable were the administration's recurring attempts to secure the deportation of Harry Bridges, the bête noir of the Hearst press (at that time supporting FDR). When the Bridges-led waterfront strike of mid-1934 mushroomed into a general strike in the San Francisco area, General Hugh Johnson, the blustering head of the National Recovery Administration, flew to San Francisco, announced that the strike was "a combustible out of which a general conflagration might grow," and demanded that it cease.[2] Anticipating a major theme of post-World War II liberals, he said that the primary responsibility to "wipe out this subversive element as you clean off a chalk mark on your blackboard with a wet sponge" was not the federal government's, but that of "responsible labor organizations. . . . They must run these subversive influences out from their ranks like rats."[3] As police and vigilante groups raided union headquarters, arresting hundreds on vagrancy charges, beating up unionists, smashing everything in sight, Johnson egged them on, calling as well for the deportation of "any alien who pretends to lead an economic group of our people in the direction of strike or bloodshed."[4] In this pointed reference to Bridges, he shouted that such a person "should be no more tolerated than an armed enemy under a foreign flag."[5]

Exactly who in the federal government was responsible for the hounding of Bridges during the 1930s was never quite clear. In her autobiography, Frances Perkins, Roosevelt's secretary of labor, portrayed Secretary of State Cordell Hull and Attorney General Homer Cummings as pushing the panic button during the 1934 strike while she remained unperturbed. She had the Immigration and Naturalization Service investigate the employers' charges that Bridges was a Communist and they turned up nothing.[6] Years later, in an oral history interview, she recalled that not only had Bridges not caused her to panic in 1934, but he had also impressed her with his intelligence, thoughtfulness, and diffidence towards authority.[7] As rumors of Bridges' Communist involvement increased, Perkins asked the conciliators working on the labor dispute about their veracity. They would invariably answer that there was no truth to them. The continuing reports of the San Francisco police about his attending meetings in a house frequented by "Bolsheviks" were counterbalanced, in her mind, by the archbishop of San Francisco who confided in her that Bridges has just shifted his (baptized) daughter to a convent school because of the hounding she was receiving from children in public school over her father's notoriety as a radical.[8]

Perkins' account of her response to the 1934 San Francisco general strike is generally supported by the record. The strike precipitated an outcry from business interests and the press calling for the deportation of Bridges and any other aliens among the leaders. Acting Governor of California Frank Merriam had wired the president demanding the arrest and deportation of the aliens fomenting the strikes, riots, and other "communistic activities."[9] In high Washington circles Perkins functioned as a voice of reason amidst a chorus of hysteria. With the press and employers crying that the Red revolution had arrived, she calmly outlined to Roosevelt the strictly union issues involved, emphasizing the generally conservative leadership of most of the striking unions, and recommended against federal intervention in the situation.[10] This was no mean feat, for not only was the conservative General Johnson warning of imminent revolution, but even Harold Ickes, the liberal secretary of the interior, wired the White House from San Francisco: "Here is revolution not only in the making but with the initial actuality." The police and National Guard were not enough to control the situation, he warned.[11] Roosevelt refused to panic. Instead, he listened to Perkins and Louis Howe, his political adviser, who had wired him that the only danger in the San Francisco situation was that the mayor was badly frightened and fear had infected the entire area.[12]

By the next year, however, as Bridges emerged as the major leftist in West Coast unionism, Roosevelt was more willing to take action against him. Prominent Bay area businessmen sent a delegation to Perkins in early 1935 demanding Bridges' deportation, and an influential Democratic party fund-raiser wrote the president complaining of the "large number of well-known malcontents and definitely-known Communists" who were fomenting disorder on the West Coast.[13] Thus, when a new strike broke out on the West Coast waterfront in mid-1935, FDR wrote Perkins: "How does Sam Darcy [a West Coast Communist leader and prominent supporter of Bridges and the strike] get in and out of the country? I think he is not a citizen but a native of Russia. Also, how about Harry Bridges? Is he not another alien?"[14]

As attacks on Bridges as an alien Communist and condemnations of the Immigration Department's inability to deport him flooded the White House, Roosevelt asked Perkins to confer with the acting attorney-general regarding Bridges and Darcy "and also in regard to the cases of others against whom we can prove propaganda directed at the destruction of the government."[15]

Roosevelt was obviously recalling the days of the Red scare of 1919-1920, when hundreds of aliens had been deported for harboring "Bolshevik" sympathies. A subsequent Supreme Court decision, however, had made this more difficult. Not only did the government have to prove that the alien was actually a member of a seditious organization, but it might also have to prove that the accused was a member when he entered the country. If he had joined after his arrival, it was doubtful if the government could secure his deportation. The administration had no unassailable proof that Bridges was then a member of the Communist party, let alone when he had entered the country. The Immigration Service and Justice Department thus agreed that there was little chance of securing Bridges' deportation at that time.

Still, the investigations continued and the pressure mounted. In 1936, the Immigration Service ran into trouble during the hearings of the all-important House Appropriations Committee over its failure to deport Bridges. The commissioner of the Immigration and Naturalization Service tried to defend himself by pleading that his men had been following Bridges "unremittingly for years."[16] Finally, in late 1937, the immigration commissioner in Seattle, who was devoting a large part of his time to "getting" Bridges, thought he was ready. He informed Perkins that he now had sufficient evidence to secure Bridges' deportation, including eyewitnesses to Bridges' attendance at party meetings. Perkins was still hesitant. Former Attorney General Cornelius Wickersham, who had recently finished a report on immigration procedures, had admitted to her privately that he had omitted from his final report a disturbing conclusion he had arrived at: That it was common for the Immigration Service to deport alien radicals and militant labor agitators on "trumped up" charges that they were trying to overthrow the government by force and violence.[17]

Meanwhile, Perkins was having trouble with the commissioner of immigration over her department's issuance of a number of extensions on the temporary visitor's permit granted Harold Pritchett, the IWA president whom the Immigration Service and the State Department were trying to exclude from the country because of his Communist associations. The president's son and secretary, James Roosevelt, who had been thrust into the role of a kind of arbiter in the case, had tried to avoid the question, but the brewing conflict between the various government departments was becoming intense.[18]

Perkins told Roosevelt that she had been advised that aliens could indeed be deported for membership in organizations devoted to the overthrow of the American government by force and violence and was given the go-ahead to begin deportation hearings on Bridges. James Landis, the dean of Harvard Law School, was selected to preside.[19]

But a federal circuit court judge had just ruled, in the so-called *Strecker* case, that Communist party membership in itself was not evidence of intent to overthrow the government violently, a ruling which, if upheld, would have undermined the government's case against Bridges. Perkins therefore ordered the hearings delayed until the Supreme Court could rule on the government's appeal against that judge's decision. This opened her up to a storm of abuse. In September 1938, Congressman Martin Dies called for her impeachment if she did not have Bridges deported. In January 1939, a motion to that effect was actually introduced in the House of Representatives by Congressman J. Parnell Thomas. Rumors and letters to the editor circulated, charging that she was protecting Bridges because she was a Jew, and therefore a Communist, which added fuel to the "Roosevelt-Rosenfeld" mania of the late 1930s. Even the august *New York Times* attacked her for delaying the hearings.[20] Finally, in June 1939, the Supreme Court upheld the dismissal of the government's case against Strecker, but on grounds narrow and convoluted enough to make possible the continuation of the government's case against Bridges.

The cabinet was split on the issue. Archliberal Harold Ickes was repelled by the idea of deporting Bridges because of his political beliefs, but the more pragmatic postmaster-general, James Farley, demanded in effect that Bridges be deported for the good of the Democratic party. According to Ickes, Farley argued that whether Bridges was a communist or not, the vast majority of the American people believed he was and therefore he ought to be deported. The failure to deport him was causing tremendous harm to the Democratic party, he warned, and it was agreed that the deportation hearings should proceed.[21]

The Landis hearings began on July 10, 1939 after the legal ground appeared to clear and lasted almost ten weeks. The government's case against Bridges was much weaker than Bridges' enemies in the Immigration Service and Justice Department had hoped. The testimony of the government witnesses, most of whom were rather shady characters, was impugned too easily. In December 1939, Landis exonerated Bridges, declaring that no convincing proof had been offered of Bridges' membership in the party, the crucial fact needed to order his deportation.[22]

By then, the administration's attitude towards Bridges had hardened. The split in the CIO over support for FDR's foreign policy was taking shape and Bridges was shaping up on the wrong side. Whereas Bridges had looked upon the Landis hearings as a chance at least to clear the air and stop the federal agents from hounding him, they soon turned out to be merely the first of a long series of judicial and quasi-judicial trials that he would be subjected to during the next twenty-odd years. Frances Perkins, "jittery these days about Communism," according to Ickes, was tempted to overrule Landis and order him deported.[23]

No sooner was Bridges exonerated, than pressure to have him deported by other means built up in Congress. In May 1940, a congressman from Louisiana introduced what was, in effect, a bill of attainder.

His bill directing that Bridges be deported sailed through the House (330 to 42).

Roosevelt was in a quandary. Attorney General Robert Jackson, repelled by the implications of the bill, recommended that when it was passed in the Senate, FDR veto it. However, Roosevelt feared that so great was the cry for Bridges' scalp that to veto the bill would be politically damaging, especially in an election year. On the other hand, to sign the bill would offend civil libertarians. Typically, he chose to avoid rather than confront the issue, He asked the Justice Department and Senator Alben Barkley of Tennessee, a respected and powerful Democratic party stalwart, to have the bill bottled up in committee.[24] This was done, but mainly on the strength of the argument that the new alien registration bill, then proceeding through Congress, would provide more than enough ammunition to get rid of Bridges.[25]

The new regulations, part of the Smith Act, allowed the deportation of anyone who had been a member of the Communist party or other subversive organization at any time in the past even if he was no longer a member. Newly armed, the government resumed its onslaught on Bridges. Roosevelt had shifted the Immigration Service from Perkins' reputedly soft Labor Department to the more punitive Justice Department, and Attorney General Robert Jackson had reluctantly fallen heir to the Bridges case. In August 1940, J. Edgar Hoover, director of the Federal Bureau of Investigation, was dispatched to the West Coast and personally supervised a new investigation into Bridges' deportability. "This investigation is the first of its kind since 1919, when I was in charge of the agents that investigated Emma Goldman," he announced. "She was deported."[26]

To the surprise of few, three months later Hoover leaked to the press that "Our investigation shows without a doubt that Bridges is a Red."[27] Bridges had not helped his case in Washington by his continuing attacks on FDR's domestic and foreign policies. In February 1941, Attorney General Jackson issued an order for his arrest and deportation.

The charges were essentially the same as those aired at the Landis hearings, with the addition of allegations that Bridges had belonged briefly to the Industrial Workers of the World in the 1920s. The FBI had managed to dredge up a new batch of witnesses, centering around Bridges' AFL rival on the West Coast, Harry Lundeberg, and the ex-publicity director of the CIO West Coast Council, James O'Neil. At the hearing, Lundeberg swore that Bridges had once confessed to him that he was a party member. O'Neil testified that he had once actually seen Bridges pasting dues stamps into his party membership book.[28] On September 26, 1941, three months after the German invasion of the

Soviet Union had put Bridges and the ILWU back behind Roosevelt's foreign policy, the presiding judge ordered Bridges deported. The now-embarrassing ball was back in Washington's court.

By this time, Jackson had gone to collect his just rewards as a member of the Supreme Court. Former Solicitor General Francis Biddle became the new attorney general. Biddle, a patrician Philadelphian who was later to become the head of the American Civil Liberties Union, was sensitive to the civil liberties of many people, but leftists were not among them.

Biddle was in a quandary. Like Jackson, he was determined to have Bridges deported. Jackson called him to his chambers and advised him that when the inevitable appeal against the deportation ruling was made, he should bypass the Justice Department's Immigration Appeals Board, which would likely rule in Bridges' favor, and, as the next level of appeal, rule directly on the case himself.[29]

Yet Biddle now found a formidable array of liberal opinion ranged on Bridges' side. The change of line in June 1941 had substantially weakened the argument that Bridges and his ilk were out to sabotage the Allied war effort. Furthermore, the CIO, the darling of liberals as well as leftists, had remained united in support of Bridges even before June 1941. In February 1941, when Bridges' second prosecution was announced, Murray attacked the government for reopening the case. Bridges had been cleared by Landis, he said, and the attack on Bridges was led by anti-union people out to break the ILWU and organized labor. He called on all CIO unions to rally to Bridges' side and announced the formation of a special committee, pointedly headed by right-wingers Sherman Dalrymple, president of the United Rubber Workers, and David McDonald, secretary-treasurer of SWOC, to publicize Bridges' side of the story and rally support for him.[30]

Bridges always hedged with Murray regarding the nature of his association with the CP, referring to his "alleged Communist affiliations" and assuring him that the testimony against him was "a complete pack of lies" that would collapse under cross-examination.[31] But Murray was not one to conclude from this that Bridges was not, therefore, a Communist. Rather, like virtually everyone else in the top CIO leadership, he assumed that if Bridges was not a member of the party, it was a mere technicality. Furthermore, Murray did not like Bridges personally and regarded him as an embarrassment to the CIO. Nevertheless, for Murray to support Bridges' deportation was another matter. Like many other non-Communists in the CIO, he was extremely wary about employers' anti-Communist attacks, and the origins of Bridges' problems clearly lay in employer dissatisfaction with the gains his union managed to wring from them. Furthermore, not to defend

Bridges would have provoked exactly the kind of Left-Right split in the CIO that Murray was still trying to avoid, a division which would have wrecked the organization.

Roosevelt also harbored few illusions about Bridges. After the second hearing was over, a hullabaloo erupted in the liberal press when FBI agents were caught red-handed, illegally tapping Bridges' telephone. When Hoover and Biddle told their side of the story to Roosevelt at the White House, FDR grinned in delight, slapping Hoover on the back and exclaiming, "By God, Edgar, that's the first time you've been caught with your pants down."[32] Later, in 1942, when Eleanor sent him a pro-Bridges pamphlet, he returned it with the notation: "About 90 percent of this is just plain untrue."[33]

Although the Bridges cases were the best known of the government's prewar attempts to curb Communist influence in the CIO, Communist refusal to go along with the administration after September 1939 provoked a swelling offensive against the CIO Communists by various government agencies. In September 1939, Roosevelt authorized the revival of the notorious General Intelligence Division of the Federal Bureau of Investigation[34] and directed the Department of Justice to conduct a general inquiry into "subversive activities." It was clear from the start that leftists would be more suspect than rightists. J. Edgar Hoover had built his early career in the bureau on the basis of his success as the original head of the General Intelligence Division and was a notorious Red-hunter. FBI "anti-subversive" activity soon mushroomed. Agents began "covering" meetings of CIO leftists, taking the license plate numbers of cars in the vicinity, bugging the hotel rooms of Bridges and, presumably, others.[35] By December, although still unable to prosecute people for mere membership in the party, the government, according to Ickes, was making "every possible effort" to indict Communists for any violation of the law it could find.[36]

In early 1940, Roosevelt ordered a purge of Communist sympathizers in the National Labor Relations Board bureaucracy. One of the three members of the board itself, Nathan Witt, was widely regarded as a Communist, and Communists played a major role on its staff. Congressional investigations were stirring up these coals, and there were widespread charges by businessmen, congressmen, and AFL unionists that because of Communist domination the board was biased in favor of the CIO. In response, Witt was let go and William Leiserson, an anti-Communist, was appointed to reorganize the board and eliminate Communist influence.[37]

Communist party members were not the only Communists the Roosevelt administration turned against. In one of the century's grosser miscarriages of justice, a small band of Trotskyists, who led the important Minneapolis local of the Teamsters union, were prosecuted under an old 1861 statute against "seditious conspiracy" and the newly passed Smith Act, which made it a crime to advocate the overthrow of the government by force and violence. The Trotskyists had defied the attempts of President Daniel Tobin of the Teamsters union and his emissary in Minneapolis, Dave Beck, to wrest the local from their control, and had attempted to desert to the CIO. The Teamsters, who had supported Roosevelt in 1940, complained to the president, who told various government departments and agencies to see what could be done.[38] The result was the arrest and conviction of the Trotskyist union leaders in a trial which could have been regarded as sheer farce, had its consequences not been so serious, for nineteen of them were sentenced to substantial prison terms and the local was handed over to the Teamster gangsters.[39]

Communist reaction to the case, the first prosecution under the Smith Act, became a source of controversy for years, held up in later years, when Communists attacked the Smith Act with such vigor, as an example of their hypocrisy regarding civil liberties. There is some justice in the criticism, but not in the exaggerations that portrayed the Communists as gleefully egging the government on, demanding the Trotskyists' scalps. Instead, the Communists seemed mainly taken aback by the case and unable to come up with a coherent response, especially since the prosecution began shortly after their line changed back to a pro-Roosevelt one in response to the German invasion of the Soviet Union.

The initial reaction of Minnesota Communists was to oppose the prosecution while maintaining the proper abhorrence of the Trotskyists themselves. They issued a statement saying that the Trotskyists were a discredit to the labor movement but that "Rank and File labor" were learning "their treacherous misleading role" and would "free themselves from them *without* government interference."[40] The Communists would have been wise to stick to this line, for it would have avoided future embarrassment, but it was not picked up in New York. Rather, the headquarters on Twelfth Street maintained a discreet silence regarding the case. The only report on the indictments in the *Daily Worker* was a short one off the United Press wire.[41]

It took over a month for the party to come up with an official view of the trial. Then, in mid-August, Milton Howard wrote that Communists should indeed support the prosecution of the Trotskyists but not, as the indictment stated, because they were revolutionaries, but because they were "wreckers." Communists, he continued, should call for the indictment to be changed. Trotskyists should be prosecuted for being "fifth columnists," in the same camp as Nazis, Bundists, and their ilk.[42]

Even this was a position that the Communists would soon try to forget, but the liberals' record was no better. Not only was the prosecution an obviously cynical political payoff, but it was personally supervised by Attorney General Francis Biddle. With the exception of *The Nation*, for whom I. F. Stone wrote a devastating exposé of the government's case, none of the liberal media defended the Trotskyists' rights either.

The executive was not the only branch of the federal government to get an early start on hounding Communists in labor. Indeed, in this field, it was a bit of a Johnny-come-lately in Washington. The House Un-American Activities Committee, under the chairmanship of Congressman Martin Dies of Texas, had carved out a sizeable stake in this area almost two years before the Roosevelt administration had begun to push panic buttons regarding the situation.

The committee had been puttering along during the mid-1930s, unsure of its direction and generally losing the all-important battle for headlines, when suddenly, in mid-1938, it struck pay dirt. Its hearings into subversion that year had dabbled with the German-American Bund and other matters which did little to arouse headline and editorial writers. Suddenly it took a different tack: testifying before it was none other than John Frey, the aging head of the AFL Metal Trades Department, one of the two or three most powerful men in the AFL. Perhaps the AFL's best mind, Frey was a rabid, conservative anti-Communist.

A self-described Jeffersonian, Frey had been concerned over what he saw as the paternalism and centralization inherent in the New Deal since its inception, but had been unwilling to break publicly with it until now. His explosive testimony, linking the CIO with communism and the administration with the CIO, constituted his final, "wholehearted" break.[43]

Frey had an informant on the national committee of the CPUSA, a Catholic who was a secret anti-Communist, whom he trusted and believed. The informant had worked for British Intelligence, had written anti-Communist magazine articles under pseudonyms, and had attended every CPUSA convention since 1922. He fed Frey information indicating that John Abt, Hillman's lawyer and a top dog in the NLRB, and Lee Pressman had been members of the same CP cell in the Department of Agriculture. He identified AFL and CIO leaders who were party members but too prominent to take out cards.[44]

Frey's testimony to Dies caused a sensation. He claimed that he knew of 238 full-time CIO organizers who were Communists and 150 more card carriers who were part-time organizers. He charged that at least ten unions in the new CIO were Communist-dominated.[45]

Before Frey's testimony, Dies had gone to Lewis with the evidence, asking for his cooperation in rooting out the Communists. Dies later complained that "instead of getting help, he read me a lecture and refused to help." Then, Lewis wrote a public letter attacking the committee. "What did we get out of it?" sighed Dies to FDR, "abuse and attacks and evasions."[46]

Actually, the Dies committee got much more than abuse from it. It got what it was looking for: an issue that would galvanize at least some of the public. Frey was deluged with supportive letters, albeit mainly from the usual array of crackpots.[47] More important, the Dies committee now had a promising new course to follow. Led by its new chief counsel, J. B. Matthews, a defector from the CP in the early 1930s who had surfaced as an "expert" on communism, it now began a series of investigations of communism, concentrating much of its fire on the CIO. The main message of its hearing in 1938 and 1939 was exactly what large segments of the business and press communities wanted to hear: that the CIO equalled communism.[48]

Some of the dissidents in Communist-controlled unions grasped at the Dies evidence like drowning men grabbing for a life raft. "We told you so," said "A Group of Rank and File Members" of the NMU in a mimeographed handout. The Dies committee wanted to prove that the Communists controlled the CIO and were trying to "capture the whole American labor movement and turn it into a Communist Political Party with headquarters in Soviet Russia." The committee meant to show that the Communists were causing strikes, violence, disorder, and "general unrest in the entire labor movement" financed by $5 million a year of Moscow's money, said the dissidents.[49] They got little mileage out of these revelations, however. The charges evoked little response from sailors inured to Red-baiting attacks on their union.

In fact, the Dies committee of 1938 and 1939 was slightly ahead of its time, and was hampered by many factors. In the first place, it was too obviously a part of the conservative Democratic revolt in Congress against the liberal New Dealers and thus aroused suspicion, rather than cooperation, from the administration and liberal Democrats, who had no compunctions about cavorting with those the committee was denouncing.[50] While the committee was holding hearings on communism in the TWU in September 1938, Mike Quill was trading jokes with liberal Democratic Governor Herbert Lehman at the New York State CIO convention.[51]

Only occasionally would the FBI, which later became an important source of information for later mutations of the committee, secretly provide it with information. Instead, Hoover, the master bureaucratic jungle fighter, would ingratiate himself with Roosevelt by reporting on Dies to FDR.[52] The committee was unable to pin the "Red" label on the most important leftist union, the UE.[53] When in 1938 the committee charged that the UE was Communist-dominated, Carey, Matles, and Emspak raced down to Washington to buttonhole committee members and try to force a retraction from them. Although able to obtain retractions from most members, Dies would not reopen hearings and issue an official retraction.[54] Nevertheless, from then on, the committee concentrated its fire on only two of the CP-led unions, the NMU and TWU. The small Fur Workers and Cannery Workers unions were also mentioned with some frequency.

Even after September 1939, when liberals began turning against Communists, Mike Quill emerged as something of a liberal hero by turning the committee's hearings on the TWU into a shambles, harassing and defying Dies.[55] On an anti-Communist offensive of his own, Roosevelt still refused to cooperate with and be identified with Dies' brand of scattershot witch-hunting. Even in his letter to Dies supporting the strengthening of the anti-subversion laws that emerged as the Smith Act, he warned against "hysteria" and repressive and undemocratic action.[56] Later in the year, in a conference with Dies over security, Roosevelt tried to make it clear, without offending Dies, that he thought the committee's methods were not appropriate for excising subversives from the body politic. Roosevelt told Dies it was unfair to persecute people for their beliefs, rather than their actions, and to make charges based on hearsay.[57]

In addition, the unsubstantiated charges, the wild fusillades that labelled friend and foe of Communists alike as "Reds," alienated many CIO anti-Communists from the Dies committee. John Brophy, for example, found himself forced again to defend himself against the hoary charge that he was a crypto-Communist, because in 1926, the Communists had supported him against Lewis in the election for the presidency of the UMW.[58] One reason why James Carey was so incensed at the committee was that it had also labelled him as a Communist.[59] John P. Frey's testimony regarding the large number of CIO organizers who were party members was reasonably accurate. Yet his simultaneous charge that the La Follette committee, which was then holding hearings into the terrorization of unionists and the denial of their civil liberties, was also part of the CIO and Communist conspiracy only served to alienate liberal anti-Communists from him, the Dies committee, and their methods.[60]

Although the Dies committee was an important source of publicity for prewar opponents of Communists in the CIO, the committee was not nearly so effective a force against Communists in the CIO as it and its imitators were in the postwar era. Its effectiveness was concentrated in the area that is least measurable, i.e., in the stereotypes that gradually built up in the minds of those exposed to the media. In this sense, by constantly hammering at the simple "CIO equals Communism" theme, it provided important groundwork for the next generation of Red-hunters. Perhaps more important, it provided a basis for the increasing concern of non-Communists such as Murray that, whatever their merits or demerits, the Communists were ultimately the CIO's Achilles heel in national politics.

NOTES

1. Robert Leiter, "The Fur Workers Union," *Industrial and Labor Relations Review* (June 1950), 173. The convictions were eventually overturned by the circuit court of appeals.

2. Estolv E. Ward, *Harry Bridges on Trial* (New York: Modern Age, 1940), 7-11.

3. Charles Larrowe, *Harry Bridges: The Rise and Fall of Radical Labor in the United States* (New York: Lawrence Hill, 1972), 85.

4. Ibid., 88.

5. Bridges-Robertson-Schmidt Defense Committee, *The Law and Harry Bridges* (San Francisco: n.p., 1952), no page numbers; also cited in Larrowe, *Harry Bridges*, 139.

6. Frances Perkins, *The Roosevelt I Knew* (New York: Viking, 1946), 314.

7. Indeed, she and Ed McGrady, the ex-AFL man who was handling the dispute for her on the West Coast, were so impressed that they thought Bridges should be encouraged to become the longshoremen's leading spokesman, although she thought that perhaps he was a little too shy and retiring for a leadership position. Frances Perkins, Oral History Interview, Oral History Collection of Columbia University, New York, N.Y. (hereafter COHC), vol. 6, 320-36.

8. Ibid., 380-84. Perkins was by no means eminently qualified at spotting who was and who wasn't a Communist. During the GM sit-down strike of early 1937, she and Governor Frank Murphy spent considerable time worried about and speculating on the identity of "strangers" who were "infiltrating" into the plants. "We hadn't thought of Communists as having much interest in strikes," she later recalled. "They never had previously had much interest in strikes. That wasn't the way they operated. They were political and theoretical people." She concluded, then, that the strangers were likely thugs hired by the Communists. Ibid., 222.

9. Marvin McIntyre to FDR, July 18, 1934, FDR Papers, Franklin D. Roosevelt Library, Hyde Park, N.Y., OF 407-B.

10. Ibid., Perkins to FDR, July 15, 1934.

11. Ibid., McIntyre to FDR, July 16, 1934.

12. Ibid., Louis Howe to FDR, July 15, 1934.

13. Larrowe, *Harry Bridges*, 100, 106.

14. Franklin D. Roosevelt to Frances Perkins, August 29, 1935, FDR Papers, PPF 1750.

15. Ibid., FDR to Perkins, September 18, 1935.

16. Larrowe, *Harry Bridges*, 139; Bridges Defense Committee, *The Law and Harry Bridges*, no page numbers.

17. Perkins, COHC, vol. 6, 449.

18. Pressman to Perkins, December 4, 1937, Pressman to Taussig, January 1, 1938, in Charles W. Taussig Papers, Franklin D. Roosevelt Library, Hyde Park, N.Y., Box 23, Folder "P"—Miscellaneous; Memos, J.H.R. to James Roosevelt, January 22, 1938,

January 25, 1938, February 3, 1938, James Roosevelt, Papers, Personal File, Franklin D. Roosevelt Library, Hyde Park, N.Y.

19. Perkins, *The Roosevelt I Knew*, 319.

20. Perkins, COHC, vol. 6, 425-69.

21. Harold Ickes, *The Secret Diary of Harold Ickes*, vol. 2 (New York: Simon and Schuster, 1954), 550.

22. The hearing is described in detail by Estolv E. Ward in *Harry Bridges on Trial*, and Larrowe, *Harry Bridges*, chaps. 5-6.

23. Harold Ickes, *The Secret Diary of Harold Ickes*, vol. 3 (New York: Simon and Schuster, 1955), 103.

24. James Rowe, Jr., to FDR, August 13, 1940, FDR Papers, PPF 1750.

25. Dalton Trumbo, *Harry Bridges* (Hollywood: League of American Writers, 1941), 9-12; Larrowe, *Harry Bridges*, 233; Bridges Defense Committee, *The Law and Harry Bridges*, no page numbers.

26. Larrowe, *Harry Bridges*, 224.

27. Ibid.

28. Ibid., 228-37.

29. Francis Biddle, *In Brief Authority* (New York: Viking Press, 1962), 297.

30. "Murray to All National and International Unions," February 15, 1941, Adolph Germer, Papers, State Historical Society of Wisconsin, Madison, Wisconsin.

31. Bridges to Murray, April 24, 1941, CIO Papers, Files of the Office of Secretary-Treasurer (hereafter Carey Papers), Wayne State University Archives of Labor History and Urban Affairs, Detroit, Mich., Box 52.

32. Francis Biddle, *In Brief Authority*, 166.

33. FDR to Eleanor Roosevelt, June 12, 1942, FDR Papers, PPF 1750.

34. It had been disbanded in 1924 when, after the frenzy of the Red scare of 1919-1921 had died down, it was discovered that it had broken into the office of liberal Senator George Norris to search his files and had attempted to do the same to Senator Robert La Follette.

35. Harry Bridges Defense Committee, "Press Release," September 18, 1940, copy in CIO Papers, Catholic University of America, Box A7, Folder 27. The bugging of Bridges room was the subject of an exposé in the New York liberal newspaper, *PM*, during the summer of 1941. Larrowe, *Harry Bridges*, 234-35.

36. Ickes, *Secret Diary*, vol. 3, 97.

37. There is little indication that Communists on the National Labor Relations Board exercised anything more than a pro-CIO, influence. Despite all the painstaking attempts to prove otherwise, there is no concrete evidence that they exerted a pro-Communist, as opposed to a more general pro-CIO, influence. Of course, the party's labor line then was simply a general pro-CIO one, so Communists with the Board could feel that they were working to further the party's aims in helping the CIO. See Daniel Bell, Interview with David Saposs, October 20, 1955; Jack Barbash to Daniel Bell, November 3, 1955; unsigned interview with Henry Kaiser, December 14, 1955; Morris Weisz to Bell, October 21, 1955, October 28, 1955, Daniel Bell, Collection of Material on Socialism and Communism in the U.S.A., Tamiment Institute Library, New York University, N.Y., N.Y., Box 3.

38. *The New York Times*, June 14, 1941. "All public officials are with us one hundred per cent," wrote the AFL's lawyer on the scene to William Green, June 16, 1941, American Federation of Labor Collection, Files of the Office of the President, William Green, State Historical Society of Wisconsin, Madison, Wisc. (hereafter referred to as Green Papers).

39. I.F. Stone, "The Great G-String Conspiracy," *The Nation*, July 26, 1941.

40. *NYT*, June 29, 1941.

41. *Daily Worker*, July 5, 1941.

42. *DW*, August 16, 1941.

43. John P. Frey, Oral History Interview, COHC, 596.

44. Ibid., 573-80, 625.

45. Ibid., 650-51; U.S., Congress, House, Special Committee on Un-American Activities, *Hearings,* 75th Congress, 2nd sess. (1938), 90-148.

46. Stenographic Report, "The President's Conference with Representative Martin Dies, November 29, 1940," FDR Papers, PPF 3458.

47. Frey Papers, Box 8, "Dies-2" Folder. Orders for copies of the testimony in pamphlet form were nevertheless disappointing, under the 1,000 minimum necessary to warrant publication. Frey to Thomas Donnely, December 2, 1938, Frey Papers, Box 8, "Dies-4" Folder.

48. Kenneth Crawford, "History of a Hoax," *The Nation*, October 3, 1942, 321; Walter Goodman, *The Committee*, chaps. 2, 3.

49. A Group of Rank and File Members, "Bulletin No. 291," Earl Browder, Papers, George Arents Research Library, Syracuse University, Syracuse, New York, Series 11, Box 9, "Labor" Folder.

50. Goodman, *The Committee*, Chap. 3.

51. L.H. Whittemore, *The Man Who Ran the Subways: The Story of Mike Quill* (New York: Holt, Rinehart and Winston, 1960), 77.

52. See Hoover to Watson, FBI Report 693, March 22, 1941, FDR Papers, OF 10-B.

53. "The CP Column," *Fortune*, vol. 22, no. 5 (November 1940), 107.

54. Carey, COHC, 100-101; Julius Emspak, COHC, 261-64.

55. Whittemore, *The Man Who Ran the Subways*, 86-92.

56. FDR to Dies, June 10, 1940, FDR Papers, OF 1661-A.

57. Stenographic Report, "The President's Conference with Representative Martin Dies, November 29, 1940," FDR Papers, PPF 3458.

58. Brophy to Martin Dies, September 11, 1939, John Brophy, Papers, Catholic University of America Library, Washington, D.C., AS-7.

59. Carey, COHC, 100-101.

60. Jerold S. Auerbach, *Labor and Liberty. The La Follette Committee and the New Deal* (Indianapolis: Bobbs-Merrill, 1966), 164.

6 1941: THE SHOWDOWN POSTPONED

Murray's hopes of avoiding the breakup of the CIO over the Communist issue dimmed soon after he assumed his new office. Barely a month after the CIO convention, Roosevelt reorganized defense planning, elevating Sidney Hillman, along with William S. Knudsen, the head of General Motors, to the cochairmanship of the newly created Office of Production Management, which would have much more power than the National Defense Advisory Commission. Hillman and Knudsen were now regarded as the co-czars of the mobilization effort. The administration seemed to have granted the CIO the greatly increased voice in defense mobilization which it had been demanding. Yet while Murray's doubts regarding the government's policies were thus being assuaged, John L. Lewis remained as hostile to Roosevelt and his policies as ever, gradually forcing a reluctant Murray to choose between him and the president.

Lewis had been deeply scarred by the experience of the AFL, and especially of the UMW, during and after World War I. Then, Samuel Gompers had traded AFL support for Woodrow Wilson's mobilization program and war policies in return for a kind of junior partnership in the administration. When the war ended, most of the benefits went down the drain, dissolving under the onslaught of postwar economic dislocation, the great open shop campaign, and the desertion of the labor movement by its former bedmates, the federal government and the Democratic party. The outbreak of war in Europe in 1939 evoked fears of similar disasters for Lewis. He was thus very hardheaded in his approach to the government. Above all, he wanted labor to be treated as an equal to big business (and even government), not as a junior partner. The CIO could not depend on the sympathy of liberals like Roosevelt for favors, but must rely on its own power to back up its demands. Ultimately, and perhaps unconsciously, Lewis was aiming for something like the British unions' relationship with the Labour party: unions would get what they demanded because of their economic and political power, not because liberal reformers felt kindly towards them.[1]

Murray and Hillman, on the other hand, were less sure of labor's bargaining power vis-à-vis the government and giant corporations, and less willing to make demands on Roosevelt. Rather, they asked for and were grateful for favors.[2] Craven as this may sound, they may have been more realistic than Lewis in assessing the debt that the CIO owed the federal government. Whereas Lewis was obsessed with the hundreds of thousands of dollars he had given to FDR's 1936 campaign and the little he felt that he had received in return, they thought that the administration had been more than generous. After all, it was the Wagner Act that had allowed most of the CIO's industrial unions (and especially Murray's SWOC) to flourish. Now, in the mobilization effort, the government was forcing the AFL to accept the CIO as a legitimate rival, if not an exact equal.

Moreover, Hillman especially, but Murray increasingly as well, thought of Roosevelt as genuinely sympathetic to the cause of the CIO and of workingmen everywhere. Whereas Lewis despised Roosevelt, Hillman and Murray revered him. Furthermore, as the war in Europe became more serious, and as American involvement on the British side deepened, Hillman and Murray became more genuinely concerned about helping the war effort than did Lewis. The Jewish Hillman, of course, was obsessed with the Nazi threat but both of these European-born men were also stirred by the patriotism of the successful immigrant. A journalist who was close to them both saw them as sharing this deep love of the country which had allowed them to rise so high. "They loved the United States the way you love a woman," he recalled. "It was personal. Seeing these two men, . . . I got a brand new concept of what patriotism can mean."[3]

In this context, the Communists' attacks on Roosevelt's foreign policy, along with their willingness to ignore calls for restraint in pursuing bread-and-butter gains, put them on a collision course with Murray. They had already collided with Hillman, but both sides were still seaworthy. The first six months of 1941 saw the Communists narrowly avert a major showdown with Murray as well, one that would probably have resulted in a sustained government-backed attempt to crush them. Only the German invasion of the Soviet Union headed off this major confrontation.

Although arguments over the Communists' overall political strategy from September 1939 to June 1941 may go on forever, there can be little doubt that their zeal in pursuing the line alienated many key liberals more than necessary. Although their new policy line was explicable, and even supportable in liberal terms from September 1939 until June 1940, it rapidly ceased to be so thereafter. Until the fall of France, the Communist line that the war was essentially an imperialist war, with little to do with democracy and fascism, was at least arguable. After all, the two greatest imperialist powers, Britain and France, who together ruled hundreds of millions of people in a most undemocratic fashion, were ranged on one side, apparently not too anxious to engage the forces of Nazism during those long months of the "phony war." Rather, they, along with the United States government, seemed to be devoting an inordinate amount of energy to cultivating Italy, the home of fascism, trying to achieve at least Italian neutrality and at best, it was often rumored, Mussolini's adhesion to the Allied cause. It was easy, then, to dismiss claims that the war was a moral one as anglophile propaganda.[4]

When Italy entered the war on the German side in June 1940, and France and the rest of the democracies in western Europe fell to the Nazis, however, the leftist interpretation lost much of its credibility. With Britain facing the Nazis and Fascists alone and an invasion of the British Isles seemingly imminent, it was too facile to dismiss the war as just another struggle for empire. Yet, as sympathy for Britain swelled in America, the CP line remained essentially the same. As the Roosevelt administration eased the country towards increased support for the Allied war effort the party tried (rather feebly) to make its opposition to this policy relevant to unionists by pointing to the close conjunction that had historically existed between war and the suppression of the civil and economic rights of the working classes.[5]

While Communist support for "isolationism" hardly affected their rank-and-file labor support at all, it alienated interventionist liberal union leaders who had previously cooperated with them. Yet the Communists were not content to soft-pedal it. In convention after convention, in union paper after union paper, the CP kept harping on the foreign policy issue. Liberal union leaders were aghast at the attacks on Roosevelt and shuddered at the sight of CIO unions apparently siding with Charles Lindbergh and the "America First" movement. People like Germer were enraged by sights such as one that greeted his arrival in the Pacific Northwest: the newspaper of a union in a desperate fight against extinction devoting much of its space to proclamations that "The Yanks are not coming" rather than extolling the virtues of unionization. It was not just the foreign policy line that horrified him; it was time and effort devoted to a cause that could never recruit potential members, but only alienate them.

Yet the future effects of this alienation of liberals were not apparent at the time, for they were camouflaged by a closening relationship with Lewis who, despite having stepped down from the CIO presidency, was still widely regarded as the most powerful man in American labor. Moreover, in terms of garnering rank-and-file support, the new tack seemed to give the Communists the kind of opportunities on which they thrived. Indeed, they could reinforce their reputation as effective militants. Not only was the new surge in demand for labor creating a favorable climate for strikes, but also, unlike their pro-Roosevelt rivals, the Communists had no concern about embarrassing the administration with strikes that might hamper mobilization. It is no surprise, then, that the first major showdown between the Communists and Roosevelt supporters in the CIO came over that issue.

Roosevelt's appointment of Sidney Hillman as codirector of the OPM (Office of Price Mobilization) in December 1940 set the stage for the sharpening of the battle. The administration seemed to give unionists the power to ensure the enforcement of the NLRA (National Labor Relations Act). With Hillman, Murray, and a number of other CIO leaders on new labor mediation boards, there was hope that, with the backing of new governmental agencies, the job of organizing the unorganized could be accelerated to the benefit of the CIO.

Murray could no longer avoid the consequences of having chosen Roosevelt over Lewis, and his deteriorating relationship with Lewis reached the breaking point. However, virtually all CIO liberals went along with Murray, leaving Lewis with the Communists as his only allies in the CIO. It was not just Rooseveltian magnetism that drew the liberal unionists to the president. After all, Lewis had an even more magnetic personal hold over many of them. But the Roosevelt connection seemed the most sensible path, not just for the CIO, but for themselves as well. To follow Lewis and the Communists meant to confront head-on the force that had helped make and protect them, the federal government. It was easier for Lewis, secure in his private UMW fief, to defy Roosevelt than for them to do so in their more exposed positions.

Moreover, to desert Lewis and go along with Murray, Hillman, and the government had its unique attractions for arriviste labor leaders. Glimmerings of fame, prestige, power, and material benefits shone for those who chose to rub shoulders with the powerful in the top decision-making circles in Washington. The CIO career of James Carey, the ambitious young president of UE, well illustrates the way these various strands were tied together. Within three years, from 1938 to 1941, he shifted from travelling with the Communists and reverence for Lewis to violent anticommunism and the protective wing of Eleanor Roosevelt.

He had originally caught the eye of Lewis' daughter, Kathryn, in 1938, and she had persuaded her father to make him the CIO's first secretary (later changed to secretary-treasurer.)[6] Although the position was a part-time one, and he retained his UE presidency, the politically charged atmosphere of Washington intoxicated Carey. He spent much of his time there, leaving the day-to-day operations of the UE to Julius Emspak and James Matles,[7] who were busily tightening the hold of their Communist supporters over the union.

Carey's political activities, some of which were in Communist "front" organizations,[8] brought prominence but little influence. Although he idolized Lewis, the older man ignored him. He garnered little respect from the others around Lewis, who regarded him as an immature braggart.[9] In the UE, it was becoming obvious that he was being turned into a Communist figurehead, one whose usefulness was declining as suspicions of his ineptitude in collective bargaining grew.

A last minute Communist attempt to change the foreign policy plank at the August 1939 UE convention to make it more amenable to the new post-Hitler-Stalin Pact line gave Carey a dramatic opportunity to break away. He liked to think that it was this, "the first opportunity of seeing a real Communist in action, making a switch," that awakened him to the extent of Communist influence in the UE,[10] but to believe this is to believe that he was one of the most naive men in American unionism. For almost two years thereafter, he tried to rally UE non-Communists to his side, using his president's column in the otherwise Communist-controlled *UE News* to lambaste the Communists, especially their foreign policy. His relations with Lewis became strained, although he still leaned over backwards to avoid openly attacking the politics of his putative boss in the CIO.[11]

While to his Communist opponents Carey's shift smacked of sheer opportunism,[12] there is no indication that he was ever insincere in his fervent internationalism or in his growing fear that international communism posed a grave threat to the labor movement and the country.[13] This concern seemed to pay off in December 1940 when he was named Hillman's alternate on the OPM, an event that led to Communist charges that he was selling out the labor movement to the Roosevelt administration and its "warmongering" foreign policy.[14] He then came to the attention of Eleanor Roosevelt, who flattered him by making him one of her prime sources of information about union affairs.[15] This developing relationship raised Carey's stock among politicians who believed that Eleanor really was the president's eyes and ears on the world in which he could not circulate.

Carey soon learned, to his chagrin, that rising status in Washington could not be easily translated into union power. Indeed, in his case, rather the reverse was true. His attacks on the Communists' foreign policy fell on largely deaf ears. The vast majority of union members cared only for bread-and-butter issues. "What's it to us?" was their attitude to foreign policy, he later recalled ruefully.[16]

His involvement with the administration's mobilization effort struck a crucial blow at his union power, for, as an alternate member of the National Defense Mediation Board, he had little choice but to vote in favor of a back-to-work order aimed at a number of defense industry strikes which had broken out in defiance of the board in spring 1941. Among the locals ordered back was a UE local at a Phelps-Dodge plant in Bayway, New Jersey. As a result, he was thrown on the defensive in the UE. In May 1941 he barely avoided censure at a special meeting of its powerful District 4 in New York. In September, he was defeated for the union presidency by Albert Fitzgerald, the genial Communist-backed candidate from Lynn, Massachusetts.[17]

Murray, meanwhile, had moved hesitantly towards confrontation with the Communists. Early 1941 saw him swerving from one side to another in the debate over Roosevelt's proposal for Lend-Lease aid to Britain. At first, he indicated that the CIO would support the idea, having sounded it out at a meeting of CIO vice-presidents where only Reid Robinson had openly opposed the plan, while Joseph Curran had waffled.[18] Soon, however, the forces of the Left joined the Lewis supporters in an offensive against the proposal. Struggles between leftist and pro-Roosevelt forces were already wracking CIO Industrial Union Councils. The leftist-Lewis forces concentrated their fire, not on tottering Britain, which, they often said, held their sympathy, but on the provisions of the bill which greatly expanded the power of the presidency. Under its provisions, they warned, the United States would be opening itself up to the threat of presidential dictatorship and giving the president a blank check to lead the nation into war. The labor movement would see all of its hard-won rights, the protection of the Wagner Act, the wages and hours law, and free collective bargaining drown in a sea of presidential fiats.[19] Within weeks, Murray changed his mind. In early February, he filed a brief to Congress opposing the proposed legislation for almost exactly the same reasons the leftists had used.[20]

The defiance, in spring 1941, by significant groups of Communists in CIO unions of the orders of the National Defense Mediation Board, of which Murray had become a member, set him back on an anti-Communist course. The UE's Phelps-Dodge strike had been only a minor sore, and the strikers had responded to the NDMB and gone back to work. However, these new strikes appeared to Murray to be a direct threat to all that he was trying to achieve in Washington.

Furthermore, because two of them took place in industries that were producing directly for the defense effort, they seemed to provide proof that not only were the Communists out to sabotage the CIO's political policy, but also that they were intent on sabotaging the United States defense effort.

The strikes, it was charged, were not really aimed at improving the lot of workers in the affected industries. Rather, they were part of an attempt to support Stalin's policy of courting the Nazis by crippling American aid to the Allies and retarding the American defense effort. They took place amidst a swelling drumbeat of media warnings that Communists in the CIO were out to sabotage the mobilization effort. Communists had gained a vise-like grip on the defense effort, warned Victor Riesel.[21] The strike at Allis Chalmers in Wisconsin was a "rehearsal for revolution," *Reader's Digest* readers were warned. "We Are Already Invaded," its readers discovered the next month.[22] Readers of the more liberal and sedate *Current History* were warned that the cause of labor was suffering because of Communist "penetration" of unions.[23] Later, supposedly more sober historians would lump these strikes together with rubrics such as "a series of strikes designed to hamper and embarrass America's defense efforts."[24]

It is difficult to take seriously the charges that the strikes were part of a well-coordinated master plan designed to sabotage the defense effort. The strikes in the "series" were few: A California UAW local's strike in November 1940 against the Vultee Aircraft Corporation, UAW Local 248's April 1941 strike against the Allis-Chalmers Corporation in Wisconsin, the May 1941 strike of the IWA in the Puget Sound area, and the June 1941 strike of UAW members against North American Aviation in southern California.[25]

The most noteworthy feature of the list is the absentees. If the CP really were intent on sabotaging the defense effort, why the absence of strikes by those unions most capable of doing it? Why did not the NMU and ILWU try to paralyze the waterfronts, blocking the shipment of arms to Britain and the Orient? Why did the UE, engaged in so much defense work, hardly strike at all and return so meekly at Phelps-Dodge after being ordered to do so by the NDMB?[26]

Leftist policy seems to have aimed at conducting "business as usual" in the unions while their liberal competitors affixed themselves to the Roosevelt administration. The speedups in production and the rising demand for labor provided more than enough raw material to create situations that could lead to strikes. Murray and Hillman had committed themselves, through the NDMB, to government-imposed solutions to disputes that would inevitably arise. The CIO would have a major voice in these decisions, they thought, thanks both to its participation in the mediation process and its growing influence in Washington.

Clearly, some Communists were unwilling to go along with this and lusted for an all-out confrontation with Murray, Hillman, and the FDR collaborationists on the question of holding the lid on strikes and Communists were often highly visible and vocal in urging defiance of the NDMB orders. Wyndham Mortimer was perhaps the most notable of this group, and the UAW contained a number of leftists who shared his views. But their willingness to do battle with both the government and the CIO hierarchy was not shared by many of those who followed the party line. Indeed, "the line" on this question was, at best, vague, and Communist union leaders were left more or less on their own in deciding what to do.[27] Even a cursory examination of the contentious strikes shows they had little to do with foreign policy and sabotage.

In actuality, the IWA strike was part of a desperate attempt by the union's leftist leaders to keep from being toppled by either their AFL competitors on the outside or the Germer-supported insurgents from within. Trying to put their most militant foot forward, they had rejected an NDMB strike settlement which the employers had accepted. Months before, in December 1940, Under Secretary of the Navy James Forrestal had begun complaining to Murray of the loggers' supposed interference with the defense effort.[28] When IWA President Joe Orton attacked the NDMB as "an all-out labor busting and strike breaking device," Murray hit the ceiling. He testily pointed out that he personally had recommended that the IWA accept the board's recommendations and that in rejecting them, the IWA leadership was also rebuking him. "In doing so," he said, "they have indulged in a campaign of misrepresentation, slander, and abuse...." Orton's charge that the board was a union-busting device was "a most reprehensible, lying defamation," said Murray.[29]

Orton's public conflict with Murray was clearly not part of any overall Communist plan. Orton was regarded as wild by other CIO leftists. When a CIO committee which investigated Orton's complaints against Germer issued its report in February 1941, its leftist member, Reid Robinson, voted with the majority to reject the IWA complaints.[30] It was rumored that Bridges and Curran had joined John L. Lewis in trying to calm Murray down and smooth over the conflict. With little support from other CIO leftists, the IWA leftists backed down and the striking loggers returned to work.[31]

It is difficult, therefore, to see the IWA strike as part of any larger Communist plan of sabotage. Although important, the logging industry could hardly be regarded as central to the defense effort. If anything, the role of other CIO leftists in the affair was conciliatory, not inflammatory. Moreover, if the party were to order all-out attacks on the war effort, surely it would have them led by unions that were more firmly under Communist control than the IWA, unions in which the leadership was more tractable and reliable than Orton and his associates.

Neither was the strike of the large Communist-led UAW local against Allis-Chalmers in Wisconsin in February 1941 part of an overall plan of sabotage. When the local struck for union security, its president, Max Babb, a prominent America Firster, called it an attempt to sabotage a vital defense industry. Although this cry was widely echoed by government officials and the media, the strike was really the product of the bitter background of labor relations at Allis-Chalmers, and Babb's recurring dreams of reverting to the good old days of the open shop. Even leaders of the anti-Communist faction within the union admitted that the strike resulted from valid union grievances and had widespread rank-and-file support.[32]

Yet Washington portrayed the strike as sabotage. On March 27 Secretary of the Navy Frank Knox and the codirector of the OPM, William Knudsen, ordered the strikers back to work, and had state troops called in to keep the plant open. Murray protested the ultimatum and Hillman made it clear that he had been out of town when it was issued, but after violence erupted over the "back to work" movement, both union and company agreed to submit the dispute to the new National Defense Mediation Board and the workers returned to their jobs.[33] By that time, despite the abundant evidence to the contrary, the dispute had already been enshrined in anti-Communist lore as an act of sabotage. Indeed, some months later a *Collier's* article appearing under Roosevelt's name called the strike "not a bona fide labor dispute, but a form of alien sabotage, inspired and directed by Communist forces, interested not in the advancement of American labor, but in the defeat and overthrow of the United States."[34]

The growing hysteria over Communist "sabotage" was brought to a head by the strike at North American Aviation in Inglewood, California, in June 1941, a strike allegedly instigated by Wyndham Mortimer, perhaps the most famous Communist in the UAW.

The strike had broken out when the North American Aviation local's negotiating committee, responding to growing unrest among its youthful membership, lost patience with the NDMB panel appointed to mediate its contract dispute and called a strike that had not been authorized by the UAW head office. Mortimer had been banished to the wilds of Seattle, where he had been frustrated in his attempts to organize Boeing for the UAW by the ironfisted domination of the area by Dave Beck and his Teamsters. On hearing that North American workers had walked out, he rushed back to the southern California local which he had been instrumental in organizing, anxious to be where the action was. Meanwhile, UAW Director of Organization Richard Frankensteen had taken the lead in the negotiations, trying to thrash out a quick settlement of the grievances and end the wildcat strike.[35] Mortimer initially supported Frankensteen's attempts to get the men back to work but soon turned and supported the mushrooming strike. When Mortimer refused to use his influence to have the strikers return to work, he was fired.[36]

In Washington President Roosevelt decided that the time for a showdown with the Communists had arrived. He personally ordered the strikers back to work. If they did not return to the line on Monday, June 9, he warned, troops would be sent in to break the picket lines and reopen the plant.

Murray was enraged at the Communists, in part for putting him in an exceedingly embarrassing position. He was convinced that they had provoked the strike for their own devious reasons.[37] Rumors had been snowballing, warning that the leftist unions were about to desert the CIO. The most common scenario had them forming a new federation with Bridges' ILWU and Curran's NMU as the foundation. Now, Frankensteen told Murray and Hillman that the strike had been instigated by Harry Bridges and other West Coast Communists, who hoped to use it as a jumping off point for forming a new organization, to be called "the Pacific Federation of Labor."[38] The fact that Murray was a member of the National Defense Mediation Board, which the strikers were defying, made matters worse. He sent Frankensteen a message of support and the strikers a direct order to return to work.[39] When they did not obey, there seemed no alternative but to go along with Hillman, Forrestal, and Knox and acquiesce to the sending of troops to break the strike, which Roosevelt did forthwith.

Like any good unionist, Murray abhorred the idea that the army be used to break strikes, but the Communists, he felt, had left no alternative open. He was not averse to employing more subtle means to curb the leftists in the CIO. In February 1941 the truce between Adolph Germer and the IWA leftists broke down when Germer continued to rally their opponents against them. When leftists asked Murray to terminate their organizing agreement with the CIO and to order the withdrawal of Germer, he refused.[40] Consequently, Germer pursued his anti-Communist activities with more vigor than ever. Germer's campaign had been aided by State Department and Immigration Service refusal to allow the leftists' most competent leader, union president Harold Pritchett, a Canadian, to cross the border to union headquarters. This left the union in the hands of Joe Orton, who would not cooperate with Germer. Murray thereupon approved a secret plan of Germer's to concentrate CIO organizing efforts in anti-leftist areas, thus providing enough delegate votes at the next IWA convention to oust those whom Germer's chief assistant called "the COMRATS."[41]

Germer and his organizers then mounted a furious campaign, first covertly, then overtly encouraging the anti-leftist Columbia River locals to set up a "CIO Woodworkers Organizing Committee," something that seemed to teeter on the brink of "dual unionism." Although Murray and Director of Organizing Haywood were initially reluctant to fund it, they did provide a token $5,000.[42] More important, the anti-Orton locals were able to send their money directly to it, and it was successful enough in organizing new locals so that by the time the IWA convention assembled in October 1941 the "right-wing" slate was swept into power.[43]

Murray also tried to prevent the Communists from adding another independent union to their bonnet by pressing the newly-formed Farm Equipment Workers Organizing Committee (FEWOC), which the Communists dominated, to abandon its hopes for a CIO charter in favor of merging with the UAW, apparently firmly controlled by anti-Communists and his friend and supporter, R. J. Thomas. Merger would have been natural and rational because workers in both industries were engaged in similar kinds of assembly-line employment, and in some cases they even worked for the same companies. Yet both the Communists and the Murray-Hillman forces were very much aware that the conditions of the merger would be all-important in deciding the internal balance of power in the UAW. Thomas' conditions for integration would have considerably weakened the farm equipment Communists. The new UAW farm equipment department would be headed either by himself or UAW Secretary-Treasurer George Addes, not President Grant Oakes or any of the other Communists on the FEWOC executive. Also, FEWOC Organizer Robert Travis, a Communist whom Thomas had driven from the UAW, and Publicity and Educational Director Dewitt Gilpin would have to be fired as a condition of merger.

Murray pressed the FEWOC to accept the UAW's terms, withholding organizing funds from the impoverished committee to make his point better understood. He personally warned Oakes that merger with the UAW was the only way the weak union would be able to secure the finances to campaign in the upcoming NLRB elections at International Harvester. However, Travis and the leftists argued that Thomas was playing politics, trying to take over FEWOC for the Hillman side of the Hillman-Lewis split in the CIO, and the FEWOC board unanimously rejected the Thomas offer. The money to carry on the Har-

vester campaign would be raised through assessing FEWOC members
and appeals to other CIO unions, they decided.[44]

Hillman, meanwhile, had been feverishly working on schemes to
enlist government aid to purge Communists from the defense industries. The idea of purges aroused sympathetic echoes within the administration from the White House down. The troops sent to Inglewood
were regarded as the opening salvo in an offensive against Communists in the labor movement. Defending the use of the army to break
the strike, Secretary of the Navy Frank Knox said that the administration had decided to accept the challenge flung at it by "subversive and
communistic elements." From now on, he said on June 11, they would
be treated as they should be, "as enemies of the country."[45]

For the next two weeks, rumors that a purge was imminent circulated widely;[46] they were well-grounded. In June, Hillman pressed
the administration to create a special mechanism to weed out Communist employees in defense industries. He suggested to Roosevelt that a
board be appointed to investigate "communistic" and "subversive"
activities in defense industries and to tell employers that the government wished certain people fired. When Roosevelt agreed and ordered
Attorney General Francis Biddle to investigate how it could be im-
plemented, Biddle found Hillman unconcerned about the details of
the board's makeup or nature, as long as some mechanism for firing
Communists was created. In Biddle's words Hillman was "less interested
in any particular method of dealing with subversive activities in defense plants than working out some solution for the problem, which he
considers pressing."[47]

Murray was less enthusiastic than Hillman about government-backed
firings. He was more comfortable with the quiet purge from within.
Not only was he completing the process of weeding out the Communists remaining in SWOC, but he did nothing to intervene when Carey
fired twenty-five Communist CIO organizers in 1941, twelve of them
in one fell swoop.[48] He feared that firings in the plants would lead to
complaints that due process was being denied and charges that they
were really disguised "union-busting" techniques, aimed at getting rid
of militant unionists. He agreed, however, that individuals might be
fired at the War Department's request with the approval of the Department of Labor and Hillman's office. Roosevelt agreed that this was the
most desirable course, in terms of both political reality and effectiveness, and he ordered Biddle to set up such a system.[49]

The Nazi invasion of the Soviet Union on June 22, 1941, and the
Communists' consequent support of Roosevelt and the Allied war effort clearly saved them from some kind of joint offensive by the administration and CIO liberals. How successful such an anti-Communist

offensive would have been is problematical; the Communists, able to portray themselves as fighting those who wanted to sacrifice the interests of workers to the contract-bloated giant corporations benefiting most from mobilization, would have had strong cards to play in any intra- and inter-union struggles that might have developed. Hillman and Murray would have found it difficult to impose the kind of self-discipline and self-sacrifice necessary as long as powerful labor leaders like Lewis refused to go along. Unity in sacrifice was an absolute necessity if the policy was not to break down. They would have been forced into a Hobson's choice: Either abandon the attempt to make labor a responsible part of the mobilization effort by curbing its demands or watch the Communists rally growing support from a depression-weary working class ready to take full advantage of the new bargaining power the rearmament boom was placing in its lap.

It is no wonder, then, that the Communists were welcomed back into the fold with rather good grace by the leaders who only weeks before were hoping to destroy them. In fact, the change of line deprived the Communists of their most powerful weapon ever and the springboard from which they might have soared to new heights of power within the labor movement. The line that they abandoned was the one congenial to the great mass of their union members and followers, calling for the kind of qualities in which they excelled. Yet the party's political leaders were calling on Communist unionists to convert themselves into industrial statesmen, who would persuade workers to sacrifice for the war effort. The suddenness of the change, and its obvious link to events in the Soviet Union, did not help. Among the middle levels of the budding union bureaucracies, the Communists soon became the butt of many jokes. Every anti-Communist local treasurer or business agent worth his salt soon had a sidesplitting story to tell about the embarrassing situations resulting from the volte-face for the "comrades" in his union.

In fairness to Communists such as those at North American Aviation, from which much anti-Communist lore emanated, it should be pointed out that it was not quite a case of the same individuals turning, en masse, from wolves into sheep. Many of the Communists and militants were purged from North American, fired and blacklisted by the company, the government, and the union. Most of their supporters were quieted, not by the change in line, but by the threat of mass drafting. According to an FBI informant, although they had been forced back to work and Frankensteen had negotiated what he, the company, and the government thought of as a generous adjustment of their wages, a "considerable number" of the workers still preferred the leadership of Mortimer and the Communists "because of their insistent fight for wage increases."[50]

Mortimer's defiance of the Executive Board ended his career in the UAW. The change in line among the Communist union leadership left no room for militants like him in the left-wing CIO network. He was clearly not to be relied upon to push the new policy of union coopera-tion with government and industry. However, Haywood did appoint him to a depressing sinecure in a CIO office in Salt Lake City. Then, with American entry into the war, he returned to the West Coast and worked first, for the State, County, and Municipal Workers, and then, Mine, Mill. There, he was merely standing in for organizers who were in the service. When they returned, he left the labor movement.[51]

Two weeks after the North American strike was broken, 250 CIO leaders met in a secret session in Washington, where Lewis delivered a stinging attack on Roosevelt and Hillman for having sent troops in. There is no report of leftist support for his attack. Rather, all that was overheard outside was the shrill voice of Jacob Potofsky, the acting head of the Amalgamated, counterattacking. FDR needed no defense, said Potofsky. The record of labor's gains under his administration was clear. The greatest of these gains had been made in recent months since Hillman had gone to Washington.[52]

NOTES

1. Lee Pressman, Oral History Collection of Columbia University, New York, New York (hereafter COHC), 181, 205.

2. Ibid.

3. Edwin Lahey, Oral History Interview, COHC, 77.

4. For example, years later, the following passage from a 1940 speech was held up to Donald Henderson, the head of the Communist-dominated FTA, as an example of how he followed "the line":

I have no more sympathy and have no more desire to support a reformed reprobate like the British Empire than I do that dastardly coward Hitler in the German Empire.

The British Empire has one of the rottenest, dirtiest, bloodiest records of autocracy and oppression of any empire in the world.

How much democracy does that empire have in relation to India, Africa, colony after colony, or Ireland? How much democracy did that empire have when we kicked them out?

What I am trying to make clear is that you can't simply say that is a battle between what we call democracy and totalitarian states.

Congress of Industrial Organizations, "Transcript of Hearings before the Committee to Investigate Charges against the Food, Tobacco, Agricultural and Allied Workers of America," 1950, 67-68, copy in Congress of Industrial Organizations, Papers, Files of the Office of the Secretary-Treasurer, Wayne State University Archives of Labor History and Urban Affairs, Detroit, Mich. (hereafter referred to as Carey Papers), Box 109. Although knowing what we now know about what happened in occupied Europe in the years after the speech was made, Henderson's analogy between the two empires was not apt, at the time it was certainly plausible, if not quite convincing.

5. "Review of the Month," *Communist*, vol. 19, no. 11 (November 1940), 967-76.

6. Sister M. Camilla Mulloy, "John Brophy, Militant Labor Leader and Reformer: The CIO years," (Ph.D., diss., Catholic University of America, 1966), 126.

7. James Matles, OH, 36-37; Albert Fitzgerald, OH, 4; both in Pennsylvania State University Archives of Labor History, State College, Pa. (hereafter, PSUA).

8. *Labor Leader*, February 6, 1939.

9. Jacob Potofsky, a liberal ally, confirming that this was a widely held view of Carey, recalled that in later years George Meany came to regard him as mentally unbalanced, "psychopathic and so forth," and would not call meetings of the Executive Council of the AFL-CIO for long periods because Carey got on his nerves. Jacob Potofsky, Oral History Interview, COHC, 634-38.

10. Carey, COHC, 213.

11. E.g., Carey to Joseph England, Secretary of U.E. District Council No. 1, February 7, 1940, Harry Block Papers, Reel 1, microfilm copy in PSUA.

12. Julius Emspak, COHC, 264; Matles, OH, 41-43.

13. Even after his conversion to anti-anticommunism, Father Charles Owen Rice recalled that he and Carey were both "very much teed off" at the Communists over the Stalin-Hitler Pact, an event which he regarded as crucial in turning Carey against the Communists. Rice, OH 2, PSUA, 15.

14. *Daily Worker*, December 28, 1940, January 11, 1941; *UE News*, December 20, 1940, January 11, 1941; "Review of the Month," *Communist*, vol. 19, no. 11 (November 1940), 968-76; "Review of the Month," *Communist*, vol. 19, no. 12 (December 1940), 1059-63.

15. See Carey Papers, Box 3, "Eleanor Roosevelt" Folders.

16. Carey, COHC, 213-14.

17. Digest of press reports of UE, 12, Daniel Bell, Collection of Material on Socialism and Communism in the U.S.A., Tamiment Institute Library, New York University, NewYork, N.Y., Box 6.

18. *The New York Times*, January 19, 1941.

19. Ibid., January 24, 1941.

20. Ibid., February 6, 1941.

21. Victor Riesel, "Communist Grip on Our Defense," *American Mercury*, 52 (February 1941):202-10.

22. Stanley High, "Rehearsal for Revolution," *Reader's Digest*, vol. 38, no. 6 (June 1941), 89-93; "We Are Already Invaded," ibid., vol. 38, no. 7 (July 1941), 122-26.

23. Hugh Lee, "Menace to Labor: The Cause of American Labor Is Suffering from the Penetration of Communists into Its Unions," *Current History and Forum*, 52 (January 10, 1941):20-22.

24. Max Kampelman, *The Communist Party vs. the CIO* (New York: Praeger, 1957), 25.

25. Ibid.

26. Years later, Matles and Emspak would trot out their union's virtually strike-free record during this period to confuse and confound their anti-Communist critics. U.S. Congress, Senate, Committee on Labor and Public Welfare, *Hearings on Communist Domination of Unions*, 82nd Cong., 2nd sess. (1952), 490.

27. Emspak later described them as taking various sides on the question, with some going along with the Murray-Hillman policy while others did not. Emspak, COHC, 235.

28. Murray to Forrestal, December 9, 1940, Adolph Germer, Papers, State Historical Society of Wisconsin, Madison, Wis.

29. Vernon Jensen, *Lumber and Labor* (New York: Rinehart, 1945), 264-65.

30. "Suggestions made by Chairman Dalrymple and Committeeman Robinson to Conference," n.d. [February 3, 1940?]; Memorandum, February 23, 1941, Germer Papers. This is another indication, as well, that the Communists and their supporters in

the CIO were never so well-coordinated and mutually supportive as their opponents often alleged.

31. Jensen, *Lumber and Labor*, 266-67.

32. Robert Ozanne, "The Effects of Communist Leadership on American Trade Unions" (Ph.D. diss., University of Wisconsin, 1954), 220.

33. Bert Cochran, *Labor and Communism* (Princeton: Princeton University Press, 1977), 174-76; Matthew Josephson, *Sidney Hillman, Statesman of American Labor* (Garden City, N.Y.: Doubleday, 1952), 543.

34. *Collier's*, October 18, 1941, cited in Ozanne, "Communist Leadership," 55.

35. Even inveterate opponents like Walter Reuther admitted at the time that Mortimer had neither started the strike nor created the conditions which led to it. Reuther and Frankensteen admitted that the origins of the strike lay in the company's wage policies and the bulk of the sentiment for the illegal walkout came from the workers themselves; they charged mainly that Mortimer had stirred up muddy waters. See Walter Reuther, "Mortimer's Letter to President Murray and Answers," undated [July 1941?], Walter Reuther, Papers, Wayne State University Archives of Labor History and Urban Affairs, Detroit, Michigan (hereafter WSUA), Series 1, Box 7, "Executive Board" Folder.

36. Wyndham Mortimer, *Organize! My Life as a Union Man* (Boston: Beacon Press, 1971), 183.

37. Edwin Lahey, Oral History Interview, COHC, 85. He told this to Lahey, a friend who was the labor reporter for the Chicago *Daily News*. Yet when Lahey went to southern California to investigate the strike, he became convinced that it had broken out over purely economic grievances, fully justified ones at that. Ibid.

38. J. Edgar Hoover to Edwin Watson, secretary to the president, June 9, 1941, FBI Report 807; Hoover to Watson, June 18, 1941, FBI Report 833, Franklin D. Roosevelt, Papers, Franklin D. Roosevelt Library, Hyde Park, N.Y.

39. Brophy, COHC, 865.

40. Alan Haywood to Germer, February 10, 1941; Haywood to McCarty, February 10, 1941; Ivan Koivenen to Murray, February 20, 1941, Germer Papers.

41. Richard Francis to Germer, March 15, 1941, Germer Papers.

42. Germer to Haywood, March 26, 1941; Haywood to Germer, March 29, 1941, Germer Papers; Lorin Cary, "Adolph Germer, From Labor Agitator to Labor Professional" (Ph.D. diss., University of Wisconsin, 1968), 140-44.

43. Cary, "Adolph Germer," 142-44; Jensen, *Lumber and Labor*, 268-70.

44. "Minutes of the FEWOC Executive Board Meeting," April 27, 1941, Walter Reuther, Papers, WSUA, Series 1, Box 57, "FE Merger" File. Although it may have seemed like good politics at the time, in retrospect the Communists likely made a grave tactical error, for George Addes had emerged as a most effective ally of the UAW Communists. With him as head of a UAW farm equipment department, protecting and nurturing the FEWOC Communists, the anti-Reuther forces in the UAW would likely have received a large enough shot in the arm to emerge in control of the union in the touch-and-go battle that was to wrack it during the next six years. The interesting thing about the episode, though, is how it bespeaks of a lack of coordination between UAW and FEWOC Communists. Indeed, it would seem to be an instance in which, in the pinch, Communists placed their union loyalties ahead of their political loyalties.

45. *NYT*, June 11, 1941. In the same press conference in which he portrayed the North American strike as part of a conspiracy to sabotage the defense effort, Knox revealed that from January 1 to June 10, 1941, companies working on War Department contracts had lost 2,370,716 man-days of work due to strikes. The five-day strike of 11,000 men at North American was hardly a drop in this very large bucket. A list of the strikes still in progress when the North American one was broken not only indicates no left-wing bias among the unions involved, but if anything, reveals a relatively high

number of AFL and anti-Communist unions on strike, including Murray's own Steelworkers. Indeed, it was a strike by two hundred skilled AFL operatives against thirteen
steel fabricating plants in St. Louis that was holding up the construction of an airplane
plant and a naval ordnance factory. *NYT*, June 11, 12, 1941.

46. *U.S. News and World Report*, 10 (June 27, 1941):18-19.

47. Biddle to FDR, June 23, 1941; Biddle, "Memo for the President: Subversive
Employees," June 26, 1941, FDR Papers, PSF Box 76, Justice Department File.

48. Most of them were either CIO organizers or employees of CIO District Councils.
Daniel Bell, Interview with James Carey, October 27, 1955, Bell Collection, Box 4,
"CPUSA" Folder.

49. Biddle, "Memo for the President," June 26, 1941.

50. J. Edgar Hoover to Edwin Watson, June 26, 1941, FBI Report 845, FDR Papers,
OF 10-B.

51. Mortimer, *Organize!*, 192.

52. *NYT*, July 7, 1941.

7 WORLD WAR II: THE GRAND STRATEGY FORMULATED

The invasion of the Soviet Union caught the CPUSA as unprepared as it did Stalin. Clearly its line would have to change and change fast, but there was little time to ponder the new stance. Thus, the initial response of Communist unionists was confused and hesitant, and it took some time for the political leadership to map out a specific trail to follow.

There was little confusion regarding what the United States should do. Almost from the moment that news of Hitler's invasion arrived, a swelling chorus of leftist unions demanded that the United States aid the Soviet Union. Within days of the invasion, the party's political leadership decided that the new line would be summed up in the slogan: "All aid to Britain, aid to Russia, for convoys and for an American expeditionary force."[1]

This was decided upon easily, but the abrupt shift caused embarrassment to Communist unionists. In Detroit, for example, a CP-dominated UAW local had submitted a resolution condemning the war as an imperialist war and branding FDR a warmonger to the Wayne County CIO Council. The Germans invaded before the meeting was held to consider this resolution, prompting another from that local, this one calling for all-out support of Hitler's foes. The council's anti-Communist president later recalled having "a great deal of fun" reading out both resolutions at the same time, pretending not to know which was the one the local wanted considered, and provoking "a great deal of hilarious comment" and some biting attacks on the Communists.[2]

But most unionists were not as obsessed with foreign policy as were the Communists in mid-1941. The domestic implications of the new policy were of greater concern. Perhaps sensing this, the party's political leadership hesitated over how the new European situation would affect their union activity, especially their militancy in leading strikes. An FBI informant reported in early July that the party was:

no longer inclined to call for strike action on every issue which confronts a labor union nor is the Communist Party the first to raise the strike question. . . . The Party will support a strike only when the majority of workers in a given factory are in favor of such action.[3]

The new approach may have appeared as waffling to some, but it was perhaps the wisest choice that could be made. On the one hand, it reflected a fear of losing the hard-won support of militant workers by trying to dissuade overwhelming numbers of them from striking when they were determined to do so. On the other hand, by refusing to encourage strikes which might damage the defense effort, the Communists could claim to be helping the flow of aid to the Soviet Union.

The obvious problem with the new line was that it was open to various interpretations, or so it appeared at first. The invasion did not cause an orderly about-face by the Communists and their followers in the unions, with everyone marching in lockstep to the same cadence. Rather, the turn was executed in a ragged fashion, with a number of leftists ambling off in different directions.

The NMU, for example, hewed to a militant interpretation of the new line at its convention in early July. In a speech to the convention, Joe Curran denied that the invasion of the Soviet Union had caused any shift in NMU policy. It had always opposed fascism, he said, and now recognized that the struggle of Great Britain and the Soviet Union against it deserved the support of freedom-loving people everywhere. He hailed Murray as a "great leader," but saved his most effusive praise for the still anti-interventionist Lewis, whom he called "the founding genius of the CIO."[4] A convention resolution applauded both Lewis and Murray for attacking those who wanted to sell out the interests of workers in the name of the defense program.[5]

In the IWA, the leftists interpreted the new line as a mandate to end factional struggle by making generous concessions to their opponents. They accepted reforms in the union constitution and convention procedure which were certain to deprive them of power. They dropped their opposition to Germer's presence and the agreement with the CIO and tried to form a "unity" slate with the rightists for the next elections for the union executive board.[6]

In the UE, on the other hand, only some Communists were willing to sacrifice power for unity. At its convention, held shortly after the invasion, the word was passed to party members and fellow-travellers that they must strive for unity above all. Carey would therefore be the

CP choice for president. However, since Carey refused to stop attacking Communists in return, many members and fellow-travellers refused to go along and voted for Albert Fitzgerald anyway.[7] Later, Communists on the UE Executive Board persuaded it to support Carey's reelection as secretary-treasurer of the CIO, and even asked Murray to convert it into a full-time job. Emspak later called these acts a sop to the CP's desire for unity that were done over his objections.[8]

The haziness of their mandate was only one of the impediments to formulating and applying rigid new guidelines for Communist unionists. Another was that the party's chief theoretician, its "great and farsighted leader,"[9] Browder, was serving time in Atlanta Penitentiary, along with a number of CP leaders. Despite Browder's "all-American" background and protestations that communism was becoming as American as apple pie, the party still functioned internally in a very Stalinist fashion under Browder's leadership. A mini "cult of personality" had been built around him and a steady stream of party functionaries visited Atlanta, asking for direction and trying not to contravene his wishes. But the site, with every conversation almost certainly overheard by the authorities, was not the best for communicating orders, especially secret ones to be passed on to union "notables."

Thus, while some Communist unionists did abruptly change from wolves to sheep after June 22, 1941, this may just as well have been the result of the looseness in the ties that bound them to the party rather than their strength. In the one documented case where Roy Hudson, the party's labor man, met with unionists to work out the new line (an FBI summary of a conclave he held with CP waterfront leaders), and, Hudson cautioned against changing directions suddenly. It was decided not to agitate for protected convoys for American ships entering the war zone because it would be too obvious a reversal of the party's position during the past year.[10]

The Japanese attack on Pearl Harbor on December 7, 1941, was a kind of blessing to the party, for it placed the party's growing admonitions to place production above all else in the indisputable mainstream of American patriotism. The immediate response of the CPUSA National Committee to the attack was virtually identical to that of the AFL and CIO. It became more urgent to resolve industrial disputes "without interruptions in production," declared the CP the day after the attack.[11] Soon the line was being proclaimed with greater shrillness ("No idle plants, no idle machines—FOR ANY REASONS!" said Roy Hudson in a front page article in the *Daily Worker*)[12] but it deviated from official AFL and CIO policy mainly in tone rather than in content.

The adoption of a "no-strike pledge" by virtually all American unions shortly after Pearl Harbor helped smooth the Communist transition further. They could respond to charges that they were subordinating the economic interests of American workers to their fealty to the Soviet Union by claiming that they were simply following CIO policy, a policy adhered to by the largest of the non-Communist unions.[13]

Browder later claimed that the Communists in the CIO went along with the "no-strike pledge" against his wishes, while he was still in jail. He favored a "no-strike *policy*." A "pledge," according to Browder, implies that something will never be done. A "policy" leaves room for striking when conditions so warrant.[14] However, the record of Browder's actions and statements during the war lends little credence to this claim. Rather, his single-minded pursuit of labor peace and maximized production during the war helped provide a basis for the rout of the Communists in the CIO in the postwar period.

The war severely hampered CPUSA communications with Moscow and, even before the dissolution of the Comintern in 1943, gave Browder considerable leeway in interpreting Moscow's mandate, which was a predictable but very general one. Apparently, shortly after Pearl Harbor, Comintern Chairman Georgi Dimitrov instructed Robert Minor, the acting general secretary of the CPUSA, that the party was to support FDR, work for a national united front against fascism in the United States, and publicize the Soviet Union's struggle against Nazi Germany. Communists in the trade union movement were to push for greater lend-lease aid for the Soviet Union.[15] There was nothing in Dimitrov's message regarding strikes, wages, or productivity.

In early 1942, while Browder still languished in Atlanta Penitentiary, the CPUSA National Committee issued a directive on labor emphasizing the need for labor unity and hailing efforts to work out a joint AFL and CIO strategy for speeding up production. It distinguished between the majority of AFL union leaders, patriots all, and a small minority of those who followed William Hutcheson into the "pro-fascist" camp. The former included the previously anathematized William Green, whereas the latter were trying to work out secret deals with John L. Lewis to sabotage the war effort. On the specifics of increasing production, nonetheless, the party went no further than the official CIO line. It merely reaffirmed its support for the recent CIO National Executive Board declaration that increased production should not be accomplished at the expense of the living standards of the working class, that "the continued existence and growth of the labor movement be guaranteed" and an equitable tax program be instituted. The CPUSA declared that the spiralling cost of living must be controlled, social security and unemployment insurance must be expanded, and labor must be represented in government decision-making bodies.

Significantly absent was any reference to the "no-strike pledge" and how the party interpreted it. Also absent was any reference to another source of tension in the ensuing war years, the question of "piece work."[16]

By the time Browder was released from prison and reassumed his direct grip on the reins of power in May 1942, he was already developing Stalinesque delusions of omniscience. Wartime Communist propaganda portrayed Stalin as personally directing every aspect of the war effort, from the relocation of Soviet industry behind the Urals to practical suggestions for the improvement of agricultural yields, while supervising the formulation of grand military strategy. His brilliance as Marxist philosopher, writer, and cultural critic was the subject of awed praise by American and other Communists. In the face of such multiple talents and interests on the part of the leader of world communism, could the leader of the CPUSA admit a lack of expertise in any important area? If he did not have a great enough mastery of Marxism-Leninism to apply it to the entire panoply of economic and political problems, then who did? Thus, the war saw Browder throw himself into a frenzy of detailed study of the minutiae of the war production effort. He had ideas about how to run everything better, from grand military strategy to the New York subway system. He engaged in lengthy correspondence with union and business leaders regarding bottlenecks in war production and produced endless tomes on how they could be overcome.[17] Through intermediaries, he established a regular connection with President Roosevelt, warning the president that some apparent liberals such as Reuther and Carey were really part of the "Trotskyite" attempt to sabotage the war effort.[18] The emphasis on labor sacrifice for production's sake came to take precedence over virtually all else. Everything had to be subordinated to winning the war and preserving the United States-Soviet partnership, efforts in which American Communists were indispensable.

The shift was soon reflected in the party's official stance on labor policy. Hudson's report on labor to the National Committee in April 1942 had been primarily an elaboration of the earlier statement, adding that Negroes and women should be included in the revived war effort and that equality of employment opportunity and wages be assured to these groups.[19] Upon his release from the penitentiary in May, Browder declared his satisfaction with the labor course being followed,[20] but soon began to emphasize the necessity of increased production. In his book *Victory and After*, published in the summer of 1942, Browder said business would have to be allowed adequate profits to keep it patriotic and prevent it from sabotaging the war effort. Wages must be set "upon the basis of providing the most efficient working class."[21] It soon became apparent that this meant wages should be tied to productivity, something that was approved in a special party conference in November 1942 and codified in Browder's pamphlet, "Production for Victory," over 100,000 copies of which were distributed to unionists around the country.[22]

By then, the party's view of the course of action for the CIO had begun to reflect the growing passion for productivity. Reporting on the CIO's November 1942 convention in Boston, Roy Hudson was much less concerned about safeguarding labor's rights and standards during the war than he had been in April. He placed much more emphasis on cooperating with the government to win the war. The speech of Under Secretary of War Robert V. Patterson, the notorious Red-baiter who only the year before had been trying to goad the CIO into an anti-Communist purge, was "a reflection of the place that the labor movement has already won in the nation and in the hearts and minds of most patriotic Americans irrespective of their class position," said Hudson. Sidney Hillman was praised for his "constructive and active role," as was Murray, of course. Hudson even saw good news in the elevation of another recent enemy, Allan Haywood, to a vice-presidency of the CIO, claiming that it was a recognition of the importance that the convention placed on new organizing. The "no-strike pledge" and "piece work," two sources of increasing controversy, were not mentioned. Hudson's main criticism of the CIO convention was that it did not condemn with sufficient vigor those who had not worked hard enough in the recent congressional elections to ensure the victory of "New Deal Win-the-War Democratic" candidates.[23]

Browder and Hudson did not stop with praise for Murray, of whom they had so much reason to be wary. Browder decided that the CIO and the war effort were endangered by Murray's apparent weakness at the helm of the CIO, the result of his previous dependence on Lewis. He convinced the party and its unionists to mount an active campaign to "build the authority and prestige of Murray within the ranks of labor and tear down that of Lewis."[24]

Driven by his growing obsession with maximizing production, Browder soon metamorphosed into a self-styled expert on all phases of production, from the level of national planning down to the shop floor, with rather extraordinary results. In 1943, for example, opportunity knocked at the CP door when a number of disgruntled longshoremen sought them out for aid in overthrowing the corrupt leadership of Joseph Ryan in the gangster-ridden International Longshoremen's Association. Thousands of workers in the Port of New York, basking in the labor shortage, were defying Ryan and the ILA; they ostentatiously worked without their union buttons and disobeyed union orders. The dissidents wanted the Communists to help them defect from the ILA and replace the Ryan-dominated shape-up system with the hiring hall system the ILWU had won on the West Coast. They complained of the corruption, gangsterism, dictatorship, and inefficiency that characterized the ILA in the Port of New York.

Remarkably, it was the slowness in ships' turnaround times and the inefficient use of waterfront labor that galvanized Browder and Hudson. Thus, rather than seizing the opportunity to make a dramatic breakthrough by supporting the creation of a new Communist-influenced East Coast waterfront union, or at least calling in the ILWU, Hudson and the CP functionaries discouraged a breakaway from the ILA. They told the dissidents to stay in the ILA and stick to war-related issues; attacks on Ryan should concentrate on the inefficiency of the cargo handling system which he oversaw. Not surprisingly, Ryan merely kicked his critics out of the union and off the waterfront, retaining his iron grip on the Port of New York.[25]

On the national level, Browder and the CP thought that they had valuable advice to give the government: the war economy must be centrally planned through strong executive action.[26] Despite the obvious debt to Stalin, the only significant way in which this advice differed from that of Bernard Baruch was that the Communists, like most CIO liberals, were more interested in labor participation in the planning process. Browder held few illusions that this had anything to do with socialism. The main objective of centralized planning, he told the party's plenum, was to increase production.[27]

To maximize production, Browder warned, the Communists must avoid alienating employers. They must recognize that there was a split in the bourgeoisie between one segment of it, the "Lamont-Morgan defeatists," and those who sincerely wanted to win the war. The party must "crystalize the will to victory" and isolate the "defeatists." The progressive sector of the bourgeoisie must be shown that the way to increase production was to cooperate with unionists.[28]

Browder recognized that some employers might be tempted to appropriate the benefits of higher worker productivity for themselves. How to prevent this was a problem because strikes were out of the question. Two things were therefore necessary: federal government action to prohibit employer exploitation of increased productivity and "piece-work." "Incentive wages," as Browder delicately called them, would tie wages to productivity and head off this possibility.[29] It was an idea that would soon plunge many Communist unionists into scalding water.

By March 1943 Browder found much more to be impressed by in the "progressive" sector of the bourgeoisie than their patriotism. He rejected the charges of leftists such as *PM* columnist Max Lerner that the "no-strike pledge" was a "betrayal" and the doubts expressed by *PM* editor Harold Levine over the wisdom of continuing the pledge at the same time that employers such as Henry Ford seemed to continue their efforts to crush unionism. American capitalism was changing, according to Browder, and a new enlightened group of big businessmen was emerging. These people saw the necessity to raise "the general level of well-being and democracy" in the country. "There is something new under the sun today," he said, and "people who go by old formulas and preconceptions cannot find their way in the present world."[30]

Browder's rightward shift picked up steam after the Tehran Conference in October 1943, which he saw as inaugurating a new era of United States-Soviet friendship. Using the conference's pledge to maintain Anglo-American-Soviet unity into the postwar era as his jumping-off point, he projected the desirability of peaceful coexistence between capitalism and socialism in the international sphere back into the American domestic scene. At home, Tehran would be complemented by a new area of cooperation between Communists, "progressives," and any capitalists who were willing to work for reform. Capitalists of all kinds should be able to see that their interests would benefit from full employment and higher wages, which would increase the purchasing power of the working class. In a sensational speech in Bridgeport, Connecticut, in December 1943, he said that Communists must cooperate with everyone who supported the Anglo-American-Soviet coalition. "If J. P. Morgan supports this coalition and goes down the line for it," declared Browder, "I, as a Communist am prepared to clasp his hand on that and join with him to realize it. Class divisions have no significance now except as they reflect one side or the other of this issue."[31]

The remark about J. P. Morgan aroused considerable unease in the party, yet Browder pressed on, displaying again and again his inability to settle for half measures and his apparent horror of ideological and programmatic loose ends. In early 1944 he analyzed the logical conclusions of the path he had embarked upon in his great theoretical work, *Tehran and America*. He explained that in his remark about J. P. Morgan "I was not making a verbal abolition of class differences, but I was rejecting the political slogan of class against class as our guide to political alignments in the next period." American Communists must choose one of two paths: either to devote themselves to helping to achieve the goals of the Tehran agreement or to try to push a reluctant United States into socialism. The prospects for success in the latter path were "dubious . . . especially when we remember that even the most progressive section of the labor movement is committed to capi-

talism, is not even as vaguely socialistic as the British Labour Party."
The correct path, then, was the first one, a struggle for "national unity"
and support for the "progressive, democratic majority."[32]

Browder's rigidity in applying the new line ultimately brought about
his downfall. Policy had to be applied thoroughly and consistently.
How much more consistent could one be than Browder, who persuaded the party to take the next logical step in the new direction, the
abandonment of the party as a political party? In May 1944 he presided
over the official dissolution of the Communist Party of the United
States and its reconstitution as the "Communist Political Association,"
an organization which was to function not as a political "party" striving
to achieve power in its own right, but as a progressive pressure group
supporting those in the two major parties who endorsed its program.
He later acknowledged that his vision of its function was similar to that
of the not-yet-founded Americans for Democratic Action.[33]

Browder's rightward tack aroused disquiet among the party's political leadership, but no one on the National Committee had the prestige,
self-confidence, or perhaps gumption to challenge him openly. Only
William Z. Foster, brooding over the complexities of reconciling the
"spirit of Tehran" with his continuing suspicion of "finance capital,"
confronted him and then mainly for the record. In January 1944 he
sent a long critique of Browder's line to all members of the party's
National Committee. It was intended not as a clarion call for Browder's
overthrow, which would foment disunity and undermine the war effort,
but to document formally but secretly his disapproval of Browder's line
for use at an appropriate future time. While agreeing that the party
must support Roosevelt in the 1944 election, he emphasized that this
must be done as the lesser of two evils, or rather of two kinds of imperialism. He disagreed with Browder's assumption that American "finance
capital" or "monopoly capital" was being domesticated and could be
worked with after the war. Labor must be rallied both during and after
the war to confront it, and not nurse false hopes of cooperating with it.
Nor did he share Browder's confidence that the United States would be
able to avoid a postwar economic crisis. Although Browder was correct
in saying that socialism would not be the main issue in postwar America,
it would "nevertheless be a question of great and growing mass interest
and influence." If the Communist party took merely a negative attitude
towards socialism, as Browder seemed to call for, "the Social-Democrats
will be left with a free hand to pose as the party of Socialism."[34]

The political aspect of Browder's line aroused little concern among
leftist labor leaders. If anything, the closer identification with the New
Deal and New Dealers smoothed the way for collaboration with powerful ex-enemies such as Sidney Hillman. However, the economic aspects of

Browder's program helped weaken the leftist position in the CIO by undermining their reputation for militancy in the all-important UAW.

NOTES

1. Hoover to Watson, July 9, 1941, FBI Report 859, Franklin D. Roosevelt Papers, Franklin D. Roosevelt Library, Hyde Park, N.Y., OF 10-B.

2. Tracy Doll, Oral History Interview, Wayne State University Archives of Labor History and Urban Affairs, Detroit, Mich. (hereafter WSUA), 40.

3. Hoover to Watson, July 9, 1941.

4. *New York Times*, July 8, 1941.

5. NMU, "Resolution No. 1, supporting Murray and Lewis," in Curran to Murray, August 5, 1941, Congress of Industrial Organizations, Papers, Office of the Secretary-Treasurer, James Carey, WSUA (hereafter Carey Papers), Box 53.

6. Lorin Cary, "Adolph Germer, From Labor Agitator to Labor Professional," (Ph.D. diss., University of Wisconsin, 1968), 141-45.

7. James Carey, Oral History Collection of Columbia University, New York, N.Y. (hereafter COHC), 237-39; Emspak, COHC, 274-77; *NYT*, September 3, 1941; James Wechsler, "Carey and the Communists," *The Nation*, September 13, 1941. Emspak subsequently attributed the closeness of the vote to the number of Communists who voted for Carey, and even Carey admitted that a number of Communists had indicated they wanted him to stay in the presidency and that he was surprised by the number of leftist votes he garnered. Emspak, COHC, 272; Carey, COHC, 237.

8. UE, "Minutes of the General Executive Board Meeting," November 17, 1941, in Harry Block, Papers, Pennsylvania State University Archives of Labor History, State College, Pa., Reel 2; Emspak, COHC, 357. Yet within months, as Carey continued to encourage opposition to them, they were complaining to Murray that the CIO was paying the salary of someone using his office to overthrow the leaders of one of its unions. Although he had little respect for Carey, Murray would not go along with their demands that he be dumped for fear that this would be seen as an indication of the inordinate power wielded by the Communists in the CIO. Pressman, COHC, 402-7.

9. Editorial, "Toward Labor Unity," *Communist*, vol. 21, no. 2. (March 1942), 100.

10. Hoover to Watson, July 9, 1941.

11. *Daily Worker*, December 8, 1941.

12. Ibid., March 3, 1942.

13. E.g., see James Matles, OH, PSUA, 62.

14. Browder, COHC, 391.

15. Hoover to Watson, December 16, 1941, FDR Papers, OF 10-B.

16. "Toward Labor Unity," 105-9.

17. E.g., see his eighty page summation of his efforts in that direction in the "1942-Plenum" Folder, Browder File, Daniel Bell, Collection of Material on Socialism and Communism in the U.S.A., Tamiment Institute Library, New York University, N.Y., N.Y., Box 3, and the copies of businessmen's speeches and material from employers in other folders in the Browder File.

18. Joseph P. Lash, *Eleanor and Franklin* (New York: New American Library, 1973), 904-7.

19. Roy Hudson, "Labor and the National War Effort," *Communist*, vol. 21, no. 4 (May 1942), 310-23.

20. The only serious "distortions" which he tried to "correct" upon gaining his freedom were the adoption of the idea that the struggle for Negro rights and Puerto

Rican liberation must be postponed until after the war. Earl Browder, "Speech to the National Committee, C.P.A.," June 18, 1945, copy in Earl Browder, Papers, George Arents Research Library, Syracuse University, Syracuse, N.Y., Series 11 Box 6, "Duclos" File.

21. Earl Browder, *Victory and After* (New York: International Publishers, 1942), Ch. 20.

22. Browder, "Speech to National Committee," June 18, 1945.

23. Roy Hudson, "The CIO Convention," *Communist*, vol. 21, no. 11 (December 1942), 992-99.

24. Browder, "Speech to National Committee," June 18, 1945.

25. Roy Hudson to Browder, May 28, 1943; Roy Hudson, "Report on Longshore Conditions in the Port of New York" (May 1943) in Bell Collection, Box 3, "Browder" File.

26. Earl Browder, "The Economics of All-Out War," *Comunist*, vol. 21, no. 9 (October 1943); Roy Hudson, "The CIO Convention."

27. Earl Browder, "Report to Plenum," November 29, 1942, Browder Files, 1942, Bell Collection, Box 3, "Plenum" Folder, 32, 66.

28. Ibid., 32-36.

29. Ibid., 50-55.

30. Earl Browder, "Labor Relations at the Ford Plant" (March 1943), Browder File, Bell Collection, Box 3.

31. Earl Browder, *Communist*, vol. 23, no. 1 (January 1944), 8.

32. Earl Browder, *Tehran and America* (New York: International Publishers, 1944), 20.

33. Browder, COHC, 409.

34. Foster to Members of the National Committee, CPUSA, January 20, 1944, Browder Papers, Series 11, Box 6. Phillip Jaffe says that when Browder concurred with Foster's demand that a copy of the letter be sent to Moscow, Dimitrov replied that Foster should cease his opposition. Phillip Jaffe, "The Rise and Fall of Earl Browder," *Survey* (Spring 1972), 42-62.

8 THE STRATEGY APPLIED

The wartime labor line had been shaped in characteristic fashion: by the party's political leadership acting alone. Its effects on the upper echelons of the CIO were almost instantaneous, so quick was the apparent reconciliation between Murray, Hillman, and the leftists. Pressman acted as the go-between in a hastily arranged conference in which the two sides pledged mutual cooperation and unity in the face of the looming Nazi danger.[1] Lewis was now isolated, with only his UMW behind him. He soon began to pull the UMW out of the CIO.

Communist unionists turned against Lewis with great reluctance. For almost three months Pressman tried to convince him to abandon his continuing commitment to "isolationism." Even after August 6, 1941, when Lewis joined Herbert Hoover and Alf Landon in signing a manifesto declaring that the Anglo-Russian alliance had destroyed any idea that the war was one between tyranny and freedom, the Communists kept alive the flickering hope that he would come around to their view. According to James Wechsler, Lewis offered them a deal: agreement to disagree on foreign policy along with continued cooperation on domestic policy.[2] The possibility was slim that they would accept such a deal, especially after the attack on the Soviet Union. For the Communists', foreign policy was the overriding consideration. Their domestic policy was too tied in to their foreign policy for the two to be surgically separated. Finally, the Communists gave up, and, in September 1941 the *Daily Worker* began a systematic campaign of attacks on Lewis.[3]

Murray's attitude towards the Communists became an ambivalent one. Like Lewis, he needed them and wanted their support. Like Lewis as well, he feared them and did what little he could to clip their wings and undermine their power without disrupting the CIO. At first,

Murray had to move cautiously. He was even more dependent on leftist support than Lewis had been during his presidency because he had to deal with a charismatic Lewis glowering at him from outside. Lewis had had his servile UMW as a secure power base while Murray had nothing comparable. Murray and Lewis had come to a complete parting of the ways in October 1941 when Murray told Lewis that he was going along with FDR one hundred percent. In 1942, when Lewis and the UMW left the CIO, SWOC stayed and reconstituted itself as the United Steel Workers union, but Murray's grip on it was not as strong as Lewis' had been in its formative years. Also, especially during the early war years, SWOC-USW's influence in high CIO councils came nowhere near matching that of the UMW-SWOC nexus of the 1930s. Furthermore, Lewis' attitude towards the war held a great temptation for unionists, especially militant ones. Many of them shared his fears of a repetition World War I experience, that Murray and Hillman, like Gompers, were settling for crumbs from the administration's tables while big business was reaping huge profits.

Although some leftist union leaders echoed the party's attacks on Lewis,[4] Browder encountered difficulties in recruiting many of them into the anti-Lewis onslaught. When Browder prepared to denounce Lewis for allowing the UMW to strike in April and May 1943, he was unable to find any Communist union leaders who would join him in "sharp and unequivocal public declarations."[5] However, when a vast media-stimulated public outcry against Lewis arose, the CIO unionists, Communist and non-Communist, fell into line. Spurred on by the Communists, a special meeting of the CIO Executive Board denounced Lewis for "exploiting the injustices of the mining industry in furtherance of his personal and political vendetta against the President of the United States, our Commander-in-Chief." His activities were endangering "the very existence of the Nation and the lives of millions of Americans on the front." Browder thought that Murray had to be pushed into this confrontation with Lewis by the Communists because he was still too unsure of his position in the CIO to confront Lewis directly and publicly.[6] It is equally likely that Murray's reluctance was based on understanding, as Browder did not, that the miners and many other unionists did not regard Lewis' defiance of the War Labor Board as ipso facto traitorous and reprehensible. Whereas Browder hardly thought twice about subordinating their safety and their pocketbooks to the Soviet Union's struggle for survival, the miners had different priorities.[7]

Lewis tried to turn the Communists' prominent role in the attacks on him against Murray and Hillman. Murray was a prisoner of the Communists, Lewis charged in February 1944. They controlled him and the CIO and, Lewis said, "There isn't a blessed thing he can do about it. Sidney Hillman is just as badly off. Both of them have to play ball with the Communists now, or die."[8]

Murray reciprocated leftist support by shunning confrontations with them. Despite repeated warnings by anti-Communists such as James Carey and Clint Golden that Pressman was taking orders directly from CP envoys such as Roy Hudson at CIO conventions, Murray, who developed a paternal affection for the New Yorker and a great respect for his ability as a lawyer, kept him on as general counsel and continued to rely upon him as a close personal aide. Len De Caux was also retained as editor of the *CIO News*. He and Hillman's counsel, John Abt, another lawyer with close Communist connections, maintained a kind of "placement bureau" for leftists in the CIO and, after its creation in 1943, the CIO-Political Action Committee.[9]

Furthermore, Murray did not heed the warnings of anti-Communists such as Adolph Germer regarding the growing power of Communists within the CIO state industrial union councils. Rather, he encouraged the councils to play a larger role especially in rallying support for the war effort and ignored the warnings of Germer and other anti-Communists in the CIO bureaucracy who saw the state IUCs as undermining the power of the CIO regional directors, who were primarily anti-Communists directly responsible to Murray and Allan Haywood in Washington.[10]

Nevertheless, behind the Communists' backs, Murray was doing his bit to ensure that their wings were clipped. Although they had a relatively free hand regarding CIO-PAC and the state IUCs, the Communists did not make inroads into the CIO's full-time bureaucracy with its crucial regional directorships and full-time organizers under Haywood's direction. Murray also defied the growing number of people who felt uncomfortable with Carey, a man without a union, as secretary-treasurer. Despite the widespread unease over the CIO paying a salary to a man who was trying to unseat the leadership of one of its largest unions, Murray made sure that Carey was never challenged for reelection at a CIO convention. Although Murray had little regard for Carey personally and was not at all close to him, one of Murray's close friends recalled that he kept Carey on because "Murray regarded Jimmy as a sort of good irritant for the Communists."[11] Murray also kept his lines of communication open with the organized Catholic anti-Communists, attending ACTU Communion breakfasts and special services presided over by ACTU priests.[12]

Furthermore, in his own Steelworkers union, Murray used the war as an excuse to continue the quiet purge he had been conducting since 1938. According to Clint Golden, a prominent USW aide, Murray said,

"With war on, we don't want those fellows in the union." The highly centralized nature of power in the union made the task easy. Suspected Communists were merely fired from the union staff.[13]

Murray also intervened against the Left in Mine, Mill, when anti-Communist insurgents made a bid to take power in 1942. The insurgents, led by ex-organizer John Driscoll, were centered in the Communist-dominated Connecticut district. They charged Robinson with padding the union payroll with Communists and using them for extraneous purposes. Secretly, Murray encouraged the insurgents, as did Father Rice and some local Actists. At a Mine, Mill Executive Board meeting that they attended in late 1942, Murray and Carey accused the union of veering too far to the Left and demanded that a number of Communists on its staff be fired. Robinson and the leftists refused to cave in although they only controlled a minority of the board. Murray thereupon put the Connecticut district into receivership, charging that Communists had been using their position in the union to recruit party members.[14] Luckily for the leftists, a rightist board member died and an anti-Communist board member switched to their side. This, as well as Robinson's regaining his right to vote on the board, allowed them to regain control of the union before the war's end.[15]

The reconciliation with the Communists appears to have been more wholehearted for Hillman. He shared their overriding concern for foreign policy and for making the defeat of Nazism the CIO's main objective. Furthermore, with their desire to play a more active role in the Democratic party, there was the basis for mutual advantage emerging through cooperation on the domestic front. Whereas in 1944 David Dubinsky broke from the New York manifestation of the Popular Front, the American Labor Party, because of its refusal to purge the Communists who were so important in it, Hillman stayed in and cooperated with the Communists to make it, along with the CIO-PAC, an important funnel for labor support for what they all hoped would be a new, more progressive Democratic party.[16]

The Communists' wartime line met with mixed success in the various CIO unions and on the shop floor. Support for the no-strike pledge caused little trouble, at least at first, but in characteristic fashion in mid-1942 the party's political leadership went too far. In their zeal to demonstrate that they were doing everything possible to aid the war effort while the battle for the Soviet Union's survival hung in the balance, they decided that unions should demand only those wage increases that could be justified by gains in productivity. They called together the party's trade union leaders to explain the new policy. In effect, the party leadership tried to persuade the unionists to pass up the magnificent opportunity that the war seemed to be laying at labor's feet to catch up on the losses of the depression. Workers whose wages had not caught up in the period of rearmament from 1939 to 1941 would thus have to wait until the war's end to press substantial wage demands.

There was considerable unease among leftist unionists over the new posture, and Browder and the political leadership had to do a lot of convincing. But in the end, the line was approved with only minor modifications,[17] in part because it coincided with that of most CIO liberals. All had promised to uphold the "no-strike pledge" and had agreed, albeit with some reluctance, to have their wage demands limited by the "Little Steel" formula of July 1942, which limited wage increases to the 15 percent rise in the cost of living since January 1, 1941.[18]

Also, despite government attempts to discourage it, the wartime labor shortage in fact led to competition among companies for labor, a competition that was often reflected in wages that were raised without union prodding. Furthermore, in many industries overtime pay was a sufficient boon to defuse discontent over wage rates. Finally, wartime price controls, although by no means totally effective, worked well enough in preventing inflation in consumer prices to head off explosions of wage discontent arising from that source. Nevertheless, in some industries, Communist unionists found the new policy uncomfortable, playing into the hands of their opponents.

The wartime line had the most untoward consequences for Communists in the UAW. Communist fortunes in the UAW's Byzantine factional struggles had sagged during 1941, primarily because of the rising star of Walter Reuther, who was using every weapon at his disposal against them and their defiance of the union leadership during the "defense strikes." Yet, although it easily passed a Reuther-backed ban prohibiting Communists from holding union office, the union's convention in August 1941 did not turn into quite the anti-Communist romp Reuther had presaged. A standoff occurred in the distribution of union power: the leader of the Communist-backed faction, George Addes, retained his post as secretary-treasurer and Richard Frankensteen began to disassociate himself from the Reuther coalition.[19]

Over the next year and a half, the power balance within the union tilted back somewhat towards the Communists. As Walter Reuther solidified and expanded his base within the union, creating around his powerful General Motors Department a well-organized machine personally devoted to him, the equally ambitious Frankensteen went over to the Communist-Addes coalition. By September 1943, the FBI reported that Frankensteen, whose fulminations against the Communists at the 1941 convention had known few bounds, was meeting secretly with Roy Hudson and Addes to work out a joint strategy for the upcoming UAW convention, including the creation of a joint committee to direct the collaboration between his forces and those led by the Communists.[20]

The new coalition, along with a somewhat more reluctant Reuther, managed to commit the UAW to following the general CIO policy of sacrifice for the war effort. Most touchy at first was ramming the CIO's abandonment of premium pay for overtime work down an obviously reluctant membership's throat. The Communists were in the forefront of those urging abandonment, despite the portents of impending trouble which appeared on the horizon. In organizing drives in the aircraft industry in the Midwest (led by Frankensteen's men) and the West (led by the Communists), the UAW's emphasis on its contributions to the war effort fell flat among the workers. Unorganized workers found the promises of the IAM and other AFL unions to extract more rewards more attractive.[21] Moreover, the rank and file in the defense industries where the UAW was concentrated were becoming increasingly restive with government-imposed wage restraints and were looking for union leaders who could break through those barriers.

The various UAW factions had managed to live in uneasy balance during the first year of the United States war effort. The UAW's convention in August 1942 was proclaimed a "Unity Convention." Walter Reuther genially supported the CP-originated resolution, introduced by Victor Reuther, calling for the opening of a "Second Front" and seconded Addes' renomination as secretary-treasurer. Addes, in turn, seconded Reuther's nomination as a vice-president and all of the top officers were elected by acclamation.[22] Beneath the surface, however, large segments of the membership were clearly seething over the effects of the union's "Equality of Sacrifice" program on their earnings and working conditions.[23]

It was precisely at this time that Browder hit upon "incentive pay" as the solution to the problem of ensuring equality of sacrifice. When the UAW Communists, as well as Addes and Frankensteen, began to advocate at least permitting it, Reuther and his supporters began to distance themselves from what they accurately sensed to be an unpopular idea among much of the rank and file.

Reuther's conduct during the war constituted an extraordinary display of political acumen, substantiating the widely-held view that he was the smartest, ablest, and wiliest of the many ambitious young people who were jockeying for power in the "new unions." From the outset, he had managed to retain his reputation for militancy in the face of employers without opening himself to attack for being un-patriotic. He stole a march on the employers in 1941 when he advo-cated the conversion of unused capacity in the auto industry to the production of warplanes, presenting a plan which he claimed would turn out fifty thousand planes a year. Adroitly he forced the com-panies to hem and haw over the plan that they ultimately turned down because it would have involved more concessions to the union than they wished to make. Thereby he succeeded in garnering very favor-able nationwide publicity for himself as both a patriot and a militant unionist, and in putting the companies on the defensive regarding contributions to the defense effort. He showed himself equally adept at putting the UAW leftists on the spot over "incentive pay."

Browder's stand on "incentive pay" was a millstone around the necks of the UAW Communists and their allies. Communists could and did use his argument that it provided a means whereby the benefits of increased productivity would go into the pockets of workers rather than into the bank accounts of capitalists. Unionization had made the threat of an actual "speed-up" without employee consent a thing of the past, in the Communists' view.[24] But it was just a short step from using "piece work" to reward employees to using it to entice them to work faster and produce more. Reuther successfully exploited this fear. In March 1943, the UAW Executive Board followed his lead and adopted such strict guidelines on the introduction of "incentive pay" schemes as to bar them, beating back the attempts of the Communist-backed Addes-Frankensteen coalition to loosen them. The next month, it again refused to loosen its strictures against "piece work," reaffirming what it now called "its traditional opposition to incentive pay plans."[25]

The Communists could not leave bad enough alone. Goaded on from New York and barraged by Browder's ponderous speeches, they persisted in their attempts to have the union soften its stance on the issue and played right into Reuther's hands. As the breech between Reuther and the Communists widened into a chasm, Browder pushed the leftists from the frying pan into the fire, taking out an ad in the Detroit *News* in which he accused Reuther of wrecking the automobile industry. It did little good. Addes and his supporters were defeated on the issue at the next UAW convention.[26] Years later, a UAW Commu-nist recalled ruefully that Reuther's most effective wartime slogan had been "Down with Earl Browder's Piecework in the UAW."[27]

Although he relied on the piece work issue to differentiate his faction from the other, Reuther also bested the leftists on the no-strike issue. Here again, he let them paint themselves into a sloganeering corner while he managed to carve a more militant yet still not "un-patriotic" position for himself. When John L. Lewis threatened to bring the precarious wartime detente between business and labor crumbling around Roosevelt's ears by taking his Mine Workers out on strike in April 1943, Reuther managed to take a position on both sides of the fence. He attacked Lewis for exploiting the miners' just grievances in calling the strike and went along with the rest of an enlarged CIO Executive Board when it unanimously condemned the strike. However, at the same time, his lieutenants, especially those such as Emil Mazey with ties to the Socialist party, refused to condemn the strike. Rather, they seized the opportunity to question the no-strike pledge.[28]

Much of the debate over these grand principles took place on the national level, and was dominated by the stratum of full-time union officials jockeying for power. It is significant that, in practice, many UAW Communists on the local union level either ignored or defied the main outlines of Browder's line. For example, the Communist-dominated local that bargained with Allis-Chalmers in Wisconsin ignored the party's admonitions to cooperate with management to increase production. Grievances were magnified and, although both union and management had long approved incentive pay, the union stubbornly refused to have it applied to the brass foundry. It also opposed the fifty-six-hour week that the navy had requested to speed up production on navy orders.[29]

Significantly, in 1943 when the Communists scored their greatest wartime gain in the UAW in the elections for control of the 80,000-90,000 member Ford Local 600, the largest union local in the country, they did so by repudiating two of the hallmarks of Communist wartime labor strategy, the party line on incentive pay and Browder's admonitions to abandon the drive for equal rights for Negroes for the duration of the war. They won on a platform demanding equality in pay and advancement opportunities for the approximately 20,000 black workers at Ford, most of whom were relegated to the foundries. This neutralized their opponents' attacks on Browder and incentive pay, which they had pointedly refused to support anyway, and rallied most of the black work force to their side.[30]

By the next year, the situation of the Communists and their allies had become desperate. A real rank-and-file movement was developing around the demand to rescind the no-strike pledge. That would be the overriding issue at the 1944 UAW convention, Addes told an emissary of Browder's. The UAW's strong public backing for the pledge was "so much double-talk," said Addes, intended for newspaper and public consumption. Reuther was backing off, and the rumblings of the membership were making Thomas uneasy and unsure of himself.

The weakness of the UAW commitment to the no-strike pledge was confirmed by a gloomy agent of Browder's in talks with the Communist rank and file, but there was no thought of altering or adjusting the CP line in the UAW to fit its unusual circumstances. Rather, Browder's man thought it was disgusting to see people playing internal union politics with something as serious as the war effort.[31]

The new rank-and-file movement composed of anti- or non-Communists made large inroads into Reuther's natural constituency. At the UAW convention in September 1944, Reuther took the middle ground between the "Rank and File Caucus," which demanded outright abandonment of the no-strike pledge, and the leftists, who wanted its retention. He suggested that it be retained, but only in factories engaged directly in war production. When none of these positions won a majority, Reuther proposed putting the question to a referendum of the membership, a suggestion accepted by a majority of the convention.[32]

The leftists were enraged, in part because they had again been outmaneuvered. Reuther was in fact no more nor less "democratic" than they were but was using the referendum as a desperate device to wriggle off a very uncomfortable hook. Indeed, Reuther came almost as close to being crucified on the issue as they did. The 1944 convention represented a severe setback to his ambitions. His waffling on the no-strike pledge alienated non-Communist militants whom he had already disappointed by supporting the disciplining of wildcat strikers. Disgusted by his apparent failure to seize the lead of a swelling militancy originating on the shop floor, many of his former supporters turned their backs on him. For the first time, he was defeated for the first vice-presidency of the UAW by his former ally, Richard Frankensteen, and retained his seat on the UAW Executive Board only by winning a subsequent contest for the second vice-presidency.[33]

Yet somehow, the referendum call enabled Reuther to wriggle off the hook. The UAW Communists, who were following the line set down by Browder, Hudson, and the general staff in New York could not bail out so easily. When they were swept by a fear of sticking their necks out on the issue, Browder sent Roy Hudson, the party's labor head, to devote himself full-time to rally a frenetic pro-pledge campaign.[34]

Despite Reuther's continued official support for the pledge, he was reviled by the Communists for having brought on the referendum. It was "instigated as part of a conspiracy against the war effort, President Roosevelt and labor," charged Roy Hudson. The issue was becoming hopelessly confused, fumed Browder, and the referendum might not reflect the true feelings of the majority of the membership; it had been called "merely to serve the factional advantage of a group of ambitious men."[35]

Browder's fears were not realized. Neither were the pessimistic soundings of rank-and-file attitudes towards the pledge. Thanks in part to the desperate leftist effort, 65 percent of those who voted favored retention of the pledge. The Communists were lucky, for a vote against the pledge would have left them in a vulnerable position, opposing the expressed will of the majority of what was at the time the most democratic of all major unions. But the leftist victory was merely a negative one. Again, Reuther had managed to have his cake and eat it. He emerged from the conflict with both his "militant" and "patriotic" reputations reasonably intact and perhaps reinforced.

The only other union in which the CP's wartime line also had perceptible untoward consequences was the Transport Workers Union. The effect there was like a time bomb that did not explode until after the war. The change in line had come at a time when Michael Quill's union was finally feeling its oats. Its position in the crucial New York City transit system was secure, and it had made substantial gains in a number of cities. Thus it could expand to other occupations, including airline pilots and mechanics, groups on which the UAW had designs as well. The CP political leadership felt that to go further would disrupt a key sector in the war effort and damage labor unity, but Quill plunged ahead, organizing an important local of Miami-based Pan Am pilots into his union. From his perspective, the CP's wartime program was "a complete surrender to the bosses in return for full production."[36] Quill found himself facing the unanimous opposition of the CP sympathizers on the CIO Executive Board.[37] No one would even second his motion to give his union jurisdiction over the airline field.[38]

He proceeded to organize Miami-based pilots anyway. In March 1943, he defied the CP political leadership when they advised him not to accept a local of eleven hundred Los Angeles track workers who had fled the AFL into the TWU. Later, he again defied the CP political leadership and their CIO counterparts when he ignored their demands to put "national unity" above all else and gave a charter to a group of San Francisco transit workers who also wanted to change unions.[39] The CP also tried to hold Quill back in his ongoing struggle with Mayor Fiorello La Guardia in New York City. For example, in February 1943, when he organized an anti-La Guardia demonstration of non-operating subway workers, the CP tried to hold down its size. While the other city papers reported that thousands had stopped work, the *Daily Worker* put the number at three hundred.[40] Although his leftist ideals and dependence on Communist support within his union kept him in the party, all of these incidents rankled and facilitated his subsequent defection.

In the UE, the ILWU, and Mine, Mill, the top leadership managed to minimize the potentially damaging impact of Browder's mania for productivity. They often echoed Browder's rhetoric but were generally careful to avoid being labelled insufficiently militant in defending their members' pocketbooks.

In the UE, for example, only after the war did James Carey seriously raise the charge that the leftist leadership had sacrificed the interests of the membership to the Soviet Union.[41] Even then, the ineffectiveness of the charge probably explains the infrequency with which it was used. It was more likely an imitation of Walter Reuther's success with it in the UAW than the result of any significant disaffection of the membership over their officers' conduct during the war.

Indeed, the UE leaders were about as adroit as Reuther in appearing to combine patriotism with union militancy. Soon after Pearl Harbor they, like Reuther, put the employers in their industry on the defensive. They offered to drop higher pay rates for overtime work for the duration of the war if the money saved would go directly to the United States government as a union contribution to the war effort. They argued that the companies had already negotiated their contracts with the government until 1945 on the assumption that normal overtime rates would be paid and, barring a revision of these contracts, the savings would otherwise be merely a windfall for the companies. Similarly, they offered to begin a union campaign to increase worker productivity by 15 percent, but with safeguards to ensure that the money saved went into workers' pay envelopes rather than corporate profits.[42] Apparently, no employers took them up on the offer.

While the UE leaders were sincerely interested in stepping up production, they did not fall into the trap of becoming totally identified with the Roosevelt administration's war production effort. Soon after Pearl Harbor, members of the union's Executive Board did go to Washington to discuss ways of increasing production,[43] and UE leaders did join other leftist CIO leaders in their repeated exhortations for all-out production for the war effort, expressing the de rigeur condemnations of "unionism as usual" and calling on workers, as did James Lustig, to "work first and argue later."[44] Yet, from early 1942 the leadership displayed a propensity to criticize various government agencies, expressing its displeasure over the War Production Board, for example, while continuing to offer "unlimited" cooperation in the war effort.[45]

The UE leaders were also not particularly affected by Browder's commitment to "incentive pay" because "piece work" was already a common feature in many occupations they represented. Thus, they were able to maintain their reputation for militancy without contravening the new line by remaining vigilant against employer attempts to rate various classifications downwards, not much of a threat because of the labor shortage during the war. They were not suicidal enough to offer to have jobs re-rated to raise "norms" except under conditions that the companies found completely unacceptable.[46]

Opponents to the UE leftists thus found their pickings slim during the war. According to Harry Block, one of the most important opposition leaders, there was little they could do during the war because

the rank and file are interested in two things . . . how much do I get in my pay envelope and don't increase the dues. And if they got service and they got their wage increases, it was pretty hard to shout "Commie" in 1943, '44, '45, to '46 because the Soviet Union was the ally of the United States.[47]

The accommodationist line also wrought little harm for Harry Bridges and the leftist leadership of the ILWU. Shortly after the invasion of the Soviet Union, Bridges proposed a plan to increase productivity and defuse labor troubles on the West Coast by appointing a joint union-employer-government board to settle disputes and oversee the implementation of plans for increasing efficiency in the ports. The employers, reluctant to give up any of their traditional powers, demurred. After Pearl Harbor, he revived his proposal, but it was vetoed by Admiral Emory Land, the head of the War Shipping Board, who despised Bridges as a Communist. Only the burning of the liner *Normandie* in February 1942 as it was being converted to troopship duty in New York harbor changed Land's mind. Reluctantly, he acquiesced to the "Bridges Plan." Within months, West Coast longshoremen were setting records for loadings and unloadings, winning effusive praise from the army and navy.[48]

Yet suspicions of Bridges ran deep in the administration and in the army. When, shortly after Pearl Harbor, Bridges had the California State CIO Council set up an anti-sabotage committee, a production committee, and a civilian defense committee, the army commander on the West Coast, General John DeWitt, told J. Edgar Hoover that the plan constituted unwarranted interference in the defense effort. Hoover, outraged because the committee members seemed to be enjoined from cooperating with the FBI, warned FDR of Bridges' "obviously sinister designs."[49]

Bridges also knew not to force his plans to increase productivity down an unwilling membership's throat. When, in mid-1942, Bridges came down to Los Angeles to convince dockworkers to go along with an army request to raise the sling load limit for bags of cement, he soon backed down genially in the face of worker opposition.[50]

Bridges faced some embarrassment in late 1944, when, adhering to the no-strike pledge, the ILWU local at the Montgomery Ward branch in St. Paul, Minnesota, refused to join a strike called by the CIO Retail Workers Union to protest the company's defiance of the War Labor Board and its refusal to bargain seriously. However, not only did Bridges have a long-standing jurisdictional dispute over control of warehouse workers, impeding cooperation with the anti-Communist Retail Workers leadership, but he also had the support of the powerful New York local of the union, which was Communist-led and opposed to the strike as well.[51]

In general, the war and the new accommodation the party was promoting between capital and labor worked in Bridges' favor. As a result of the new line, "Red 'Arry," so feared and despised by the owners of the West Coast shipping fleets, was able to metamorphose into a "labor statesman" of sorts, creating the kind of cooperative relationship with employers that came to characterize the West Coast waterfront throughout most of the postwar period. He convinced them that, despite his militant bearing, he was someone with whom they could work. To the general public, however, Bridges still remained a wild radical, primarily because his deportation case dragged on through the war and he remained the object of American Legion and other superpatriotic attack.[52]

The great upsurge in employment in the mass production industries where the CIO was concentrated brought swelling union membership figures in its wake, and Communist and non-Communist unions benefited equally. However, it also brought a subtle change in the nature of the membership and the major unions. The new members were normally workers who took out union cards as a condition of employment, people who had not experienced the great organizational struggles of the 1930s. They were even less union-minded than their predecessors. At the same time, the growth in union membership was accompanied by a proportionally greater expansion of CIO union bureaucracies. Once the wild days of hectic organizing campaigns were over, the unions produced comfortable jobs for those who fancied themselves able administrators, people who developed an overweening commitment to the preservation of their own jobs and a concomitant reluctance to rock the boat. This phenomenon affected leftist and non-leftist alike.[53] A Browder aide sent to investigate the UAW in 1944 found widespread cynicism among the rank-and-file regarding all who held union office. By and large, they said, organizers were "nothing more or less than ward heelers" who "might easily kill a man to maintain their well-paid jobs, but not organize him."[54]

Although many of their best young organizers were in the service, the Communists managed to expand the base of their unions into difficult new territory. The wartime boom helped the previously impoverished Farm Equipment Organizing Committee win enough important contracts to demand and receive a CIO charter in 1942.

The Food and Tobacco Workers, hitherto facing an almost solid wall of fear and employer-government opposition in the South and West, managed to organize some canners in California and over ten thousand tobacco plant workers in North Carolina, as well as workers in scattered large food processing plants in the North. The tobacco factory workers were their special pride and joy, for the 10,000 at the R. J. Reynolds plant in Winston-Salem, North Carolina, constituted something unheard of in that part of the South, a huge racially-integrated union local with large numbers of white members in a predominantly black union. The tiny Communist-led United Furniture Workers even managed to organize some furniture factory employees in Tennessee and the equally small United Public Workers had some success organizing black federal government cafeteria workers in Washington, D.C., workers for the Panama Canal Company in the Canal Zone, and perhaps most spectacularly the guards at Alcatraz penitentiary.[55] The Office and Professional Workers even organized those seemingly quintessential capitalists, Prudential Life Insurance salesmen.

None of these small unions made breakthroughs into major league status during the war, but most did enough to stake out claims for continuing their independent existence. This gave some of their leaders seats on the CIO Executive Board and helped reinforce the approximately one-third of the votes the Communists could consistently rely on there to support their political causes. It did not add appreciably to the proportion of CIO members in Communist and fellow-traveller-led unions. That, not counting the UAW, remained between one-fifth and one-fourth of total CIO membership.

Despite the general euphoria over the impending Allied victory in the war, there was growing unease among American Communists over the wartime line. By mid-1944, the party's National Committee was receiving many complaints from its functionaries in the trade unions over the overriding commitment to the no-strike pledge and productivity increases. According to an FBI informant, many party members felt that the party was "folding up," abandoning its role as the vanguard of the working class, allying with the reactionary wing of the labor movement, cooperating with capitalism, and abandoning class struggle. Their complaints all received the same response: "We have got to win this war!"[56] Many more members, like Jessica Mitford, a United Public Workers activist, did not complain, but were "secretly disappointed to discover that its revolutionary goals seem to have faded away."[57] All it would take would be a gentle shove from abroad to bring Browder's house of cards tumbling down.

NOTES

1. John Brophy, Oral History Interview, Oral History Collection of Columbia University (hereafter COHC), 867.

2. James A. Wechsler, *Labor Baron: A Portrait of John L. Lewis* (New York: William Morrow, 1944), 138-48.

3. *Daily Worker*, September 17, 1941.

4. Lewis was not above exacting retribution. Reid Robinson, who became one of Lewis' more vociferous detractors in late 1941, was beaten up at the CIO convention that December, allegedly by a gang of hoodlums in the service of Lewis' son Denny. Lee Pressman, COHC, 402.

5. Earl Browder, Speech to the National Committee, C.P.A., June 18, 1945, copy in Earl Browder, Papers, George Arents Research Library, Syracuse University, Syracuse, N.Y.

6. Browder, COHC, 397, 402; CIO, Executive Board, "Resolution on John L. Lewis," May 14, 1943, copy in Nat Ganley, Papers, Wayne State University Archives of Labor History and Urban Affairs, Detroit, Mich. (hereafter, WSUA) Box 8, Folder 17.

7. Dubofsky and Van Tine make the point that Lewis' wartime militancy was also based on his intimacy with miners and a keen awareness of the relationship between increased productivity and accidents in the mines. In mid-1943, Lewis pointed out that since Pearl Harbor, more miners had died as a result of their occupation than American soldiers on the battlefield. Melvin Dubofsky and Warren Van Tine, *John L. Lewis* (New York: Quadrangle, 1977), 315-40.

8. *The New York Times*, February 29, 1944.

9. Daniel Bell, "Interview with Clint Golden," October 26, 1955, Daniel Bell, Collection, Box 3; "Conversation with Jim Carey," October 27, 1955, Bell Collection, Box 4, "CPUSA" Folder; Edwin Lahey, COHC, 101, 105.

10. Germer to Haywood, March 16, 1943, Adolph Germer, Papers, State Historical Society of Wisconsin, Madison, Wis.

11. Lahey, COHC, 70.

12. E.g., see clippings from *Catholic News*, n.d.[late 1942?]; Detroit *News* and *Detroit Free Press*, January 25, 1943, in Association of Catholic Trade Unionists, Detroit Chapter, Records, Wayne State University Archives of Labor History and Urban Affairs, Detroit, Mich., Box 1, "Clippings, 1939-1943" Folder.

13. Bell, "Interview with Golden."

14. Chase Powers, Oral History Interview, Pennsylvania State University Archives of Labor History, State College, Pa. (hereafter, PSUA), 32-33; Robinson, OH, PSUA, 37-38; Vernon Jenson, *Non-Ferrous Metal Industry Unionism, 1932-1952: A Story of Leadership Controversy* (Ithaca: Cornell University Press, 1954), 102-15.

15. Powers, OH, 39.

16. Matthew Josephson, *Sidney Hillman, Statesman of American Labor* (Garden City, N.Y.: Doubleday, 1952), 604; Max Danish, *The World of David Dubinsky* (Cleveland and New York: World, 1957), 140-42.

17. Browder, COHC, 391.

18. Joel Seidman, *American Labor from Defense to Reconversion* (Chicago: University of Chicago Press, 1953), 109-24.

19. Roger Keeran, "Communists and Auto Workers, The Struggle for a Union, 1919-1941" (Ph.D. diss., University of Wisconsin, 1974), 345-51; Bert Cochran, *Labor and Communism* (Princeton: Princeton University Press, 1977), 184-95; James Prickett, "Communism and Factionalism in the United Automobile Workers, 1939-1947," *Science and Society*, vol. 32 (Summer 1968), 262-65.

20. "Communist Activities in Organized Labor" (1943-1944), FBI Report 2580, OF 10-B, Franklin D. Roosevelt, Papers, Franklin D. Roosevelt Library, Hyde Parke, N.Y.

21. Nelson Lichtenstein, "Industrial Unionism Under the No-Strike Pledge: A Study of the CIO during the Second World War" (Ph.D. diss., University of California, Berkeley, 1974), 259-69.

22. UAW, *Proceedings of the Annual Convention*, 1942, 62-66.

23. Lichtenstein, "Industrial Unionism," 269-71.

24. E.g., "Resolution on Production Incentives," introduced by Richard Frankensteen, UAW-CIO Executive Board Meeting, April 19-20, 1943, copy in Ganley Papers, Box 8, Folder 17.

25. Ibid., excerpt from "UAW-CIO Executive Board Minutes—Relative to Incentive Plans," March 9, 1943, April 19, 20, 1943.

26. Detroit *News*, May 14, 1943, cited in Irving Howe and B. J. Widick, *The UAW and Walter Reuther* (New York: Random House, 1949), 118.

27. Ganley, OH, WSUA, 40.

28. Executive Board, Local 155, UAW-CIO, to Edward Levinson, May 14, 1943; "Statement," Executive Board, Local 155, UAW-CIO, May 14, 1943, Ganley Papers, Box 8, Folder 17.

29. Robert Ozanne, "The Effects of Communist Leadership on American Trade Unions" (Ph.D. diss., University of Wisconsin, 1954), 316.

30. Lichtenstein, "Industrial Unionism," 385-88. Another indication that Communist fealty to "the line" was not as abject on the local level as often depicted came later, when Herbert Sorrell, the party line leader of the weak Confederation of Studio Unions, defied the no-strike pledge and the party in calling a strike against some major Hollywood studios over a jurisdictional dispute, and shrugged off the wrath of the *People's World*, the West Coast counterpart of the *Daily Worker*. David Saposs, *Communism in American Unions* (N.Y.: McGraw Hill, 1959), 58.

31. Unsigned, undated report, Browder Papers, Series 11, Box 19, "UAW" Folder.

32. UAW, *Proceedings of the Annual Convention*, 1944, 72; Howe and Widick, *UAW and Walter Reuther*, 123-24.

33. Lichtenstein, "Industrial Unionism," 659-71.

34. Browder, "Speech to National Committee," June 18, 1945.

35. *Daily Worker*, December 24, 1944; January 7, 1945.

36. [?] Levering, Interview with Michael Quill, November 21, 1948, Bell Collection, Box 3; CIO, "Transcript of Hearings Before the Committee to Investigate Charges against the International Longshoremen's and Warehousemen's Union," Washington, D.C. June 1950, 160, copy in CIO, Papers, Office of the Secretary-Treasurer, James Carey, (hereafter Carey Papers), WSUA.

37. He later said there were sixteen of them at the time. Levering, Interview with Michael Quill, Bell Collection.

38. Ibid., another indication that if there was a CP master plan to gain a stranglehold on transportation, it certainly sat on the back burner most of the time.

39. Ibid.

40. Ibid.

41. James Matles, OH, PSUA, 65.

42. UE, "Recommendations by the General Officers," March 24, 1942, copy in Harry Block Papers, PSUA, Reel 2, "UE-1942" Folder.

43. *UE News*, December 20, 1941.

44. *DW*, March 7, 1942.

45. UE, "Some General Considerations on War Production Presented by the General Secretary-Treasurer, to Donald Nelson, Chairman, War Production Board, March 1942," in Block Papers, Reel 2, "UE-1942" Folder.

46. E.g., UE, "Recommendations by the General Officers."

47. Block, OH, PSUA, 19.

48. Charles Larrowe, *Harry Bridges: The Rise and Fall of Radical Labor in the United States* (N.Y.: Lawrence Hill, 1972), 251-54.

49. Hoover to Watson, December 22, 1941, FBI Report 1068, OF 10-B, FDR Papers.

50. In Larrowe, *Harry Bridges*, 256.

51. Aaron Levenstein, *Labor Today and Tomorrow* (New York: Knopf, 1946), 161-66.

52. In contrast, on the other coast, tough Joseph Curran became something of a darling of the media, reaping favorable publicity as head of the union whose members were daily risking and losing their lives to keep the troops supplied. Curran appreciated the irony enormously and enjoyed rubbing his CIO anti-Communist enemies' noses in his new respectability. When in 1942 *Life* magazine ran a laudatory feature on him and his union, he made sure to send a copy to James Carey. Leo Huberman to Carey, September 1942, Carey Papers, Box 53.

53. Julius Emspak noted this ruefully in his recollections, altering, as it did, his original conception of what a growing CIO would become. Emspak, COHC, 317-19.

54. Unsigned, undated, [April 1944?] memorandum, Browder Papers, Series 2, Box 19, "UAW" Folder.

55. Jessica Mitford, *A Fine Old Conflict* (London: Michael Joseph, 1977), 49.

56. "Re: Communist Party, U.S.A., May 16, 1944," FBI Report No. 2536, FDR Papers, OF 10-B. The informant appears to have worked for the *Daily Worker*. He may have been Louis Budenz, the managing editor from 1940 until 1945, when he quit the party and became a recurring witness on communism for congressional committees.

57. Mitford, *A Fine Old Conflict*, 61.

9 ONE WAR ENDS AND ANOTHER BEGINS

Roosevelt's election victory in 1944 was a close one. It came at a time when the New Deal coalition that had been constructed out of such disparate parts in the 1930s seemed to be on its last legs. The coalition had collapsed in Congress in the wake of Roosevelt's attempt to pack the Supreme Court in 1937 and his unsuccessful intervention to unseat his conservative Democratic opponents in the 1938 congressional primaries. Buffeted by the war and growing dissatisfaction with the government in various quarters, the seemingly unstoppable Democratic party juggernaut of 1936 and even 1940 seemed but a shell of its former self. The only part of the old coalition that remained reasonably intact was labor. The CIO's new Political Action Committee, headed by Sidney Hillman, and the money, men, and materiel it had channelled into the Democratic campaign were widely regarded as crucial in reelecting Roosevelt and preventing a conservative sweep of Congress.[1]

The CIO did not have a particularly favorable image among the voters. Indeed, if anything, to large sectors of the electorate, CIO endorsement amounted to a kiss of death. A Gallup Poll in mid-1944 said that 53 percent of the respondents declared that a CIO endorsement would make them less likely to vote for a candidate, whereas only 10 percent said that they would be more likely to vote for the office-seeker.[2] But official endorsements are much less important than the kind of contribution Hillman and the Communists who gave so much support to PAC were able to funnel into the Democratic campaign: money, printed literature, and dedicated legs to distribute the literature and round up the voters. Many Americans became convinced that the labor movement, and most particularly the CIO, would henceforth play a greater role than ever in national politics, becoming, in fact, the mainstay of the Democratic party.

The Communist leadership found satisfaction in this apparently fundamental change in American politics. Roy Hudson was pleased that after the election Eugene Meyers, the owner-publisher of the pro-Dewey Washington *Post*, told the 1944 CIO convention that "in breaking precedent and in taking an organized part in the political campaign" the CIO had inaugurated the beginning of a "new era," the significance of which few had fully realized. Labor had "emerged as a political force in its own right," Hudson wrote, and "a historic milepost" had been reached. The day that American Communists had awaited for generations had finally arrived.[3]

By early 1945, Browder was pressing resolutely past the milepost, ignoring the growing signs of dissatisfaction within the party. He spoke eloquently on the benefits of the new Tehran-inspired interclass alliance. The war, in his view, had made a large part of the business community more progressive,[4] and Communists must support the progressive elements of the capitalist class against the Right. "The problem is no longer how to combat the whole bourgeoisie," he said, "but how to strengthen the progressive against the reactionary sector."[5] Nowhere was there an indication that this would be a short-term, tactical alliance. Rather, as the party's dissolution would indicate, the alliance with the progressive bourgeoisie was to last a long time.

In a report on labor in March 1945, Roy Hudson, the most sincere supporter of Browder's line, attacked Reuther-Lewis-Dubinsky followers who wanted to abandon the no-strike pledge after the war. Strikes would not provide the 60 million jobs which would be needed in the postwar period to protect the wage gains of the war. Only political action and total support for President Roosevelt's program could do that.[6]

Shortly thereafter, Eugene Dennis, a less sincere supporter of Browder's line, hailed the proclamation of the "New Charter for Labor and Management" proclaimed by the AFL, CIO, and the U.S. Chamber of Commerce in March 1945 for recording "labor's pledge, under present social conditions, to recognize capital's property rights and to promote increased production." He also lauded its assertion that continued cooperation between labor and capital was essential in the postwar era. Dennis dismissed those who thought that this was "class collaborationism" of the Gompers variety as misguided "progressives," Socialists, and Trotskyists. Gompers' class collaborationism had been one of a skilled aristocracy of labor working in its own interests to the detriment of the great mass of workers. It aimed at destroying the Soviet Union and allowing the rise of fascism. The Washington Charter, on the other hand, was "a collaboration of classes within our own country directed towards welding post-war national unity in support of our government's foreign policy entered into at Cairo, Tehran, and Yalta, and its domestic program for 60,000,000 peacetime jobs."[7]

To Browder, the wartime line and its end-of-the-war variations seemed eminently successful. He later claimed that the response among trade unionists was especially favorable. "A lot of new people came in from the trade unions," he recalled. "They were the most active, of course, the ones who responded most enthusiastically."[8] There was some statistical support for him. The number of party members in the auto industry doubled in the year 1943 alone, and membership among steelworkers increased by 50 percent.[9] In May 1945 when the party was officially dissolved, Browder claimed that membership had reached an all-time high of 80,000, and that did not include an estimated 10,000 members in the armed forces.[10]

There were other signs of Browderism's growing acceptability. Spurred on by the Yalta Conference in February 1945, public opinion was now favorably disposed towards the Soviet Union and the possibilities of continuing wartime cooperation with it after the war.[11] The CPUSA was playing an active, open, and relatively successful role in New York City politics and, especially from the vantage point of Union Square, it no longer seemed a political pariah. Rather, it was rapidly becoming accepted as a respectable part of the American political structure. A public opinion poll taken soon after the war revealed increased toleration towards Communists among the general public.[12]

Yet, beneath the surface all was not so rosy, especially in the labor movement. Although the party had recruited a considerable number of new working class members, many of its young militant cadre had volunteered or been drafted into the service. Many of the new members joined the party to smooth their quest for secure positions in leftist union bureaucracies. Furthermore, especially in mass production industries, the exodus of the generation of the late 1930s into better-paying jobs and the recruitment of large numbers of new workers who had not fought the bitter organizational struggles of the 1930s led to a general decline in the political sensitivity of the work force.

In August 1945 party leaders lamented that "even in unions under progressive leadership we find cases where only a fraction of the membership attend meetings or participate in the life of the unions."[13] To many, it seemed that the gap between the increasingly bureaucratized union leadership and the rank and file was becoming wider. Stan Weir, a leftist union activist, was struck by the chasm that seemed to separate the two during the 1946 strike wave. For a moment, he had thought that "the pre-war period that had such a wonderful confidence that the movement would result in progressive social change" had returned. But, he recalled, although thousands of leftists were still seeking real change, "we were not operating from strength. Our prewar power was based on our close knowledge of and familiarity with the people we worked and lived around. . . . The war removed us from those people and changed our world. . . ."[14] In the crunch, as the Communists would soon discover, both the new union members and the new bureaucrats could be weaned away from Communist leadership if their pocketbooks led them in that direction.

Although relatively successful in recruiting new members, especially among blacks and women, the Communists began to experience a perceptible drop in active union followers. By the time the CPA was founded in May 1944, a shift in the class composition of the party membership was noticeable. The party was gaining middle class members, but seemed to be losing working class ones.[15] Moreover, its control over its trade union membership was weakened by the abolition of Communist "cells" and "clubs" in many unions with the formation of the CPA.

If Browder were correct in claiming a membership of 80,000 in May 1944, it seemed that large numbers of them were either inactive or dissatisfied with the new line. As the French Communist Jacques Duclos pointed out in his critique of Browder, as of July 16, 1944, almost two weeks after the deadline for doing so, only 45,000 adherents were reported by the *Daily Worker* to have converted their CPUSA membership into CPA membership.[16]

Duclos' sensational attack on Browder's revisionism led directly to Browder's downfall and Foster's resurrection. It was made public by the New York *World-Telegram and Sun* on May 22, 1945, and published in full by the *Daily Worker* two days later. Duclos accused Browder of leading the CPUSA off the revolutionary trail and onto the kind of reformist path that meant the abandonment of class struggle as a method and of communism as a goal.

Soon thereafter, the Duclos article would be cited by anti-Communists as a kind of opening shot in the cold war: a call for a return to policies of sectarianism and sabotage by the Communist parties and labor unions of the capitalist world. A more dispassionate reading of the article today shows that it probably represented nothing of the sort. Duclos did not object to the CPUSA's alliance with bourgeois progressive forces. Indeed, he applauded the party's fervent support for Roosevelt. He called for a policy of preserving the unity forged with progressive bourgeois forces into the postwar era. But Browder had gone too far. In effect, Duclos said, for Communists alliances with the bourgeoisie were short-run or medium-run ones. French and other Communists throughout the world had been busily constructing fruitful alliances of that sort. But this did not mean doing what Browder and the CPUSA appeared to have done, to abandon class struggle in the long run and thereby abandon the hope of ever bringing communism to the United

States. To Duclos, the dissolution of the party, the instrument of the proletariat, signified just that. As he pointed out, a number of parties other than the French were cooperating with bourgeois liberals and yet vehemently refused to follow the Americans into abandoning the party.[17]

The article proved to be just what Browder's opponents needed. Clearly it represented the opinion, not just of Duclos, but of someone much more important in Moscow, probably Stalin. Members of the CPA National Board soon fell all over each other to disassociate themselves from Browder and recant their errors. Among the top leadership, only Roy Hudson did not confess the error of his ways.

An irony of the crisis was that, in the short run, at least, the change in leadership did not bring a substantial change in line. In fact, under Foster, who now stepped into Browder's shoes, the party continued to search for an alliance with bourgeois liberal forces. It courted anyone who would support the continuation of Big Three unity into the postwar period, and it had few illusions about the imminence of communism in the United States.[18] But the CPUSA's line became more like that of the French party: a search for a pro-Soviet alliance of all possible forces, but based on the assumption that big business, the "trusts" or "cartels," were by nature reactionary and out to destroy the Soviet Union. In the end, Foster, like Duclos, could accept an alliance with the Devil himself for tactical purposes, but to base his politics on the notion that the capitalists he had spent a lifetime fighting had undergone permanent transformation was out of the question: It was "class collaborationism" of the worst sort, worse even than that of those "shameless revisionists" Eduard Bernstein and Samuel Gompers.[19]

Despite Foster's bitter invective, he and his group brought little change in the crucial area of labor relations. Indeed, with regard to labor, the roaring lion gave birth to a mouse. The party's first labor program after the repudiation of Browder was still very Browderist, although there were marked rhetorical returns to the old militant camp grounds. True, "big business" was assailed, and no Browderist distinctions were made between its "progressive" and "reactionary" wings. A crisis was imminent because big business had sabotaged plans for orderly reconversion to peacetime production in the hope of repeating the post-World War I experience and using massive unemployment to weaken the labor movement, it said.

Yet, the party's nostrums for the coming economic crisis were totally reformist: measures such as increased severance pay for workers laid off by war industries, which the party took pains to point out was supported by Eleanor Roosevelt. It was hardly the program of a movement that wanted to unleash maximum turmoil in the country. Indeed, the emphasis in the new program was still on working with liberals to secure New Deal reforms and cooperation with the Soviet Union.

In the attempt to construct a national coalition of progressive forces, the labor movement, which had "gained a new status in the nation," was to play the leading role. The wartime no-strike pledge was hailed as "correct policy," but where victory was won there should be "correct application of the strike tactic, with disputes settled through direct collective bargaining between employers and employees," hardly the kind of program with which liberals would take issue.

The Communists were somewhat more confused about the role of the Communist party in the labor movement. There was the feeling that, under Browder, the party had been thrust into the background in the trade unions in which Communists and sympathizers were important. Now, if the leftist unions, with their headstrong and secure leaders flexing their new political power, were to play a vanguard role in promoting the progressive united front, there was the danger that the party itself would become merely a silent and junior partner in the coalition. The only solution proposed was for the party to "begin to develop activity in the name of the Communist party itself."[20] Shortly thereafter, the order went out to reestablish the "cells" which had been dismantled in the unions, but in many industries disrupted by the war's end this proved impossible. In the electrical industry, for example, many of the Communists had been laid off and dispersed, making it difficult to reestablish shop floor contacts.[21]

For the party's trade unionists, the change in leadership in itself made little difference in their approach to union problems. In fact, in terms of militancy in the pursuit of bread and butter gains, they were practically indistinguishable from the mainstream of the CIO. When the end of the war failed to inaugurate a new era of labor-management harmony but instead led to a surge of labor conflicts, CIO non-Communists and Communists alike backed off from their optimistic dreams for postwar harmony. Moreover, both groups shared a profound disappointment with the new Truman administration. Truman's bumbling attempts to stem the postwar wave of strikes through alternating threats and cave-ins, his hasty advances and retreats on the price control question, and the replacement of many Roosevelt liberal advisers with more conservative ones aroused disquiet among CIO unionists of all stripes in late 1945 and 1946. All felt the pressure from their memberships to produce wage increases to make up for the years of wartime restraint and to keep pace with postwar inflation. They all responded as militantly as they could.

However, as Stan Weir and his friends noted, the new militancy was not like the old militancy of the embattled 1930s. The depression that was so widely expected to follow the war never came. Instead, many workers coasted through the postwar years on new automobiles purchased with their wartime savings. They worried more about buying their first homes than about their unions' leadership. When he returned to the southern mill towns he had struggled to organize before he joined the army during the war, Junius Scales, one of the party's top southern leaders, found "an altogether transformed situation." The cotton industry had boomed during the war and the mill workers were finally free of fear of the companies. In his home town, the leftist textile local he had helped organize had been transformed by prosperity. Now it was "like an old, rather comfortable and conservative union. . . . For the first time the company couldn't tell you how to live and what to do. It was no paradise but wages were now living wages. Consumer goods were just becoming available and the villagers just revelled in it. And so my proletarians had become practically middle class."[22]

But prosperity itself was not enough to substantially weaken the Communist position in the labor movement. Union members who cared little about what their union leaders did as long as they produced satisfactorily at contract time were just as willing to abide Communist leadership as they were conservative, liberal, and/or simply corrupt leadership. The growing cold war in Europe and its ramifications for the American political scene made communism an issue again in American unionism. The rapid deterioration of relations between the United States and the Soviet Union soon demonstrated that anticommunism had not died out within American unionism and American politics, it had merely hibernated for the duration of the war.

By 1944, the AFL was mounting a well-financed anti-Communist crusade among unionists abroad, with Jay Lovestone and his shadowy assistants laying the groundwork for American labor's postwar foreign policy. It refused to join the CIO and the British and Soviet trade unions in founding a World Federation of Trade Unions in London in January 1945 on the grounds that the Soviet trade unions were not real unions. The implication was that the new organization was merely a Communist "front" and the CIO was at best being duped and at worst being run by Communists.[23] At home, the rudimentary requirements of labor unity had served to mute the AFL's attacks on communism in the CIO. Nevertheless, dragging that skeleton from the CIO closet remained a knee jerk response to criticism of the AFL. In 1943, when defending the AFL against the usual charges of gangster infiltration, William Green responded with a gratuitous attack on Communist influence in the CIO, unconsciously feeding the old saw that each organization had its own poison.[24]

In 1944 Green could not resist aligning himself with Congressman Martin Dies, who by this time was charging that "Sidney Hillman will soon succeed Earl Browder as head of the Communists in the United

States."[25] Despite the refusal of a number of AFL locals in Dies' home district to go along, Green endorsed Dies for reelection. Roosevelt aides had heard that this was part of a deal: in return for Green's endorsement, Dies had promised a drive on Hillman and "the leftist element" in the CIO by his House Un-American Activities Committee.[26]

But Green and the AFL old guard were swimming against the White House stream. Roosevelt, whose wife had been badly burned by the disruption caused in Popular Front organizations by the Communist change in line after the Stalin-Hitler Pact,[27] nevertheless tacitly accepted and encouraged Communist support. Not only was a reluctant Eleanor enlisted to act as a go-between, passing advice from Browder to FDR, but Roosevelt let it be known that he was kept apprised of the Communist contribution to the war effort through his regular contacts with party-line labor unionists.[28]

As a result, not only was Browder's prison sentence commuted in May 1942, but Roosevelt worked quietly to protect Communists from witch-hunting. Earlier that year, when Dies tried to add an amendment to a bill requiring the registration of foreign agents that would have specifically named domestic Communists, FDR secretly instructed his men on Capitol Hill to head it off.[29] A year and a half later Roosevelt took a deep personal interest in encouraging CIO-PAC's efforts to get out the vote among CIO oil refinery workers in Dies district in the successful effort to defeat him in the Democratic primary.[30]

At Attorney General Biddle's insistence, the pursuit of a deportation order against Harry Bridges was taken all the way up to the Supreme Court, but only because Roosevelt was convinced that the Court would never let him be deported and that a decision on it would be a long way off, after Bridges' contribution to the war effort was no longer needed. He was right on both counts.[31]

But the scars left by the attacks during the Stalin-Hitler Pact years on Roosevelt and the liberal internationalists would never heal. Roosevelt, Hillman, and those involved in the day-to-day effort of mobilizing America's resources could cooperate with Communist union leaders, but would never trust them or doubt that their primary loyalty was to Moscow. In fact, despite their growing euphoria over Roosevelt, the Communists could take heart only in the fact that the war had neutralized the federal government as a force trying to crush them in the labor movement.

The same could not be said of the Catholic church. Throughout the war, the Communists kept looking over their shoulders at the people they lumped together under the rubric "ACTU." Like the Communists, the war took its toll among Actists as well. Many ACTU members ended up in the armed forces, including George Donahue, its president, and a number of the lawyers who had guided anti-Communists through court actions against leftist unions.[32] Dissension and rivalry continued to wrack the Catholic anti-Communist crusade, and the Communists' new-found superpatriotism weakened their case, but there was still hay to be made.

Although the conflict between ACTU's New York and Detroit locals over the nature of the organization had persisted, keeping the national organization an ineffectual shell, Actists had continued their struggle on the local level in a number of areas. For a while an ACTU-supported slate gained control of the giant UAW Local 600, and an ACTU vice-president was elected chairman of the Ford Council of the UAW.[33] The Connecticut-based rebellion against Mine, Mill's leftist leadership was aided by the Reverend Charles Owen Rice[34] and New York Actists kept poking away at Michael Quill, trying to organize opposition to him, and supporting dissidents in the courts.[35]

Michigan Actists managed to emulate the Communists by infiltrating CIO-PAC. By 1945 their cells had been so successful that despite Communist strength in the Detroit area, most key posts in the Wayne County CIO-PAC were held by Actists and their sympathizers. When one of the masterminds of the coup, Harry Read, moved to Washington in 1945 as an assistant to Carey, he was able to feed ACTU priests secret information on Communist unionists from CIO files for use in their resurgent anti-Communist struggle.[36]

The Catholic labor schools had continued functioning during the war, expanding considerably towards its end. Although the war had brought a drop in enrollment at the largest and most famous of them, the Jesuit-run Xavier Labor School in New York, it still boasted 190 students in 1944.[37]

The labor priests, meanwhile, aided by supporters in the hierarchy such as Archbishop Mooney, kept up their close personal contacts with CIO leaders throughout the war. They kept quietly cultivating Philip Murray, awaiting the purge they knew he must someday lead, backing Carey's attempts to curb Communist influence in CIO industrial union councils, asking for more anti-Communist CIO representatives in the field to aid anti-Communist uprisings in the CIO, and aiding anti-Communist unionists wherever they found them.[38]

By early 1945 with the war drawing to an end, Catholic pressure on Murray to begin the long-awaited purge began to build up. In late 1944, ACTU-Detroit President Paul Weber fired the opening salvo in the campaign when he called for a purge of PAC. ACTU had supported PAC through the 1944 elections and had helped enormously in registering and getting out hundreds of thousands of working-men's votes, he wrote. PAC was in danger of losing much of this support because of Communist influence in it. "Whose support does PAC want?" asked Weber. "Does it want to win the confidence of about 300,000 working class Catholics in this area (to be specific) or would it rather have the doubtful services of a couple of thousand Reds?"[39]

As 1945 drew on, comments such as Weber's became increasingly common. Friends of Murray's such as Charles Owen Rice had spent the war years assuring Catholics that Murray's alliance with the Communists was merely a temporary one. As the war ended, an ever-increasing chorus of opinion made it clear that many Catholics expected Murray to produce. Always the refrain was phrased in terms of praise for Murray coupled with support for the CIO and its objectives. Murray and Carey, said labor columnist Victor Riesel, "are friends of the Catholics who are leading the anti-Communist campaign. Murray and his colleagues know these men are honest in their views and friendship for the CIO."[40] But Murray, still fearful of splitting and wrecking the CIO, would not move.

Even before the breakdown of American-Soviet relations became apparent, some of the forces that would seek to renew the anti-Communist offensive of 1939-1941 were mobilizing again. On the surface, their chances of success were slim. The government was generally neutral. Their sympathizers within the CIO were unwilling to mount the kind of crusade they wanted. Although the war had not led to an appreciable shift of union power towards the Communists, neither had it perceptibly weakened them. There were obvious troubles at the top of the party, but the expunging of the Browderist heresy had caused only minor ripples in the union movement. The new generation of workers may have been relatively unresponsive to leftist and unionist slogans, but they soon proved to be just as militant in the pursuit of bread-and-butter gains as their predecessors in the 1930s, a militancy that the Communists, once shed of some embarrassing carry-overs from the days of wartime cooperation, were as willing as anyone else to lead. Only in the UAW did the wartime experience severely weaken Communist fortunes, but it was the turnaround in this union that would prove to be crucial in destroying Communist influence in the CIO and the rest of American labor.

NOTES

1. One can argue, as James Foster has, that CIO-PAC's influence on the outcome of the 1944 election was vastly exaggerated, but the important point here is that the exaggeration was widely subscribed to by Communist and non-Communist alike. James C. Foster, *The Union Politic. The CIO Political Action Committee* (Columbia: University of Missouri Press, 1975), chaps. 2-3.

2. George Gallup, *The Gallup Poll: Public Opinion, 1935-1971* (New York: Random House, 1972), 453.

3. Roy Hudson, "Two Conventions of Labor," *Political Affairs*, vol. 24, no. 1 (January 1945), 41.

4. To prove this, he apparently collected "progressive" sounding statements by big business leaders whenever he could find them. E.g., see Daniel Bell, Collection of Material on Socialism and Communism in the U.S.A., Tamiment Institute Library, New York University, N.Y., N.Y, Box 3, for part of Browder's collection of progressive statements by luminaries such as the vice-president of Inland Steel.

5. Earl Browder, "The Study of Lenin's Teachings," *Political Affairs*, vol. 24, no. 1 (January 1945), 4.

6. Roy Hudson, "Labor's Victory Wage Policies," *Political Affairs*, vol. 24, no. 4 (April 1945), 312.

7. Eugene Dennis, "Post-War Labor-Capital Cooperation," *Political Affairs*, vol. 24, no. 5 (May 1945), 418.

8. Earl Browder, Oral History Collection of Columbia University, New York, New York (hereafter COHC), 398.

9. Sidney Lens, *Radicalism in America* (New York: Crowell, 1969), 335.

10. Jacques Duclos, "On the Dissolution of the CPUSA," *Political Affairs*, vol. 24, no. 7 (July 1945), 669.

11. Gallup, *Gallup Poll*, 453, 471, 492.

12. David A. Shannon, *The Decline of American Communism* (New York: Harcourt, Brace and Co., 1959), 3.

13. Unsigned, "Labor and the Problems of Reconversion," typescript of draft program, CAP National Board, August 1945, Bell Collection, Box 3, in "Browder" File.

14. Stan Weir to James Green, June 23, 1974, cited in James Green, "Fighting on Two Fronts: Working Class Militancy in the 1940's," *Radical America*, vol. 9, nos. 4-5 (July-August 1975), 39.

15. Communist Political Association, Proceedings of the Constitutional Convention, 52, cited in Frank Emspak, "The Break-Up of the Congress of Industrial Organizations (CIO), 1945-1960" (Ph.D. diss., University of Wisconsin, 1972), 45.

16. Duclos, "On the Dissolution," 669.

17. "Speeches in Discussion on the Draft Resolution of the National Board at the Plenary Meeting of the National Committee, C.P.A., June 18-20, 1945, Speech by Gilbert Green," *Political Affairs*, vol. 24, no. 7 (July 1945), 591; see Joseph Starobin, *American Communism in Crisis, 1943-1957* (Cambridge: Harvard University Press, 1971), chaps. 4-5, for a good description of the effects of the crisis on the party's political structure.

18. CPA National Board, "The Present Situation and Next Tasks," resolution adopted June 2, 1945, copy in Earl Browder, Papers, George Arents Research Library, Syracuse University, Syracuse, N.Y., Series 11, Box 6, "Duclos" Folder.

19. William Z. Foster, "The Struggle Against Revisionism," *Political Affairs*, vol. 24, no. 9 (November 1945).

20. Communist Party, U.S.A., Labor Committee, "Labor and the Tasks of Reconversion," August 1945, typescript copy in Bell Collection, Box 3, Browder File.

21. U.S. Congress, House, Committee on Un-American Activities, *Hearings on Communist Activities in the Philadelphia Area*, 82nd Cong., 2nd sess. (1952), 4398-4400.

22. Michael Friedman, "Recorded Time: The Story of an American Family. Junius, Gladys, and Barbara Scales, 1920-1973" (oral history ms. in possession of Michael Friedman, Great Barrington, Mass.), 57.

23. Significantly, although he had no real objection to joining the WFTU, especially since it seemed consonant with United States foreign policy and gave the CIO a leg up in its running battle with the AFL for equality in foreign policy, Murray could not bring himself to go to the founding conference. According to Pressman, he was "instinctively

reluctant to sit there with Russians, with part of the Russian labor movement. It just simply went against his grain, to sit down with Communists like that and deal with them." Lee Pressman, COHC, 443.

24. *The New York Times*, May 23, 1943.

25. Walter Goodman, *The Committee* (New York: Farrar, Straus and Giroux, 1968), 159.

26. Memorandum for the Files, May 23, 1944, summarizing unsigned political report to Eleanor Roosevelt, April 1, 1944, Franklin D. Roosevelt, Papers, Franklin D. Roosevelt Library, Hyde Park, N.Y., PPF 3458.

27. Joseph Lash, *Eleanor and Franklin* (New York: New American Library, 1973), chap. 48.

28. Browder, COHC, 409.

29. James Byrnes to FDR, undated, filed February 20, 1942; FDR to McIntyre, January 13, 1942, FDR Papers, PPF 3458.

30. Memorandum for the Files, May 23, 1944, summarizing unsigned political report to Eleanor Roosevelt, April 11, 1944. This was part of a larger PAC drive to secure the defeat of seven of the eight members of his committee. Goodman, *The Committee*, 158.

31. Francis Biddle, *In Brief Authority* (New York: Viking Press, 1962), 302-6. When the Court handed down its decision in April 1945, there was a separate, concurring opinion by Justice Frank Murphy, ex-governor of Michigan, which was a blistering attack on Biddle's hounding of Bridges. As Murphy glowered down at Biddle and said that "The record in this case will stand forever as a monument to man's intolerance to man. . . . When the immutable freedoms guaranteed by the Bill of Rights have been so openly and concertedly ignored, the full wrath of constitutional condemnation descends upon the actions taken by the Government . . . ," Biddle thought to himself, "What a windbag. . . ."Ibid., 307.

32. *New York Post*, May 3, 1943.

33. The anti-Communists kept control of Local 600 until 1944, when the leftists won it back. In May 1945 the Right won control again, only to lose it again the next year. "Report of the Detroit Chapter," National ACTU Convention, June 30-July 1, 1956, Association of Catholic Trade Unionists, Detroit Chapter. Records. Wayne State University Archives of Labor History and Urban Affairs, Detroit, Michigan, Box 1; Frank Emspak, "The Association of Catholic Trade Unionists and the United Automobile Workers" (M.A. thesis, University of Wisconsin, 1968), 65-67.

34. Reid Robinson, OH, Pennsylvania State University Archives of Labor History, State College, Pa., 37.

35. Phillip A. Carey, S. J., to James Carey, November 28, 1944, CIO, Papers, Office of the Secretary-Treasurer, Wayne State University Archives of Labor History and Urban Affairs, Detroit, Michigan (hereafter Carey Papers), Box 11. *The New York Post*, May 3, 1943.

36. Foster, *The Union Politic*, 83-85.

37. Phillip Carey, S. J., to James Carey, November 24, 1944.

38. E.g., Carey to Carey, Reverend John F. Cronin to Carey, May 31, 1943; Carey to Cronin, June 23, 1943; Cronin to Carey, December 19, 1943; Cronin to Carey, June 17, 1944, Carey Papers, Box 11. Cronin, a Baltimore labor priest, became so involved in the partisan factional struggles that by mid-1944 he was writing of "our right-wing caucus" of a UE local "running things here." Cronin to Carey, June 17, 1944, Carey Papers.

39. Undated clipping [December 1945?], Victor Riesel's column, *New York Post*, in ACTU Papers, Series 2, Box 33.

40. Ibid.

10 THE UAW FALLS

Walter Reuther had learned an important lesson in his battles in the UAW's factional quagmire. Although anticommunism could be effective in rallying union leaders and bureaucrats behind him, it fell flat among the membership as a whole. The way to best the Communists, he concluded, was to avoid grand ideological confrontations and concentrate on pocketbook issues.[1] Reuther recognized that workers would care about Communist affiliations only if they were shown that such ties weakened their leaders' ability to produce at the bargaining table.

Reuther's aversion to grand ideological confrontations was also grounded in the diverse coalition that had gathered around him by 1946. It ranged from social democrats such as Emil Mazey through lapsed Socialists, such as himself, who now called themselves liberals, to the ACTU group, many of whose activists were quite conservative, to Gompersian business unionists. Thus, on the level of those participants in the coalition who were active in union affairs, a high degree of anticommunism was necessary because it was the only commonly-shared sentiment that could keep the diverse group together.[2]

The opposing coalition, in which the Communists and their supporters played a major role, was equally diverse. By 1946 it included former anti-Communists such as Frankensteen who had made deals with the leftists to further their own ambitions, the followers of Richard Leonard, the head of the UAW's Ford Department who had recently defected from the Reuther camp, and UAW President R. J. Thomas. According to UAW Communist Nat Ganley, even though it commanded the loyalty of the large majority of the union's black members, it also included "certain anti-Negro forces . . . which played havoc within that grouping."[3] In the same way that anticommunism was the only broad idea unifying the Reuther coalition, fear and hatred of Reuther was the glue of the faction in which the Communists placed their hopes.

During the war, UAW President R. J. Thomas, playing a balancing game, had allowed Reuther to build up his base as head of the General Motors Department, but so successful was Reuther in the headline-hunting derby that in the eyes of many UAW members he became the de facto spokesman for, if not leader of, the UAW, a man whose strategic and tactical acumen could produce dividends on the shop floor and in the pay envelope.

The image was almost shattered during the 113-day GM strike that began on November 21, 1945. Prodded by Reuther, the UAW Executive Board had approved a strike against General Motors in principle, but decided to keep the target secret until all preparations were in order. But Reuther, anxious to seize the mantle of leadership, publicly declared the strike approved while Thomas denied that any decision had been made. The impression was widespread, therefore, that Reuther had called the strike, a feeling that Thomas took pains to reinforce as it became apparent that Reuther's calculations that GM would cave in quickly had been painfully askew.[4]

The 200,000 GM workers striking to leap ahead of rampant inflation were soon joined by about 1.5 million workers in other industries, bringing with them a flurry of fact-finding, arbitration, and cajoling from Washington. When a consensus seemed to emerge in January that in the mass production industries an 18.5 cents an hour raise would be a fair basis for a return to work, and the steelworkers and others did so, Reuther miscalculated again, holding out for the 19.5 cents an hour raise the union was demanding. Finally, on March 10, the union gave in and accepted the hourly raise of 18.5 cents.

Normally, keeping strikers out for two extra months in an unsuccessful attempt to wrest an extra one cent an hour from an employer would severely weaken the position of a labor leader. Reuther's opponents assumed this and took the offensive. Less than two weeks after Reuther caved in to GM, when the UAW annual convention convened, Thomas told the press that the strike had been "too early, lasted too long, and accomplished little," a charge that the leftist press enthusiastically echoed.[5]

Yet the attacks were quite ineffective because there were two factors working for Reuther. In the first place, the strike had achieved something, if only the pay raise that the other unions had received. More important, however, was the fact that it was against GM, the widely-despised and even more widely-feared giant of the industry, which the union had not struck since the initial sit-down strikes for union recognition. Reuther and his supporters were able to deflect the leftist attacks and claim that Communist sabotage lay behind their loss. They charged that the Communists' attempt to "get Reuther" had undermined the strike when the UE, representing 30,000 GM workers, which had struck along with the UAW, had broken ranks and settled for 18.5 cents.[6] So successful was Reuther at this that the leftist-supported coalition avoided a floor fight on the issue at the UAW convention.

Thomas faced up too late to what had long been apparent: that Reuther had his eyes squarely fixed on Thomas' job. Belatedly he threw in his lot with the Communist and other anti-Reuther factions and came to the 1946 convention prepared to battle. But the GM strike did not provide enough anti-Reuther ammunition to counter the determined Reuther thrust. While the Communists and other pro-Thomas forces heaped calumny on Reuther, Reuther and members of his well-oiled machine went from caucus to caucus, from hotel room to hotel room, sounding the refrain that the Thomas coalition was dominated by Communists and was therefore crippled in its ability to produce bread-and-butter gains for the membership. Their willingness to sacrifice the interests of American workers to those of Moscow had already led them to support "piece work" and a "draft labor" bill during the war. The UE "stab in the back" during the recent strike was further proof.[7]

Philip Murray's support for his friend Thomas was neutralized by the threat that a victorious but alienated Reuther might take the UAW into the AFL. It was no secret that David Dubinsky was secretly subsidizing Reuther's campaign,[8] and Murray suspected that John L. Lewis, now back in the AFL, was doing the same. He feared that Carey might be a defector as well. In an obvious reference to these suspected machinations, he told the CIO Executive Board in mid-March that he was sick and tired of politically ambitious people dividing and disrupting the CIO.[9] Moreover, Murray must have wondered whether Thomas had become a prisoner of the Communists. Murray's speech to the UAW convention endorsing Thomas was a mild, half-hearted one that could have changed few votes. Reuther consequently eked out a narrow (4,444 to 4,320) victory over a stunned Thomas.[10]

Reuther's victory constituted a spectacular demonstration of how anticommunism could be an effective weapon only if it were directly connected to bread-and-butter issues. Yet it demonstrated little else because there was little except their attitudes towards the Communists in the UAW that separated Reuther from most of his intra-union opponents.

Both sides were implacable during the year-and-a-half between the 1946 and 1947 UAW conventions. Reuther had won the presidency, but the Communist-supported coalition still held a majority of the seats on the UAW Executive Board. At the Michigan CIO's important convention in June 1946, the Communists pushed hard to help their people assume the leadership of the Addes coalition, alienating many of their allies and paving the way to power for the Reuther forces in a shift that reflected the change taking place within the union as a whole.[11] The fact was that Reuther seemed destined to win, and canny office-holders and office-seekers throughout the union flocked to his side.

Despite his public stance portraying a vast struggle of the "armies of light" versus the "armies of darkness" for control of the labor move-ment, in private Reuther emphasized that little, aside from personal ambition, divided the two groups. At his first Executive Board meeting as president he said that he recognized the fact that there was no basic disagreement between the factions over union issues and asked for an end to the factional strife and the reestablishment of unity.[12]

In retrospect, many leftists agreed with Reuther. Years later, Nat Ganley compared the differences between the two coalitions to those between Republicans and Democrats.[13] Addes said that, aside from some minor squabbles, there had been complete agreement on issues during the war and that, although some differences became more pronounced after the war, they were "neither too numerous nor too serious."[14]

At the time, however, most of Reuther's opponents were too embit-tered by his tactics to let bygones be bygones. Moreover, few of them trusted him enough to contemplate compromise. Thomas was perhaps the most vituperative of the lot, infuriating Reuther by dropping anti-Reuther bombshells in what Reuther called the "anti-labor, re-actionary press" (mainly the Detroit *News* and Detroit *Free Press*). He accused Reuther of supporting the restrictive Taft-Hartley Act of 1947 and moved in an UAW Executive Board meeting that it be called the "Taft-Hartley-Reuther Act." Both sides bombarded each other with distorted propaganda in the local union papers that they controlled. Communist-dominated publications tried to turn the tables on Reuther and label him as favoring "speedups." They dubbed him "More Pro-duction Reuther," and stickers with that slogan were affixed to ma-chines at a number of GM plants.[15]

The two issues that most exacerbated relations between the factions involved the strength of the Communists in the UAW: the controversy surrounding the Allis-Chalmers strike and the proposed merger with the Farm Equipment Workers Union. The large Communist-led Local 248 at Allis-Chalmers in Milwaukee had battled unsuccessfully the anti-union company for a union shop since 1937. At the end of the war, the company walked out of negotiations on a contract that would at least have perpetuated the lesser right of maintenance of membership granted by the War Labor Board. According to Robert Ozanne, it was "a declaration of war by management. The long eleven month strike which followed was the way any self-respecting union acts in a struggle for survival."[16] Refusing to bargain with the local's leadership and rejecting their offer to submit the dispute to arbitration, the company waited while a rival group formed to contest Local 248's right to represent Allis-Chalmers workers and to encourage a back-to-work movement. When the rival group won a Wisconsin state labor relations board ruling that a certification election be held, Local 248 was forced to conduct a resource-sapping campaign for renewed certification in the midst of its debilitating strike, a campaign conducted in the face of a barrage of vituperation in the local media (especially in the Hearst-owned *Milwaukee Sentinel*), harassment by the FBI, and investigations by anti-Communist congressional probers. Moreover, many anti-Communists in the Wisconsin CIO, including some Reuther-supporting UAW locals, refused to support the strikers, thousands of whom returned to work.[17]

For the UAW leadership, the most sensitive issue involved the company's refusal to bargain with the local's leaders. Reuther, who loathed the local's president Harold Christoffel and his "machine," was in a difficult position: to acknowledge Allis-Chalmers' right to refuse to meet with the democratically elected bargaining committee of the local would be tantamount to giving employers the power to decide with whom they would deal. Yet the local seemed headed for disaster.

At first, Reuther tried not to divide the UAW Board on the issue. He asked Addes to work out a settlement and, when Addes demurred, the job was given to Thomas. He also threatened to repudiate his right-wing supporters in the Wisconsin UAW if they did not lend their support to the strike;[19] most did, albeit reluctantly and sullenly. Inevitably, though, the dispute became an issue in the factional struggle for survival among the top leaders.

In early January 1947, a Milwaukee clergyman told Reuther that the company would be willing to meet with Reuther and Philip Murray to resolve the conflict. Reuther agreed, as did Murray, who appointed John Brophy to represent him. The UAW Policy Committee, dominated by Reuther's opponents, approved the meeting on the understanding that Reuther and Brophy negotiate only the issue of the company's refusal to meet with the local leadership. When Reuther and Brophy did discuss wages and other strike issues, Thomas charged that they were dealing with the employer behind the local leadership's back in contravention of the union's constitution. Reuther was forced to take along Thomas, Addes, and Leonard, as well as Robert Buse, Local

248's president, to the next meeting with management. When these discussions proved fruitless, Thomas charged it was because the presence of the union's other officers had forced Reuther to renege on the settlement he had secretly committed himself to impose on the local.[20]

Local 248 won the certification election in February, but by only thirty-one votes out of over 8,000 cast. The company still refused to negotiate with the local leadership, and an estimated five thousand workers were back in the plant by early March. When Reuther's suggestion that the local be put under an administratorship was rejected by the UAW Executive Board,[21] he and Brophy, along with Allan Haywood, reopened negotiations with the company, persuading it only to accept the strikers back with no reprisals. There was no contract. That would still be negotiated.

Reuther, Brophy, and Haywood thought they had salvaged all they could from the situation.[22] When Thomas and the Local 248 leadership balked at the settlement, Reuther said he had done all he could and would now "be guided and governed by [Thomas's] recommendation."[23] A few days later, faced by a massive strikers' return to work, Local 248 asked the Executive Board to end the strike on essentially the terms worked out by Reuther, Brophy, and Haywood, and the remnants of the shattered local voted to return to work without a single concession from the company.[24]

Perhaps only Reuther could have turned the Allis-Chalmers debacle into the victory that it became for him. As in the aftermath of the GM strike, he blamed the Communists for the defeat. During the strike he had readily acknowledged that it had been forced upon the union by a ruthless employer determined to smash the union,[25] but it soon became part of Reutherite lore that, (although it affected farm machinery rather than ships), it was a "political" strike against America's defense industry conducted in conjunction with the concurrent wave of Communist-led strikes in Europe. The strike was lost, said Reuther, "because there were people in positions of leadership in that local who put their loyalties outside of their union, outside of the rank and file, and outside of the country."[26] John Brophy took pride in having helped Reuther work out the settlement that, as he saw it, discredited Thomas completely and gave Reuther "enough of a weapon to smash Communist opposition in the UAW."[27]

Thomas and the Communists tried to counterattack with "stab-in-the-back" and "back door negotiation" charges, but to no avail. In fact, little could be pinned on Reuther. Although his Wisconsin supporters had not supported the strike through most of 1946, he could not assume total responsibility for them and their attitudes towards their intrastate opponents. Moreover, he did intervene in December and force them to cooperate. As for "back door" negotiations, by early January the company was in a virtually impregnable situation and could not be forced to negotiate with the local leadership. By March, even Addes had recognized that something must be done to get around this roadblock and had agreed to consider putting the local under a CIO administratorship to negotiate a new contract.[28]

The circumstances of the "wrecking" of Local 248 allowed Reuther to preside over the debilitation of an important focus of Communist power in the UAW and emerge unscathed. The Communists, left barely hanging on to the tattered local, were even more on the defensive. After Reuther won total control of the UAW later in 1947, his Executive Board appointed an administrator for the local who, with the help of the local police, charter revocation, extension of his term of office, and expulsion of key leftist leaders, finally managed to bring the recalcitrant local into the Reuther camp.[29]

Even more important in deciding the ultimate fate of the UAW was Reuther's parry of the thrust to have the UAW merge with the leftist Farm Equipment Workers Union before the crucial 1947 UAW convention, a merger that would have decisively shifted the balance of power against him. In 1941, when FEWOC had rejected Philip Murray's proposal for a merger with the UAW, the UAW convention laid the groundwork for significant incursions into the farm equipment field by tacking on "and Agricultural Implement Workers" to the "Automobile" in its name.

In the feisty days of war-contract-stimulated organizing, the UAW managed to organize a number of farm implement manufacturers from under the noses of the still relatively weak and poor FE, the main jewel in whose modest crown was its contract with International Harvester, the giant of the industry. When a number of jurisdictional disputes between the two erupted during the war, a CIO Executive Board subcommittee, composed of three anti-Communists,[30] again recommended a merger, which was again rejected by the FE leadership, this time on the grounds that submersion of farm equipment workers into the UAW would weaken their bargaining power. Their unique interests and identity would be swamped in the larger union. Perhaps more to the point, they also charged that the merger proposal was a right-wing attempt to get rid of a "progressive" union by forcing it into a "shotgun" marriage. Their rejection of merger was approved by a large majority of FE members in a referendum.[31]

The Reuther victory at the UAW convention in 1946 brought great changes in the FE attitude towards merger. The reasons were obvious: Reuther's winning margin was razor-thin. The leftist coalition still dominated the Executive Board. The addition of the FE's 80,000 members to the UAW would effectively tip the balance back towards the Left, adding about 500 convention votes. However, their effectiveness as a left-wing force would depend on their continued cohesion. If the FE was simply merged into the UAW on a local by local basis, as the CIO committee had recommended, not only would a number of leftists on the FE staff lose their positions of influence, but the leftist leadership would lose control of a number of non-leftist locals. Thus, FE president Grant Oakes and the FE leadership came up with a merger agreement that would maximize their political strength and destroy Reuther's chances of gaining control of the union. The FE would merge with the UAW, but would retain its identity, becoming a virtually autonomous "FE Division" in the UAW.[32] The overall aim of the new proposal was clear to all involved. "It was dreamed up in a caucus," Reuther charged at a UAW Executive Board meeting. "It was worked out with Grant Oakes and their boys as a political maneuver."[33]

Realizing he was battling for survival, Reuther at first fought for a delaying action and called for increased cooperation with FE before giving consideration to a merger. Oakes and Reuther's other opponents on the UAW Executive Board replied that time was of the essence and that the merger must be approved by the UAW in time for the FE's next convention, which would then be able to ratify it.[34]

Reuther saw that the real deadline was the next UAW convention. When in June 1947 Addes showed up at an Executive Board meeting with a merger agreement that he, representing the majority coalition of the UAW Executive Board, and Oakes had agreed upon, Reuther and his supporters managed to have the proposal submitted to the UAW membership in a referendum to be held in one month.

To Reuther, the referendum campaign provided the final proof of the value of his anti-Communist tactics. The political motives behind the merger proposal were obvious enough, but he did not dwell on them. To emphasize the Communist issue in the campaign, he thought, would "confuse" the membership and the Communists would have cried "Red-baiting." They could then have pushed the plan through on the basis of their general appeal to unity. Reuther thus concentrated on the union issues, emphasizing that the creation of an autonomous farm equipment division would open the door to that most dreaded Trojan horse: craft unionism in the UAW. To grant autonomy to farm equipment workers would make it impossible to resist the similar demands of machinists and other skilled workers in the UAW. It would be a small step from there to separate bargaining sessions for the skilled and unskilled and a loss of bargaining power for the unskilled.[35]

The leftists were more awed by the potency of Reuther's machine than by his arguments. After the voters rejected the merger proposal, a

stunned left-wing leader admitted: "We give Reuther credit, his workers covered the country from coast to coast and down to the Gulf."[36]
Deprived of the hope that FE delegates would come riding over the
crest of the hill to save them, the leftists gave up the hope of heading
off the Reuther forces at the next convention, still five months away.
Reuther slates swept local after local, including some CP strongholds
in the fall 1947 elections for representation at the November convention. By the time the convention met, it was clear that it would be
completely dominated by Reuther. The Addes-Thomas coalition did
not even run a candidate against him for the presidency. Emil Mazey
demonstrated the tremendous new strength of the Reuther forces by
handily defeating still-popular George Addes for the post of secretary-
treasurer. The Executive Board, elected on a regional basis, was swept
by Reuther supporters, who now held eighteen of its twenty-two
seats.[37]

Some UAW Communists blamed the rout on wartime changes in the
auto industry's work force, especially the influx of new workers from
the South and Appalachia and the failure of many prewar militants to
return to the industry after their demobilization.[38] But Reuther's success had little to do with politics or political radicalism. Furthermore,
black workers, heavily concentrated at Ford, provided a disproportionate amount of support for the Communists. As for WASPs from
Appalachia, later studies in the Detroit area showed them to be class
conscious, determinedly pro-union, and quite radical in their political
views.[39]

John Williamson, from the Olympian heights almost overlooking
Union Square, blamed defeat on the failure of the Communists to
come up with a program that would distinguish them from other
factions and on their enmeshment in the job-seeking factional scramble for union office spoils.[40] In fact, the Communists were involved in
the degrading scramble for jobs because that is precisely what the
conflict was all about. As many on both sides recognized, there were
few irreconcilable differences on union issues separating Reuther and
the Communists. Certainly some of those who enlisted under the
Reuther banner did so because of a sincere fear of a Communist takeover of the union.[41] But more important was the feeling among hundreds of "pork-choppers," the local union bureaucrats who emerged
from the war with comfortable jobs they wished to keep, that Reuther
was the destined winner of the struggle for power. It was common
knowledge that if you were not with Reuther you were considered to be
against him, but it was also well-known that he could forgive the attacks
of his most vituperative detractors if they would cross over and sign on
with him. These men in the middle, practicing the politics of self-

preservation, defected in droves from the Addes coalition to line up behind the man who had so adroitly stolen the militant image that the Communists had abandoned for the duration of the war.

Reuther's victory indicated little about the pro- or anticommunism of auto workers. Indeed, it was based on his assumption that the vast majority of the UAW membership simply did not care about their leaders' politics, something that had been borne out in the crucial referendum on the FE (whose ramifications were so political), in which only seven percent of the membership voted.[42] The political affiliations of union leaders would be an issue only if "outside" political loyalties led leaders to subordinate shop floor interests of the membership to other considerations. As long as the new class of CIO union apparatchiks could line up with a machine that was perceived by the membership as acting forcefully and efficiently in their interests, their jobs appeared safe.

If anything was crucial in ensuring this victory that owed so much to tactics and so little to strategy, it was Browder's intervention in the 1939 UAW convention. This victory might never have occurred if Communist-supported Addes had been selected as president rather than Thomas. It is stupefying to think that something so important as the political structure of the postwar American labor movement may have been decided by a puffed-up Communist bureaucrat rushing to Cleveland on an overnight train to head off leftist sectarianism.

Irving Howe and B. J. Widick were right when, in 1949, they called Reuther's 1947 victory "the decisive event in the gradual destruction of Stalinist power in the CIO."[43] They were not correct, however, in seeing the alternative as a Communist triumph. The Communists never comprised a majority in the Addes caucus, and would have been hard put to assemble a coalition that could have successfully shunted aside Addes and the other non-Communist leaders of that caucus for some of their own people. But neither is there any solid evidence to support the hypothesis that, had Reuther been turned back, within two or three years Addes and his non-Communist allies would have thrown the Communists out of their caucus.[44] Aside from the question of Addes' own compatibility with the Communists, it is difficult to see a situation developing in which the Reutherites were so decimated that the victors could then devour their own.

Thus, the importance of Reuther's victory lay not in preventing a Communist takeover of the UAW and, consequently, the CIO, but in shifting the UAW into the aggressively anti-Communist camp. Now, of the three largest CIO unions, the UE, with its 650,000 members, was far outweighed by the combined membership of the anti-Communist UAW and USW, each of which hovered close to the one million member mark. With two of the three major unions in the anti-Communist camp, the prospect of an anti-Communist purge could be thought of as one involving major excisions rather than a split down the middle.

NOTES

1. Walter Reuther, "How to Beat the Communists," *Collier's*, February 28, 1948.

2. Al Leggat, OH, Wayne State University Archives of Labor History and Urban Affairs (hereafter WSUA), Detroit, Mich., 60.

3. Nat Ganley, OH, WSUA, 43.

4. UAW, Minutes of Executive Board Meeting, September 22-24, 1947, 72, UAW Executive Board Minutes Collection, WSUA, Box 9.

5. Jean Gould and Lorena Hickock, *Walter Reuther, Labor's Rugged Individualist* (New York: Dodd, Mead, 1973), 239-40.

6. Ibid., 233.

7. Ibid., 239-40.

8. Leggat, OH, WSUA, 57; Frank Cormier and William J. Eaton, *Reuther* (Englewood Cliffs, N.J.: Prentice-Hall, 1971), 236.

9. Philip Murray, Report to CIO Executive Board Meeting, March 15, 1946, Walter P. Reuther, Papers, WSUA, Series 1, Box 7, "Philip Murray" Folder.

10. UAW, *Proceedings of the Annual Convention*, 1946, 190-220. As usual in a close electoral victory, various groups saw their votes as crucial to the win. The small band of Trotskyists, never averse to overestimating their own importance, were especially conscious that the small bloc of votes which they threw on Reuther's side tipped the balance. It was something they came to rue in later years. John Anderson, OH, WSUA, 114.

11. Bert Cochran, *Labor and Communism* (Princeton: Princeton University Press, 1977), 264-65.

12. UAW, Minutes of Executive Board Meeting, April 16, 1946, 6.

13. Ganley, OH, WSUA, 43.

14. George Addes, OH, WSUA, 33.

15. UAW, Executive Board Minutes, September 22-24, 1947, part 2, 48-88.

16. Robert Ozanne, "The Effects of Communist Leadership on American Trade Unions" (Ph.D. diss., University of Wisconsin, 1954), 254.

17. Speech by Congressman Melvin Price to U.S. House of Representatives, January 23, 1947, copy in Ganley Papers, WSUA, Box 1; Reuther to R. J. Thomas, February 11, 1947, John Brophy, Papers, Catholic University of America Library, Wash., D.C. (hereafter CU), Box A5-12; Ozanne, "The Effects of Communist Leadership," 229-54.

18. UAW Executive Board Minutes, December 9, 1946, 10-11.

19. In announcing the turnabout, Walter Cappel, the leader of the right-wing bloc in in the Wisconsin UAW-CIO, made it clear that they were coming out in support of the strike only because Reuther had twisted their arms. His new-found support for the strike, he said, "in no way changes my attitude toward the leadership of Local 248." *Milwaukee Journal*, December 10, 1946.

20. Thomas to Reuther, January 26, 1947, Ganley Papers, Box 1; Reuther to All Local Unions, February 13, 1947, Reuther to Thomas, February 11, 1947, Brophy Papers, Box A5-12.

21. UAW, Executive Board Minutes, March 17, 1947, 18.

22. John Brophy, *A Miner's Life* (Madison: University of Wisconsin Press, 1964), 292-93.

23. UAW, Executive Board Minutes, March 17, 1947.

24. Milwaukee *Journal*, March 23, 24, 1947, cited in Frank Emspak, "The Break-up of the Congress of Industrial Organizations (CIO), 1945-1950" (Ph.D. diss., University of Wisconsin, 1972), 165.

25. UAW, Executive Minutes, December 9, 1946, 10-11.

26. Ozanne, "The Effects of Communist Leadership," 241.

27. Brophy, *A Miner's Life*, 293.

28. UAW, Executive Board Minutes, March 17, 1947, 19. Earlier in December, when he broached the idea of a UAW administratorship, Reuther said that Addes had suggested it too. Ibid., December 9, 1946, 10-11. In March Reuther reported that Philip Murray had suggested the idea to him, but Addes, who had attended the meeting with Murray, insisted that it was vice versa. Ibid., March 17, 1947, 39.

29. *The New York Times*, December 2, 3, 12, 1947.

30. They were John Green of the Shipbuilders, Frank Rosenblum of the Amalgamated, and Sherman Dalrymple of the URW.

31. CIO, "Report of the Jurisdiction Committee in re: UAW-CIO and Farm Equipment Workers," July 16, 1945; Carey to Gerald Field, July 17, 1945; George Weaver to Carey, October 11, 1949, CIO, Papers, Office of the Secretary Treasurer, WSUA, Box 50; FE Executive Board, "Report to the Membership," June 22, 1945; "Stewards Bulletin," FE Local 105, July 25, 1945, in Walter Reuther, Papers, WSUA, Series 1, Box 57, "FE Merger" Folder; CIO, "Report of the Committee Dealing with the UAW-FE Dispute," April 4, 1949, CIO, Papers, CU A7-25.

32. "FE-CIO Proposal to the UAW-CIO for an Autonomous Merger," CIO, Papers, CU, A7-25.

33. UAW, Executive Board Minutes, September 22-24, 1947, Part 2, 69-70.

34. Ibid., April 22-28, 1947, 168.

35. Reuther, "How to Beat the Communists," *Collier's*, February 28, 1948.

36. *Detroit Free Press*, July 20, 1947.

37. Gould and Hickock, *Reuther*, 250-52.

38. Saul Wellman, "The Party and the Trade Unions," *Emphasis*, n.d., Ganley Papers, cited in James R. Prickett, "Communists and the Communist Issue in the American Labor Movement, 1920-1950" (Ph.D. diss., University of California at Los Angeles, 1975), 303.

39. John C. Leggat, "Sources and Consequences of Working-Class Consciousness," in Arthur Shostak and William Gomberg, *Blue-Collar World* (Englewood Cliffs, N.J.,: Prentice-Hall, 1964), 235-47.

40. John Williamson, "Trade Union Problems and the Third Party," *Political Affairs*, vol. 27, no. 3 (March 1948), 234-35. Earl Browder, now outside the tent, also ascribed the UAW debacle to the failure of Communists to distinguish themselves from the Reuther forces by adopting a more militant policy than that on wages. Earl Browder, "The Decline of the Left Wing of American Labor," mimeo (New York: the author, 1948), 25-26.

41. For example, Tracy Doll, who recalled that a number of his allies shared this sincere fear. Tracy Doll, OH, WSUA, 37.

42. *Wage Earner*, July 18, 1947, cited in Cochran, *Labor and Communism*, 276.

43. Howe and Widick, *The UAW and Walter Reuther* (N.Y.: Random House, 1949), 150.

44. Cochran argues this with considerable vigor. Cochran, *Labor and Communism*, 277-79.

11 THE TURN OF THE TIDE
1945-1948

Philip Murray had not supported the anti-Communists in the UAW in large part because of his friendship for Thomas and his enmity towards Reuther. From late 1945 until late 1947 while the UAW battle was taking place, a variety of forces, external and internal, pushed Murray towards the kind of confrontation with the Communists that he both feared and anticipated.

The greatest single factor was, of course, the cold war. Leftist opposition to the very cornerstones of United States foreign policy threatened to upset the relationship that Murray, Hillman, and liberals like Carey had created with the New Dealers in the Democratic party, a relationship that assumed critical proportions with the passage of the apparently anti-union Taft-Hartley Act in 1947. The anti-Communist union leaders had come to think that they were travelling a different road from the "pure and simple" business unionism of Samuel Gompers. They believed that workers' gains would come, not just at the bargaining table, but through participation in the broader political life of the nation. They were now acutely conscious that "what you could get in collective bargaining could be taken away from you through the enactment of unfavorable social or labor laws," according to James Carey.[1] Communist opposition to the government's foreign policy threatened to turn the CIO into the core of an opposition political movement that would be strong enough to spread disquiet in Washington but weak enough to invite massive retaliation by a government armed with extensive formal and informal power over the labor movement. Moreover, because the conflict involved opposition to United States foreign policy, the leftists were working against the strong patriotic grain in people like Murray, whose chauvinistic feelings had been strengthened by World War II. American unionists were used to dissenting with the government's domestic policy, but had often responded to charges that they were subversive by demonstrating their patriotism in foreign affairs.

Murray, Carey, and the CIO liberals had joined the Soviet labor movement in the WFTU because it seemed to be consonant with the Roosevelt administration's foreign policy. Almost everyone seemed to agree on the necessity to maintain "Big Three" unity into the postwar era, and the WFTU seemed an apt vehicle for doing this in the labor field. However, as Washington became increasingly suspicious of Soviet intentions in late 1945 and more hostile to Soviet policy, CIO liberals became more open about their doubts over the possibility of successful cooperation with the Russians in the WFTU. By early 1946, with the cold war clearly taking shape in Europe, foreign policy was becoming an increasingly important and divisive issue in the CIO.

One of the reasons was the existence and nature of local state and regional CIO Industrial Union Councils. They had proliferated after 1940 as vehicles for the expression of CIO opinion on state and local issues, invariably becoming involved with national issues as well. In the mobilization crisis preceding the German invasion of the USSR they had been wracked by conflicts over resolutions praising or condemning FDR's foreign and defense policies. During the war, with the Left-Right splits temporarily healed, they had become centers for rallying union support for the war effort. They had also played an important part in organizing support for the CIO-PAC during and after the election of 1944.

In wartime, when their enthusiasm for the mobilization effort knew few bounds, leftist unionists had come to exercise power in the IUCs all out of proportion to their numbers. Not only were they personally more active, but a higher proportion of their unions belonged and contributed to the IUCs. Thus, the leftists sailed into the cold war with a strong base in many of these organizations that by now took frequent stands on foreign policy.

As United States-Soviet relations deteriorated, the leftist-controlled IUCs became an acute embarrassment to CIO anti-Communists. As early as November 1945 the leftist-controlled Greater New York CIO Council denounced administration policy in China, calling the presence of United States troops there and the use of lend-lease arms by Chiang's troops armed intervention in China's internal affairs.[2] At the same time, alarmed West Coast anti-Communists were writing Adolph Germer asking for help against the Communists (who were "running wild") in control of the Washington State CIO Council.[3] But in 1946 many liberals shared the Communists' concern over the administration's growing toughness with the Soviets. In itself this was not enough to push those in the middle, such as Murray, into a possibly suicidal purge. Moreover, the Communist attacks on Truman's foreign policy were not much out of step with the disillusionment over his domestic policies that swept the labor movement in 1946.

Therefore, Murray hedged, zigzagging on the Communist issue through much of 1946. In May 1946, at his Steelworkers' convention, he took a moderate stand on demands for formal purges of leftists. The Steelworkers would not tolerate "efforts by outsiders—individuals, organizations or groups—whether they be Communist, Socialist or any other group, to infiltrate or meddle in our affairs," he said. But this remark was not directed at "any one person or group." What he had in mind was "any attempt by any force outside our own membership to interfere in the functioning of our union. . . . We engage in no witch hunts. We do not dictate a man's thoughts or beliefs."[4] In July 1946, he responded positively but cautiously to anti-Communist demands that Harry Bridges be sacked as California regional director of the CIO, slicing Bridges' jurisdiction into northern and southern California districts on the grounds of administrative efficiency.[5] The man who had begun as CIO director of the entire West Coast was now left with only northern California, which meant primarily the Bay area, as his bailiwick. A month later, Victor Riesel reported that Murray had secretly met in Pittsburgh with the anti-Communist insurgents in the UE, advising them on strategy.[6]

To dampen these rumors, Murray tried to assuage UE leaders' unease by extolling their virtues at the UE convention.[7] This, in turn, aroused disquiet among anti-Communists. The New York ACTU's *Labor Leader* complained that Murray "cut the ground from under the anti-CP caucus by getting up and telling the delegates what wonderful guys their pro-CP officers were. Is Phil Murray for the CPs or against them? That one puts you out for the count."[8] Disgruntled Actists in the UE began thinking seriously of secession to the AFL.[9] The large circulation Brooklyn *Tablet*, the newspaper of the Brooklyn Catholic diocese, attacked Murray's belittling of "the Red issue": Murray would have to "face the ideological battle, break himself loose from Lee Pressman and the others who seem to hold him as a prisoner, and to oppose the disintegrating subversive forces." It warned that "He will have to stop giving aid and comfort to the Communists in the CIO. . . ."[10]

As if to correct the anti-Communists' mistaken impression, within two weeks of the UE convention Murray departed from his prepared speech at a conference of liberals and leftists opposed to the rightward drift of the Truman administration to deliver a seemingly gratuitous swipe at the Communists in the CIO. Organized labor wanted "no damn Communists meddling in our affairs," he cried, as cheering liberal delegates leaped to their feet.[11] The next month, the Detroit *Times* reported that he had told a secret meeting of the Executive Board of the UAW that he had declared open warfare on communism and all other "anti-Americanisms" in the CIO.[12] No doubt exaggerated (after all, if one is declaring "open warfare," why do it in secret?), the report was probably based on a Murray warning that he would take a stronger stand against the Communists in the CIO.

Quietly and secretly, he had already begun the war. Only Victor Reisel suggested that Murray was in the same hotel in Pittsburgh where the UE insurgents were meeting to form the UE-Members for Democratic Action in August 1946. But by that time he had begun secretly channeling steelworkers' money into the organization, using Father Rice as the intermediary[13] and subsidizing his trips to various union conventions where he helped anti-Communists organize.[14]

Meanwhile, Murray's aides at CIO headquarters were mobilizing anti-Communists in CIO unions across the country. Alan Haywood did what he could to help anti-Communists in the elections for city and state CIO councils.[15] In May 1946, a leftist-rightist conflict in the Cleveland CIO council led to a walkout by the Amalgamated delegates and a plea for Murray's intervention. Murray sent Haywood, who placed the council in the hands of a "receiver" and proceeded to restructure its composition and rules to prevent the leftists from using it to support their causes.[16] Later, the Milwaukee council was "reorganized" in reprisal for sending a delegate to the convention of a "Communist-dominated" organization.[17]

Concerned about their continuing attacks on United States foreign and domestic policy, Murray reversed his attitude towards leftist-dominated CIO councils. Whereas at the 1942 CIO convention he had admonished them to be more active, he now set Haywood to drafting new rules which would severely restrict their activities and expenditures regarding national and international affairs.[18] Patterned after the successful wing-clipping job he had done in Cleveland, these rules were pushed through the CIO Executive Board just before the November CIO convention. These limited the councils' activities "to issues of local and state concern." They could make statements of policy on more general concerns only if they were in consonance with official CIO national policy. The CIO national office would also now have the power to assign "duly accredited CIO representatives" to "work closely" with the councils to see that they "comported themselves" in line with the directive.[19]

Meanwhile, James Carey had begun conducting an energetic campaign, not just to regain his position in the UE but to rally anti-Communist forces throughout the CIO. Following the lead of Harry

Block, a leader of the Carey faction in the UE, the Philadelphia CIO council passed a resolution in August 1946, barring Communists from office.[20] In September Carey delivered an inflammatory speech to the shipbuilders' convention in which he accused the Communists of having a "basic desire to operate your international union solely in the interests of the foreign policy of Soviet Russia."[21]

Carey's attacks were taken especially seriously by outsiders because he was widely regarded as "Murray's mouthpiece."[22] UE leaders often complained of his activities, but Murray kept him on because he valued him as a good irritant for the Communists.[23] Yet, when pressed, Murray would acknowledge neither his own anti-Communist scheming nor his support for Carey's activities. He tried to convince the leftists that he simply could not control Carey.[24] Some believed him and ascribed his inaction not to agreement with Carey but to his unwillingness to cross ACTU, which backed Carey.[25]

In fact, Murray's erratic course and duplicity resulted from the two seemingly irreconcilable goals he pursued: first, to preserve and strengthen the unity of the CIO and second, to cut down the power of the Communists and, someday, rid the CIO of Communist influence altogether. Because that day had not arrived, he saw his role as that of the honest broker betwen the pro- and anti-Communists in the CIO, whose overriding concern was unity and the survival of the CIO. To the Communists, who were just as concerned about preserving the CIO as Murray, he remained the best hope for avoiding a disastrous split. In November 1946 the party's political leadership reaffirmed the importance of working for CIO unity under his leadership.[26]

Then, the greatest threat to unity seemed to come from the Right. During Reuther's run at the UAW presidency, Murray had been unnerved by the support Reuther received from Lewis and Dubinsky and was plagued by fears that he would ultimately lead the UAW into the AFL to join them. The fears were heightened by the artful rumor campaign the Reuther forces had started, charging that Murray and the USW had stabbed the GM workers in the back during their strike by accepting the 18.5 cents hourly wage increase.[27]

Other potentially divisionist tendencies were springing up as well.[28] In October 1946, CIO anti-Communists began organizing formally. Led by Jack Altman, the vice-president of the Retail Workers Union, thirty-four CIO union officials formed a "CIO Committee for Renovative Trade Unionism" to combat the Communists. It was graced with the surprise turncoat, John McGrath, president of the small, leftist United Shoe Workers, who said he was resigning his post because Communists were trying to seize control of his union.[29] As the anti-Communists, buoyed by Reuther's victory, began to formulate their demands for the CIO convention in November, rumors circulated that they intended to replace Murray with Reuther.[30]

Reuther and the anti-Communists arrived at the convention demanding passage of a resolution proclaiming the CIO "an American institution" which rejected "policies emanating from totalitarianism, dictatorship and foreign ideologies such as Communism and Fascism." It condemned "Communism and Fascism as inimical to the welfare of labor and destructive of our form of government" and called on all CIO unions to "vigorously resist all anti-democratic and totalitarian philosophies or forces wherever they raise their ugly heads in American life."[31]

The Communists, on the other hand, came to the convention proclaiming their determination to head off the anti-Communists. Any "knuckling down" to them, wrote *Daily Worker* labor editor George Morris, "would only whet the reactionary appetite."[32] But their hand had been weakened by Reuther's victory, which deprived them of much UAW delegate support. They could now count on the solid support of unions representing 20-30 percent of the CIO membership.[33] Equally important was the spreading feeling that the tide was shifting against them.

Murray avoided open warfare over the proposed resolution only by threatening to resign and thereby shatter the CIO. The two sides then agreed to the appointment of a six-man committee consisting of three men from each of the opposing camps who fashioned a compromise resolution which declared that the convention delegates "resent and reject efforts of the Communist Party or other political parties and their adherents to interfere in the affairs of the CIO."[34]

The resolution amounted to a major setback for the Communists. Their representatives on the committee, Ben Gold, Michael Quill, and Abraham Flaxer of the United Public Workers Union, accepted it only after considerable arm-twisting by Murray.[35] Given the changing power balance in the organization, this was likely the best they could hope for. At least it did not sanction purges, or so they were assured. Before the full General Executive Board voted on the resolution, Donald Henderson of the FTA extracted assurances from Murray that the resolution did not mean that "there shall be purges or that men shall be assassinated or deprived of employment."[36]

The Communists' main justification for accepting the resolution was that it preserved CIO unity. They also insisted that it was a kind of Gompersian statement, proclaiming that the CIO was not the creature of *any* political party, including the Democratic party. Once forced to accept it, they portrayed it as a kind of victory. After the Executive Board voted unanimously to adopt the resolution, Flaxer and Ben

Gold thanked Murray effusively. Michael Quill added that "I found out for the first time that no matter what side of the fence we are on, we are all CIO members."[37]

Armed with Murray's assurances that the resolution would not encourage purges, the Communists dragooned their supporters into voting for it. When two well-known Communist supporters in the NMU broke ranks and voted against the resolution, they were buttonholed by party pooh-bahs and harangued publicly. With tails between their legs they went to the platform to speak to Murray, who announced that he was pleased to say that they had withdrawn their votes, thus giving the resolution unanimous approval.[38]

As usual, the party had problems with members unable to leave bad enough alone. George Morris proclaimed that the party "had always favored a statement telling the world the CIO isn't Communist." Lewis Merrill, the Communist president of the United Office and Professional Workers, and his Communist-dominated Executive Board issued an astounding directive ordering union members and officers not to "become identified with this or that wing" of the labor movement, including the Communist party, and threatening severe disciplinary action against "any effort to impose the viewpoint of outside organizations" on the union. As witness to the seriousness of Merrill's resolve, he publicly resigned as a contributing editor of the *New Masses* magazine and from the board of directors of the party's Jefferson School in New York.[39]

The weakness of coordination among Communist unionists was again apparent, for Merrill and his union's Executive Board had obviously gone off half-cocked with their own interpretation of the meaning of the convention compromise. Within days they were attacked in a withering editorial in the *Daily Worker*, entitled "Appeasement of Redbaiting Never Paid," and called to account by the party. They were accused of not having rid themselves of all the influences of "Browderism" and threatened with "sharp disciplinary action." Within twenty-four hours, they recanted.[40]

Party labor coordinator John Williamson darted about "clarifying" the Communist position on the CIO resolution to CIO Communists. It was adopted only because it was necessary to maintain the alliance of Left and Center at all costs, he explained to a secret meeting of FTA Communists before their mid-January convention.[41] In an article in the Communist theoretical journal, *Political Affairs*, he called the resolution "inaccurate and unjust," accepted only to head off the "Social Democrats" who wanted to equate communism with fascism. The leftists had acquiesced only after Murray had given assurance that it did not mean the CIO would favor "repression." The election of Ben

Gold to the CIO Executive Board, he said, was understood as a "guide to action for everyone within the CIO."[42]

The more militant of the anti-Communists were no more satisfied with the resolution than the Communists. The Jewish *Daily Forward*, which reflected the views of the "Social Democratic" labor leaders whom the Communists so despised, declared that Murray "betrayed the Right-wingers" who had a "right to expect help from him." It would have been better for them to have accepted his challenge and let him "abdicate." The "unity" that Murray's compromise resolution created was "no less of a fake than the fake resolution which he . . . put through," said the *Forward*.[43]

While most eyes were on the anti-Communist resolution and the lesser issue of the compromise foreign policy resolution, new Executive Board regulations governing the CIO councils promulgated on the eve of the convention proved to be a much more important anti-Communist weapon. Anti-Communists were now assured of more effective help from CIO headquarters in either overthrowing or defanging leftist-dominated CIO councils.

Almost immediately after the convention, anti-Communist delegates returned to their local CIO conventions and councils with demands that they endorse the national "resent and reject" policy. In most cases, the wording was changed to make it a much more explicit rejection of Communist participation in the CIO. In New Jersey, for example, anti-Communists in the state CIO council pushed through a resolution to endorse the national CIO policy and to "resist and fight, in democratic fashion, any and all attempts of the Communist Party, in and out of the CIO, to foist their policies on our organization." The Massachusetts CIO convention barred Communists and members of "Communist organizations" from holding office and restructured its executive committee to cut down on Communist influence there.[44] In Milwaukee, armed with the national resolution, spurred on by the relentless exposés of Communist domination of the Wisconsin State CIO council by the Milwaukee *Sentinel*, and assisted by the disarray in the leftist stronghold, UAW Local 248, rightists scored a sweeping victory in the December elections for the crucial Milwaukee county CIO Executive Board. Then, they moved to take control of the Wisconsin state council from Communist hands.[45]

However, the Communists could not be dislodged from control of many key CIO councils, including important and powerful ones such as the Greater New York CIO council, Detroit's Wayne County council, the Los Angeles CIO council, and the Bridges-dominated Northern California and Washington state councils. The anti-Communists relied on the new rules limiting the activities of the CIO councils to keep them in line. With Director of IUCs Brophy aggressively clipping their wings, leftist councils found themselves restricted in a number of ways. When the Los Angeles CIO council voted to contribute some money to the National Negro Congress, which the anti-Communists considered a Communist-front, Brophy forbade their doing so. He directed all CIO councils to stop all aid to the NNC and decreed that they could support only National Association for the Advancement of Colored People.[46] Brophy soon expanded on this approach and circulated a list of thirty-six approved organizations to whom funds might be contributed, none of which were Communist-front organizations but some of which were anti-Communist.[47]

In New York, defeated in their attempts to wrest control of the Greater New York CIO council from Communist hands, anti-Communists led by Jack Altman walked out of the council and organized a new parallel anti-Communist council. Formed on the basis of an earlier organization created to rally CIO support for the reelection of Senator Herbert Lehman, whom the New York CIO had refused to support in 1946,[48] the Trade Union Committee for Democracy tried to usurp the political function of the Greater New York CIO council.[49] This type of "dual" organization was too much for Murray and Brophy, and it died without their support.[50] Such drastic, divisive tactics seemed unnecessary when the new regulations were taking their toll. By May 1947 Father Rice could report with satisfaction to readers of the *Catholic Digest* that new rules regarding IUCs had automatically weakened the "Red stranglehold" on them, "closing down these bodies completely as sounding-off devices for the communists."[51]

Meanwhile, political events both at home and abroad were making the Communist position more precarious, rapidly converting the leftist unions in the CIO into liabilities. The November 1946 congressional elections saw liberal Democrats swamped by a tidal wave of conservative Republicanism, much of it violently anti-union and especially anti-CIO. In state after state, anti-union legislation was proposed and passed. Successful anti-union offensives in various southern states seemed to give heart to employers throughout the country. There were fears in the CIO that the recent employers' defiance of NLRB decisions was linked to a feeling that the tide had turned, with the government on the run. Murray and Haywood became pessimistic about the near future. The feeling that the time had come to draw the wagons in a circle swept the CIO's Washington office.[52]

The new Republican-dominated Congress arrived in Washington determined to right the imbalances of the New Deal. It was especially intent on clipping the wings of the labor movement it had created and was reckoned to have endowed with excessive power. But one of the arguments for the restrictive labor legislation that began to wend its way through Congress was the need for government intervention to curb Communist power in the labor movement. The major piece of legislation that emerged, the Taft-Hartley Act of June 1947, included the requirement that all union office holders sign affidavits affirming that they were not members of the Communist party. Those who perjured themselves would be open to prosecution and stiff prison sentences. Any union whose officers refused to sign the affidavits would be deprived of its certification and bargaining rights under the NLRA. Unable to have its name on NLRB ballots, a union would be extremely vulnerable to raiding by rivals. Moreover, even if it were to retain the support of the vast majority of the employees, intransigent companies could legally refuse to bargain with it.

The entire CIO, along with the AFL, was united in opposition to the Taft-Hartley Act as a whole, mainly because of its other provisions. Murray, Reuther, and most CIO liberals agreed that whatever the merits of the anti-Communist provisions, the act as a whole had to go, and a powerful movement to secure its repeal must be mounted. Yet there were deep divisions within the Murray-Reuther bloc, as well as between it and the leftists, over how the new act should be combatted and what should be done about the affidavits.

The UE proposed that the CIO organize a twenty-four-hour general strike against the act and pursue a militant policy of mobilizing massive worker opposition to it, especially the affidavit requirement. This suggestion was rejected by the CIO General Executive Board. While declaring itself opposed to the act as a whole, the Board left the question of compliance with the affidavits up to individual unions. Almost immediately upon passage of the act, the auto and textile workers unions announced that they would comply with the affidavit provision. In the UAW, Reuther had shrewdly maneuvered the Executive Board, which he still did not control, into voting to comply, by persuading the UAW's Canadian regional director, George Burt, to turn on the Addes group, which he had previously supported, in exchange, it was rumored, for a promise he might continue in the position for the foreseeable future.[53]

Murray, on the other hand, had civil libertarian qualms about the affidavit and was concerned that it would encourage witch-hunters to run roughshod over the union movement. Just two months before, he had vigorously protested Truman's executive order calling for loyalty checks on all government employees and the firing of those who belonged to "subversive" organizations. Not only were thousands of people being deprived of due process, but the government had assumed the power to declare any labor, consumer, religious, or educational organization "subversive" without explanation.[54] Murray called the Taft-Hartley affidavit "presumptuous" and unconstitutional and resisted pressure to comply from within his own Steelworkers union until mid-1949.[55] Gradually, however, most anti-Communist labor leaders overcame similar qualms and signed the affidavits. By August 1948, one year after the act went into effect, affidavits had been signed by 81,000 union officers, including officials of 89 of the AFL's 102 unions and 30 of the CIO's 45 unions.[56]

As the adverse effects of not signing the affidavits piled up, leftist labor leaders began searching for ways to comply with the letter but not the spirit of the law. Even this was resolutely opposed by the party's political leaders who were convinced that what was needed was labor militancy on all levels. Labor had successfully withstood the employers' postwar offensive, they pointed out, and avoided a repetition of the disastrous post-World War I experience. Militancy in the drive for higher wages and a resolute determination to fight Taft-Hartley would pay off. Typically, they blamed the leftist leaders' problems on their ineffectiveness in explaining the issue properly to union members.[57]

Aside from being self-evident, this kind of analysis helped no one. The party was therefore forced to reaffirm in October 1948 what had been grudgingly conceded in June, that "if and when this question is pushed to a point that threatens the life of the majority of a union, the issue can best be settled by taking it to a referendum vote of the rank and file." However, this happened only in the NMU, whose leftist leaders were being routed on the issue. For the rest, the party warned, "It is a matter of concern that a few Left-wing union leaders have had illusions about the benefits to be gained by signing. Such leaders are certainly living in a fool's paradise, and this 'adjustment' might well lead them to make further concessions on questions of principle."[58]

The Taft-Hartley Act had an unanticipated untoward effect on the Communists. As it became by far the most important item on labor's political agenda, union leaders' assessments of the domestic political scene came to be shaped by a virtual obsession with securing its repeal. Harry Truman's veto of the bill and his vocal opposition to the act after Congress overrode his veto helped reverse labor's disaffection with him. Clearly if labor wanted to achieve repeal, it would have to stick with the Democrats. It was unthinkable that the GOP would come up with a presidential candidate who favored repeal, and a third party had no chance. Truman, who was looking better with each passing day of Republican control of Congress, became the labor movement's only hope.

The drastic changes that Taft-Hartley brought to the political atmosphere are illustrated by the stance of A. F. Whitney, the president of the independent Brotherhood of Railway Trainmen. In 1946, alienated by Truman's proposals for tough legislation to control strikes in the railroad industry, Whitney flirted with the leftists. Vowing to spend the entire $47 million union treasury on securing Truman's defeat, he joined the disaffected liberals and leftists rallying around Henry Wallace in late 1946 and became a vice-president of Wallace's Progressive Citizens of America. In March 1947 he joined in Wallace's attacks on the Truman Doctrine. Then came Taft-Hartley. In July 1947, Whitney proclaimed that Truman's veto of that act had "vindicated him in the eyes of labor." Stating that there was no potential liberal GOP candidate and that a third party was "out of the question," he was soon back in the Democratic fold. The reconciliation culminated with a visit to the White House on January 20, 1948, two days after he resigned from the PCA, and his endorsement of Truman.[59]

The Communists were in substantial agreement with Murray on Taft-Hartley and were initially heartened by his stand against the affidavit. Throughout 1947 he was able to continue his delicate balancing act, all in the name of avoiding a rupture in the CIO. Anti-Communists such as Father Rice still nursed their hopes; Rice assured a bishop that Murray (who "hates" the Communists) wanted to get rid of them but favored "letting the rank and file do it."[60]

Murray's firing Len De Caux from his position as publicity director of the CIO in mid-July 1947 was widely regarded as the opening shot in a campaign to purge the CIO bureaucracy of Communists, but in fact it was the product of a misunderstanding. Although there had been considerable pressure on him to fire De Caux and Pressman because of their Communist sympathies, De Caux's dismissal came after the *CIO News* published an article on the horrors of British rule in India in ignorance of the fact that Murray had just signed an ADA statement praising the British Labour party's policies in India. De Caux actually had nothing to do with running the *CIO News* story; the editorial content of *CIO News* was decided by an assistant, who had simply pulled the story from the "refrigerator" where it had been lying around for use during a slow news week.[61] Nevertheless, De Caux's firing did mean the elimination of a Communist from a very sensitive position. Moreover, he was replaced by an anti-Communist and from then on the line of the *CIO News* was that of Murray and the CIO anti-Communists. This was especially important when serious conflicts were emerging over foreign policy.

The growing conflict over foreign affairs had a disastrous impact on the Communist position in the CIO. Ultimately, as Joseph Starobin wrote, its international ties proved to be the "Achilles heel" of American communism.[62] In the CIO, this was true, not because the union membership at large was galvanized by foreign policy issues, but because the Communists' opposition to United States foreign policy led them to support Henry Wallace's crusade. Not only did their dissent bring the tremendous weight of the federal government down on them, but it pushed Murray and those in the middle, who were casting their lots with Truman and the Democratic party because of Taft-Hartley, into summoning up all their resources to crush the leftists in the CIO.

Many CIO liberals had shared the leftists' concern over the Truman administration's tough line towards the Soviets as well as its support for right-wing regimes in Greece and Italy. They too were disturbed over the continuation of West European colonial rule in Asia and Africa and discomfited by events in China. Among those who had attended the National Conference on Progressives in Chicago in September 1946, the last formal meeting at which Communists and anti-Communist liberals worked out agreements on foreign and domestic policy, were Murray, Carey, and Potofsky. Called by CIO-PAC to try to stop the rightward drift of the Truman administration, the conference unanimously passed a resolution supporting Henry Wallace in his opposition to Truman's betrayal of the Roosevelt heritage in foreign policy.[63] As part of the overall attempt to avoid a breakup of the CIO at its November 1946 convention, Murray and the liberals had little trouble swallowing a compromise foreign policy resolution which leaned heavily in Wallace's direction, a position very similar to that held by the Communists. Drafted and introduced by Pressman, the resolution called for peace, disarmament, antifascism, and "above all," the continuation of FDR's policy of preserving Big Three unity in the postwar era. The CIO proclaimed that it rejected "all proposals for American participation in any bloc or alliance that would destroy the unity of the Big Three."[64]

The spring of 1947 saw a widening of the incipient rift, however. The Truman administration's proposal of March 1947 to send economic and military aid to Greece and Turkey and the Truman Doctrine that accompanied it seemed, to many leftists, to be opening shots in a new kind of world-wide offensive against communism, using the Soviet threat to rationalize the creation of an expanded American empire. They were thus wary of the next major initiative, the proposal by Secretary of State George Marshall in June 1947 that the United States mount a massive program of economic aid to help rebuild the war-shattered countries of Europe, East and West. As the details of the Marshall plan emerged, it became apparent that it would involve the kind of coordination with and therefore subordination to the capitalist economies that the Soviet Union and her clients could never accept.

The CPUSA therefore joined most other Communist parties in attacking the proposal as simply an extension of the Truman Doctrine, an attempt to assert American dominance over Europe and rebuild West Europe as an anti-Soviet bastion.

This interpretation was not unreasonable, but it was hardly saleable in the United States. Marshall's proposal struck a chord of liberal generosity at a moment when Americans were feeling privileged amidst their resurging affluence, for Europe had just passed through its coldest and most deprived winter in memory, and capitalized on growing fears that western Europe would be driven by internal discontent into Stalin's hands. Yet the Communists in the CIO opened a determined offensive against the Marshall Plan, urging CIO councils to condemn it.

The struggle climaxed in October, with the dramatic appearance of Marshall himself at the CIO national convention, the first secretary of state to address a labor convention. The world was faced with a choice between freedom and dictatorship, he warned. The labor movement, which would be the first victim of a dictatorial regime, must support aid to Europe because the peace and security of the United States as well as the survival of "western civilization" depended on the survival of Europe.[65]

Marshall's warnings were echoed by Walter Reuther, who, with one eye reputedly on the 1948 Democratic vice-presidential nomination, delivered a ringing attack on "totalitarianism" and a defense of American foreign policy. Those who accused the administration of following a provocative policy, he warned, were the same people who in 1940 attacked Roosevelt and others opposed to Hitler as warmongers. Now, they were calling Truman the same.[66]

Clearly, the basis for a massive split on foreign policy was there. The moment either to crush the leftist unions or force them out of the CIO had arrived. Yet was it really the right moment? Was it the right issue? Murray thought not. Desperately, he tried to head off a floor fight on the foreign policy resolution the way he had avoided a split over the "resent and reject" resolution at the 1946 convention: by calling leaders of the opposing factions together to try to hammer out a compromise resolution. In the course of a four-and-one-half hour meeting in his hotel room, he finally hit on an idea that all could at least live with. The Marshall Plan was not really a plan, he said, in the sense that it was a single written document. It was merely a set of general proposals outlined by Marshall in a Harvard University commencement address. Therefore, the CIO need not do more than express its opinion of the general idea of aid to Europe. The compromise resolution expressed the CIO's support for the general principle of giving food and economic aid to a Europe devastated by war, with the proviso that it not be used to support oppression. He personally favored the "Marshall idea," said Murray, and saw it as compatible with the resolution. He promised that he would "lend every constructive aid in the development of a satisfactory plan that will provide substantial relief and economic aid to all of the people of Europe...." "After all," he said, the "heart, soul, and pulse-beat" of the resolution provided "a means to feed the hungry and clothe the naked and shelter the homeless and give medicine to the sick."[67]

While Murray was able to interpret the foreign policy resolution as essentially in consonance with the Marshall Plan, the Communists were able to emphasize other aspects of the grab bag of ideas it contained which were more congenial to their position. Irving Potash of the Fur Workers declared that his union would support it because it laid down good basic principles for the government to follow: universal disarmament, demilitarization, decartelization, and the destruction of Nazism and fascism in Germany and Japan. It meant the continuation of FDR's policy of Big Three unity and a sound program of postwar rehabilitation "because it is not the Marshall Plan nor anybody else's plan, but because it is the CIO plan." In declaring that food should not be used to stifle freedom, the resolution was censuring administration policy, for exactly this was being done in Greece and Italy.[68]

Despite Potash's disclaimers and his attempts to put the best face on it, the CP had lost ground on the Marshall Plan issue. Indeed, even before the convention they had realized that their view would not prevail, and they decided to "lay low" on the issue at the convention itself.[69] After the convention, they insisted that the CIO had neither endorsed the Marshall Plan nor commended the Truman administration's foreign policy. In his report to Mine, Mill on the CIO convention, Secretary-Treasurer John Clark said, "It is my opinion that on the question of foreign policy the delegates were confused. Marshall's speech was vague and indefinite. The only positive position he took was to advocate U.S. aid to the peoples of Europe."[70]

The Communists were forced into an abrupt change of tactics, however, that led straight to disaster. Shortly before the convention, the Soviets had begun assuming a much tougher posture towards the United States, a change that had important effects on the foreign Communist parties. A secret conference of representatives of nine European CPs in Poland under the leadership of Andrei Zhdanov agreed to mount an offensive against the Truman Doctrine and the Marshall Plan. Stalin's wartime gesture of dissolving the Comintern was partially reversed with the establishment of a new Communist Information Bureau, which, although comprising only the nine European parties, was a clear signal of the Soviets' intention to continue to ride close herd on the Communist parties of the world.

The Communist parties were to take the lead in organizing opposition to the Marshall Plan and American policy in Europe in their own countries. They were to become the "vanguard" of new anti-imperialist and anti-Fascist coalitions. To American Communists, the message seemed clear. Citing the resolutions of the new Cominform, the *Daily Worker* said that the United States needed a "strong anti-monopoly, anti-war coalition based on the Roosevelt-Wallace line."[71]

But what shape should the coalition take? Should it work within the Democratic party or should there be a new national third party, the recurring dream of Communist political planners? In the two years since the war had ended American Communists had wavered between the two, flirting with the tantalizing idea that the time for a real third party had finally arrived and then recoiling in fear of its implications.[72] After the conservative triumphs in the November 1946 elections, party members were warned not to panic, à la Browder, and begin forming alliances with bloated capitalists. Communists were to continue working for the united front of all progressive forces, but it must be a front united against the capitalists and their representatives, the Truman administration. The goal of their political activity must be the formation of a new people's party, anti-monopolistic and anti-imperialistic, but not immediately. Although the chances of reforming the Democratic party from within were slim, the "Wallace-Pepper" forces should be aided in their efforts to win the 1948 presidential nomination.[73]

Although reform of the Democratic party was supposedly subordinate to the preparations for a new party, Communists concentrated more on boosting Wallace and Pepper within the Democratic party than on preparing for a third party. Indeed, in the UAW, the most notable proposal that "concrete action in the building of an independent labor party of workers and farmers" be taken came in a letter to UAW local presidents in April 1947 from Walter Reuther's Socialist aide, Emil Mazey.[74] Months later, on Labor Day 1947, Harry Bridges announced that his union would support "the progressive forces in the Democratic Party led by Henry Wallace and other Roosevelt New Deal Democrats." Although he added that "the time has come to decide that the evils of the two-party system cannot be tolerated for the rest of our lives,"[75] it seemed that it was tolerable at least through the next presidential election.

By December the party's political leadership had changed its mind. The party's top union leaders were called together in New York and told that Wallace would soon be announcing his candidacy on a third party ticket and that the party would be going down the line with him. They were urged to prepare to swing their unions behind the ticket.[76]

Again as in 1940, in the political crunch, most of the party's unionists put self-preservation above the party line. Taft-Hartley had changed the nature of the political game in union circles, and it would have been difficult to rally non-Communists to a cause that would clearly close the door on any chance of repeal. Communist unionists were distinctly reticent in pushing their unions into all-out support for Wallace, something that upset the Communist political leadership's calculations and played a major role in Wallace's humiliating defeat.[77]

The only major leftist-led union to endorse Wallace was Mine, Mill. Otherwise, only the Fur Workers, the FTA, and the tiny Furniture Workers and Marine Cooks and Stewards gave him their official endorsement.[78] Even the UE, whose leaders played an active role in the Wallace campaign, did not officially endorse Wallace; it left the question of whom to support up to its locals. Its officers supported Wallace only as individuals, and Fitzgerald became head of the Labor Committee for Wallace.[79]

Murray and the liberals were unimpressed with such legalistic strategems, aimed, it appeared, at avoiding the charge of defying national CIO policy. The leftists seemed now to be trying to destroy the Democratic party. No sooner had the leftist unions begun their hesitant mobilization for Wallace than Murray and the anti-Communists opened an offensive against them. At the CIO Executive Board meeting in January 1948 they proposed that the board resolve that it was "unwise to inject a third party into the political scene in 1948." Another resolution pledged to work for peace and the Marshall Plan.[80]

The leftists tried to have the third party resolution tabled, arguing that for the CIO to dictate a political stance to its member unions infringed on their autonomy. Their opponents countered with reminders of the leftists' enthusiasm for the CIO-dictated no-strike policy during the war and, in any event, denied that the resolution ordered CIO unions to support Truman, the Democratic party, or any other political force. It was merely an expression of opinion by the national CIO about where it thought its unions should stand on the third party issue, said the anti-Communists.[81] The resolution carried the day easily by a vote of thirty-three to eleven.[82]

Despite the vagueness about its mandate, the third party resolution was an important defeat for the leftists. Even those who agreed that it was merely an expression of CIO feeling rather than a mandate still thought that it would provide an important weapon in the fight against Wallace and the Communists.[83] Similarly, the resolution on the Marshall Plan represented a decisive step to the Right from the position approved by the CIO convention just three months before. Now the CIO expressed its support for the Marshall Plan itself, rather than simply the principles which purportedly underlay it. It was a short step from there to regard opposition to Wallace and support for the Marshall Plan as the twin hallmarks of CIO national policy.

The open parting of the ways had been reached. At the Executive Board meeting some leftists had difficulty restraining the bitterness they felt towards Murray.[84] Murray also felt forced to take the CIO's new posture to its logical conclusion. Within weeks, he fired Pressman. Despite Murray's continuing respect for him, Pressman, who was committed to Wallace, had become in effect a hostile spy in the CIO national office.

Pressman was let go as gracefully as possible. As he was being forced to resign, Murray gave him a CIO case to take before the Supreme Court, a case for which Pressman was paid a $25,000 fee.[85] Pressman broke down and cried at the press conference announcing his departure, but he anticipated a bright future in the Progressive party and embarked on a vigorous campaign for a congressional seat from Brooklyn.[86]

Murray and his aides in Washington thereupon marshalled their forces. It was almost impossible to impose a political stance on unwilling national unions. The IUCs, however, as creatures of the national CIO, were a different story, especially since the recent administrative changes giving the national headquarters increased control over them. Furthermore, as the center of state and local CIO-PAC activity in many areas, they were of crucial importance in the effort to keep the CIO solidly in the Democratic party.

From the beginning of the offensive that was now mounted against them, the leftists were on the defensive in the IUCs and the CIO-PACs. For the most part, they did not even try to secure IUC endorsement for Wallace, but concentrated on heading off IUC endorsements of anyone. For a while, these tactics helped stave off confrontation. When Brophy recommended a showdown to a meeting of CIO vice-presidents in late February 1948, they temporized, sending Allan Haywood and R. J. Thomas to Los Angeles to investigate the situation in that explosive IUC.[87] Within two weeks, unencumbered by the minority of leftist vice-presidents, Murray had decided to proceed with the crackdown on his own. On March 8, 1948, Brophy sent a letter to all state and local IUCs ordering them to pass resolutions supporting the CIO stand on the third party and Marshall Plan issues.[88] This forced a showdown with the leftists on the two issues on which they were most vulnerable: their apparent desire to hand the election to "Taft-Hartley Republicans" and their "slavish" devotion to Soviet foreign policy.

Even in the places where they dominated the IUCs, leftists tried to avoid a vote on the issue because Brophy's letter and the arguments of

anti-Communists had put the issues on the ground of either supporting or opposing "national CIO policy." Aside from the as yet unknown
consequences of opposing "national policy," this also represented an
important emotional weapon for the anti-Communists. Divisiveness is
what breaks strikes. "Unity" is the cement of strong union movements.

Murray himself led the way. In mid-March he relieved Bridges of his
post as CIO regional director in northern California, a move that West
Coast anti-Communists rightly regarded as a clarion call for a wholesale offensive against the leftists.[89]

In Washington state, as well as in San Francisco, Denver, and other
centers, the leftist-dominated IUCs tried to avoid a confrontation by
refusing to vote on the Brophy resolutions. Throughout most of the
nation, the issue that wracked the IUCs was not support for Wallace.
This was rarely even proposed. The issue was whether or not to support the Democratic party, the Marshall Plan, and, soon, Truman.

When the Washington state IUC refused to support "national policy,"
the anti-leftists defected and set up a rival IUC to which they contributed their per capita tax.[90] In Newark, New Jersey, anti-Communists
withdrew from the Newark CIO Council in March and formed the
Confederation to Support CIO Policy.[91] In some places leftists who
worked for Wallace were brought up on charges of contravening
policy and expelled from the IUCs.[92]

Leftist refusal to stay in the Democratic party fold was likely the
major factor in convincing Murray that the time had arrived to purge
them from the CIO. In the words of Father Rice, "That was the big
[reason] . . . Murray was finally convinced by me and a lot of other
people that they were a damage to the movement."[93] By April 1948
Brophy reported in his diary that Murray stalked about the CIO head
office, fulminating against "the machinations of CP re Wallace and 3rd
Party."[94] Mike Quill had apparently told him that the CP had ordered
its unionists to back a third party the day after the CIO convention in
October 1947 had resolved against one. Thus Murray denounced the
Wallace party as nothing more than the creature of the CP, charging
that there was "no question" but that the CP was "directly responsible"
for its creation.[95] The idea of a purge was becoming more thinkable
among top CIO officials. John Brophy, for one, became convinced that
the conflict "could only be resolved by a purge."[96]

The party's political leadership was as inflexible as ever in responding to Communist unionists' complaints about the problems the Wallace
candidacy was creating for them. Quill later reported that when he met
with William Z. Foster in the spring of 1948 and questioned the policy,
he was told two things: first, the party was going down the line with
Wallace and its unionist adherents were to do the same, even if it meant

splitting every CIO union. Second, anticipating a split, the party was prepared to start a third labor federation.[97]

Foster's rigidity on the Wallace issue helped force Quill out of the party. As for the other party-influenced labor leaders, Curtis Mac-Dougall reported that they "sat on their hands," doing little to mobilize their membership for Wallace.[98] Like Quill, they realized that the party had embarked on a path that was severely endangering their position in the union movement and, despite their personal pro-Wallace inclinations, they had few kamikaze-like inclinations.

In October 1948, as the Wallace campaign faltered and began to sour, the party's political leadership began to pile much of the blame on the leftist trade unionists. The broad network of tens of thousands of Wallace committees in shops and unions on which they had counted had not materialized, reported John Williamson to the party's national convention that month. The best work on that front had been in the auto industry, where two hundred of them had been set up. The situation was especially disappointing in the "Left-progressive" unions, for much more had been expected of them. The ILWU, Mine, Mill, FTA, and Office and Professional Workers had done the best job, he reported, but the rest, including the UE and the furriers, were clearly disappointments. Worse, the pro-Wallace forces in certain unions, such as Packinghouse, NMU, and TWU, had "allowed themselves to be completely disoriented by internal union developments."[99] In fact, the "disorientation" of the Left in the unions was as much the result as the cause of their feeble support for Wallace.

"Sitting on their hands" during the Wallace campaign was at best a holding operation for the leftist unionists. It merely headed off alienating even more of the CIO membership drifting back, en masse, to Harry Truman and the Democrats. The spectacular events abroad in 1948—the Communist takeover in Czechoslovakia in February, the Berlin blockade of March, the continuing civil war in Greece, the resurgent Red army in China—all helped create an atmosphere in which it was easy to portray Wallace supporters as at best dupes of the Communists and at worst willing servants of Moscow. As portrayed in most of the American media, these events simply confirmed what Truman and his Republican opponents now agreed on: that there existed a vast, worldwide movement directed from Moscow which aimed to conquer the world. Support of Wallace, the obvious candidate of this movement, was therefore tantamount to treason. More important for unionists relatively unimpressed by foreign policy and appeals to patriotism, the bread-and-butter necessity to defeat Dewey at any cost was hammered home when Dewey, as expected, came out in favor of Taft-Hartley. For Murray and the CIO liberals, then leftist inaction on Wallace was not enough. In order to stay in their good graces, the leftists would have to make the same choice presented to Pressman: either Wallace or "the CIO position." Nothing less than an endorsement of Truman and open defiance of the CPUSA would suffice.

The division over the Marshall Plan and Wallace was accompanied by a breakdown of unity over the CIO's foreign labor policy as well. Murray now began using the Marshall Plan to force a showdown with the Soviets and their European Communist union supporters in the WFTU. In December 1947 he dispatched James Carey to the meeting of the WFTU Executive Bureau in Paris to demand that the Marshall Plan be placed on the agenda. If the Communist-dominated organization refused to support the Plan, the basis would be laid for CIO withdrawal. Louis Saillant, the French Communist director of the WFTU, saw the ploy and resisted. After a long wrangle, the item was placed on the agenda of the Bureau's next meeting, to be held in April.[100]

In the interim, the Communist unions in Europe expanded their campaign against the Marshall Plan while, with American government and union aid, anti-Communists defected from the two major Communist-dominated union movements, those of France and Italy, and set up new, anti-Communist labor confederations. Murray and the CIO liberals joined the AFL and the state department in encouraging these unions to form a new anti-Communist international labor organization which would support the Marshall Plan.

The British Trades Union Congress was persuaded to take the lead in this. When Saillant refused to advance the next meeting of the WFTU Executive Bureau from its April date, they called a conference in London for early March, at which they set up a trade union advisory committee to the newly formed European Cooperation Administration that would implement the Marshall Plan. The committee included the new, breakaway French and Italian unions, plus most of the non-Communist West European ones still affiliated with the WFTU. Significantly, for the first time, the AFL and the CIO both sent delegates. The United States government, acknowledging their quasi-official function, provided them with free transportation plus sixty dollars a day.[101]

Armed with the threat of defection, Carey went to the meeting of the Executive Committee of the WFTU in Rome from April 30 to May 4, attacked Saillant for having issued an anti-Marshall Plan manifesto in the name of the WFTU, and declared that "The CIO will not pay a single cent towards the salary of Louis Saillant while he is engaged in attacks on the policy of CIO."[102] Saillant was forced to resign his post in the French *Confedération Général de Travailleurs*. His powers in the WFTU were restricted and anti-Communists in WFTU headquarters were given a veto over any pronouncements coming from that center. A victorious Carey went to the Vatican, where he received the blessing of the pope.[103]

Although for the moment everyone expressed pleasure over the new arrangements, ultimately they did not satisfy Murray and Carey, who wanted more than silence or neutrality on the Marshall Plan issue. Murray and the CIO liberals were soon working to replace the WFTU with an organization that would actively support their government's policy.

NOTES

1. James Carey, Oral History Interview, Oral History Collection of Columbia University (hereafter COHC), 141.

2. *Daily Worker*, November 10, 1945.

3. Adolph Germer, Diaries, State Historical Society of Wisconsin, Madison, Wis., November 21, 1945.

4. *The New York Times*, May 15, 1946.

5. Murray to All CIO Unions, July 4, 1946, Walter Reuther, Papers, Wayne State University Archives of Labor History and Urban Affairs, Detroit, Mich. (hereafter WSUA), Series 1, Box 16, "CIO, Murray" Folder.

6. *New York Post*, August 21, 1946.

7. James Matles, OH, Pennsylvania State University Archives of Labor History, State College, Pa. (hereafter PSUA), 65.

8. *Labor Leader*, September 21, 1946.

9. Michael Harrington, "Catholics in the Labor Movement," *Labor History*, vol. 1, no. 2 (fall 1960), 250.

10. New York *World-Telegram*, September 27, 1946, cited in James Morton Freeman, *No Friend of Labor*, pamphlet (New York: Fulfillment Press, 1948), 24.

11. *NYT*, September 28, 1946.

12. *Detroit Times*, October 28, 1946, cited in Freeman, *No Friend of Labor*, 24.

13. The Rev. Charles Owen Rice, OH 2, 20 PSUA.

14. Harrington, "Catholics in the Labor Movement," 259.

15. Haywood to Germer, November 4, 1946, Adolph Germer Papers, State Historical Society of Wisconsin, Madison, Wis.

16. *NYT*, December 1, 1946; Art Preis, *Labor's Giant Step, Twenty Years of the CIO* (New York: Pioneer Publishers, 1964), 328-29.

17. *NYT*, December 1, 1946. The organization was the National Negro Congress.

18. Haywood to Germer, November 11, 1946, Germer Papers.

19. Quoted in Preis, *Labor's Giant Step*, 329.

20. Ibid.

21. Max Kampelman, *The Communist Party vs. the CIO* (New York: Praeger, 1957), 39.

22. Ibid.

23. James Matles, OH, PSUA, 65; Edwin Lahey, COHC, 20. Characteristically Carey had a more inflated view of his role. He thought of himself as "a quarterback in the fight to throw the Communists out of the CIO." Carey, COHC, 104.

24. Matles, OH, PSUA 65.

25. Albert Fitzgerald, OH, PSUA, 17.

26. John Williamson, "Problems and Tasks Before Labor Today," *Political Affairs*, vol. 25, no. 11 (November 1946), 986.

27. Jean Gould and Lorena Hickock, *Walter Reuther, Labor's Rugged Individualist* (New York: Dodd, Mead, 1973), 238-39.

28. Phillip Murray, Report to CIO Executive Board Meeting, March 15, 1946, Reuther Papers, Series 1, Box 7, "Phillip Murray" Folder.

29. *NYT*, October 3, 1946. United Shoe Workers officials retorted that McGrath had simply "deserted his post" for reasons unconnected with communism.

30. UAW, Press Release, November 8, 1946, in Walter Reuther, Papers, WSUA, Series 1, Box 16, "CIO, Murray" Folder.

31. "Declaration of Policy," Reuther Papers, Series 1, Box 15, "CIO Convention 1946" Folder.

32. *DW*, November 17, 1946.

33. The figure depends on how one defines the various camps and the basis for calculating strength. There is no accurate measure of CP and anti-Communist strength, one that would compensate for the inflated membership estimates of unions such as the Textile Workers, yet which also takes into account the disproportionate influence of unions such as the Amalgamated, which exercised an influence in the CIO much greater than its small size. Joel Seidman estimated that the CP controlled one-third of the CIO in 1946 while Max Kampelman gave a low, 15 percent estimate, saying this represented unions with approximately one million members. Neither is very explicit about the method of calculation. By most rules of thumb, Seidman would seem to be much closer to the mark. Joel Seidman, "The Labor Policy of the Communist Party during World War II," *Industrial and Labor Relations Review*, vol.4, no. 10 (October 1950), 55-69. Max Kampelman, *Communist Party vs. the CIO*, 37. Arnold Beichman, who did a detailed breakdown for the Research Institute of America in 1946, said that in that year, "by universal admission," the CP controlled unions with 20 percent of the membership. *Christian Science Monitor*, October 16, 1958, cited in Joseph R. Starobin, *American Communism in Crisis, 1943-1957* (Cambridge: Harvard University Press, 1972), 257. The problem with this type of figure, though, is that in talking of "control" by the CPUSA, it does not take into account unions such as the Packinghouse Workers which the CP did not "control" yet which were highly influenced by it.

34. CIO, *Daily Proceedings of the Constitutional Convention*, 1946.

35. Interview with James Carey, October 27, 1955, Daniel Bell, Collection of Material on Socialism and Communism in the U.S.A., Tamiment Institute Library, New York University, New York, N.Y., Box 4, "CPUSA" Folder.

36. Extract from Minutes of CIO General Executive Board Meeting," November 1946, in Carey to Curran, September 1947, CIO, Papers, Office of the Secretary-Treasurer, WSUA (hereafter Carey Papers), Box 54.

37. Ibid.

38. Preis, *Labor's Giant Step*, 332.

39. Ibid., 333-34.

40. Unsigned Confidential Report of Meeting of FTA Communists with John Williamson, January 10, 1947, Carey Papers, Box 109; Preis, *Labor's Giant Step*, 334.

41. Report of Meeting of FTA Communists, January 10, 1947, Carey Papers.

42. John Williamson, "The Situation in the Trade Unions," *Political Affairs*, vol. 26, no. 1 (January 1947), 25.

43. Cited in Preis, *Labor's Giant Step*, 334.

44. Ibid., 333; *Washington Post*, January 9, 1947.

45. *Washington Post*, January 9, 1947; *Milwaukee Sentinel*, March 2, 1947.

46. *Washington Post* January 9, 1947; Preis, *Labor's Giant Step*, 333.

47. Preis, *Labor's Giant Step*, 336.

48. Kampelman, *Communist Party vs. CIO*, 36.

49. Altman to Murray, March 13, 1947, John Brophy, Papers, Catholic University of America Library, Wash., D.C., Box A5-12.

50. Freeman, *No Friend of Labor*, 27.

51. The Rev. Charles O. Rice, "Phil Murray and the Reds," *Catholic Digest*, May 1947, 99.

52. Haywood to Germer, November 6, 1946, February 28, 1947, Germer Papers.

53. Matles, OH, PSUA 68; Haessler, OH, WSUA, 194-96.

54. Murray to Truman, April 14, 1947, copy in Reuther Papers, Series 1, Box 16, "CIO, Murray" Folder.

55. Charles Madison, *American Labor Leaders* (N.Y.: Harper, 1950), 323. Another anti-Communist labor leader who opposed the affidavit on principle was John L. Lewis, who withdrew his UMW from the AFL in December 1947 primarily because the AFL refused to take a strong stand against it.

56. Arthur F. McClure, *The Truman Administration and the Problems of Postwar Labor, 1945-1948* (Rutherford: Fairleigh Dickinson University Press, 1969), 145.

57. John Williamson, "Defeat the Drive Against the Unions," *Political Affairs*, vol. 27, no. 10 (October 1948), 857-60.

58. Ibid., 861.

59. Curtis D. MacDougall, *Gideon's Army* (New York: Marzani and Munsell, 1965), 178-79.

60. Father Rice to Bishop Hugh C. Boyle, June 7, 1947, Rice Papers, PSUA, Roll A-B. Rice was writing specifically about the UE, and was likely thinking of Murray's secret contributions to the anti-Communist "rank-and-file" movement.

61. Daniel Bell, Interview with Henry Fleisher, editor, *CIO News*, October 20, 1955, Bell Collection, Box 4.

62. Starobin, *American Communism in Crisis*, 47.

63. David A. Shannon, *The Decline of American Communism* (New York: Harcourt, Brace and Co., 1959), 129. It was also at this conference that Murray departed from his prepared text to blurt out his attack on Communists meddling in the CIO's affairs.

64. CIO, *Proceedings*, 1946, 10.

65. CIO, *Proceedings*, 1947, 262.

66. Ibid., 284-86.

67. Ibid., 289-91.

68. Ibid., 290.

69. Testimony of Michael Quill, CIO, "Transcript of Hearings before the Committee to Investigate Charges against the International Longshoremen's and Warehousemen's Union," Washington, D.C., June 1950 (hereafter CIO, "ILWU Hearings"), copy in Carey Papers, Box 110, 139-41.

70. John Clark, "Report on the Ninth Constitutional CIO Convention," November 3, 1947, mimeo copy in Carey Papers, Box 111, "Mine, Mill" Folder.

71. *DW*, October 7, 1947; Shannon, *Decline*, 137.

72. Shannon, *Decline*, 114-21; Starobin, *American Communism in Crisis*, ch. 5, 6, 7.

73. Fred Blair, "Report at Meeting of Wisconsin State Committee," CPUSA, Fred Blair, Papers, State Historical Society of Wisconsin, Madison, Wis., Box 1.

74. Emil Mazey to Local Union Presidents, Region 1 and 1A, April 30, 1947. Mazey did not choose to or was not allowed to follow up the suggestion, perhaps because of Reuther's coolness to the idea, as well as the heated opposition of Tracy Doll, the anti-Communist head of the crucial Detroit area IUC and CIO-PAC. Tracy Doll to Addes, May 9, 1947, Reuther Papers, Series 5, Box 38, "Emil Mazey" Folder.

75. Starobin, *American Communism in Crisis*, 167.

76. Ibid., 167-69; Michael Quill subsequently charged that the decision was announced to the union notables the day after the CIO convention, in October 1947, but there is no corroboration of this from other sources. Harry Bridges, in his cross-examination of Quill, cast grave doubts on Quill's recollections by proving that although Quill claimed to recall his active participation in the meeting clearly, he could not possibly have been there. CIO, "ILWU Hearings," 65-72.

77. Eugene Dennis, "The Main Lessons of the 1948 Elections." *Political Affairs*, vol. 27, no. 12 (December 1948), 1050.

78. MacDougall, *Gideon's Army*, 613.

79. Matles, OH, PSUA 68. MacDougall, *Gideon's Army*, 613.

80. CIO General Executive Board, Press Release, January 22, 1948, copy in Germer Papers.

81. Excerpts from Minutes of CIO Executive Board Meeting, January 22, 23, 1948, in Carey to Ferdinand Smith, April 12, 1948, Carey Papers, Box 54, "NMU" Folder.

82. CIO, Press Release, January 22, 1948.

83. Excerpts from Minutes of CIO Executive Board, January 22, 23, 1948.

84. See ibid., remarks of Ferdinand Smith.

85. Daniel Bell, Interview with James Carey, October 27, 1955, Bell Collection, Box 4, "CPUSA" Folder. Murray Kempton put the total value of the parting favors considerably higher. Murray gave Pressman a $15,000-a-year retainer from the tiny Marine Engineers Beneficial Association, Kempton wrote in 1955, as well as the CIO challenge to a minor section of the Taft-Hartley Act. Pressman and Nathan Witt, his co-counsel, sent Murray a bill for $83,000, said Kempton, "which Murray paid with pain." Murray Kempton, *Part of Our Time* (New York: Simon and Schuster, 1955), 77.

86. Kempton, *Part of Our Time*, 77-78.

87. John Brophy, Diaries, February 25, 1948, in John Brophy, Papers.

88. Brophy to All CIO IUC's, March 8, 1948, Brophy Papers, Box A5-12.

89. Murray to Germer, March 24, 1948, Germer Papers.

90. Brighton Erwin to All CIO Unions and Councils Dissident to Washington State IUC Policy, April 1, 1948, Germer Papers.

91. Freeman, *No Friend of Labor*, 27.

92. Fullerton Fulton to Brophy, April 19, 1948; Fulton to R. Jacobson, April 19, 1948, Germer Papers.

93. Rice, OH 2, 24.

94. John Brophy, Diaries, April 22, 1948, Brophy Papers.

95. Starobin, *American Communism in Crisis*, 174.

96. Brophy, COHC, 949.

97. Testimony of Michael Quill, CIO, "ILWU Hearings," 159. Earlier in his testimony (p. 72), Quill had placed Foster's third labor federation idea in January. It is not clear whether Quill was simply confused about the dates or whether the proposal was ever seriously entertained. It never passed the stage of rumor.

98. MacDougall, *Gideon's Army*, 642.

99. John Williamson, "Defeat the Drive Against the Unions," *Political Affairs*, vol. 27, no. 10 (October 1948), 863.

100. John Brophy, "Autobiography," chap. 23, 4, Brophy Papers.

101. Wyndham Mortimer, *Organize! My Life as a Union Man* (Boston: Beacon Press, 1971), 238.

102. Brophy, "Autobiography," chap. 23, 6. There is no indication that he saw any irony in echoing so faithfully the kind of attacks which the UE leftists had made on his use of his CIO post to undermine them.

103. Freeman, *No Friend of Labor*, 29.

12 OUTSIDE PRESSURE MOUNTS, 1945-1948

Leftist refusal to support Truman was the event that galvanized the determination of Murray and other CIO liberals to crush communism in the CIO. Still, the postwar offensive against them was the product of other forces as well. There is considerable evidence to support the view of Father Rice that "they were kicked out regardless of what they said, because of the gathering cloud of McCarthy."[1] The postwar years witnessed a resurgence of the very same anti-Communist forces that had almost coalesced in 1941. This time, they had the cold war and the growing alarm over the external and internal Communist threat to support them, and no German invasion of the Soviet Union or Pearl Harbor to head them off. Their pressure reinforced the growing belief among CIO liberals that the Communists were the Achilles heel of the CIO.

Employer anticommunism surged after the war, fueled by alarm over the wave of strikes in late 1945 and 1946. Inextricably combined with anti-unionism, it gained new momentum with the Republican victory in the November 1946 congressional elections, a victory that clearly presaged a congressional clipping of labor's wings. The postwar strikes in the mass production industries confirmed many employers' worst fears about the CIO's militancy. It seemed natural to assume that the CIO was somehow connected with communism. Conversely, the well-known power of the Communists in the ranks of the CIO made it vulnerable to the attacks of employers who, although professing patriotic anticommunism as their motive, were much more concerned about crushing militant unionism than Communist unionism.

In 1946, the United States Chamber of Commerce, representing the most anti-union segment of organized business, advocated a purge of leftist government employees. It also demanded that the government publish a list of Communist-controlled front organizations and labor unions.[2] It soon did so itself, publishing its widely circulated pamphlet, *Communists in the Labor Movement, Facts and Countermeasures*.[3] Simultaneously, it began to have anti-Communist clauses inserted in what was to become the Taft-Hartley Act, hoping, in its words, to "modify the Wagner Act so that employers can work more effectively and without fear of law violation with American-minded employees in opposing Communists within the labor movement."[4]

As in the prewar period, employer charges of Communist domination of the CIO found ready echoes in the AFL, whose president, William Green, said that the basic difference between the AFL and CIO was the difference between "a foreign-controlled organization and an American organization."[5] In 1946, when the Gallup Poll asked AFL members what was their main criticism of the CIO, the most frequent response was that it was "run by communists and radicals."[6]

By 1946, the term "Communist" was taking on the worst connotations possible. Thanks to the cold war and the interpretation of it disseminated by the government and most of the media, the American public was quickly disabused of the illusions about the Soviet Union encouraged by wartime propaganda. Whereas in February 1945, 55 percent of those queried by the Gallup Poll had said that they thought Russia could be trusted to cooperate with the United States after the war, one year later only 35 percent thought so. Two weeks later, in March 1946, 71 percent of the respondents said they disapproved of Russia's foreign policy whereas only 7 percent said they approved.[7]

The growing opposition to the Soviet Union took its toll on the reputation of American Communists, who were so closely identified with it. In mid-1946, 48 percent of Gallup's pollees thought that members of the CPUSA were basically loyal to the USSR rather than the United States, whereas only 23 percent thought they were loyal to America. By April 1948, 65 percent of the respondents had become convinced that the Communists were loyal to the USSR while only 16 percent thought them loyal to the United States.[8]

As a result, sentiment for crushing communism in the United States increased markedly from 1945 to 1948. By June 1946 over half of all Americans thought that something should be done to curb Communists in the United States. Thirty-six percent thought they should be killed or imprisoned, 16 percent thought they should be curbed and forced into inactivity, and 7 percent thought they should be watched carefully. Only 16 percent thought they should be left alone. Manual workers were about average in their hostility to the Communists.[9] By March 1947, 61 percent of Americans thought membership in the CP should be forbidden by law while only 26 percent thought it should remain legal.[10]

These sentiments were carefully nurtured by the business community and the media. After the war's end, Americans were subjected to an increasing tide of frightening stories about Communist domination of labor unions. Columnists such as Victor Lasky, the "Red expert" for the New York *World-Telegram,* joined Victor Riesel of the *New York Post* and the swelling chorus of people who had discovered that exposés of Communist domination made good copy that pleased publishers and readers alike. A common theme was the supposed Communist master plan to dominate and sabotage American transportation and communications. When Bridges' ILWU began organizing Hawaiian fishermen and longshoremen in Alaska, Lasky had a field day: "The Japanese also used fishermen for their espionage prior to Pearl Harbor," he warned. "High Japanese naval officers, posing as fishermen, photographed naval installations from every angle. Their work paid off on December 7, 1941." It was no secret, he warned, that the Pan-Pacific Institute in Vladivostock and the Communist school on Haight Street in San Francisco were turning out "well-trained agitators . . . by the hundreds. . . . At Vladivostock, Japanese, Filipinos, Portuguese and Spanish half-castes have been schooled for special missions throughout the Pacific, with Hawaii as the special object for their Stalinist tactics." As for Alaska, he warned that

Bridges has his tentacles reaching throughout the Pacific and Caribbean. He has organized sugar workers in Cuba, longshoremen in Panama. His agents are now in Alaska where there is a minute labor movement. Labor sources report that Germain Bulcke, ILWU second vice-president, was sent there to organize some 250 longshoremen. Bulcke's expenses were $1000 a month, an inordinate sum considering the number of longshoremen. But it is a small figure compared to the importance of having a Communist machine in America's nearest approach to Russia. A fifth column in Alaska would paralyze that territory more readily in the event of war.[11]

The hysteria was by no means restricted to the sensationalist media. By 1948 even staid *Harper's Magazine* ran a story warning of Communist attempts to control New York's transportation facilities. "With such control," it said, "they could tie up the commercial center of the United States. If New York's transportation was disrupted, wheat would pile up on Kansas sidings, textiles would rot in the Midwest. The Communists would hold a weapon that could effectively impair the national economy."[12]

Leftist unions also felt the power of the media on a local level. A large number of newspapers in the country were anti-union[13] and an even larger majority were also violently anti-Communist. It was natural for them to jump at the chance to link the two, "exposing" and attacking Communist domination of unions wherever and whenever possible. For many leftist unionists, this meant having to face a constant barrage of charges in the local press, which could not be easily answered because of the absence of any sympathetic large circulation newspapers. In some areas, press hounding of leftist unionists was especially intense. In Wisconsin, for example, CIO leftists faced a steady barrage from the state's major morning newspaper, the Hearst-owned *Milwaukee Sentinel*, which worked closely with the Allis-Chalmers Company in a concerted attempt to oust the leftist leadership of UAW Local 248. In September 1946 the paper began a series of attacks on the Communists in the state CIO that ran for fifty-nine consecutive days. Signed by "John Sentinel," supposedly the pseudonym for a *Sentinel* reporter, the series was in fact written by an Allis-Chalmers research man. The series and the *Sentinel* played an important role in breaking the grip of the leftists on the Milwaukee County CIO Council and the Wisconsin State CIO Council in the elections that were held after the series appeared.[14] The *Sentinel's* continuing attacks on the leaders of Local 248, in secret cooperation with Allis-Chalmers, played a major role in crushing their strike and ousting them. That achieved, the paper experienced a distinct loss of zeal in continuing the anti-Communist crusade against labor. The paper's labor reporter, the supposed author of the "John Sentinel" series, became disillusioned by evidence that it was anti-unionism and the *Sentinel's* desire to do Allis-Chalmers' bidding rather than sincere anticommunism that had motivated the crusade.[15]

Newspaper harasssment was not limited to the right-wing or Hearst press. Indeed, the Milwaukee *Journal*, one of the most liberal papers in the nation, was hardly fairer to the leftists than the *Sentinel*. It even refused the local's bids to buy ads in the *Journal* and commercials on the *Journal*-owned radio station to state its case. Only when the UAW International intervened and offered to take out the advertisements in its name did the *Journal* relent.[16]

Catholic anti-Communist labor activists, sensing the opportunities presented by the rising tide of anticommunism in 1946, frantically stepped up their activities. Many were concerned that Philip Murray might miss the boat. Father Tom Darby, a leader in the anti-Communist movement in UE, wrote Father Rice in August 1946, expressing his concern that Murray and Carey were "out of touch with the growing rank-and-file dislike of the CP's. All or most Americans are turning against CPs [*sic*] as vs. Americans and if Phil Murray doesn't do something he will be left holding Lee Pressman's bag."[17]

As in the prewar period, the Catholics were never able to achieve the unity of strategy and purpose to which they aspired: the well-oiled coordination they imagined characterized their Communist opponents. They remained divided among a myriad of groups and tendencies. The Jesuits and ACTU remained deeply at odds over strategy and tactics. Both were suspicious of the increasing activity of the National Catholic Welfare Conference, whose social action department was led by energetic liberal priests such as Father George Higgins. Nevertheless, the objective of all their activity remained the same: ridding the CIO of Communist influence. The cumulative effect of the various kinds of activity was important; different activities and different approaches appealed to different Catholic constituencies, but they complimented rather than contradicted each other. Furthermore, by 1946, more priests, especially younger ones, had been attracted to the liberal industrial unionist but anti-Communist line.[18]

Most noticeable were the renewed activities of ACTU, the various Catholic "labor schools," and individual priests in mobilizing insurgencies in leftist-dominated unions. ACTU, as the most controversial and visible of the organizations, received a disproportionate share of the credit or blame for this revival. As in the prewar era, enemies and supporters tended to attribute to it all kinds of activities with which it was either unconnected or only remotely involved in.[19] Militants who had been in the service returned. Labor schools began to revive and expand. In Detroit, Father Clancy, the ACTU chaplain, was soon presiding over a network of forty-one labor schools in the Detroit parishes. Thanks to the support of Cardinal Spellman, within a year after the war's end the New York chapter had doubled the circulation of its newspaper and increased its activity in every sphere.[20] Among the unions in which it was most active was the UE, and it is little wonder that the UE leadership took the lead in denouncing ACTU, labelling its opponents the "Carey-ACTU" bloc.

In fact, though, ACTU was merely one of three major opposition groups in UE, and its postwar relations with Carey were strained. Father Rice, who led the anti-Communist insurgency in the UE's Pittsburgh district, supported Carey for the UE presidency in 1946, albeit reluctantly. "Over the years, I have found him of damn little assistance," he wrote a New York counterpart. The Reverend Thomas Darby, who organized anti-Communists in the UE's New York City area district, was even less enthusiastic about Carey. He supported other priests who were searching for a "rank-and-filer" of the "right caliber" to run for the presidency. "Jim C. is a little bit too much a chameleon," he wrote Rice.[21] A few months later, he told Rice that he still opposed "bringing Carey into the picture" because he did not "seem to have lasting convictions" and was not "reliable."[22]

Nevertheless, ACTU was a very active component in the movement that eventually led to the defection of the pro-Carey forces from the UE and the formation of a rival union. The problem was that it never acted as a cohesive, disciplined unit. Despite the aspirations of many of its activists to emulate Communist tactics, ACTU was too diverse, its power over its members was too dispersed and unenforceable, and the organization was simply too loose to maximize the impact of its militants. In the UE especially, its adherents had a tendency to work at cross purposes, shifting their ground on the crucial strategic question of whether or not to support secessionist movements without apparent consultation and coordination with each other.[23]

Actists were particularly important in the early stages of organization of the UE anti-leftist coalition. Father Tom Darby, who organized the first UE insurgent movement in the crucial New York City area district in March 1946, was an ACTU associate who taught at the New Rochelle Labor School. He and ACTU leader George Donahue organized a special educational program for UE dissidents and suggested to them the tactics to follow in their struggle to oust the union's leadership. Under their direction, the anti-Communist movement expanded its base to encompass opposition groups in seven UE locals in the area. With an expanding basis in the New York metropolitan region, the group called a national meeting in Pittsburgh in August 1946, out of which emerged the UE Members for Democratic Action, the core of the anti-leftist insurgency for the next three years.[24]

In Pittsburgh, Father Rice was again a "One-Man ACTU," recruiting insurgents in the UE's huge Westinghouse locals 601 and 610, writing their manifestos, addressing their meetings, and trying to coordinate policy with other leaders such as Father Darby.[25] Although officially opposed to secession, he helped the insurgent leaders of two UE locals steer them into the UAW after Reuther's victory.[26] Secretly subsidized by Murray, Rice would attend UE conventions and direct the anti-Communists from a balcony overlooking the convention floor.[27]

ACTU was also very active in the UAW, where the militant and conspiratorial Detroit chapter threw its weight behind the Reuther forces. More than any other local, it tried to emulate the CP, caucusing before union conventions and conferences and laying down the line to be pursued on all questions. It even improved on the CP technique by issuing mimeographed secret summaries of the line to be taken on all questions and detailed lists of what positions to take on every item on the agenda, replete with summaries of the arguments to be made for each stand.[28] Its "Basic Training Course" taught that "Catholics must form cells in all social groups to bring the world back to Christ."[29]

ACTU had swung behind Reuther even before the war, and in 1946 its newspaper was one of the first to leap on Walter Reuther's presidential bandwagon.[30] Since 1941 its members had been especially active in UAW Local 600, the Ford local which, with 65,000 members, was the largest in the country, and gained control twice in the seesaw battle for power during the war. Although the leftists regained control of the local itself in 1946, thirty-three of the seventy-six delegates elected to the Ford council were rightists. At the 1946 UAW convention, these delegates cast 228 votes, more than enough to account for Reuther's 100-vote margin. ACTU then could and did claim, with some justice, that its work had provided the crucial margin of victory for Reuther.[31] The press picked this up and ACTU was given credit for the Reuther victory by a wide variety of sources, from *Fortune* magazine to the "Voice of America."[32]

Exactly who is responsible for the crucial margin in close electoral victories is, of course, impossible to decide. (Indeed, *Fortune* could just as easily have credited the Trotskyists for that particular triumph of anticommunism.)[33] Nevertheless, ACTU did play a major role in the Reuther victory in the crucial eastern Michigan area. Indeed, to some UAW leftists, it began to appear that the struggle within the union was taking the form that Actist ideologists had predicted: a struggle between the Communists and the Catholics, with Reuther being forced to throw in his lot with the latter.[34] This, however, is to look at the union through the perspective of Wayne County, and ignore the powerful nationwide machine that the Reuthers created entirely independently of ACTU or any other Catholic group in the union.

Aside from its activities in the UE and the UAW, the impact of ACTU itself was not particularly great. Its labor schools did train anti-Communist leaders in a number of unions in the parliamentary skills that enabled them to hold their own against Communists in the interminable parliamentary wrangles that wracked union meetings,[35] but ACTU labor schools were often given credit in the media for the achievements of much more numerous labor schools run by other Catholic anticommunist groups.[36] For example, ACTU was described as leading the assault on Michael Quill's leadership in the Transport Workers Union when its rivals, the Jesuits, were more involved. The two leaders of the major insurgency against Quill were office workers who had attended the New York Jesuits' Xavier Labor School during the war. Upon graduation in 1944 they tried to form a rival to the TWU by organizing the unorganized in the New York transit companies into an independent union. When their efforts proved futile, they joined the TWU where, under the tutelage of Xavier priests, they managed to get control of one segment of the bus drivers' section of the union.

They and the priests carefully recruited 125 men to be leaders of the insurgent movement and sent them to Xavier, where they were instructed in parliamentary procedure, anticommunism, and the usual curriculum. These men then fanned out in the union and began working arduously to loosen the leftist grip on it. By 1948, every one of the officers of the New York Omnibus unit of the TWU was a Xavier grad, and the Jesuit-trained rebels had made real inroads into such Quill strongholds as the IRT subway workers.[37]

Catholic labor schools were just part of a much larger stream of Church-influenced anti-Communists in CIO unions. A group of radical Jewish social workers attempting to overthrow the Communist leadership of the United Office and Professional Workers found themselves deluged with the unwanted aid of priests sent from the "power house," the Madison Avenue mansion which was the headquarters of Cardinal Spellman and the New York City archdiocese.[38] Some priests, afraid of an anti-Catholic backlash, acted in secret. When in 1946 a Jesuit professor of Commerce at St. Louis University wrote Father Rice about his organizing the opposition in the leftist-dominated St. Louis CIO-IUC and his supporting the anti-Communists in the local UE, he warned that disclosure of his involvement "would be disastrous."[39] Other priests were not as discreet about their activities. Indeed, leftist unionists often thought of themselves as facing invasions of the priesthood. Chase Powers, leftist vice-president of Mine, Mill, observed that at the union's 1946 convention "at no time were there less than ten priests on the floor, including a set that relieved each other, taking it down verbatim in shorthand, sitting right opposite . . . which is a hell of a situation."[40]

Catholic activity at the 1946 Mine, Mill convention was the climax of a loosely coordinated campaign by a number of disparate churchmen to overturn the union's leftist leadership. Two of the Catholics running on the anti-Communist slate had given some priests lists of the anti-Communist candidates. The priests then sent the lists to clergymen friends throughout the country, asking their help in this vital battle. Compunctions over interfering in internal union politics were easily overcome. As a priest at St. Louis University explained to a colleague in El Paso, Texas, the election campaign provided "a rare opportunity to implement our opposition to communism in a practical decisive way."[41] Far to the north in Cleveland, priests at John Carroll University recruited their students to distribute handbills at factory gates in support of the anti-Communist slate.[42]

Father Rice was most effective as a pamphleteer and publicist, and in this way the church effort probably had its greatest ramifications. Catholics were inundated with articles calling for purges of Communists in the CIO by Rice and national Catholic magazines such as *Our Sunday Visitor* and the *Catholic Digest*, whose material was often reprinted in local Catholic journals. Rice himself was responsible for a plethora of material. His 1946 article, "How to De-Control Your Union of Communists," evoked a tremendous response. Thousands of copies were reprinted in pamphlet and other forms and distributed in churches and unions throughout the country. His regular articles in *Our Sunday Visitor* were widely read, and his papers are packed with requests for help from as far away as the Panama Canal Zone.[43] He also had a weekly radio program in Pittsburgh and a weekly column on labor in the *Pittsburgh Catholic*. At times, especially when he was attacking Communists in the labor movement, his program would have a national hookup.[44]

The requests for information on fighting Communists in unions led Rice to set up an informal reference service. In 1947, at the end of a widely circulated article called "Philip Murray and the Reds," he asked all unionists who were in doubt as to whether their union or local had "a clean bill of health" to write him for information.[45] The back page of *How to Decontrol Your Union of Communists* had a list of Communist-dominated national unions. Unionists were assured that if they belonged to one of those unions, their locals were bound to be Communist-dominated as well.[46] When hundreds of members of leftist unions wrote in asking for advice, Rice sent them regular mimeographed letters analyzing recent trends in the anti-Communist struggle and giving advice on how to "defeat and thwart the Communists."[47]

The most significant phenomenon, however, was that so much effort accomplished so little with the vast majority of Catholic unionists. More often than not the priests were frustrated by the ineffectiveness of their efforts with Catholic workers. The Communists always seemed well supplied with Catholic leaders whom they could rally to their side, whether they were slyly cynical, occasional churchgoers like Michael Quill, devout Catholics like George Addes, or those like Julius Emspak, Albert Fitzgerald, Harry Bridges, or Martin Durkin (the head of the Office and Professional Workers Union) who could at least produce Catholic baptismal papers.

Furthermore, many Catholic union members not only did not respond to the pleas of the clergy but resented them. Two Catholic leaders of a UE local wooed by Father Rice told him to "go to hell" and trounced his supporters in the local elections. When they worked through local churches, said Rice, some good churchgoers would tell them to "go to hell." Parish priests would sometimes oppose the efforts of the labor priests as well.[48]

Another problem was that the anti-Communists could often find little wrong with the way the Communists were running the unions.

This was the reason why they were forced to over-emphasize foreign policy, despite the conventional wisdom which said that union members were less responsive to foreign policy issues than to anything else. According to Rice, the opposition to the UE leadership had to concentrate on foreign policy because they could not find anything else to criticize. "We'd look and look and we couldn't [find anything]," he recalled; "we examined it with a fine tooth comb to try to find things wrong with them other than that. The indictment was very weak."[49]

But the Catholic hammering on foreign policy issues did have a wider impact. When combined with similar charges of disloyalty from other sources, it spurred federal government intervention on the side of those trying to cleanse the CIO of Communist influence.

There was initial ambivalence and division over the issue at the highest levels of the executive branch. Truman had engendered so much suspicion of himself among CIO leaders during the strike wave of 1946 that he was unwilling to risk alienating them further by publicly attacking Communist influence in the unions. Privately, however, he displayed his concern. In September 1946 with leftist and labor opposition to his domestic and foreign policies on the rise and a waterfront strike led by the NMU and ILWU in swing, he wrote in a private memo: "The Reds, the phonies and the 'parlor pinks' seem to have banded together and are becoming a national danger. I am afraid that they are a sabotage front for Uncle Joe Stalin."[50]

But Truman found it politically prudent to keep his fears private. An attack on communism in the CIO might drive it from his camp. Angered at a threatened railroad strike in 1946, he almost lapsed and wrote a statement attacking Communist influence in labor, but his aide Clark Clifford convinced him to shelve it.[51] However, Undersecretary of War Kenneth Royall was allowed to condemn the strikes for interfering with the national defense program and to call on labor to oust Communists from its ranks. Communist strength within the union movement weakened the United States in the face of the enemy, he said, and might therefore cause war.[52]

Pressure against the Communists in the CIO from within the executive branch mounted in 1947, led primarily by the Justice Department and FBI. During the Allis-Chalmers conflict, for example, an FBI agent gave the company information on the sex lives of leftist leaders in Local 248.[53] When a congressional committee came to town to investigate the local in 1947, FBI agents met with representatives of the *Sentinel* and Allis-Chalmers to help them prepare a case that would lead to perjury charges against the local's leaders.[54] In Washington, FBI agents followed and harassed members of the Public Workers Union, a Communist-dominated union with a substantial black membership. The vast program of FBI sabotage and harassment of the CPUSA which it has admitted existed in the 1950s was likely well under way by 1948 with untold effects on Communist unionists.

Meanwhile, Communists such as the TWU's John Santo, whose immigration status made them susceptible to possible deportation, had cases against them which had been dropped during the war, renewed. In Santo's case, not only was a 1941 charge of illegal entry and false claim of citizenship revived in 1947, but a charge of advocating the overthrow of the government by force was added to the indictment, all of which eventually led to his deportation. The IWA leftists, with their strong Canadian base, were hamstrung by United States immigration officials who blocked the border.[55]

By 1947 anti-Communist unionists who had been appointed to important federal government positions were using their powers against the Communists. CIO leftists thus faced hostility, rather than sympathy, from a purged NLRB. They also contended with the secret machinations of the liberals who staffed the Department of Labor, which was often called in to mediate labor disputes. In June 1947 John Gibson, a UAW anti-Communist who had been appointed assistant secretary of labor in Washington, bragged to Adolph Germer about having used his power as mediator to help the newly-converted Joseph Curran.

I just settled a nation-wide maritime strike in which we gave the Communist Party and Mr. Bridges the soundest trouncing of his career as a labor leader and Joe Curran has been elevated to the position of top dog in the maritime industry, as a result of his East Coast fight for improvements for the workers after Mr. Bridges had started a movement extending agreements without any improvements.[56]

There was no need to concern himself over his boss' reaction, for Secretary of Labor Lewis Schwellenbach, although opposed to Taft-Hartley, declared himself in favor of outlawing the CPUSA and barring its members from unions.[57]

President Truman's Executive Order of March 1947 authorizing "loyalty" investigations of all federal employees and the firing by special boards of those found suspect was a body blow to the United Public Workers. Already harassed by congressional investigators because of a UPW-led strike of congressional cafeteria workers and because it represented over 10,000 federal employees in the strategic Panama Canal Zone, the UPW watched helplessly while many of its activists were fired from their jobs. By the end of 1947 the union's leadership was contemplating divesting itself of the federal workers and setting up a separate, presumably less Communist-implicated, national union of federal employees.[58]

After the January 1948 split in the CIO over the Wallace campaign and the Marshall Plan, the administration became much more overt in its drive on the CIO Communists. In early 1948 it ordered an expanded deportation drive against Communists. John Williamson, Ferdinand Smith, and Irving Potash were detained without bail on Ellis Island while deportation proceedings began.[59] Simultaneously, Justice Department officials went to San Francisco to work on reinstituting deportation proceeding against Harry Bridges. They began by securing indictments against Bridges and two other ILWU executives for perjury and conspiracy regarding Bridges' 1945 naturalization hearing.[60]

The administration was not simply trying to reconstruct its damaged alliance with Murray and the CIO liberals by persecuting their opponents.[61] Internal pressures from within the Cabinet and external ones from public opinion were building up as well. Secretary of Defense James Forrestal, for one, was upset over Truman's veto of the Taft-Hartley bill because he found its anti-Communist aspects attractive. He recorded in his diary that in a Cabinet meeting, he "recalled our experiences during the war with the Brewster strikes, with the Allis-Chalmers strike, and I called attention to the fact that . . . there were many Communists in the CIO organization." He warned that further deterioration of the international situation would lead to Communist sabotage unless the Communists were driven from the CIO.[62]

By March, 1948, administration pressure on Murray was becoming intense. When Truman learned that Communist propagandists in Europe were circulating a denunciation of the Marshall Plan by the San Francisco CIO Council, he called Murray into his office and urged him to take strong action against the "disruptive tactics of certain elements." It was soon after this conference that Murray swung behind the clampdown on the CIO Councils that Brophy had been urging.[63] Lunching with Forrestal on March 30, Murray assured him that they were making progress in weeding out Communists from the CIO, although there were some problems with the UE and some other unions.[64]

The UE leaders received a somewhat different message from Murray, who acknowledged that he was under intense pressure from the administration. He told Albert Fitzgerald several times that, with United States-Soviet relations deteriorating, the heat on the trade union movement was increasing and there was great pressure from the administration on the CIO to clean out the Reds. Murray gave Fitzgerald the impression that Forrestal was pressuring him at Truman's request. Trying to wean Fitzgerald from the Communists (whose "front man" he was thought to be), Murray told Fitzgerald that he was all right, but a number of UE men in the field had "questionable records" and should be let go.[65]

Meanwhile, the administration did what it could to undermine the leadership of the UE and other leftist unions. During 1948 it began to apply pressure on defense contractors who recognized leftist unions to change their bargaining agents. When General Electric constructed a new plant in Schenectady to produce equipment for the Atomic Energy Commission, the AEC ordered GE not to recognize the UE as the bargaining agent for the new plant, although it was the agent for the other GE plants in the area. Furthermore, the AEC said that GE should continue bargaining with the UE in other plants working on equipment for the AEC only if their union leaders confessed to past and present Communist activities and passed loyalty checks.[66]

While the stick was being wielded against the leftists, the CIO liberals were enticed by the carrot. The wartime system of appointing union leaders to government boards and positions expanded in the postwar period. CIO-PAC and its AFL counterpart provided sound political reasons for cutting unions in on their share of Washington-dispensed patronage. Thanks to the cold war there were outlets for the talents of unionists in all sorts of agencies concerned with foreign policy. As the administration became convinced of the benefits to be gained from enlisting American unions behind it in the cold war crusade, the number of foreign policy positions for unionists multiplied, ranging from posts as labor attachés at American embassies abroad through special "advisory" positions with the burgeoning new foreign aid organizations to secret appointments to carry out the suborning of foreign unions.[67]

Executive branch persecution of leftist unionists was paralleled by a similar trend in Congress. The Taft-Hartley Act, whose most damaging effects on Communists began to be felt in 1948, was of great importance, but so was the growing pattern of harassment of embattled leftist unionists by congressional committees. Congress got off to a relatively slow start in November 1945 with the hearings of the House Un-American Activities Committee, which starred the testimony of Louis Budenz, a top Communist functionary who had just defected from the party. Although his testimony warning that the Communists were on the verge of taking over the CIO and naming Harry Bridges and Julius Emspak as top party members caused a minor sensation, Bundenz seemed too much the opportunist to be of much use to other labor anti-Communists. After a speech in Milwaukee in which he charged that the UAW Local 248 leaders were Communists, he was quite uncooperative in giving more information to Milwaukee *Sentinel* reporters hoping for more fuel for their anti-Communist crusade. They discovered that, like many anti-Communist witnesses before and after him, Budenz realized that his future was dependent on having a steady stream of fresh material to divulge. They decided that he wished to make his revelations piecemeal, exploiting them to the utmost, and found him "a rather contemptible person."[68]

Congressional investigations of communism in the union movement proliferated in 1947 and were characterized by a similar pattern: congressional committees were brought in by influential local employers or anti-Communist unionists to "expose" the leaders of leftist union locals who could not be ejected by conventional means as Communists and hopefully to prepare the way for their prosecution for perjury or contempt of Congress.

This worked especially well against the leaders of UAW Local 248 in Wisconsin. Thanks to the intervention of Allis-Chalmers and the editor of the Milwaukee *Sentinel* with his friend, "Charlie" Kirsten, the head of the House Education and Labor Committee, Kirsten's committee summoned the leftist local leaders first to Washington and then to specially convened hearings in Milwaukee. Working with FBI and Allis-Chalmers investigators, the committee staff managed to trip Harold Christoffel, the most talented and dangerous of the leftist leaders, into apparent perjury, for which he was indicted. This played a major role in the leftist loss of control over the local.[69]

Also in 1947, the pattern was repeated in Hollywood, where Communist sympathizers had made inroads in some of the unions, most notably in the CIO's Screen Writers' Guild and the Confederation of Studio Unions. Hollywood people concerned over hints of pro-Soviet and anti-capitalist attitudes in some wartime movies had recruited 1,100 members into an organization called the Motion Picture Alliance for the Preservation of American Ideals, but it had little effect in an America still enthralled with Big Three unity.[70] After the war, though, the anti-Communist campaign was pursued tirelessly by Ray Brewer, the liberal, ex-Socialist president of the AFL's International Association of Theater and Studio Engineers, the rival of the CSU.

At first, Brewer's warnings were ignored by most movie "moguls," who suspected him of using the issue to gain industry support for what was essentially a jurisdictional dispute. IATSE's reputation for corruption also made outsiders reluctant to join it on the barricades.[71] As the political climate changed, however, Brewer was able to rally more support. By October 1946 the AFL's Matthew Woll charged that movie houses were showing the films of "treasonable stars and writers." "Light-minded" stars such as Orson Welles and Myrna Loy imagined that they were working for the oppressed, he warned, but were in fact working for a tyrannical organization.[72]

The Motion Picture Alliance for the Preservation of American Ideals, the Teamsters union, the California State Federation of Labor, and even the CIO's Screen Actors' Guild soon lined up behind Brewer's calls for a Hollywood anti-Communist crusade. A prolonged CSU strike in 1947 and 1948 strengthened his hand. Brewer and the anti-Communists (as well as the obvious gold mine of headlines to be garnered) convinced HUAC to step in. The committee's 1947 investigation of Communist influence in Hollywood put the leftists to rout. In an industry so susceptible to publicity and public opinion, hostile congressional hearings were a devastating weapon. In November 1947 RKO studios became the first to announce that it would not hire Communists.[73]

In the Screen Actors' Guild, liberals worked furiously to sever their ties with Communists. Its new, "moderate" executive board announced that it would require all officers to sign the Taft-Hartley affidavit, a decision ratified by an overwhelming vote of the membership.[74] After HUAC's first investigation of Hollywood, even the sophisticated leftists who had dominated the Screen Writers' Guild could not resist the pressure against them. In the next elections, the "progressive" slate went down to defeat.[75]

With the atmosphere in Hollywood changed so markedly, it was easy for the studios to resist the CSU strike, and the CSU was destroyed.[76] Later, in 1952, Brewer acknowledged that the crucial factor in eliminating Communist influence in Hollywood unionism was HUAC, whose 1947 hearings "hit Hollywood like a broad slap in the face."[77]

The split in the CIO over Wallace and the Marshall Plan brought a great upsurge in congressional investigation of communism in labor unions. HUAC still kept its hand in the labor pot,[78] and in June 1948 the House Committee on Education and Labor (or Kirsten committee) began a lengthy series of hearings on communism in labor unions, hauling before it leaders of the UE, Fur Workers, NMU, and TWU in obvious attempts to expose them to perjury indictments. Although it lost the headline-grabbing Hollywood investigation to HUAC, the Kirsten committee provided stiff competition for HUAC in investigating other leftist labor unions. After starting with New York Local 65 of the Retail Workers Union in July 1948,[79] it sank its teeth into the largest of the leftist unions, the UE. Its hearings on UE during September and October of that year followed essentially the same pattern as HUAC's "investigations": a series of comparisons of the foreign policy line of the union newspaper and conventions with that of the Soviet Union, followed by evidence from relatively uninformed informers and "experts," and climaxed by the reluctant appearance of leftist "witnesses" who were, in fact, defendants. Matles and Emspak were suitably defiant and sensitive to their rights, while Carey was unsure whether he needed the aid of these outsiders from Congress, opposed as he was to the activities of their competitor, HUAC. Like the HUAC hearings, the main objectives seemed to be to force the leftists to perjure themselves and to "expose" them to UE members who would throw out their Communist leaders.[80]

Leftists had to face persecution by legislators outside of Washington as well. In Wisconsin, where the so-called "Little Dies Committee" had pursued leftist unionists in 1941, there was a revival of legislative hounding of the strong leftist element in the state CIO. In the state of Washington, a newly-created state HUAC pursued the IWA leftists. In February 1948 it held hearings in which over forty witnesses labelled Harry Bridges, Harold Pritchett, Mickey Orton, and most of the top leftist leaders in the IWA as party members. The CIO liberals aiding the right were overjoyed. Roy Atkinson, the CIO regional director for Washington, wrote Germer that "The Party machine is getting the worst licking and upset that it ever received in this area."[81]

State governors also saw the advantages of carving out an anti-Communist reputation and even intervened in local union elections. In February 1947, as elections approached in the Communist-dominated UAW Local 155 in Detroit, Governor Sigler of Michigan announced: "I want to give the right kind of support to anti-Communist union leaders. . . . I want to give the decent union leaders every chance to clean this situation up."[82]

On the local level, municipal politicians and police forces could be especially helpful or harmful to embattled union leaders. Allis-Chalmers and the *Sentinel* received the full cooperation of the Milwaukee police department in their battle in support of the anti-Communists in the Wisconsin State CIO. The Milwaukee Police anti-subversive squad threw open its files to the rightists as they searched for material to incriminate the leftists.[83] In New York, when Joseph Curran turned against the Communists, Mayor William O'Dwyer assigned a squad of twenty New York City policemen to protect him from jeering NMU members as he entered and left his office. When Curran held a meeting to eject the elected Port Agent of New York and his democratically-elected slate from the union, 250 city policemen were assigned to protect him from the thousands who tried to howl him down, allowing him to railroad his wishes through despite the large majority against him.[84]

O'Dwyer also helped Michael Quill keep his opponents at bay in 1948 after he defected. According to Quill's biographer, at a secret meeting with Quill before the transit negotiations that year, "O'Dwyer patiently asked how much Mike needed to beat the Reds' appeal to his membership." He then conceded all that Quill asked in terms of wages and allowed the TWU to control the checkoff of union dues to strengthen Quill's hand even further. Then, they both went through the charade of public negotiations, with O'Dwyer yielding to Quill in full view of everyone to ensure that Quill received all the credit.[85]

The many-layered pattern of opposition to leftist unionism was repeated in many ways in different localities. Throughout the nation, entrenched leftists found themselves facing the combined onslaught of virtually every powerful group in the community. Whereas in cities such as Pittsburgh and Detroit in the North the UE and UAW found the Catholic church arrayed against them, in the South, Mine, Mill faced the Klan, opposed to its integrationism as well as its leftism. For leftists on the local level, it seemed that the most powerful forces in society had concentrated on one objective: to get rid of them. For many, there was little hope of holding off that vast array of forces. Years later, Nat Ganley, a Communist business agent in a Detroit UAW local, recalled his defeat in 1947: "A Nat Ganley, for example," he said, "to win an election had to fight the entire pressure coming from the Federal Government of the United States, the National CIO leadership, the Catholic Church, employers as a group. . . ." His voice trailed off.[86]

Yet of all these elements, the crucial one was clearly the federal government. The Justice Department and Taft-Hartley stand out as the most effective outside forces in destroying Communist power in the union movement, forces whose suppression of civil liberties was sanctioned by the cold war. Yet neither of these forces would have been able to do so had it not been for the split between Communists and liberals in the CIO itself. As Clark Clifford told Truman in 1946, a Democratic administration would not have been able to mount a wholesale onslaught on communism in a united CIO.

NOTES

1. The Reverend Charles Owen Rice, OH 2, Pennsylvania State University, Archives of Labor History, State College, Pa. (hereafter PSUA), 24.

2. Arthur Eggleston, "Labor and Civil Liberties," *The Nation*, vol. 174, no. 126 (June 28, 1952), 648.

3. Richard Boyer and Herbert Morais, *Labor's Untold Story* (New York: Marzani and Munsell, 1955), 345.

4. Eggleston, "Labor and Civil Liberties," 649.

5. C. Wright Mills, *The New Men of Power, America's Labor Leaders* (New York: Harcourt, Brace, 1948), 198.

6. George Gallup, *Gallup Poll: Public Opinion, 1935-1971* (New York: Random House, 1975), 601.

250 Communism, Anticommunism, and the CIO

7. Ibid., 492, 565, 567.

8. Ibid., 593, 690.

9. Ibid., 587.

10. Ibid., 640.

11. Victor Lasky, "Red Wedge in Hawaii," *Plain Talk* (May 1948), 41.

12. Jules Weinberg, "Priests, Workers, and Communists," *Harper's Magazine* (November 1948): 50.

13. See A. J. Liebling, *The Press* (New York: Ballantine Books, 1960), for some rather bizarre examples of this.

14. Affidavit of High Swofford, ex-*Sentinel* labor reporter, January 23, 1950, copy in Nat Ganley, Papers, Wayne State University Archives of Labor History and Urban Affairs, Detroit, Mich. (hereafter WSUA), Box 7, Folder 15.

15. Ibid.

16. Al Leggat, OH, WSUA, 52.

17. Father Thomas Darby to Rice, August 12, 1946, The Reverend Charles Owen Rice, Papers, PSUA, Reel C-D.

18. A 1946 survey of junior clergy in Connecticut indicated that a large majority now gave a qualified yes to the question of whether workers were morally obliged to join a union. They generally thought there was too much communism in the CIO, but preferred it over the AFL because of its industrial unionism and non-restrictive policies. *Time*, July 22, 1946.

19. Michael Harrington, "Catholics in the Labor Movement," *Labor History*, vol. 1, no. 2 (fall 1960), demonstrates this quite effectively. Frank Emspak, "The Association of Catholic Trade Unionists and the United Automobile Workers" (M.A. thesis, University of Wisconsin, 1968), came to similar conclusions.

20. John Cort, "Nine Years of ACTU," *America*, April 6, 1946.

21. Rice to the Reverend Thomas Darby, June 13, 1946; Darby to Rice, June 14, 1946, Rice Papers, Reel C-D.

22. Ibid., Darby to Rice, August 12, 1946.

23. Harrington, "Catholics in the Labor Movement."

24. Ibid.

25. Ibid.; Rice to Darby, June 14, 1946, Rice Papers, Reel C-D.

26. Rice, OH 2, 19; Harry Block, OH, PSUA, 28.

27. Fitzgerald recalled that Rice attended the conventions in grand style, and lived in a hotel suite, but this was likely the product of charges that emerged from the 1950 convention when Rice used a suite rented by UEMDA for some meetings. He himself stayed at a different hotel. Albert Fitzgerald, OH, PSUA, 18; Rice to Martin [?], August 28, 1950, Rice Papers, Reel C-D.

28. ACTU, Confidential memoradum to Actist delegates to Michigan State CIO Convention, July 7, 1945, Association of Catholic Trade Unionists, Detroit Chapter, Records, WSUA, Series 1, Box 3.

29. "ACTU Basic Training Course. Lecture Number IV. 'The Errors of Collectivism.' " ACTU Records, Series 1, Box 1.

30. *Wage Earner*, February 8, 1946.

31. *Commonweal*, 43 (March 22, 1946): 577, cited in Emspak, "ACTU," 67.

32. See clippings in ACTU Records, Series 1, Box 1, especially those from *Fortune*, *Michigan Catholic*, and United States Department of State, Voice of America, Labor Analysis no. 24, May 18, 1948.

33. Their hatred of the CPUSA had led their small band of delegates to hold their noses and throw what they later realized was the critical number of votes behind Reuther, a move most would soon regret.

34. Carl Haessler, OH, WSUA, 267.

35. Emspak, "ACTU," 49; Phillip Taft, "The Association of Catholic Trade Unionists," *Industrial and Labor Relations Review*, 11 (January 1949): 208; *Fortune*, 39 (January 1949): 208.

36. Weinberg, "Priests, Workers," 53. By 1948 there were over 100 permanent labor schools in the country, twenty-four of which were run by Jesuits, thirty-two by diocesan authorities, and the rest by Catholic fraternal organizations. There was at least one in every industrial city in the nation. Each year approximately 7,500 students graduated from their two-year courses.

37. Ibid., 50-56.

38. Paul Jacobs, *Is Curly Jewish?* (New York: Atheneum, 1966), 153.

39. Leo Brown, S.J., to Rice, June 28, 1946, Rice Papers, Reels C-D.

40. Chase Powers, OH, PSUA, 43.

41. Sam Twomay to "Jim P.C.," October 15, 1946, in CIO, Papers, Office of the Secretary-Treasurer, James Carey, (hereafter Carey Papers), WSUA, Box 111.

42. Statement of Alex Balint, March 20, 1947, in Edward Hadden to Richard Stern, March 20, 1947, Carey Papers, Box 111.

43. See Rice Papers, Reels C-D, *passim*, and Rice to George Roland, May 22, 1948, Reels C-D.

44. Rice to Religion in Life Program, YMCA, January 30, 1952, Rice Papers, Reel A.

45. "Rice, Murray and the Reds," *Catholic Digest*, 11 (May 1947): 101.

46. The Reverend Charles Owen Rice, *How to Decontrol Your Union of Communists* (n.p., 1948). When Harry Bridges wrote inquiring as to why his ILWU was on the list, Rice replied: "My chief reason for listing the ILWU as a Communist-controlled union is that you control it." Bridges to Rice, July 17, 1948, Rice to Bridges, July 22, 1948, Rice Papers, Reel A.

47. Rice, "ACTU. Exchange" [January 1949?], ACTU Records, Series 1, Box 3.

48. Rice, OH 2, PSUA, 19, 23.

49. Ibid., 13.

50. Lloyd Gardner and William O'Neill, *Looking Backward* (New York: McGraw-Hill, 1973), 411.

51. Richard Freeland, *The Truman Doctrine and the Origins of McCarthyism* (New York: Alfred Knopf, 1972), 300.

52. *The New York Times*, September 25, 1946.

53. "Swofford Affidavit," Fred Blair, Papers, State Historical Society of Wisconsin, Madison, Wis.

54. Fred Blair to Robert Friedman, July 13, 1948, Blair Papers.

55. Irving Abella, *Nationalism, Communism, and Canadian Labour* (Toronto: University of Toronto Press, 1973), 119.

56. John Gibson to Germer, June 23, 1947, Adolph Germer, Papers, State Historical Society of Wisconsin, Madison, Wis.

57. *NYT*, October 15, 1947.

58. CIO, *Daily Proceedings* of the Constitutional Convention, 1949, 208-13. The idea was dropped.

59. *NYT*, March 2, 1948. Deportation proceedings against others, including John Santo of the TWU, had begun earlier in mid-1947.

60. Ibid., May 27, 1948.

61. Richard Freeland suggests this, as well as that it wished to attack labor opponents unprotected by the CIO. Freeland, *Truman Doctrine*, 301-2.

62. Walter Millis, ed., *The Forrestal Diaries* (New York: Viking, 1951), 280.

63. O. J. Dekom, "The Washington Reporter," *Plain Talk*, April 1948, 34.

64. Millis, ed., *Forrestal Diaries*, 69, 406.

65. Fitzgerald, OH, PSUA, 20.

66. U.S. Congress, House, Committee on Un-American Activities, *Hearings Regarding Communist Infiltration of Labor Unions*, 81st Congress, 1st sess. (1949), 866-71.

67. See Ronald Radosh, *American Labor and United States Foreign Policy* (New York: Random House, 1969); Harvey Levenstein, *Labor Organizations in the United States and Mexico: A History of Their Relations* (Westport, Ct.: Greenwood Press, 1971), ch. 10-13, and Philip Agee, *Inside the Company: CIA Diary* (Harmondsworth: Penguin, 1975).

68. "Swofford Affidavit," 25.

69. Ibid.

70. David J. Saposs, *Communism in American Unions—A Bibliography* (Ithaca: Cornell University Press, 1969), 69.

71. Ibid., 67-68.

72. *NYT*, October 1, 1946.

73. Ibid., November 23, 1947.

74. Ibid., November 23, 1947, January 16, 1948.

75. Saposs, *Communism in American Unions*, 78.

76. Ibid., 70.

77. U.S. Congress, House, Committee on Un-American Activities, *Hearings Regarding Communist Infiltration in Hollywood*, 82nd Cong., 2nd sess. (1952), 492.

78. U.S. Congress, House, Committee on Un-American Activities, *Hearings Regarding Communist Infiltration in Hollywood*, 80th Cong., 1st sess. (1947).

79. *Daily Worker*, September 6, 1948.

80. U.S. Congress, House, Committee on Education and Labor, *Investigation of Communist Infiltration of UERMWA*, 80th Cong., 2nd sess. (1948), *passim*. James Carey, Oral History Interview, Oral History Collection of Columbia University, New York, N.Y., 231-32.

81. Roy Atkinson to Germer, February 2, 1948, Germer Papers.

82. Detroit *News*, February 14, 1947.

83. "Swofford Affidavit."

84. *Labor Action*, November 28, 1949.

85. L. H. Whitemore, *Man Who Ran the Subways: The Story of Mike Quill* (N.Y.: Holt, Rinehart and Winston, 1960), 151.

86. Nat Ganley, OH, WSUA, 67.

13 THE LEFTIST FRONT CRACKS

Successful insurgencies are rare in American unionism, especially on the national level. Outside of periods of employer-employee conflict, most unions are characterized by low levels of member activity. Compared with British and European unions, post-World War II American unions have a very high proportion of full-time job-holders who can be mobilized to turn back insurgencies. Furthermore, the immense size of the United States makes it prohibitively costly in time and money for unionists who are not full-time union employees to assemble movements diverse enough to overthrow a leadership with a number of regional bases of support. It is no surprise then that two key events destroying leftist power within the CIO were not insurgencies but were shifts by individual leaders who succeeded in taking large groups of union job-holders with them. The departures of the NMU and TWU from the Communist camp were the result of coups from above rather than eruptions from below.

The shift in the NMU was in large part the result of a split among the Communists themselves. Although the Communist machine that built the union managed to stay reasonably united during the hectic days of prewar organizing, the war and the period of bureaucratic stability it inaugurated led to conflicts among the leftists in the union bureaucracy. Disagreements over issues such as how to deal with the government degenerated into deep personal hatreds. Jealousies over the division of power and suspicions that some officials had enriched themselves in office turned Communist against Communist.

The relationship between Curran and the Communists had worked to their mutual advantage before the war. The Communists had used his image and reputation as an organizer, and he had used their organizational talent to run the day-to-day operations of the union and extend its sphere. With the end of the initial organizing phase of the union and the maturing of its bureaucracy, Curran's usefulness to the Communists seemed to diminish. Moreover, one group of Communists, headed by the union's top Communist functionary, Vice-President Frederick "Blackie" Myers, began to suspect that the union leaders closest to Curran, a number of whom were Communists and fellow-travellers, were crooked. In 1942, Myers was vexed by rumors that M. Hedley Stone, the union's Communist treasurer, was embezzling money from the treasury and taking kickbacks on union construction contracts. Myers, who was regarded as scrupulously honest, was also disturbed by even more sinister stories that Stone and Al Lannon, head of the Waterfront Section of the CP, were being paid by Standard Oil to sabotage the union's efforts to organize its ships.[1]

In the fall of 1943, Myers, angered by Stone's inflexibility regarding a minor dispute with a shipping line, charged into a meeting in Curran's office and accused Stone, Harry Alexander, and Tommy Ray, all party members on the NMU Executive Board, with fomenting an uneccessary strike that would damage the war effort. Stone's reply was hardly oil on troubled waters: "You know, Blackie," he said, "I would as soon kill you as look as you." For six hours the suspicion and hatred that had been building up, dividing the union's Communists, welled to the surface. Finally, Myers broke down and cried, claiming that his nerves were on edge and he was not himself, and the five repaired to a nearby bar.[2]

But the alcohol could not heal the deep division that opened between the Communists surrounding Myers and those around Curran. The union bureaucracy, dominated by Myers, reported to Myers and Ferdinand Smith, the union's West Indies-born secretary. Curran, Stone, and Vice-President Jack Lawrenson (another Communist supporting Curran) were bypassed. Tensions heightened in October 1944 when a union committee rejected Curran's objections to Smith's candidacy for the secretaryship, a challenge based on the constitutional requirement of American citizenship for incumbents of that post.[3] Curran feared that control of the union was slipping away from him; he was being treated as a mere figurehead, his directives ignored by people who listened only to Myers.[4] Seething because Myers and the Communists took an increasing share of the credit for having organized the union, Curran was infuriated by a report by Myers which he interpreted as saying, "if it were not for Blackie Myers, there wouldn't be any union."[5]

The contempt of the Myers' faction for Curran and his supporters was reinforced by continuing suspicion that they were personally profiting from their union offices. In 1945 rumors circulated that

Stone had purchased an $18,000 bungalow, was depositing $50 a week in banks, and was profiting on real estate he bought for the union. When Curran went to Europe in the fall of 1945, the Myers group hired an auditor to check the books. The auditor seemed to confirm their worst suspicions when he reported, wrongly it turned out, that Stone had "misplaced" some $340,000 in union funds.[6] Stone was expelled from the party, along with Tommy Ray, the party "commissar" who had protected him during the war, and Harry Alexander, the union's New Orleans port agent.

Curran was infuriated and refused to pay the auditor's bill. Meanwhile, he discovered that an order he had issued to port agents in August 1945 to hire "no more people than necessary" was being ignored. From August to December, the union's monthly payroll had jumped from $78,000 to $112,000. Most of the new officials, he suspected, were Communist retainers with sinecures.[7]

In October 1945 while in Moscow with a CIO delegation, Curran slipped into James Carey's room and confided that he was having trouble with the Communists in the NMU. They used the union for party purposes and had tapped the wires between his wife's and secretary's phones, he said; he gave Carey the distinct impression that a break was near.[8] On the same trip, Len De Caux noted that Curran was "a sophisticate on communists" and came to think that the NMU Communists underestimated him.[9]

If anything, this was an understatement. Curran and his supporters were convinced, likely with reason, that rumors of peculation on their part were being circulated by the party.[10] The party people realized too late that they might have spread the seeds of their own rather than Curran's destruction. Their belated attempt to appease him failed.

In December the union's National Council set up a subcommittee to investigate the "disunity" at union headquarters. Composed entirely of Communists, with the exception of Curran, the subcommittee nevertheless found valid Curran's complaints over being bypassed and kept in the dark by Myers and his group. There had been a "breakdown of administration" in the union, the report said, and "the refusal in some cases of officials to accept the President as the executive officer of the union has been a large contributing factor to this condition."[11] But it was too little too late. Curran, his ego badly bruised, and his allies expelled from the party vowed to cut the puppet strings that the Communists seemed to be attaching to him. He added his "dissenting comments" to the report, charging that the union had become the prisoner of a "machine." He would be satisfied only by the resignations of the machine's leaders, Myers, Smith, and Vice-President Howard McKenzie. "I will not be a party to a machine," he declared, calling on the membership to help "smash it" and "bust it up."[12]

Curran's alienation doomed one of the Communists' pet projects: the Committee for Maritime Unity, formed in 1946 by the NMU, the ILWU, and Bridges' satellite unions to coordinate maritime union policy and provide the basis for another assault on Joseph Ryan's control over the East and Gulf Coast waterfronts.[13] Curran suspected that the project might serve to extend Bridges' control to the East Coast, and make him more subservient to the party's leaders. His fears were exacerbated by the aftermath of the CMU-sponsored maritime strike in the summer of 1946 when he suspected the Communists of circulating rumors that the settlement to which he agreed had "sold out" the membership.[14]

Bridges met with Curran in the fall of 1946 trying to patch up their differences but the mission failed.[15] Curran still saw the CMU as a vehicle for imposing control over him by Bridges and the party. In December 1946 he signalled his irrevocable break with the party by resigning as co-chairman of the CMU.

The NMU was by then wracked by an acrimonious, often violent civil war. Curran's reelection as president in late 1946 by a three-to-one margin confirmed his personal popularity. Significantly, his 1946 campaign had centered not on communism but on the Communists' alleged extravagance, waste, and "misuse" of union funds for political purposes. He had absolved the CP itself of any desire to take over the union, but concentrated on charging that some party members wanted to get control of all union offices and discredit him. A major theme of his campaign was to return power to the rank and file.[16] But the war was by no means won; the Communist-supported caucus retained control of half of the executive board and the large majority of the union's elected and appointed officials.

Although in the anti-Communist climate of 1947 and 1948 Curran's battle was widely regarded outside the union as one motivated by anticommunism per se, within the union, Curran continued to emphasize Communist waste and mismanagement: the inflated payroll and the union money diverted to Communist political causes remained the main theme of his campaign. Indeed, until 1948 Curran had agreed with the Communists' foreign policy and, although he supported Truman rather than Wallace, he continued to regard himself as a leftist. The main benefit to be derived from ejecting the Communists from control of the union's national council, he said in 1948, would be a salary cut for union bureaucrats and a return to a tight budget.[17]

Curran had the support of the national CIO and the federal government, as well as that of the municipal government and most of the media in the all-important New York district. The anti-Communists in the Federal Conciliation Service, who imposed a settlement favorable to the union in the 1947 negotiations, helped to neutralize the Communist charges that Curran had "sold out" to the bosses in 1946.[18]

Curran concentrated much of his initial fire on one of the weakest links in the Communist chain, Joseph Stack, a New York Jew who had been elevated to a union vice-presidency in 1946. Curran portrayed Stack as typical of the kind of people who were trying to grab control of the union. When anticommunism was in fashion, charged Curran, Stack had been one of the most vicious "Red-baiters" in the union. Then, when the wind changed, he joined the Communists. Curran charged him with disrupting the union by not reporting on organizing drives to its president, ignoring the "advice and counsel" of the president, and misusing union funds through contributions to left-wing causes.[19] The battle over Stack became the crucial test of strength between the two sides, climaxing in a formal hearing at which Stack was removed from office by a trial committee; it was followed by two uproarious meetings of the New York membership which at first failed to ratify the order but finally succeeded. As the results of the second vote were announced, Curran roared that "The Waterfront Section of the Communist Party is not going to run this union!"[20]

The Communists were down, but not out. After a month-long canvass of the membership, Howard Young, a leftist with Communist support, was elected to replace Stack on the Executive Board. He won by a hair's breadth, 10,475 to 10,091, and restored the three-to-three balance on the union's Executive Board, but the victory was to be the leftists' last major one.[21] By the time the NMU convention met in New York City in October 1947, Curran's forces had gained control of a majority of the delegates and the uncoordinated Communists were in disarray. Curran and his supporters pushed through a new constitution that disabled the Communists by strengthening the presidency at the expense of the positions they controlled. Curran's victory was hailed by shipowners as a major step toward labor stability. *The New York Times* praised the new constitution for turning power back to the rank and file. Vice-Admiral Thomas Kinkaid, the head of the United States Maritime Commission, urged the union to back Curran in his struggle against the Communists.[22]

Strengthened by the new constitution, the Curran group moved in for the kill with a barrage of attacks on Communist waste and mismanagement of union funds in the crucial Port of New York district. Thanks primarily to a two-to-one majority there, they won a sweeping victory in the election for national officers in July 1948.[23]

Although Curran had promised that a victory for his slate would bring no "Communist-style purge," it was immediately followed by one of enormous proportions. As official after official was fired, Curran and Stone had a broom hoisted over the union's headquarters, the Navy signal that a clean sweep of the area had been made.[24]

Curran's victory owed little to anticommunism per se. It owed much to the Communist blunders in handling their union power, blunders whose effects they could not recoup at the October 1947 convention in part because they could not function as the smoothly running, well-coordinated machine, they were reputed to be. Too late they realized that Curran's popularity among the rank and file had been a much more important factor in the success of the union than they had acknowledged. They felt secure enough to dispense with Curran at the same time that they stacked the union bureaucracy with Communists. They might have been able to accomplish one or the other, but could not do both. They might have been able to shunt Curran aside had they built up a lean union bureaucracy with the respect of the membership. Conversely, they could have padded the bureaucracy had they continued to butter up Curran and not threatened to eliminate him completely from decision-making.

The Communists' error was compounded because, while the incipient bourgeois life-style of Hedley Stone and other Curran supporters may have fed doubts about their commitment to austere unionism, the Communists left themselves open to charges of financial waste of a different nature. Although they could never prove their suspicions about peculation in the Curran camp, the Communist hangers-on in the NMU were there for everyone to see, especially in the key Port of New York, which was too close to party headquarters for the political leadership to resist. Thus, the Communists, whose success in so many other contexts had been the result of their reputation for hard work, self denial, and honesty, were defeated in the NMU because they left themselves open to charges of extravagance and the waste of union funds. A year after Curran's victory, Daniel Bell wrote for *Fortune* magazine that Curran's victory was "a tribute to the confidence of ordinary seamen in Curran's honesty and integrity." In words that he may well wish to forget, Bell hailed the new administration for "pruning away the expensive and fancy services that the party-liners had loaded into the unions."[25]

Twenty years later, Curran had become the autocratic dictator of a dwindling union in an industry whose jobs were evaporating. He was probably the highest paid leader of perhaps the smallest union in America. From his plush office in the palatial "Joseph Curran Annex" to the NMU's equally pretentious head office building in New York, he masterminded one last plundering of the union's dwindling treasury when he pushed through a retirement pension scheme for himself that made his few remaining defenders blush. By the late 1970s, the union was almost bankrupt, the white marble buildings with the porthole windows had been sold, and Curran's successors had to resort to court proceedings to recover some of the immense amounts of money which the leader of the "rank and file" had awarded himself. Had the Communists not blundered in their handling of the vain man whom they tried to turn into a "stooge," the union might have fared better. Neither they nor anyone else could have done much to avert the decline in membership, which was directly related to the decline of the United States merchant marine, although they might have expanded into other fields. What they might have done, however, was to keep the NMU in the leftist camp in the CIO when it most mattered, during the anti-Communist onslaught of the late 1940s. Their failure to do so led to the shift of some 80,000 NMU members to the other camp, a major contribution to the growing feeling that anticommunism was snowballing in the CIO even though the origins of the move had little to do with communism.

The Communists also mishandled Michael Quill, whose defection was less expected than was Curran's and was probably even more avoidable. Quill had had squabbles with the party leadership during the war and was resentful of the lack of support for his union in the *Daily Worker* on a number of local New York issues in 1945 and 1946.[26] Moreover, Quill often turned to ousted leader Earl Browder for advice, and Browder took to ghostwriting many of his political memoranda.[27]

Nevertheless, Quill showed no signs of wanting to leave the party and gave no indication that he disagreed with its overall line. Revelling in his prominent role in New York City politics, he basked in the notoriety of being "Red Mike" on the City Council. When Curran, in breaking with the Communists, resigned as president of the Communist-dominated Greater New York CIO Council, Quill stepped into his shoes. It was only a directive from the CP political leadership threatening his power in his own union that forced Quill to break with the party.

The basis for the crisis was laid by an an anti-Communist insurgency movement led by Catholic labor school graduates advised by Xavier Labor School priests. Aided by the Crown Heights Catholic labor school, anti-Communists made their first major inroads in Brooklyn. Quill denounced the intervention of the priesthood and ACTU into union politics and managed to rebuff their challenge to his Communist colleague, Austin Hogan, in the December 1947 election for the presidency of his Brooklyn TWU local.[28] The writing on the wall was disturbing, especially since the CP's role in founding the union was widely reported in the press and top TWU Communist John Santo was interned on Ellis Island facing deportation.[29]

The Wallace candidacy added fuel to the insurgents' fires. In a number of TWU locals in the South and West, TWU organizers who were CP members enthusiastically took the Wallace bit in their teeth and tried to push locals into early endorsements of Wallace. The local members' protests forced Quill to intervene to save the organizers' necks, and impressed on him the dangers of continuing along the CP path.[30] Quill resisted party pressure for a TWU endorsement of Wallace; although he personally supported Wallace, he declared that he would not try to force his union to do so.[31] Later, in March 1948, he said that Wallace should be supported unless the Democrats came up with a strong candidate at their convention in late August.[32]

Meanwhile, the Reuther-led UAW was preparing to raid leftist CIO unions and snap up dissident rightist locals. A prime target was the TWU, whose large Miami airline local presented a tempting target.[33] It was apparent that Quill would receive more support against Reuther from his old friend, Phil Murray, if he acknowledged that the time had come to do what Murray had always expected of him when the right moment came: to split with the Reds. Furthermore, Mayor William O'Dwyer of New York City, where the core of the TWU lay, let Quill know that a break with the Communists would be amply rewarded at the bargaining and other tables.[34]

The Communist leadership, continuing to alienate Quill apace, urged on him a seemingly suicidal path over the five cent New York subway fare. The issue had always been a delicate one, especially for a left-wing union which was presumably concerned for the welfare of the working class as a whole. The party and the TWU had always insisted that wage increases were possible without fare increases, but in the pinch, in other cities, had acceded to fare increases "as a last resort."[35] The nickel fare was virtually sacrosanct in New York City working class politics, despite the dire economic straits of the subway lines and the widespread acknowledgment that they could not possibly grant substantial wage increases without abandoning it. By late 1947, John Santo, Austin Hogan, and other top Communists in the TWU had come around to favor higher fares while Quill remained opposed.[36] Abe Sacher, the Communist treasurer of the union, was able to persuade Quill that the subway lines had no money, and Quill agreed to support a proposal by O'Dwyer that would link wage raises to an eight cent fare, but only after it had been approved in a referendum of the union membership.[37] No sooner had Quill committed himself to the unpopular fare rise than the party's political leadership changed course. There could not be a fare increase at least until 1949, they decided, because support for the nickel fare was to be a major plank in Vito Marcantonio's projected campaign for the mayoralty. The *Daily*

Worker again emerged as the staunch guardian of the nickel fare, and the majority of the Communist-dominated TWU Executive Board now came out against a fare increase. Quill, supported by a minority of the board, refused to change, and the overwhelming majority of voters in the referendum agreed with him.[38]

The climax of the conflict came on March 25, 1948, at a meeting between Quill, Eugene Dennis, John Williamson, Robert Thompson, and several other CP luminaries in the New York City area. There Quill rejected their proposition that the TWU publicly endorse Wallace, condemn the Marshall Plan and oppose any increase in the subway fare. Although the CP promised to rally support for a wage increase for TWU workers in return, Quill refused to go along. At the end of the acrimonious meeting, Quill stalked out, and threatened that "If you want war, you're going to get it now."[39] When a few days later the Greater New York CIO-IUC came out in support of Wallace, Quill asked the TWU to withdraw from the council and resigned as its president, affirming that he personally continued to support Wallace, at least until the Democrats nominated a strong candidate.[40]

Quill's break with the party was reluctant, made with great difficulty. On April 18, Quill sent a long letter, drafted by Browder, to Luigi Longo, the secretary-general of the Italian Communist party, hoping it would reach Moscow. Quill wrote that he hoped to continue cooperating with the CPUSA, but not under its present leadership because that "crackpot" Foster and his henchman Robert Thompson, the New York State chairman, were driving him and his union from the party's arms. Foster's refusal to consult the union leadership on the decision to support Wallace, his insistence that Wallace be supported even if it meant the breakup of the CIO, his erratic lurching between supermilitancy and craven abandonment of principle, evidenced in the acceptance of the "resent and reject" resolution in 1946 and the Marshall Plan resolution of 1947—all were destroying the party's influence in the labor movement, warned Quill. In a clear bid for Moscow's intervention to depose the man it had put in power, Browder, through Quill, ended by citing Stalin's 1929 condemnation of CPUSA factionalism. The letter evoked no response from Moscow. Even Longo did not reply.[41] With no help to be expected from the deus ex machina, Quill rejoined Curran despite the letter's disclaimer to Longo of any intention of following Joe Curran into "the camp of professional Communist-haters, anti-Sovieteers and warmongers."[42]

Quill's misgivings about breaking with the party were not all political and ideological. The prospect of losing union office was most disconcerting. People like Santo, he thought, with the party's social security system to keep them in some post or other, could think in suicidal terms. In the words of a man who later interviewed Quill, "If the TWU were smashed, Santo would still be a Communist hero while Mike Quill would be just another Irishman looking for a job."[43]

Even though it seemed a fight to the finish, or perhaps because it did, Quill tried to temporize and compromise with the Communists. In April 1948 he offered his friend, Bill McMahon, then the top Communist in the TWU, a deal: the CP could have twelve of the twenty-six members of the union's executive board. All Quill wanted was a "leeway" of two. According to Quill, McMahon seemed to think the offer reasonable but when he returned from discussing it with the party leadership, he said, "No, we want all or nothing." "Go back and tell them that that is just what they will get, nothing," Quill recalled saying.[44]

In the ensuing conflict, Quill was aided by several factors. Although the Communists controlled a majority of the union's Executive Council, Quill had a great personal following among the membership. A majority of the union's members were concentrated in the New York City area, and in fourteen years in office Quill had been able to meet and charm a considerable proportion of them. Over the years, he stood in front of places like the subway shops at 180th Street and Lenox Avenue in New York, where 1,100 transit workers emerged for lunch, and talked to the members, repeating the process throughout the New York City area and across the country.[45] He had thus quietly developed a personal "machine" of TWU officials who would follow him rather than the party in a crisis.[46]

When the break came, many of Quill's long-standing Catholic opponents were hesitant about joining him, but Father Rice helped forge a reconciliation by writing Catholic TWU insurgents across the country assuring them that Quill's conversion really was sincere and asking them to lend their support to this new friend of anticommunism.[47]

Quill was also aided by Santo's deportation in 1948. The union constitution which Santo had drawn up gave extraordinary power to the secretary-treasurer, the position that he held. His legal problems forced him to relinquish the post to Gustav Farber, who sided with Quill and helped to compensate for Quill's lack of majority on the union Executive Board.[48]

As in most unions, "bread-and-butter" issues were paramount in the battle for control. The TWU Communists were at a distinct disadvantage on these grounds. Opposition to fare increases might have been good politics in New York City generally, but as the overwhelming vote of the TWU membership in favor of raises suggested, it cut little ice within the union. From the outset, Quill was able to establish himself as the man most able to "deliver the goods" to the membership.

He obtained the complete support of Mayor O'Dwyer who, thanks to a fare increase to ten cents, was able to grant the union a wage increase that more than satisfied most of the membership. Moreover, adopting a pattern that would characterize New York transit negotiations until the mid-1960s, O'Dwyer went through the charade of appearing to make painful concessions to Quill and allowed Quill to take all the credit for the wage increase. "Wages before Wallace" became Quill's most effective battle cry.[49]

While O'Dwyer provided ammunition for Quill, the Communists were grossly undersupplied with weapons to use against him. They charged Gustav Farber, the treasurer of giant New York Local 100 and one of Quill's major supporters, with embezzlement, but the district attorney conveniently managed to prolong his investigation of the charges until after the union's crucial December convention.[50] In any event, it was common knowledge that the modest-living Quill was above reproach on that score.[51] Communist aspersions on his ability to expand the union's membership were met by charges that the Communists had sabotaged his wartime organizing efforts.[52] When his opponents, presumably hoping to shake his Catholic support, charged him with having been a Communist, they discovered that Quill had anticipated them, and had his membership records stolen from party headquarters. Then he dramatically offered to resign his presidency if the accusations were proven.[53]

Quill's break was amply rewarded by Murray and the national CIO. In May 1947 Murray forced Reuther to call off UAW raids on the TWU locals in Miami, Brownsville, and San Francisco and let it be known that Quill was the unofficial head of the drive on leftist control of the Greater New York CIO Council, the body which Quill had so recently chaired and used so effectively as a forum for his party-lining views.[54] In many cities, CIO regional representatives, working directly under Murray and Allan Haywood, swung into action behind Quill's faction in the TWU civil war and organized it into groups that took control of various locals.[55] Office holders caught in the middle soon sensed which way the wind was blowing. In Omaha, for example, John A. Cassidy, a TWU officer, resigned as chairman of Nebraska's Wallace for President Committee after the two Omaha TWU locals demanded that he be stripped of his union job. Thanks to Quill's benign intervention, his union post was preserved as he made a swift reentry into Quill's camp, abandoning Wallace and the leftists "to preserve union unity."[56]

Meanwhile, in New York, Mayor O'Dwyer tantalized TWU members with tangible benefits for supporting Quill. In August, he let it be known that were it not for the TWU Communists, he and Quill could work out an enticing pension plan.[57] He then announced that a purge of the TWU Communists was a precondition for city approval of a new plan for collective bargaining in the New York City transit system that would be highly favorable to the TWU.[58] This support helped Quill and his supporters gain control over the crucial local in the union, Manhattan Local 100, whose 35,000 members constituted over one-third of the union's total membership, in August and September 1948. Enough other locals now scurried aboard the Quill bandwagon to make the victory overwhelming. Quill's supporters dominated the union convention in Chicago that December, which replaced the Communist-dominated international council with one beholden to Quill and elected Quill's men to all the top executive posts.[59]

Quill's victory at the international level was immediately followed by a purge of leftists in its ranks. The ballots at Chicago had hardly been counted when the firing of sixteen leftist TWU organizers was announced.[60] Within months, the Communists in the TWU, who a short time ago had been riding so high, were reduced to a tiny band of the hunted and hounded, kicked out of union office or forced to break with the party and make their peace with Michael J. Quill.

The party itself had played a major role in alienating both Curran and Quill. Nevertheless, the decision to cut their ties with the Communists also owed much to the political climate of the times: the growing opposition to Communists in the CIO outside and inside the CIO. In both cases, the defectors knew that they would not have to fight a lonely battle against an entrenched machine; they could count on a large number of officeholders in their own unions nervous about swimming against the tide and also an impressive array of powerful outside forces, ranging from the federal government through the national CIO staff to Mayor O'Dwyer and the Catholic church. Yet anticommunism per se played only a minor role in rallying the mass of union members to their side. Curran and Quill had successfully weathered enough "Red-baiting" attacks to know that union struggles were not won on that basis. In both cases, their great personal popularity helped, as did the Communists' own actions and policies, which anti-Communists were able to label a willingness to sell out the interests of the workers at the bargaining table for exotic political reasons.

Rising anti-Communist pressure also told in the International Woodworkers Association, but again it was bread-and-butter issues that brought a rightist victory. The Left had slowly rebuilt its support during the war, aided by the apparent incompetence of the rightist leadership in administering the union and heading off the inroads of its AFL competitors. At the IWA convention in November 1945, the Left came within a hairbreadth, ("too close for comfort" according to

Adolph Germer), of passing a condemnation of George Brown, an anti-Communist CIO organizer assigned to the union.[61] The next year, in late 1946, the leftist coalition regained control of the union's Executive Board. In July 1947, however, the CIO recalled Germer from Paris, where he was duelling with the Communists in the WFTU, and sent him back to the Northwest, where he immediately began reorganizing the IWA anti-Communists for a new offensive.[62]

The rightists were aided by the Taft-Hartley affidavit requirement. In July 1947 the leftist-dominated IWA Executive Board announced that it would not sign the affidavit. Acknowledging that this would deprive them of the right to participate in NRLB-supervised representation elections, they gamely said that henceforth they would strike to force recognition of their union and dispense with the elections.[63]

The leftists were bold but foolhardy. Since its inception, the IWA had been fighting a running battle with AFL unions, especially in the Pacific Northwest. Over the years the AFL unions had become more militant, more aggressive in organizing, and more successful. Many of their contests with the IWA had been settled only by close NLRB elections. The IWA was in no position to rely on the hope that those workers who supported it in any given area would feel strongly enough about being represented by the IWA rather than the AFL to strike for the privilege and, even if they did, would constitute a large enough majority to mount an effective strike.

By the fall of 1947, thanks in large part to dismay over the effects of the leftist course on the contest with the AFL, the Right had squeaked back into power. Now the purges began. One of the first moves of the new officers was to pledge the union to have its officers sign the Taft-Hartley affidavit. When an international trustee refused to sign it, the new rightist president of the union fired him. When the British Columbia District attacked the Canadian Congress of Labor's support for the Marshall Plan, the CIO representative, George Brown, who was now also the IWA's director of organization, fired four leftist British Columbia organizers for the District's stand.[64] Meanwhile, over forty witnesess were giving heart to the rightists by testifying at the Washington state HUAC hearings that Harold Pritchett, Mickey Orton, and many other leaders of the left-wing of the IWA were party members.[65] When Pritchett and other leftists demanded a CIO investigation of the case of British Columbia organizers, at Germer's suggestion Philip Murray and Allan Haywood neatly stacked the investigating committee with anti-Communists, even appointing Germer to it.[66]

The three-man committee's hearing were a forerunner of the kind that would characterize the purges of the rest of the CIO. The four organizers were charged with having voted against compliance with the Taft-Hartley Act and the Marshall Plan at the convention of the British Columbia district of the union, even though the International had declared its support for both of these things. At the hearings, the evidence against the organizers consisted primarily of copies of the British Columbia district's newspaper showing how the paper and the organizers had followed the party line in foreign policy. The committee thereupon voted that the firings were justified.[67]

Supported by Germer and the CIO and aided by state and local authorities on both sides of the border, the IWA anti-Communists were able to purge their rolls of most of the leftist organizers and reduce the position of the Communists to that of a distinct minority concentrated in British Columbia, many of whose leaders could not cross the border, thanks to the United States Immigration Service.

The rightist victory was based on a number of factors, some of which went back to the origins of the IWA union in the late 1930s. Since its founding, strong centers of opposition to the leftist factions had existed in various areas, especially in the United States. The relative weakness of the union and the competition it faced from the AFL had made it dependent on the CIO and vulnerable to anti-Communist pressure and machinations from the national CIO. Furthermore, the leftist leaders could not and did not distinguish themselves in bread-and-butter terms at the bargaining table or in the bureaucracy, a weakness that was mitigated only by the fact that their rightist opponents were no better at this. The only leftist leader with considerable personal appeal was Harold Pritchett. But, no Bridges or Quill to begin with, Pritchett's modest charms were often lost on American IWA members because the Immigration Service would not allow him into the United States.

NOTES

1. [?] Hennessey, Special Reports [to a government security agency?], September 1, September 11, September 14, 1942, copies in Earl Browder, Papers, George Arents Research Library, Syracuse University, Syracuse, N.Y., Series 2, Box 10, "Labor Salaries" Folder.

2. Kempton, *Part of Our Time*, 100.

3. *The New York Times*, February 28, 1947.

4. NMU, National Subcommittee on Policy Enforcement Report, February 28, 1946, copy in CIO, Papers, Office of the Secretary-Treasurer, Wayne State University Archives of Labor History and Urban Affairs, Detroit, Michigan (hereafter Carey Papers), Box 54, "NMU" Folder.

5. Ibid., NMU, National Subcommittee on Policy Enforcement Report, Dissenting Comments of Joseph Curran, February 28, 1946.

6. Ibid., NMU Subcommittee on Policy Report, February 28, 1946.

7. Ibid., Dissenting Comments of Joseph Curran, February 28, 1946. It was commonly thought that NMU Communists who held salaried union offices were tithed

ten percent of their salaries by the party. "Hennessey's Breakdown of NMU Financial Report" [for government security agency?], 1942, copy in Browder Papers, Series 2, Box 10, "Labor Salaries" Folder.

8. He and Carey were by no means close confidants. Indeed, they had once come to blows. James Carey, Oral History Interview, Oral History Collection of Columbia University (hereafter COHC), 340-41.

9. Len De Caux, *Labor Radical* (Boston: Beacon Press, 1970), 420, 422.

10. CIO, Hearing before the Committee to Investigate Charges against the International Longshoremen's and Warehousemen's Union, commencing May 17, 1950 (hereafter "ILWU" Hearings)," 601.

11. NMU, National Subcommittee on Policy Enforcement Report, February 28, 1946.

12. Ibid., "Dissenting Comments of Joseph Curran."

13. Al Lannon, "The West Coast Maritime Strike,"*Political Affairs*, vol. 27, no. 11 (November 1948), 963.

14. *NYT*, July 8, 1946. Hedley Stone later ventured that the party rejected a satisfactory offer from the shipowners in order to continue to sabotage the economy. CIO, "ILWU Hearings," 600-603. Max Kampelman seems to agree that the strike was part of a larger, worldwide plan. Max Kampelman, *The Communist Party vs. the CIO* (New York: Praeger, 1957), 79-80. Yet many non-Communist unions also struck that year, including the UMW, the USW, and the UAW. If the Communist advice to hold out for more was dictated by some larger plan of sabotage rather than union considerations, what can one say about Walter Reuther's holdout in the GM strike of the same period as well as the charge that the UE sabotaged the GM strike by *not* holding out for more? (See above, ch. 10.)

15. CIO, "ILWU Hearings," 603.

16. *NYT*, July 8, 1946.

17. Julian Steinberg, "Alert! The CP and the NMU Treasury," *New Leader*, January 24, 1948.

18. See ch. 12.

19. *NYT*, February 27, 1947.

20. *NYT*, March 12, 18; April 2, 3, 4, 6, 1947. Significantly among the formal charges levelled against Stack was one accusing him of opposing the Spanish Loyalists in 1938 and taking out membership in the CPUSA "for opportunistic reasons," *NYT*, April 6, 1947.

21. James R. Prickett, "Communists and the Communist Issue in the American Labor Movement, 1920-1950" (Ph.D. diss., University of California at Los Angeles, 1975), 315.

22. *NYT*, October 19, 1947.

23. *New York Herald-Tribune*, July 18, 1948.

24. Prickett, "Communists and the Communist Issue," 320.

25. Daniel Bell, draft of *Fortune* article, June 1, 1949, in Daniel Bell, Collection, Box 4, of Material on Socialism and Communism in the U.S.A., Tamiment Institute Library, New York University, New York, N.Y., "CIO-National" File.

26. See ch. 8, and Michael Quill, "As I Was Saying . . ." *Transport Bulletin*, July 24, 1948.

27. Philip Jaffe, *The Rise and Fall of American Communism* (New York: Horizon, 1975), 144.

28. *NYT*, February 17, February 18, November 24, November 25, December 7, 1947.

29. *NYT*, September 7, 18, 1947.

30. Michael Quill to Luigi Longo, secretary of Italian CP, April 16, 1948, Browder Papers, Series 11, Box 8, "TWU" Folder.

31. Ibid.

32. *NYT*, March 29, 1948.

33. *NYT*, March 21, 1948.

34. L. H. Whittemore, *The Man Who Ran the Subways, The Story of Mike Quill* (New York: Holt, Rinehart and Winston), 139.

35. Earl Browder, *The Decline of the Left Wing of American Labor* (New York: the author, 1948), 31.

36. Ibid.; Whittemore, *Man Who Ran the Subways*, 139.

37. Levering, "Interview with Mike Quill," October 21, 1948, Bell Collection; Browder, *Decline*, 32.

38. Levering, "Quill Interview"; Browder, *Decline*, 32-34; Whittemore, *Man Who Ran the Subways*, 136.

39. Levering, "Quill Interview."

40. Quill to Longo, April 18, 1948; *NYT*, March 29, 30, 1948.

41. Quill to Longo, April 18, 1948; Jaffe, *Rise and Fall*, 144.

42. Quill to Longo, April 18, 1948.

43. Whittemore, *Man Who Ran the Subways*, 136.

44. CIO, *Daily Proceedings of the Constitutional Convention*, 1949, 273.

45. Levering, "Quill Interview."

46. Levering, "Interview with Victor Riesel," November 28, 1948, Bell Collection, Box 6.

47. E.g. Rice to John Frommeyer, Philadelphia, September 11, 1948; Rice to Robert McNally, Miami, September 11, 1948, Rice Papers, Reels C-D.

48. Levering, "Quill Interview."

49. Whittemore, *Man Who Ran the Subways*, 143.

50. *NYT*, October 30, 1948; "Hillman Dispatch," Bell Collection.

51. Levering, 'Quill Interview;" Levering, "Riesel Interview."

52. *NYT*, September 9, 1948.

53. Quill to Rice, October 4, 1948, The Rev. Charles Owen Rice, Papers, Pennsylvania State University Archives of Labor History, State College, Pa. (hereafter PSUA), Reels C-D.

54. *NYT*, May 25, 1948.

55. Serrel Hillman to Donald Bermingham, December 8, 1948, Bell Collection, Box 6.

56. *NYT*, June 15, 1948.

57. *NYT*, August 19, 1948.

58. *NYT*, August 21, 1948.

59. Whittemore, *Man Who Ran the Subways*, 143; *NYT*, December 12, 1948.

60. *NYT*, December 11, 1948.

61. Adolph Germer, Diaries, State Historical Society of Wisconsin, Madison, Wis., November 17, 1945.

62. See Germer to Tucker, July 21, 1947; Germer to Hartung, July 29, 1947; and a number of other letters and replies around the same dates, Adolph Germer, Papers, State Historical Society of Wisconsin, Madison, Wis.

63. IWA, Press Release, July 24, 1947, Germer Papers.

64. George Brown to Alan Haywood, January 10, 1948, Winn to All IWA Locals, February 17, 1948, Germer Papers.

65. Roy Atkinson to Germer, February 2, 1948, Germer Papers.

66. Ibid., Haywood to Germer, April 2, 1948.

67. "Proceedings of the IWA Committee, April 7 and 8, 1948," "Report and Findings of the Committee to Investigate the Discharge of Three Organizers by George Brown, April 7 and 8, 1948," Germer Papers.

14 THE PREDATORS MOVE IN

Leftist unions that managed to head off the rightist insurgencies in the postwar years found themselves facing an equally dangerous phenomenon: raiding. One of the major motives for unions gathering together in federations such as the AFL and CIO is that they afford some sort of protection aginst unions in similar (or not-so-similar) fields who try to woo dissident locals or groups of members from one union into another. Every union has dissidents, and battles to keep them from being enticed into other unions can be very costly. Because of the hostility they aroused from government and other outside forces, the leftists were especially susceptible to raiding and knew it. This was one of the reasons there was little temptation to bolt the CIO in 1941, despite the hostility of Hillman and Murray. In 1947 and 1948, when moves to implement the affidavit requirement of the Taft-Hartley Act got under way, leftist unions whose leaders refused to sign the affidavits presented tempting targets for raiders.

Reinforcing the temptation was the fact that apparently the days of heady expansion by the CIO and its unions had come to a close. Its major postwar campaign, the Southern Organizing Drive (carefully kept at arm's length from the Communists), was a nagging failure and a massive drain on funds. The young generation of zealous CIO organizers of the 1930s had become middle-aged, cautious union bureaucrats. The temptation to swell their unions' rolls by snapping up defectors from other unions, even CIO unions, was strong. All that was needed were vague indications that the targets were legitimate ones.

Walter Reuther did not wait for anyone to give him the signal that raiding leftist unions was acceptable. Almost immediately after his faction assumed power in the UAW, he led it in a series of forays against leftist unions. In early 1948, he announced that the UAW was ready to accept rank-and-file members of any Communist-dominated unions who wanted to change to a "democratic" organization. One of his first targets was the UE, whose Pittsburgh Local 155, which had been taken over by graduates of the Catholic La Salle Labor School, had already defected to the UAW.[1] In March, the UAW announced that it would welcome disaffected UE members in the New York City area and proclaimed its intention to snap up entire locals of the TWU, the Mine, Mill, and the Farm Equipment Workers Union as well.[2] Reuther rejected Emspak's protests to Murray that the UAW was planning more raids on the UE as "preposterous nonsense...the product of Mr. Emspack's [sic] guilty conscience" and refused to meet with Murray to settle the dispute.[3] Nevertheless, at the very same time, the UAW Executive Board declared that where "the rank and file membership" were in revolt against the leadership of national unions who refused to follow national CIO policy, the UAW would be willing to charter their locals rather than see them leave the CIO entirely.[4] Reuther announced that 1,500 workers in New York City linotype companies represented by the UE had signed UAW cards, and that the UAW would request a NLRB election to decide on representation,[5] an election in which the UE would not be on the ballot.

Reuther's initial foray met with a slap on the wrist from Murray, who said that the CIO could not condone raiding.[6] Given the fact that Murray's own USW was soon engaging in the same kind of activity, it is easy to dismiss his condemnation as hypocritical. However, Murray was probably serious in regarding Reuther's game as counterproductive, because Carey, Block, and most UE anti-Communists were firmly opposed to defections from the UE. They too condemned the raids and urged members to continue the struggle within the union rather than defect.[7]

Nevertheless, the raids continued. Within six months, the UAW claimed that it had decimated the large UE Local 475 in Brooklyn, centering on machine and foundry workers, and had set up a new local to accommodate the thousands who had defected to it.[8]

Michael Quill's turnabout saved the TWU from UAW raids at the last minute. Soon after he abandoned the Communists, his union was rumored to be preparing to raid the independent leftist Packinghouse Workers, some of whose members were reputed to be dissatisfied with their leadership's failure to join the anti-Communist crusade.[9]

Mine, Mill was not so fortunate. It became the object of UAW incursions soon after Reuther won control. First, the UAW tried to woo workers in Mine, Mill locals in Michigan and Cleveland. In mid-December Mine, Mill leaders complained to Philip Murray that UAW Secretary-Treasurer Emil Mazey had urged a Detroit Mine, Mill local to come over to the UAW. Locals of other unions whose leaders had not signed Taft-Hartley affidavits would be invited to join UAW as well, Mazey allegedly stated.[10] Then, the UAW shifted its focus to the entire casting division of Mine, Mill.[11] The Mine, Mill leaders' refusal to sign the Taft-Hartley affidavits made the union vulnerable and in 1948 the UAW set up a special die casting unit and convinced the leaders of the Mine, Mill casting unit to bring their organization with its 20,000 members into the UAW fold.[12]

Most of the UAW's raids concentrated on the union whose affiliation with the UAW Reuther had so adamantly opposed until 1947, the Farm Equipment Workers. Until Reuther's takover of the union, their admittance into the UAW would have swelled leftist strength. But his victory was followed by the rapid disintegration of the anti-Reuther front. R. J. Thomas took refuge in the national CIO where his friend Murray made him a CIO staff member. He now attacked his old Communist allies and followed Murray on his rightward course in 1948. Richard Leonard, his ex-running mate, made a feeble attempt to rally the non-Communist segment of the anti-Reuther faction in 1948; his call for a new coalition of anti-Reuther and anti-Communist forces fizzled and he too was given his just rewards on Murray's payroll.[13] The disastrous strike against Allis-Chalmers had decimated the large Communist-led UAW local in the Milwaukee area and Reuther was able to place the local under an administratorship and expel Christoffel and the other leftist leaders.[14] Reuther's opponents of all stripes were on the run, desperately seeking shelter from their pursuers. The balance of power tilted so markedly in Reuther's favor that he no longer needed to fear that the addition of FE locals and members would tilt the balance against him, especially if they entered the UAW individually and not as a bloc dominated by Communist leaders.

Thus, soon after Reuther won complete control of the union, the UAW took advantage of the FE leadership's refusal to sign the Taft-Hartley affidavits and forced NLRB elections in which FE was barred from the ballot at International Harvester in Memphis and Caterpillar in Peoria; it replaced the FE in both cases as bargaining agent.[15]

The national CIO had remained in the background in the FE-UAW dispute in 1946 and 1947, with its jurisdictional committee simply noting in 1946 the lack of compliance with its recommendation for amalgamation.[16] When open warfare between the CIO Left and Right broke out in 1948, rightist CIO leaders lined up behind Reuther on the FE issue. They were unable to secure an order for the dissolution of FE at the CIO Executive Board meeting on August 30, 1948, but on November 27 after Harry Truman's presidential victory and Henry Wallace's dismal showing dashed leftist prospects, the triumphant anti-Communists moved in for the kill. The Executive Board then approved Reuther's resolution that the FE be given sixty days to agree to a merger or face loss of its charter. The FE leadership attacked this "Pearl Harbor ultimatum" and the union convention in March 1949 rejected the merger order.[17] The next meeting of the CIO Executive Board thereupon voted to recommend to the next CIO convention that the FE charter be revoked. It was officially open season on the FE.[18]

Mine, Mill was another union which was naturally susceptible to raiding. Like FE, it was surrounded by other unions of overlapping jurisdictions. Its internal problems provided an added temptation to the wolves baying at its door. The opposition to the leftist leadership of Mine, Mill had achieved some success during the war. Control over the union's Executive Board teetered between the two factions, with the opposition, centered in Montana and Connecticut, gaining an occasional majority on the Executive Board while the leftists retained control of most elected executive posts. The Connecticut opposition, led by John Driscoll, was especially active and vituperative. With a heavily Catholic constituency and aid from local churchmen, it had hammered away at the Robinson faction's Communist sympathies and affiliations throughout the war. Attempts by both sides to unify in support of the war effort broke down repeatedly in the face of Driscoll's zealous crusade.[19] The union's success in organizing many of the large brass companies in Connecticut in 1941 and afterward increased the relative weight of Driscoll's home territory within the union. In 1943, an administrator appointed by the Executive Board of the union, which had temporarily fallen into the hands of an anti-Robinson majority, had purged the district bureaucracy of leftists; effective control of the district was left in the hands of Driscoll and his supporters. From this base, they built the organization they hoped would displace the left in the entire union.

The challenge was strong enough to make the election for the union executive in late 1946 a hard-fought one. When Robinson and his supporters won all the seats, except that of the secretary-treasurer which they did not contest, the rightists called the elections fraudulent. When their protests brought no redress, in early March 1947 leaders claiming to represent forty-eight locals comprising 30,000 of the union's 100,000 members denounced the "Communist tyranny" imposed on Mine, Mill and announced that they would secede from the union but remain in the CIO. They said that they expected that the other CIO unions would welcome them.[20]

The anti-Communists were heartened by a fortuitous breakdown of leftist leadership. On March 11, 1947, Reid Robinson resigned as president of the union. Since late 1945 the opposition had been charging that Robinson had extracted a $5,000 personal "loan" from the owner of a large firm with which the union bargained.[21] He said that he resigned to clear the air and salvage the union because the secessionists had made their struggle a personal one. In reality, though, he resigned because a majority of the union's Executive Board, Left and Right, became convinced that he could not effectively deny the "shake-down" charge and had become a liability to the union, especially in its dealings with Murray.[22] What even they did not know was that the incident that had become public was not an isolated one. In fact, from 1943 to 1946 the hard-drinking Robinson had become entangled in a complex net of "borrowing" from employers to pay off the other creditors.[23] The danger of further exposures lay around the corner.

Robinson was replaced by Vice-President Maurice Travis, whom Murray despised even more than he did Robinson. A secret party member, Travis had been ejected from SWOC in 1941 during an anti-Communist purge. If Murray regarded Robinson as a Communist puppet, Travis was the puppeteer. Even Robinson and the leftists thought Travis a poor choice for the succession but he took office because, as vice-president, he was next in line.[24]

Despite their displeasure with the ruling group in Mine, Mill, the CIO anti-Communist establishment was not yet ready to approve secession of the nature and scale attempted by the Driscoll group. It would set a dangerous precedent for other unions, including their own. Murray created a special CIO committee, consisting of Jacob Potofsky, Van Bittner, and L. S. Buckmaster, all anti-Communists, to find a more acceptable way out of the imbroglio.

The committee reported that the constitutionality of the recent election was indeed questionable. Furthermore, it was apparent that "outside influences...played a material role in the affairs of the International Union." Nevertheless, it concluded, under CIO rules "no local union or group of local unions has any legal and moral right...to secede from an international union." It concluded that "John Driscoll and associates, over a period of years, have carried out a disruptive program." Their activities had been "detrimental...to the entire membership of the union." It recommended that Travis resign as president or be deposed, that the Driscoll group disband and rejoin the union, and that Murray appoint an administrator to run the union until the dust had settled enough to call a convention to devise ways to elect new officers.[25]

For the Left, to accept the committee's recommendation would have been tantamount to giving up control of the union; any administrator appointed by Murray would certainly have waited until an anti-

Communist victory was assured before calling a new convention. They therefore rejected the report and fought the secessionists alone with no aid from the CIO.

However, Travis did step aside as president after the Potofsky committee made public two letters from a deceased Utah organizer for the CP which indicated that Travis cleared leftist strategy in the union with party officials and took direction from them.[26] He was replaced by John Clark, a leftist whose connections with the CP were more removed than Travis' were. Robinson, meanwhile, remained on the union payroll and played a prominent role in the ensuing battles.

Murray was not exactly a disinterested observer of the conflict which wracked Mine, Mill. Although the national CIO was squarely opposed to the secession of whole districts and locals as units, the Potofsky committee had evaded the question of more conventional kinds of "raiding," saying that it was outside its purview.[27] Even while the committee was still meeting, some organizers from Murray's own Steelworkers union were trying to persuade individual members of Mine, Mill locals to join the USW.[28]

Defecting locals were still not welcome into the USW, at least not as whole locals, but what was there to stop the members, at the proper moment, from voting to change bargaining agents? The Mine, Mill leadership's endorsement of Wallace in February 1948 sealed their fate. After that Mine, Mill locals throughout the nation became the target of Steelworkers' organizers, who forced NLRB elections wherever possible, elections in which Mine, Mill, whose leaders had not signed Taft-Hartley affidavits, had to urge its supporters to vote "no union."[29]

By spring 1948, Mine, Mill was being assailed on all sides, with the Steelworkers leading the assault but others, such as the UAW, the Gas and Coke Workers, and the CIO Shipyard Workers Union at their heels.[30]

The politics of the Mine, Mill leadership was a liability among some important sectors of the membership. In Utah, for example, an important Mine, Mill center where a large majority of Mine, Mill members were Mormons, the leftists were severely weakened when their endorsement of Wallace, announced at a union Executive Board meeting in Salt Lake City in February 1948, provoked a stinging attack on them by Mormon leader David McKay before 14,000 Mormons at the Mormon Annual Conference, reinforcing the Mormons who formed the hard core of the opposition to the lefists in the far west.[31]

Both the frustrated secessionists within Mine, Mill and CIO unions who were raiding it received encouragement and support from national CIO staff members, especially CIO regional directors. In Colorado, secessionists received CIO assurances that although their method (secession) could not be condoned, they would receive CIO aid in their struggle.[32] The Shipyard Workers were aided by the local CIO regional director as they scoured the Utah-Nevada area, far from their oceanside home, for Mine, Mill defectors. According to the Mine, Mill leadership, raiders received open or secret help from CIO regional directors in virtually every raid on Mine, Mill.[33]

Mine, Mill's relatively small size made it particularly vulnerable to raiding. In some areas, such as that around Birmingham, Alabama, where United States Steel's huge complex dominated the local economy, Mine, Mill had played second fiddle to the Steelworkers, unable to swing enough weight against the U.S. Steel ore mining subsidiaries with which it bargained to better the settlements reached by the USW. It invariably followed the USW in wage settlements. There was little in the form of bread-and-butter benefits that the union leaders could use to counteract the mounting charges of Communist domination, charges which struck a very sensitive chord in the South. A letter to James Carey from the leaders of five Alabama ore mining Mine, Mill locals, petitioning to desert to the USW in December 1948, illustrated this dual weakness. "We do not like to take orders from Moscow," they said. The leadership's support of "the Communistic Third Party," opposition to the Marshall Plan and defense programs, and attacks on Philip Murray had alienated the miners, they said. Furthermore, the rebels added, "We are anxious to go to Steel due to the fact that in the past, the iron miners of Alabama have always waited in negotiations until the Steel contract is settled. This resulted, in some cases, with loss of retroactive pay to the iron miner."[34]

Smaller Communist-dominated unions were even more vulnerable than Mine, Mill. The struggling Food and Tobacco Workers (FTA) now faced competition from the giant AFL Teamsters union at the California canneries. Not only did the Teamsters overwhelm the FTA with size and wealth, but their ability to cut off truck transportation to and from canners at crucial times gave them power of a kind that the FTA could not muster. Instead of the more righteous FTA, local authorities usually favored the Teamsters, and cannery owners preferred to deal with the businesslike Teamsters, who were thought of as not averse to "sweetheart" contracts. Finally, in a pinch, the Teamsters in the cannery field were directed by Dave Beck, who could gather a fearsome array of toughs to support his union's cause when needed.[35]

To make matters worse, when rumors spread that union president Donald Henderson and the national FTA officers were planning to take over FTA Local 78, whose anti-Communist leaders represented

3,000 cannery workers in Salinas, California, Local 78 leaders took most of their members into the Teamsters.[36]

Help from the national CIO, crucial to struggling small unions such as FTA, evaporated. The CIO refused the union's plea for aid in its strike against the giant R. J. Reynolds tobacco processing plant in Winston-Salem, North Carolina, in 1947 on the grounds that the strike was a "political" rather than an "economic" strike, despite the fact that it involved a new contract.[37] The union had expected to benefit from the well-financed CIO Southern Organizing Drive but with the drive firmly under control of anti-Communists only a trickle of dollars reached it.[38]

The FTA leadership's refusal to sign the Taft-Hartley affidavit provided other CIO unions with an excuse for joining in with the Teamsters in the scramble for FTA-represented cannery and packing-house workers. In a number of areas, the UAW joined in. Even the non-Communist but leftist Packinghouse Workers could not resist taking over the FTA's 5,000 member local at the Campbell's Soup plants when Taft-Hartley left it ripe for plucking. In the South, the CIO's feeble counterpart to the Teamsters, the United Transportation Services Employees Union, was able to muster enough support from Murray and the national CIO to mount raids on the FTA's few footholds there.[39]

Even the FTA's grave diggers were not immune. An FTA grave diggers' local in New York had the misfortune to represent the 250 workers in the Catholic Calvary and Gate of Heaven cemeteries, which gave Cardinal Richard Spellman of New York an opportunity to strike a blow against communism in his own backyard. When their contract came up for renewal in December 1948, his adamant refusal to negotiate with the Communist leaders forced a strike. A two-month strike ensued, during which a backlog of 1,000 corpses built up. Finally, when the local's attorney, who was a member of ACTU, persuaded the local to desert the FTA for the AFL Building Service Employees Union, a settlement was quickly reached.[40] By February 1949 the beleaguered FTA had lost 16,000 workers in raids on locals since mid-1948. It maintained a brave front, claiming that only 4,000 of these members had voted to leave; this seemed to ignore those who voted in elections in which the FTA was not even represented.[41] By January 1950 the threadbare union had spent over $300,000 defending itself against raids.

The Taft-Hartley Act made the smaller leftist unions vulnerable to raids by even the weakest of unions. By August 1948 the CIO Shipyard Workers, decimated by postwar layoffs, had snapped up a number of locals of the United Public Workers.[42] The tiny Office and Professional

Workers was raided by the almost equally small CIO Paper Workers Union, which forced a number of NLRB elections where the Public Workers were not allowed on the ballot. Even Philip Murray, who despised Martin Durkin, the UOPWA's Catholic president, for acting as a kind of "House Catholic" for the Communists, condemned these raids.[43] The decimated UOPWA was forced into merger negotiations with the United Public Workers, also in full retreat.

While small CP-dominated unions were being raided, CP beach-heads in a number of smaller unions whose national leadership was non-Communist were being wiped out. Leftist nuclei were wiped out in the CIO Shipyard Workers and Gas and Coke Workers unions. The Steelworkers' mopping up operation continued as usual, although small groups of Communists in the Chicago area still managed to batten down the hatches and ride out the storm. In the United Retail, Wholesale, and Distribution Workers of America, open warfare erupted between the liberal anti-Communist national leadership and the union's Communist-led New York locals. Congressional investigators came to New York to "expose" the Communist ties of the local leaders while the leftist locals tried to find legalistic ways around the Taft-Hartley affidavit.[44] When the national leadership suspended Leon Davis, the president of Local 1199 of the Retail Drug Store Employees, and three other officers in September 1948 for refusing to sign the Taft-Hartley affidavit, the local's membership voted overwhelmingly to secede from the union.[45]

Truman's victory in November 1948 gave a tremendous impetus to President Samuel Wolchak of the national union, a strong Truman supporter. At the union's convention that month, with the leftist locals absent, Wolchak forces were able to pass easily a regulation barring Communists from holding union office and to counterattack by setting up "official" locals to represent workers in the seceding locals.[46]

The swelling wave of raids on leftist unions took place against a background of rising anticommunism in the country as a whole. Many millions of Americans were convinced that the United States faced a mortal threat to its very existence: a combination of a worldwide offensive against it abroad and a "fifth column" working to undermine it at home. Yet, although the growing hysteria did form the backdrop, and, in certain circumstances and areas, the South and Utah, for example, did adversely affect leftist unionism, it was the practical effects of postwar anticommunism that opened leftists to raids and debilitation of their unions. Most importantly, it was the Taft-Hartley Act, combined with the Communists' refusal to go along with the majority of the CIO on national political questions, that made them vulnerable to raiding.

The vast majority of the rank and file who did follow the raiders into new unions appeared to have been motivated not by the anti-Communist climate that enveloped them but by mundane bread-and-butter considerations. While anticommunism played a major role in creating a politico-legal climate that encouraged raiding as well as the atmosphere in which the top leadership of the CIO unions operated, the relative success of the raiders owed little to anticommunism among the American working class. Rather, the most noteworthy phenomenon is the degree to which American workers were able to compartmentalize their union lives, carefully segregating their views on union politics from their opinions on the political world outside the shop floor.

NOTES

1. Harry Block, OH, Pennsylvania State University Archives of Labor History, State College, Pa. (hereafter PSUA), 28.

2. *The New York Times*, March 21, 23, 1948; Frank Cormier and William J. Eaton, *Reuther* (Englewood Clffs, N.J.: Prentice-Hall, 1971), 253.

3. Reuther to Murray, March 30, 1948, in Walter Reuther, Papers, Wayne State University Archives of Labor History and Urban Affairs, Detroit, Mich. (hereafter WSUA), Series 1, Box 16, "CIO, Murray" Folder.

4. UAW, International Executive Board, Statement on Policy, March 30, 1948, in Reuther Papers, WSUA.

5. *NYT*, April 8, 1948.

6. *NYT*, March 21, 1948.

7. *NYT*, April 11, 1948.

8. *NYT*, October 7, 1948.

9. Ibid.

10. Ken Eckert to Philip Murray, December 14, 1947; John Clark to Murray, December 16, 1947, Reuther Papers, Series 1, Box 16, "CIO-Murray" Folder. Murray simply forwarded the protests to Reuther. Murray to Reuther, December 17, 1947, Reuther Papers.

11. John Clark and Maurice Travis, "Confidential Memo," March 25, 1948, copy in Adolph Germer, Papers, State Historical Society of Wisconsin, Madison, Wis.

12. *NYT*, August 5, 1948.

13. *NYT*, August 20, 1948.

14. *NYT*, December 2, 1947, October 4, 1948.

15. CIO, Report of the Committee Dealing with UAW-FE Dispute, April 4, 1949, CIO, Papers, Catholic University of America Library, Washington, D.C. (hereafter CU), A7-25; George Weaver to Carey, October 11, 1949, CIO, Papers, Office of the Secretary-Treasurer, WSUA (hereafter Carey Papers), Box 50; Reuther to Murray, March 30, 1948, Reuther Papers, Series 1, Box 16, "CIO-Murray" Folder. Reuther supporters denied that the Peoria incident actually constituted "raiding" because the IAM-AFL had applied for an election first. Germer to George Brown, May 24, 1948, Germer Papers.

16. CIO, "Report to the Committee Dealing with the UAW-FE Dispute," 1949; Weaver to Carey, October 11, 1949, Carey Papers, Box 50.

17. FE Press Release, "Statement of Grant Oakes to CIO Committee," January 7, 1948; Weaver to Carey, October 11, 1949, Carey Papers, Box 50.

18. Murray to Oakes, March 24, 1949, FE-CIO, Officers Report to the 4th Constitutional Convention, March 25, 26, 27, 1949, CIO Papers, CU, A7-25; Weaver to Carey, October 11, 1949.

19. Report to President Murray by the Committee Appointed to Investigate the Breach within the IUMMSW, May 16, 1947, Carey Papers, Box 111.

20. Ibid.; *NYT*, March 9, 13, 1947.

21. John Mankowski et al., Petition demanding Robinson's resignation, undated [November 1945?], Carey Papers, Box 111. Murray gave the rumors as the reason for dropping Robinson as a CIO vice-president in November 1946, Reid Robinson, OH, PSUA, 46, 60.

22. Robinson, OH, PSUA 46.

23. Chase Powers, OH, PSUA, 42.

24. Robinson, OH, PSUA 11.

25. Report to Murray by Committee to Investigate IUMMSW, May 16, 1947.

26. Ibid., appendix, Phil Wilkes to Henry Huff, May 13, 1946; Wilkes to Travis, May 13, 1946.

27. Report to Murray by Committee to Investigate IUMMSW.

28. Travis to Jacob Potofsky, March 29, 1947, Carey Papers, Box 111.

29. John Clark and Maurice Travis, "Confidential Memo," March 25, 1948, Germer Papers. The hope was that if "no union" won, the employer would be forced to continue to recognize Mine, Mill as the bargaining agent because it would still be able to pull the workers out on strike. Yet the struggles over representation and the fierce divisions they exacerbated made that an unlikely prospect.

30. Ibid. The Shipyard Workers had taken in some of the Mine, Mill secessionists of 1947 and assigned them to lure Mine, Mill locals to follow them.

31. Frank Bonacci to Alan Haywood, April 7, 1948, Germer Papers.

32. Matt Livoda to Germer, May 12, 1948, Germer Papers.

33. Clark and Travis, "Confidential Memo," March 25, 1948.

34. George Eliot et al. to James Carey, December 20, 1948, Carey Papers, Box 111.

35. Carey McWilliams, *Factories in the Fields* (Philadelphia: Lippincott, 1939).

36. Tim Flynn to Philip Murray, July 23, 1948, Carey Papers, Box 109.

37. CIO, "Hearings before the Committee to Investigate Charges against the Food, Tobacco, Agricultural and Allied Workers of America" (hereafter referred to as "FTA Hearings"), January 1950, transcript in Carey Papers, Box 109, 362-64.

38. CIO, "FTA Hearings," 49, 236-39.

39. Ibid., 313-16, 366-67.

40. "Memoradum on the Calvary Cemetery Strike," March 11, 1949, Carey Papers Box 109; *NYT*, December 14, 1948, March 10, 1949.

41. Local 78, FTA-CIO, "Resolution on the Rights of CIO Affiliates and Condemning Raiding," Carey Papers, Box 109, "FTA" File; CIO, "FTA Hearings," 49, 236-39.

42. *New York Herald Tribune*, August 1, 1948.

43. CIO, *Daily Proceedings of the Constitutional Convention*, 1948, 176.

44. *NYT*, February 12, July 2, August 5, 1948.

45. *NYT*, September 24, 1948.

46. *NYT*, November 18, 1948.

15 1949: LEFTISTS ON THE RUN

Political commentators in early November 1948 were too engrossed in analyzing the reasons for Truman's upset victory in the election campaign to point out what would certainly be one of its most important effects: it sealed the doom of the Communists within the CIO. Truman's triumph vindicated the political gamble of Murray and the CIO liberals. They were now assured of a friend in the White House and support from the administration. Had Dewey and the Republicans achieved the overwhelming victory that was predicted for them, the CIO would have had to draw its wagons into a circle to defend against the anti-union and, especially, anti-CIO onslaught that could be expected to follow. This was one of the reasons why Murray and the CIO liberals were so enraged at Communist refusal to line up behind Truman in the first place. Now, Truman's victory gave them a free hand, in the phrase that became current, to "clean their own house." Henry Wallace's dismal showing, which demonstrated that in national politics the Left was a paper tiger, assured the CIO liberals that they would be sailing with the wind to their back.

The Communists recognized that the election had immeasurably strengthened the hand of the CIO liberals. In his gloomy election postmortem, Communist political leader Eugene Dennis warned that they would now "reinforce their attempts to isolate the Left-progressive forces."[1]

Dennis' forebodings were, if anything, overly optimistic. The official election returns were hardly in before Murray and the liberals marched triumphantly into the CIO's national convention in Portland and turned it into an anti-Communist spree. Thanks to the election, they now aspired to much more than "isolating" the Communists and their allies in the CIO. Ultimately they would be satisfied with nothing less than the obliteration of Communist power in the organization.

Even before the convention officially opened, the leftist front began to crack. At the Executive Board meeting immediately preceding the convention opening, UE President Albert Fitzgerald deserted the leftist line in foreign affairs by voting in favor of the Marshall Plan.[2] As the convention assembled, the leftists were unable to agree on a common stance in the face of the inevitable onslaught. An "every man for himself" atmosphere seemed to sweep their ranks, coinciding, ironically, with the repeated charges that they were well-disciplined automatons marching to the party's tune.

The vicar-general of the archdiocese of Portland had hardly finished his invocation (which criticized C. Wright Mills' *New Men of Power*) and the mayoress had hardly finished the official welcome to the "City of Roses" when Murray lashed out at the Communists. The CIO had "stuck its neck out" and supported Truman with its might and money and had won. The Communists, on orders from Moscow, had determined to defeat Truman, and did not care "whether Dewey . . . or the devil was elected. They were licked!" he exulted. Now they would pay for their opposition. Murray announced that because of the Communists' "inability to organize the unorganized," he would propose the reorganization of unionism in the public worker, retail worker, and other unspecified fields where numerical weakness demonstrated the failure of unions to organize their industries.[3] Although he refrained from attacking communism in the small unions, the message was crystal clear: Murray had opened an offensive against the Communists by assaulting the weakest outposts of their empire.

Truman's victory had clearly played an important role in emboldening Murray, for the decision had obviously not been taken until after the election, too late for inclusion in the official President's Report, a compilation of various reports and proposals prepared some time in advance of the convention. Moreover, the proposal was ill-defined and poorly thought out, the signs of last-minute origin.

The Communists had not backed the right horse and would pay the price. The anti-Communists at the convention more than rose to the emotional heights demanded by the occasion. Donald Henderson's criticism of the Marshall Plan and the administration's foreign policy was greeted by a loud, hostile demonstration. When Murray, in an impassioned defense of American freedom and an attack on the Communists as "Charlie McCarthies" of Moscow who could never admit that Stalin was wrong on anything, warned of an international Communist attempt to wreck the Marshall Plan through a campaign of industrial and political sabotage, the mention of Henderson's name brought cries of "Take a walk!"[4]

It was left to Walter Reuther, however, to raise for the first time the specter of drastic action, perhaps expulsion. Some of the leftists on the

Officers' Report Committee had issued a minority report taking issue with the CIO's foreign policy stance and condemning raiding. "I wonder how long these people can exploit Phil Murray's tolerance?" Reuther asked.

"You had better make up your minds to act as trade unionists dealing with trade union problems, exercising your democratic rights, but once having exercised those democratic rights, accepting the will of the majority . . . because you are not going to be tolerated forever in this program of deliberate planned madness of destroying the American labor movement and sabotaging the basic policies of the CIO. . . . You had better repent before it is too damn late."[5]

Now vastly outnumbered, with few allies left in the "Center," and divided among themselves over tactics, the leftists could counterattack but feebly. Their attempts to present the case against the Truman administration's foreign policy were to no avail. The convention approved overwhelmingly a foreign policy resolution condemning the Soviet Union for its use of the veto in the United Nations, for the blockade of Berlin, for its charges of American "warmongering," and for its opposition to the Marshall Plan. In contrast to the vaguely worded 1947 convention resolution on the Marshall Plan, it pledged its vigorous support for the Marshall Plan and the CIO officials working with it in Europe.[6] It also approved overwhelmingly a resolution laying the basis for CIO withdrawal from the WFTU.[7]

Leftist disunity was most apparent where it had usually been most unified: on foreign policy issues. There were notable absentees among the signers of the minority report on the President's Report, which had dissented mainly on foreign policy issues. Julius Emspak of the UE, J. R. Robertson of the ILWU, and Hugh Bryson of the Marine Cooks and Stewards had abstained, signing neither report, and only Henderson, Irving Potash of the Fur Workers, and Joseph Jurich of the Fishermen signed it.[8] Moreover, in the debates over foreign policy that ensued, UE intervention on the side of the Left was noticeably absent. Indeed, Fitzgerald went so far as to criticize Soviet "sabre rattling and warmongering."[9]

By the fourth day of the convention, Murray had modified his stand on the minor leftist unions. As it emerged in a hastily-written special resolution, the proposal simply authorized the Executive Board to investigate the situation in unions where dereliction was suspected and report on it. Answering Emspak's specific question as to whether the resolution authorized the Board to revoke or suspend union charters, Murray explained that it did not. What he hoped was that when the CIO Executive Board condemned the leadership of certain unions as "incompetent," that is, unable "for one reason or another" to build up the membership of those unions, it would ask the union leaders to resign and provide strong backing for their opponents. They would not, said Murray, protect the small "political cliques" in whose interests it was to keep their captive unions small. As an example of this, Murray cited the United Office and Professional Workers. Rather than organizing the unorganized, that union had wasted thousands of dollars of CIO money. It seemed to have a special committee that did nothing but "send telegrams to the President of the CIO" asking him "to do things about organizing their industry [which] they cannot do themselves."[10]

The convention was less hesitant in imposing a final solution to the FE problem than it was regarding the more minor leftist unions. It simply ordered the FE to join the UAW.[11]

At the close of the convention Murray made it clear that the battle against the Communists would continue relentlessly, but towards a vague goal. He would not permit, he swore, "Communistic infiltration into the national CIO." He had come to know the "damaging effects, the devastating effects, the degrading effects" of the Communist party on the labor movement and he asked CIO members to join him in forcing the few CIO organizations "as may be engaging in the propagation of Communistic doctrines . . . to cease and desist."[12]

In any other kind of political party, the shattering double defeat of November 1948, the Wallace fiasco and the Portland debacle, would have produced a profound shakeup. The leadership would have been discredited or at least fighting to stay in control. Yet in the CPUSA, the Foster group weathered the crisis with remarkably little change in line or leadership.

Party political theorists blamed their dual defeat on virtually everything but their "line," which they repeatedly asserted was a "correct" one. The actual vote for Wallace was no indicator of his true support, and the Progressive party faced a bright future, they assured the Communists.[13] As usual, they found signs of increasing worker militancy and impending economic crisis.[14] "The real reason for the Red-baiting hysteria of Philip Murray at Portland," wrote John Williamson, "is that he, also, had some inkling of the moods of the members, and he knows that this militancy will mount as the economic situation worsens. With nothing but the Marshall Plan to offer the workers, since his support of American imperialism strips him of all ability to make an effective fight on economic issues, Murray tries to cover up by resorting to flagwaving and anti-Communist hysteria."[15]

The leaders blamed much of the rout of leftists in Portland on the powerful alliance which the "misleaders of labor" and their representatives in government had created with Wall Street, but the CIO "Left-progressives," who broke under the strain, came in for criticism as well. Williamson chided them for their disunity, for failing to "grasp the initiative" and for allowing Murray to turn the issue of organizing the unorganized against them. Why was there the evident division in "Left-progressive" ranks? Williamson blamed it on fear and timidity on the part of some, as well as the mistaken belief of others that if they did not "stick their necks out," they might be forgotten and passed over. "The FE delegation felt the whiplash of that mistake," he wrote.[16]

What was now needed, top party theorist V. J. Jerome soon announced, was not change in line, but the more vigorous pursuit of the present one. Disunity must be combatted, not only among the "Left-progressives," but between them and potential allies as well. The "united front" must be pursued, more vigorously than ever, and attempts should be made to expand the party's alliances within both the CIO and AFL, as well as its own working class base. But, he warned, this should not be done at the expense of falling into the heresies of "Browderism" or "economism." Yes, the coalitions must be rebuilt around basic bread-and-butter issues. Yes, workers could and should be rallied to the "Left-progressive" side by pointing out that their real earnings were falling and that only united action could defeat Taft-Hartley. But these and other pocketbook issues must always be linked to continued support for the Progressive party and opposition to the Marshall Plan. Workers should be told that they pay for United States imperialist foreign policy, and that the Marshall Plan, designed by Wall Street to assert America's hegemony over the world, could not head off the crisis.[17] Citing Engels' 1886 prediction that "even in America the condition of the working class must gradually sink lower and lower," Jerome concluded, "Clearly, there is a decline in monopoly capital's material basis for bribing a labor aristocracy in the United States."[18]

Certainly, the postmortems left much to be desired. The main problem facing the leftist unionists was sheer survival, yet the party leadership told them to mount a crusade with their most ineffective weapons: the commitment to Soviet foreign policy and a third political party that had so weakened them during 1948. Moreover, rather than careening towards a crisis, a resurgent American capitalism was priming itself for an anti-Communist crusade of enormous magnitude. The time had come for Communist unionists to crawl into the shelter and hope to survive, while trying to produce the kind of material gains that would keep members loyal to them and relying on exactly the kind of "economism" for which the party's political leadership had proclaimed its contempt. Yet the CPUSA leadership was obsessed with demonstrating a mastery of the complex current line, which demanded that a radical stance on foreign policy be linked with a reformist posture in domestic affairs. Above all, the leaders were intent on covering their tracks, reaffirming the basic correctness of the party line and the way they applied it. Suspicions that they were succumbing to creeping Browderism had to be headed off at all costs.

But their theories and directives now mattered less and less. In their relations with unionists during 1949 the CPUSA political leadership began to resemble the men who had directed the last throes of the German war effort from the bunker in Berlin. The gigantic armies they ordered about were becoming phantoms. Many faithful adherents still listened to the orders and went through the motions of complying, but their confidence in the leadership had evaporated. They concentrated on the furious fight for their own survival, complying perhaps with the letter but not the spirit of the suicidal orders emanating from the bunker.

The orders were couched in all-too-familiar tones. Again, the party's unionists were exhorted by party bureaucrats who lived a life of endless meetings, exhortations, and political infighting in New York to get down to "shop floors" and show the workers the "connections" between things which even they could not connect without resort to tedious tomes. A "most valuable weapon" in radicalizing the workers, wrote Williamson, was William Z. Foster's recent book, *American Trade Unionism*, a collection of Foster's more turgid pieces and vitriolic attacks that few party intellectuals, let alone workers, could ever really wade through.[19] Again and again, unionists whose only livelihoods were their hard-won positions in the unions they had built were exhorted to sacrifice all in the struggle, not simply for the kind of bread-and-butter gains on which their popularity rested, but for a foreign policy that was impossible to defend because of its refusal to criticize the Soviet Union and a domestic political policy that had already led many of their adherents to crucifixion on the cross of the CIO's commitment to the Democratic party. At times, the party leadership displayed a commitment to the inflexible application of the line that verged on the suicidal. In the South, the political leaders in New York helped destroy one of the apples of their eye, the racially integrated FTA local which represented R. J. Reynolds tobacco factory workers in Greensboro, North Carolina. According to Junius Scales, the head of the CP in the South at that time,

If the Italian Communists led a steel strike in Italy, don't think Local 22 didn't have to send a resolution supporting their strike. Every time someone with a brass-hat brain in New York decided we ought to support this or that international cause, they'd call on this huge local, Local 22, to come along and pass a resolution of support. And each and every resolution would be loudly announced in the local press: "Local 22 Supports a Communist Cause!"[20]

To ensure that the current hard line against "white chauvinism" was not contravened, black leaders from New York would come down and scotch any overtures to white workers concerned about participating in the black-dominated union. Scales recalled that

they would come down and meet with union leaders and fan sectarian feeling. They tended to take an extreme line on white workers. "If they got any guts," they would say, "let them stand up and fight," not realizing, as many black workers and union leaders realized, that for a white worker to just *belong* to a predominantly black union at that time was an act of great courage.

White party members could not disagree with the black leaders from the North for fear of being labelled "white chauvinists."[21]

The party and the union paid dearly for their failure to attract more white members, for the racial balance in the Greensboro work force was shifting dramatically. Black workers, previously a majority, were soon a minority of 25 percent. In mid-1949, when the FTA could no longer head off an NLRB election forced by the CIO United Transport Services Workers, which was the only union on the ballot because of Taft-Hartley, the majority of workers voted "no union," and the plant reverted to the open shop.[22]

Earl Browder, brooding outside the tent, did not represent much of an alternative to Foster and his suicide squad. He criticized Williamson for not whipping the Left into line at Portland. The party had embarked on wild crusades against Curran and Quill over relatively minor differences, he wrote, and yet Williamson had responded to Fitzgerald's description of the Soviet leaders as "sabre-rattlers" by saying that Fitzgerald had the right to say what he pleased. "But of course this is not true," wrote Browder. Fitzgerald must listen to his membership, and Williamson's comment "only means that the Left wing dare not challenge Fitzgerald's course before the membership." The real reason for the Portland debacle, said Browder, was that the Left did not have its own program. Its critique of the Marshall Plan was not specific enough regarding the possibility of a UN-directed alternative. They should have put forward the "Roosevelt Plan," as outlined in his book *Tehran and America*. Despite leftist claims to the contrary, there were no real differences with the Right over wage policy.[23] Clearly, "Browderism" would have held out little more hope for the survival of the Left in the CIO than "Fosterism."

One of the more obvious results of the November 1948 anti-Communist sweep was the transformation in the *CIO News*. Briefly, after De Caux's firing as editor, the paper tried to preserve the illusion of harmony within the CIO, but the split during 1948 produced a noticeable tilt to the Right, with the Wallace heresy a special target for attack. In 1949, however, even the vaguest pretense of impartiality was abandoned. The statements of leftist CIO leaders and unions were routinely reported with bold-faced refutations inserted in the text after each statement.[24]

The offensive by the CIO majority against the Communists was welcomed by Matthew Woll of the AFL, but he taunted them for crushing only the weak leftist unions and not the strong ones such as the UE and ILWU.[25] Murray and the CIO liberals spent much of the next year proving him wrong. One of the major tools in the ensuing attack on all the leftist unions was Murray's new-found desire for absolute conformity to all aspects of the national CIO line. As the leftists frequently pointed out, Murray seemed to have a double standard regarding union autonomy within the CIO. With regard to the Taft-Hartley affidavit, he was a consistent defender of the right of each CIO union to decide its own path, undermining the united opposition to the affidavit that the Communists thought so essential. However, when it came to foreign and domestic political issues seemingly more remote from home, he was adamant about the necessity for conformity.

Conflict over this came to a head in early April 1949 at the ILWU convention. There, Bridges complained bitterly about Murray's policies at an executive session attended by R. J. Thomas, Murray's emissary to the convention. The crushing of the independence of the CIO Councils, the attempted forced merger of FE and UAW, and the lack of consultation with the ILWU over withdrawal from the WFTU were all castigated by Bridges, who saw the CIO as trying to deprive its unions of their autonomy and deny the ILWU a voice in formulating CIO policy. Thomas reported to Murray that he strongly suspected that Bridges was preparing the ILWU membership for a withdrawal from the CIO.[26]

The revulsion that Thomas and Murray felt towards Bridges was reinforced by the feeling that he was an ingrate. In September 1948 when West Coast waterfront employers had tried to crush the ILWU by provoking a strike and refusing to negotiate with Bridges, Murray had rejected their overtures for support. Instead, by his lights, the national CIO had played a mediating role and eventually convinced them that they would indeed have to deal with Bridges.[27] But Bridges drew another conclusion from the three-month strike. As in 1946, WFTU unions throughout the world had tried to help by boycotting the ships of struck employers.[28] In recommending withdrawal from the WFTU without consulting him, Murray and the CIO officers angered the leader of the one union that felt the organization could be of practical as well as ideological use.

Murray replied to Bridges' charges with a strong telegram to the ILWU convention denying that the ILWU had been kept in the dark about CIO actions. Bridges would have had more say on important decisions had he attended more than four of the last fifteen Executive Board meetings in the past three-and-one-half years, said Murray.[29] With regard to the WFTU, the CIO officers were merely carrying out the mandate of the Portland convention to take whatever action they saw fit regarding that organization. They would submit their recommendation that the CIO withdraw to the next Executive Board meeting.[30]

By this time, personal relations between Murray and Bridges, never warm, had deteriorated beyond repair. During these last years of his life, recalled a friend of Murray's, "Phil hated Harry's guts."[31] The animosity exploded at the next CIO Executive Board meeting in New York on May 19-21, 1949. There, with Bridges present, Murray and the majority pushed through resolutions withdrawing from the WFTU, supporting the North Atlantic Pact, and calling on Board members who would not obey CIO policy to resign. As a final fillip, it urged CIO unions with leftist leaders to oust them from control of their unions.[32]

Meanwhile, the raids on vulnerable leftist unions were stepped up. Murray's Steelworkers now attacked the staggering prey. Since February 1947 the national CIO office had resisted the pleas of Nick Zonarich, the Steelworkers representative in Birmingham, Alabama, that local industrial union charters be given to Mine, Mill secessionists in his area. Then, on March 7, 1949, that policy was reversed and CIO charters were issued to six secessionist locals in the area although they were not yet assigned to any particular union.[33]

As conflict over who would represent the workers in Tennessee Coal and Iron, a United States Steel subsidiary, raged between those who remained in Mine, Mill and the new CIO locals, the company and the unions agreed to submit the question to a vote of the workers. In the campaign that followed, Mine, Mill was weakened both by the USW's dominant position in bargaining with the company and the widespread assumption that the new locals would be absorbed by it and by the Communist commitment to Negro rights in the South. Like the other Communist-dominated unions, Mine, Mill had gone out of its way to court blacks and elevate them to leadership positions. As in Greens-

boro and Tennessee, where the United Furniture Workers were on the
run, it was easy to label the union a "nigger-loving" one among whites.
During the election campaign, a Ku Klux Klan motorcade demonstrated in front of Mine, Mill headquarters with torches aflame and
horns blaring.[34]

Mine, Mill leaders later tried to link the national leadership of the
Steelworkers to the Klan and the presence of the race issue in the
campaign, but the connection was likely remote at best. Indeed, one of
Mine, Mill's arguments against the secessionists was that they were not
really a part of the USW and could not therefore bargain as effectively
with the company as could Mine, Mill.[35] Moreover, the racial composition of the USW had shifted considerably during the war and it now
contained too large a black minority for its officials to openly court
racist support without provoking trouble in the North. Nevertheless,
local Steelworkers led by Zonarich, who helped the new CIO locals,
were clearly not above accepting the benefits of the race issue, at least,
and the national leadership wired the secessionists that if they won, the
USW would act as their bargaining agent. Furthermore, Murray himself was directly implicated in the dirty campaign, for the secessionists
made effective use of a letter from Carey implying that Mine, Mill was
to be kicked out of the CIO and portrayed themselves as Phil Murray's
choice. Thus, when Mine, Mill Secretary-Treasurer Maurice Travis,
Reid Robinson (now back as vice-president), and another Mine, Mill
official were set upon and brutally beaten by a gang of fifteen, Mine,
Mill held the Steelworkers responsible.[36]

To Mine, Mill, this was but one example of their opponents' violent
tactics, and they ascribed their rivals' 2,996 to 2,233 victory in the
election to the fear of white racist thugs which kept many black workers
from the ballot boxes.[37] This may well have been true. But because of
the race issue, the South was also the only part of the country where
anticommunism was an effective weapon in the union battles. The
leaders of the Steelworkers campaign against Mine, Mill noted the
unusual effectiveness of anticommunism in rallying southern white
workers and used it with considerable success.[38] Not only were all the
usual anti-Communist canards, the appeals to patriotism and the anti-
Semitism, more effective in the white South, but the inevitable linking
in the public mind of communism and "nigger-loving" proved to be
fatal to Communist hopes of preserving their hard-won beachheads in
southern unions.

The attack on the Mine, Mill leaders was an especially brutal one,
and Travis lost the sight of one eye as a result. Nevertheless, when, at
the insistence of the leftists, the subject was raised at the CIO's May
Executive Board meeting, it was Mine, Mill that was on the receiving

end of a blistering condemnation. By a vote of 38 to 11, the Board condemned Mine, Mill for carrying on a campaign of "vilification" against Philip Murray. Mine, Mill was attempting to split Negro and white workers, the resolution said, by using "the Communist weapon of fear, intolerance, racial hatred, threats and other methods which have no place in the decent ranks of trade unionism." The Travis beating was simply a minor incident which the Communists had tried to blow up, said the majority.[39]

The Mine, Mill leaders were outraged. At the union's next convention some months later, President John Clark said that the thought of the recent CIO Executive Board meetings made him sick to his stomach.[40] Yet, despite Clark's conviction that the CIO leaders were "bent on the destruction of Mine, Mill," the idea of pulling out of the CIO was rejected because it would leave them even more exposed to raiding.[41]

The Mine, Mill decision to stay within the CIO was in consonance with CP policy, but some changes in Communist tactics were clearly in order. By August 1949 the situation had reached a critical point. The offensive of Murray and the CIO majority against the leftist unions was now open and above board. At the same time, the Communist-led unions were prostrate in the face of the mounting raids because of their refusal to sign the Taft-Hartley affidavit. Murray and the USW, the last major liberal holdouts against the affidavits, had changed their stand and signed their affidavits on July 29, 1949.[42] Not only did this remove a major moral obstacle to a Communists' turnabout on the issue, but it put the giant USW in a position to join the others in demanding NLRB elections from which noncomplying unions would be excluded. The Communists therefore decided to allow their union leaders to comply with Taft-Hartley. Taft-Hartley penalized only union officers who were presently members of the party. Now, leftist union leaders began to announce that they had quit the CP and then, some days later, submit the affidavits stating that they were not members of the party.

It was a desperation move because it threatened to leave those, who had previously denied membership in the party before congressional committees or grand juries, open to charges of perjury. On August 17, 1949, when Donald Henderson and Maurice Travis submitted their affidavits, the Justice Department was momentarily taken aback. In response to a congressional outcry, it announced that it was investigating the affidavits for possible perjury prosecutions.[43] Henderson especially, who had usually replied to investigators with the statement "It is a matter of public record that I have denied affiliation to the Communist Party many times,"[44] sent Justice Department and congressional lawyers to scouring the transcripts of the past in a search for indictable offenses.

Most leftist union leaders submitted their affidavits, some announcing resignations from the party, most not. The last to go were the UE officers, authorized to sign the affidavits by their convention in late September 1949. "The siege guns of the raids dictated the choice," wrote Matles later. "It was a bitter pill to swallow."[45] The pill was made even more bitter by the announcement, soon after the affidavits were filed, that the Justice Department had directed the FBI to investigate the UE affidavits for criminal offenses.[46]

Meanwhile, the conflict over raiding had been exacerbated during the year, and grew uglier with each passing month. In February 1949, 300 members of the FE and UAW fought a pitched battle outside the gates of the International Harvester plant in Moline, Illinois, a conflict sparked by the arrival of one hundred UAW members at the plant to distribute literature enticing the FE members into the UAW.[47]

At first, the FE Executive Board simply defied the CIO order that it dissolve itself into the UAW. The union leadership countered with a brash demand that all farm equipment workers, including those presently in the UAW and other unions, be congregated under its leadership into one big industrial union.[48] In May and June, it defied the CIO Executive Board's threat to revoke the union's charter if it did not join the UAW, citing the Declaration of Independence's charges against George III in maintaining its stand.[49]

But by that time the FE's stand was more bravado than bravery. The larger, wealthier UAW, with the prestige of Reuther's recent collective bargaining gains in the auto industry behind it, was making large inroads into the FE. Armed with its green light from the Portland convention, the UAW mounted a series of raids on FE strongholds and dropped the pretense of moving in only where there was no bargaining agent or where the employers refused to negotiate with the FE.[50] The FE leaders, soon forced to back down on their commitment to an independent farm equipment union, negotiated a hasty merger with the UE, which promised them autonomy in collective bargaining under their present leadership under the overall supervision of the UE Board.[51] The date of the referendum of FE members to decide on the merger proposal was October 25, just five days before the opening of the national CIO convention at which the FE charter would most certainly be revoked.

His health precarious, Murray had grown more intractable as the year progressed. His plan to lop off the smaller Communist-controlled unions through Executive Board action never came to fruition, probably because it was simply unworkable in practice. Executive Board condemnation of the unions' leadership would do little except expose the inability of the Executive Board to do much else. This realization, however, must have strengthened the idea that the most effective weapon the national CIO had against the Communists was the most drastic: to deprive them of their CIO charters.

Unwilling, for the moment, to take this final step, Murray became increasingly forceful in urging purges on CIO unions. The failure of the CIO's Southern Organizing Drive, belly-up despite the expenditure of hundreds of thousands of dollars, was a particularly sensitive point with Murray and the CIO liberals. From the beginning, they had studiously kept its control out of leftist hands, giving its direction first to Murray's USW and CIO aide Van A. Bittner, and then after Bittner's death in mid-1949 to George Baldizini, an even more committed anti-Communist. With Emil Rieve's fiercely anti-Communist United Textile Workers Union the main beneficiary of the drive, it was to be a showcase of what the CIO could do without the Reds. In a sense, it was to be a living, postwar demonstration that the CIO did not owe its tremendous organizational gains of the 1930s to the Communists. Yet, as the drive's failure became manifest, Murray searched for Communist scapegoats, charging in June 1949 that the drive was hampered by the refusal of the leftist-led Miami TWU to lend its support. Although the CIO was committed to autonomy, Murray urged the TWU to "put your house in order in the Miami area."[52]

Relations between Murray and the UE leadership deteriorated to the breaking point. In March 1949 the UE Executive Board had condemned him and the CIO leadership for having failed to mobilize the masses in the drive against Taft-Hartley and for civil rights. Instead, they charged, the CIO leadership was using accusations of communism and treason to "divert the attention of the membership from their subservience to the foreign and domestic policies of the administration. . . ." The national CIO was again serving the cause of "reaction," according to the UE Board.[53]

Murray and the CIO leadership, meanwhile, supported Carey and the insurgent UE Members for Democratic Acton more openly. As the UE's September convention approached and Carey became dubious of his chances for victory, he and Murray made plans for the creation of a new electrical workers union. When, as anticipated, the Carey-led faction failed to gain control but did seem to demonstrate that it had the support of about 40 percent of the membership, he and Murray agreed that this was enough of a basis upon which to form a new secessionist union, but no date or method was established for its founding.[54]

As Murray and the CIO leadership grew more open and rancorous on the Communist issue, the Communists were faced with growing pressure from among their supporters to pull out of the CIO. In mid-August, soon after the reversal on the Taft-Hartley affidavit, rumors of imminent leftist secession spread when the UE, the American Communications Association, the FTA, the Fur Workers, and a number of other leftist unions in the New York area called a conference for the end of that month on "democracy and autonomy in the CIO."[55] But despite the abuse heaped on Murray, Carey, and the national CIO leadership, the meeting resolved to stay and fight within the CIO.[56]

The leftists, facing a tidal wave of hostile forces in American society, could not face the prospect of "taking a walk" with even the same equanimity they could in 1946, or certainly in 1940. With the CP political leadership itself now considering going underground and battening down the hatches to ride out a right-wing storm of indefinite length, the trade unionists were best off trying to remain in the CIO, seeking cover among the rightists, and trying to avoid being left exposed in the face of the persecution that was clearly in the wind.

But Murray was less and less willing to tolerate their presence in the CIO. When the UE threatened to stop paying dues to the CIO unless Carey stopped "interfering" in UE affairs from his CIO office, an angry Murray said that "We will take care of Mr. Fitzgerald later," with the emphasis on "take care" given in a decidedly unfriendly manner.[57]

Actually, Murray was most incensed with the UE over an issue close to home. He was angered by leftist attacks on the report of President Truman's fact-finding board in the negotiations for a national steel contract. While Murray and the USW leadership were urging acceptance of the recommendations upon an apparently reluctant membership, the UE and other leftist unions were calling the report a sellout to the bosses.[58] To Murray, the fact that Truman had appointed a fact-finding board instead of invoking Taft-Hartley had demonstrated the benefits to be gained from support for the Democrats in 1948. The report of the fact-finding board, which recommended that employers accept the key union demand, employer assumption of pension plan costs, seemed to further justify his path, as did the moral support given by the government to the union in the one-month strike that followed.[59]

If the steel strike drew Murray closer to the administration, it pushed him over the brink in his relations with the Communists. In late September, while he fretted over his ability to deliver for the USW members walking the picket line, the UE held its annual convention. There, Matles and other UE leaders attacked both the national CIO and him personally. A leadership-backed resolution attacked the very Steel Board recommendation which Murray had accepted. A resolution condemning raiding and citing 465 raids allegedly mounted by CIO unions against UE also attacked "individuals in the top leadership of the CIO" who were trying to turn the organization into "a dictator-ship over unions and their members alike."[60] The convention also approved the FE merger and authorized the union's Executive Board to withhold its dues to the CIO if satisfaction were not achieved on the raiding issue.[61]

Murray resolved to crush the leftists once and for all, but had not yet arrived at the precise method. Almost everyone still shrank from the prospect of actually expelling a union as large as the UE. In mid-September, Murray and the CIO national officers decided to propose to the following month's CIO convention CIO Executive Board that members who refused to conform to CIO policy be ousted from the Board.[62] Although this may well have provoked the withdrawal of unions so penalized, they could not bring themselves to take the initia-tive and expel entire unions from the CIO.

As the CIO convention approached, the UE leaders tried to work out a settlement with Murray on the raiding and FE issues, but he would not even meet with them. Finally, on the eve of the convention he did consent to a meeting, but by then he had probably decided to have them expelled.[63] At the meeting, Murray and Reuther, who was to function as a floor leader for the anti-Communists at the convention, refused to sign the anti-raiding agreement that the UE leaders said would solve much of the problem. Instead, they wanted the issue to be resolved on the convention floor, where the UE faced certain defeat.[64]

Some kind of drastic action was clearly in the cards. Only its precise nature was still unclear. Expulsion was still regarded with trepidation by many anti-Communists. Even *The New York Times*, while applauding the offensive against the Communists, said that the expulsion of leftist unions might lead to self-destructive open warfare between the Left and Right, encouraged by the AFL. It would be best for the CIO to let the Communists stand "marked" for what they were and let them retain their membership, it said.[65] But Murray and Reuther remained intractable on the FE and raiding. Seeing no reason to compromise with UE on those issues, they were willing to accept the inevitable consequence: the continued refusal of the UE to pay its dues. In effect, they forced the UE to walk out of the CIO. This in turn opened the way for the expulsion of the rest of the leftist unions, for the main argu-ment against expelling them had always centered on the debilitating effects that the loss of the 400,000 strong UE would have had on the CIO. Now, with the UE on the way out of the CIO and a Carey-led electrical union already on the planning boards, literally waiting in the wings, why not get rid of the rest?

NOTES

1. Eugene Dennis, "The Main Lessons of the 1948 Elections," *Political Affairs*, vol. 27, no. 12 (December 1948), 1052.

2. CIO, *Daily Proceedings of the Constitutional Convention*, 1949, 281; *Daily Worker*, December 7, 1948.

3. CIO, *Proceedings*, 1949, 9-19.

4. Ibid., 157-68.

5. Ibid., 170-71.

6. Ibid., 228-30.

7. Ibid., 257-62.

8. Ibid., 156-58.

9. Ibid., 279-80.

10. Ibid., 342-43. This was a rather unfair characterization of the UOPWA's frantic efforts to secure his intervention against the raids on the organization from AFL and CIO unions.

11. Ibid., 212.

12. Ibid., 423.

13. Dennis, "The Main Lessons of the 1948 Elections," 1047-54; V. J. Jerome, "Lenin and Opportunism in the American Labor Movement," *Political Affairs*, vol. 28, no. 1 (January 1949), 1-15.

14. Jerome, "Lenin and Opportunism," 10; John Williamson, "Two Conventions of Labor," *Political Affairs*, vol. 28, no. 1 (January 1949), 27.

15. Williamson, "Two Conventions," 28.

16. Ibid., 28-35.

17. Ibid.; Jerome, "Lenin and Opportunism."

18. Jerome, "Lenin and Opportunism," 13.

19. Williamson, "Two Conventions," 44.

20. Michael Friedman, ed., "Recorded Time: The Story of an American Family. Junius, Gladys and Barbara Scales, 1920-1973" (unpublished ms. in possession of Mr. Friedman), 64.

21. Ibid., 63.

22. Ibid., *New York Herald Tribune*, April 23, May 6, 1949.

23. Earl Browder, *The Decline of the Left Wing of American Labor* (New York: the author, 1948), 6-29.

24. *CIO News*, September 5, 1949, which, in reporting some leftist statements, devoted twice as much space to its editorial comments than to the statements, making the article look something like the Talmud.

25. *The New York Times*, January 12, 1949.

26. Report of R. J. Thomas to Executive Board on Matters Relating to the ILWU, undated [April 1949?] in CIO, Papers, Catholic University of America Library, Washington, D.C. (hereafter CU), A7-27.

27. Ibid. Actually, Truman's victory played the crucial role in forcing them to deal with Bridges, for they had also relied on the hope that the new Dewey administration would crush Bridges once and for all.

28. ILWU, "Statement of Policy, World Federation of Trade Unions," Executive Board Meeting, November 30, December 1, 1948, copy in CIO Papers, CU, A7-27.

29. Rather a low blow, when most people still travelled by train across the continent. Bridges was the head of the only major union with a West Coast head office and the meetings were normally held in the East.

30. Murray to Timothy Flynn, April 5, 1949, CIO Papers, CU, A7-27.

31. Edwin A. Lahey, Oral History Collection of Columbia University (hereafter COHC), 67.

32. *NYT*, May 20, 1949.

33. Unsigned memo, May 16, 1949, CIO, Papers, Office of the Secretary-Treasurer, Wayne State University Archives of Labor History and Urban Affairs, Detroit, Michigan (hereafter Carey Papers, WSUA), Box 111.

34. Graham Dolan, "Eyewitness Story of Steelworkers' Attack on Travis," *The Union*, May 9, 1949.

35. Copies of Mine, Mill leaflets, Carey Papers, Box 111, "Mine, Mill" Folder.

36. Ibid.

37. Ibid.

38. E.g., see Leo Kendrick et al. to Carey, December 20, 1948, Carey Papers, Box 111 "Mine, Mill" Folder.

39. *NYT*, May 18, 1949. A report from the scene by Adolph Germer, which described Travis' injury as merely a black eye and ignored the circumstances of the clash, helped Murray push through this exoneration of his union. Frank Emspak, "The Break-Up of the Congress of Industrial Organizations (CIO), 1945-1950" (Ph.D. diss., University of Wisconsin, 1972), 231.

40. *CIO News*, September 19, 1949.

41. Ibid.

42. *NYT*, July 29, 1949.

43. "Travis Statement on Signing Taft-Hartley Law Affidavit," *The Union*, August 9, 1949; *NYT*, August 18, 1949.

44. CIO, Hearings before the Committee to Investigate Charges against the Food, Tobacco, Agricultural and Allied Workers of America (unpublished transcript), held in Washington, D.C., commencing January 6, 1950, vol. 1, p. 75.

45. James Matles and James Higgins, *Them and Us* (New York: Prentice-Hall, 1974), 194.

46. *NYT*, October 25, 1949.

47. *NYT*, February 11, 1949.

48. FE, Officers Report to Fourth Constitutional Convention, March 25-27, 1949, copy in CIO Papers, CU, Box A7-25.

49. "A statement to the membership of the FE-CIO from the International Officers," June 6, 1949; "Declaration of the Executive Board of FE-CIO," June 23, 1949, in CIO Papers, CU, Box A7-25.

50. FE, Officers Report, 1949.

51. Grant Oakes et al. "To All Members of FE-CIO," n.d.[1949?], "The UE-CIO Proposal to the Farm Equipment and Metal Workers"; UE, "Proposed Relationship between UE and FE," CIO Papers, CU, Box A7-25.

52. *NYT*, June 7, 1949.

53. *UE News*, May 2, 1949, cited in Emspak, "Break-Up," 302.

54. Emspak, "Break-Up," 312-14, 322-24.

55. *NYT*, August 19, 1949.

56. *CIO News*, September 19, 1949.

57. *NYT*, September 23, 1949.

58. Ibid.

59. Charles Madison, *American Labor Leaders* (New York: Harper, 1950), 325.

60. UE, *Proceedings*, 1949, 43, 103, cited in Emspak, "Break-Up," 317-18.

61. Ibid.

62. *NYT*, September 23, 1949.

63. The *New York Daily News* had reported that at a meeting of top CIO leaders on October 26 the decision had been made to oust the UE and charter a new union. *New York Daily News*, October 27, 1949, cited in Emspak, "Break-Up," 326.

64. *NYT*, October 31, 1949.

65. *NYT*, October 26, 1949.

16 THE PURGE

For Murray, the last straw may have been the viciousness of the attacks on him in the Communist press. Thin-skinned to begin with, the accusations that the USW was pandering to racism in its offensive against Mine, Mill in the South gnawed at him. Communist charges that the foreign policy which he supported represented a betrayal of the principles of Franklin D. Roosevelt, whose memory he revered, rankled. Allegations that he and the CIO were following a foreign policy laid down by "Wall Street" and were selling out to the employer class cut to the bone the man who had devoted his life to the betterment of the miners, steelworkers, and industrial workers of America. The leftist claims that Murray and the USW were selling out the Steelworkers in the hard-fought negotiations and strike of 1949, when they confronted the entire steel industry, were likely the last straw. It was difficult enough to keep hundreds of thousands of strikers in line without Communists telling USW members that their leaders were "lackeys" of the company owners and prepared to sell the workers out. It is no surprise that Murray's opening report to the CIO convention which gathered in Cleveland on October 31, 1949, was full of the bitterness of one who had been attacked by the Communist "slander machine" and wounded to the core. With Father Rice and, it seemed to the leftists, a veritable horde of anti-Communist priests looking benignly on as his invited guests,[1] he let loose a blistering opening salvo. "The Moscow radio has called your President a 'traitor' to American workers," he said.

Leaders of unions who wish to be judged as responsible men have accused your President of subservience to corporate interests; of selling out the interests of American workers; of race baiting; of company unionism; of repudiation of the democratic principles to which your President, through all the years of his life, has remained steadfastly loyal.

The "carping, unjustified criticism" of the USW and its leadership with which a "small group of union officials" had filled the press was "diabolical, prejudiced, and ill-founded in fact," he said, and constituted "the most flagrant approach to union strikebreaking" he had ever seen. The CIO could no longer tolerate the obstructionism of those who were interested in using the CIO, but represented only 10 percent of its membership. "It obviously has the power of disaffiliation over those organizations whose leaders' policies, statements and actions demonstrate their contempt and their hostility toward our general policies," said Murray.[2]

Then it was the UE's turn to throw down a gauntlet. The next day, after their last-minute attempts to obtain a commitment from Murray to end raiding and curb Carey's machinations against them were rebuffed, they refused to pay their per capita dues and consequently declined to take their seats at the convention. Rather than seriously entertain their proposals, they charged, the CIO leaders made it clear "that the main business of the CIO Convention would be a red-baiting spree for the gratification of the anti-labor commercial press and the politicians to whom the CIO now subordinates itself."[3]

The failure of the UE delegation to take their seats seems finally to have pushed Murray into action on expulsion. For at least six weeks, while Murray agonized over the problem, Walter Reuther had walked around with three proposed constitutional amendments which would lay the groundwork for the expulsion of UE as well as all the other leftist unions. Murray called a special meeting of the Resolutions Committee that evening that received and reported out the Reuther amendments for floor action the next day.[4]

The first amendment barred members of "the Communist Party, any fascist organization, or other totalitarian movement, or [those] who consistently pursue policies and activities directed towards the achievement of the program" of such totalitarian organizations from membership on the CIO Executive Board. The next section gave the purified Executive Board the power to expel, by a two-thirds vote, any affiliate whose policies and activities were "consistently directed towards the achievement of the program or the purposes of the Communist Party, any fascist organization, or other totalitarian movement, rather than the objectives and policies set forward in the constitution of the CIO." Although expelled unions could appeal to the national CIO convention, the expulsions would take effect when decreed by the Executive Board. The third amendment authorized a rise in per capita

dues large enough to compensate for the funds lost because of the
expulsion of the leftist unions, especially the UE, ILWU, and Fur
Workers, all of whom were consistent dues payers.[5]

The debate on the resolutions was predictable. As a *Fortune* correspondent at the convention remarked, because the representatives to
national CIO conventions were almost all "pork-choppers," paid officers and staff men, there was little spontaneous debate from the
floor, for few delegates would defy their leaders.[6] The speakers for
and against were exceptionally eloquent, because they repeated their
respective themes innumerable times: the anti-Communists denouncing the Communists' fealty to Moscow, the Communists pleading for
respect for their rights. The only new twists were the repeated expres-
sions of horror by the anti-Communists at the Communist attacks on
the beloved Phil Murray.[7] By the end of the debate, even Murray had
taken to referring to himself as "kindly, tolerant, patient, Phil Murray."[8]

Murray echoed the theme of Reuther, Reive, and the other anti-
Communist speakers. There was simply "one issue, and one issue
alone, and that is . . . Communism," he said. The unions fighting the
constitutional amendments had "supported the foreign policy of the
Soviet Union against the government of the United States" at every
meeting of the CIO Executive Board since the fall of 1946, he charged.
What they aimed for was to make the CIO "subject to the dictums of the
Soviet state, the Communist Party." As for the raiding issue, 90 percent
of the "alleged raids" were not raids at all but anti-Communist insur-
rections of the rank and file. No one could have been more tolerant
over the years than he, but he had finally given up on the futile attempt
to make the Communists "recognize that there is a trade union line" in
the United States and "it must be an independent, democratic trade
union line." As their refusal to support the CIO-endorsed candidate in
1948 had shown, the "chattels of Sovietism" wanted the benefits of
CIO membership, but were unwilling to follow the line settled upon by
the majority.[9]

The constitutional amendments passed easily, but that was not all.
The UE boycott of the convention allowed the anti-Communists to
accelerate their program. On Tuesday evening, the resolutions committee was again convened hastily, and the next morning, immediately
after Secretary of Labor Maurice Tobin had finished expressing his
hope to the convention that American trade unions would remain
"immune to the poison of subversive influences," another extraordinary resolution was circulated among the delegates. Bearing many of
the hallmarks of the Carey-Reuther style of anti-Communist rhetoric,
it began: "We can no longer tolerate within the family of CIO the
Communist Party masquerading as a labor union." It cited the UE's

support for Soviet foreign policy and opposition to that of the United States, as well as its defiance of the CIO majority and attacks on Phil Murray, and concluded that the UE should therefore be expelled from the CIO and a new union in its field should be created.[10]

The claims of the left-wingers that the UE was being railroaded and that it was being deprived of due process were derided as "a hypocritical sham" by Murray. Rather than appearing at the convention to fight their own battle, the UE leaders "ran like skulking cowards, and after they did run they left those apostles of hate behind them to defend them," he said.[11] Before the day was out, the resolution received the required two-thirds approval and the Executive Board, at a special meeting, issued a charter to the new International Union of Electrical, Radio, and Machine Workers (CIO), headed by James Carey.[12]

The convention also expelled the FE, but this had been slated earlier and was a case of closing the barn door after the horses had fled.[13] As it ended with the traditional nominations for vice-presidents to sit on the Executive Board, jarring notes were introduced into the usual display of unanimity. When the names of representatives of the left-wing unions were put forward, there were repeated objections on the grounds that their election would contravene the new anti-Communist constitutional amendment. Their names were therefore struck from the list of nominees for the new Executive Board which would meet immediately after the convention to decide their fate.[14]

The triumphant anti-Communists displayed little grace in victory. "The scummy bastards got what they deserved," said a Steelworkers organizer.[15] Sidney Hillman's widow, an Amalgamated delegate, was among the more moderate in her comments. "They've done this themselves," she said.

We tolerated them for years. We didn't care what their private thoughts were. But when they call Murray a fascist and a Nazi, we had enough. It was up to the neck, goddam it. We defended that son of a bitch Bridges for years to keep him in this country. But look what he's done. Look at what he says these past two years. Do you think I like taking this action which is against my better conscience. But what else can we do?[16]

The leftists were in disarray; any unity they had hoped to preserve had broken down at the outset of the convention, when the UE boycotted it alone. The absence of coordination was manifest. Bridges, who had called the UE withdrawal ill-advised and vowed that his union would stay in the CIO until kicked out, wryly pointed this out to reporters. "This should torpedo all that crap about us forming a bloc and the organization of a third labor movement," he said as he peered through his broken glasses.[17] Dejected United Office Workers President James Durkin said gloomily, "I don't know what the hell will happen next." His union's director of organization added, "It's a bloody mess."[18]

The day after the convention closed, the now totally non-Communist Executive Board ordered hearings to be held regarding charges laid by Board member William Steinberg, president of the American Radio Association, that ten CIO unions had been consistently following the Communist party line and should therefore be expelled from the CIO. Four three-man committees were appointed to investigate the charges and make recommendations to the Executive Board. The ten unions were the American Communications Association, the FTA, the Fur and Leather Workers, Mine, Mill, the United Office and Professional Workers, the United Public Workers, the ILWU, the Marine Cooks and Stewards, the International Fishermen's Union, and the United Furniture Workers. Each committee received two or three unions to investigate. The Furniture Workers were soon dropped from the list. Their Communist leadership was voted out of office at the union's convention before the hearings on them began.[19]

The committee hearings, begun in early January 1950, had all the makings of "kangaroo courts." The prosecutor, William Steinberg, whose small union, composed mainly of ships' radio officers, was at odds with the Bridges-dominated mariners unions, was not expected to be unbiased. However, since the Executive Board had already been purged, it was almost inevitable that all three committee members, who acted as judges, would be biased against the leftists as well. One committee, for example, was composed of Joseph Curran, a defector still battling Communist pockets of resistance in his own union, Emil Mazey, an aide of Walter Reuther, and Murray's man in the Steelworkers, David McDonald. The chairman of the ILWU hearings, O. A. Knight of the Oil Workers, was not quite impartial on Bridges' foreign policy line; subsequent revelations suggested that his union was a major conduit for CIA funds into the CIO.[20]

Leftist obedience to the dictates of the party was now more frayed than ever. The party's political leadership recommended that the accused unions make their defense on the basis of union autonomy. The trials should be exposed as "phony" and "rigged." The charge that the leftists had sold out their members in the interests of a foreign power could be easily refuted by citing the great economic gains the unions had achieved for their members.[21]

Although most of the defendants used all or part of the suggested arguments, there is little evidence that they coordinated their defensive strategy. The Mine, Mill leadership followed the general line suggested, albeit in a characteristically belligerent manner. They tried to use the hearings as a sounding board to trumpet their achievements and refused to counter most of the charges against them directly. Rather, after they returned from an adjournment to prepare their defense, they defiantly attacked the committee and the CIO for "rigging" their expulsion.[22] The FTA, on the other hand, led by ex-scholar Donald Henderson, resolved to fight to stay within the CIO and assembled a documented case to defend itself against the charges, a case which Henderson had considerable difficulty presenting because of the repeated interruptions of committee member Joseph Curran who, along with Chairman Jacob Potofsky, conducted a running commentary and refutation of Henderson's prepared statement to the committee.[23]

The most openly Communist of the unions, the Fur Workers, ultimately paid the party the least heed. It simply defied and taunted the CIO. Ben Gold wrote Carey a public letter awarding him the Nazi Iron Cross for his purported statement that whereas during the last war the liberals had united with the Communists to defeat the Fascists, during the next one they might need to unite with the Fascists to beat the Communists.[24] Although they had initially urged their members to stay in the CIO, by the time the Fur Workers' turn to be heard came up, the union leadership had given up any hope of receiving a fair hearing and the union convention voted to leave the CIO. The committee went through the motions of holding a hearing anyway, duly pondering Steinberg's evidence and voting to expel the Fur Workers.[25]

Harry Bridges fulfilled his promise to be kicked out rather than walk out, and used the hearings to display the vast amount of knowledge of courtroom and quasi-courtroom procedure he had accumulated in his almost twenty years of continuous litigation over citizenship and deportation. Using the absence of a bill of particulars and the proceedings' trampling of due process as his jumping-off points, he managed to exasperate the committee with his superior knowledge of the law regarding quasi-judicial hearings and drag the hearings out for hour after hour and day after day while he raised intricate points of order.[26]

Those who attacked the way the hearings were run had a valid basis for doing so. Not only was the bias of the "judges" evident from their backgrounds, but the procedures which they tried to impose to arrive quickly at their foregone conclusions were decidedly unfair. At the first hearing, that of the FTA, Chairman Potofsky ruled that the union was not entitled to have counsel present because the CIO position had always been "that any matter within the family can by handled in the family without counsel from outside for either side." Yet, this was a matter of such seriousness and the right of due process in such doubt that expert legal advice was clearly in order. Moreover, Potofsky would not even allow the defendants to call witnesses in their own behalf. Only an FTA-obtained court order forced him to do so.[27]

As Harry Bridges said often during his trial, the charges against the unions were also vague to the extreme. All were accused of the same thing: of having violated the new constitutional amendment by pursuing policies "consistently directed towards the achievement of the programs and policies of the Communist Party rather than the objectives and policies set forth in the Constitution of the CIO." Yet, it was easier to *know* that this was true than to prove it; in fact, the leftists could easily show that for the most part the policies they had pursued were policies followed by a large majority of the CIO's non-Communists until the fateful decision over whom to support for United States president in 1948. It was not enough to fall back on the favorite response of Carey and his followers: "If it walks like a duck and talks like a duck, it must *be* a duck." Yet, for the most part, this is what the committees did.

The leftists could and did attack the trials as attempts to impose political uniformity on the CIO. To support this charge, Donald Henderson even produced a *Washington Post* editorial expressing the concern that if the new CIO tack were not changed, "the time may not be distant when the dissident non-Communist elements within the unions will face expulsion for political heresy—if, that is, they presume to criticize the political program approved by union majorities, often at the dictation of the union leaders."[28]

The anti-Communists tried to refute these charges, and took pains to argue that Communist loyalties were *sui generis*. They argued time and time again that loyalty to the CP was *ipso facto* loyalty to the Soviet Union rather than the CIO. Indeed, in ruling against the FTA, the committee said it acted on the assumption that "by consistently pursuing the program and purposes of the Communist Party, the FTA tends to undermine the democratic goals of the CIO."

There can be no doubt about the violent clash between the constitutional objectives and policies of the CIO and the program and purposes of the Communist Party. The CIO is dedicated to advancing the cause of liberty and the never-ending struggle for equality begun by our forefathers; to the end of achieving a world of free men and women. . . .

The Communist Party is precisely the type of organization which the CIO is under a constitutional mandate to oppose—one which would use power to exploit the people for the benefit of alien loyalty. . . . In the event of conflict between the needs of the Soviet Union and the best interests of American labor, the former must always prevail.[29]

To buttress this analysis, at each hearing Steinberg would trot out the well-worn passage from Lenin's *Left-Wing Communism, An Infantile Disorder*, in which Lenin admonished Communists to "agree to any and every sacrifice . . . to resort to all sorts of devices, manoeuvers and illegal methods, to evasion and subterfuge, in order to penetrate the trade unions, to remain in them and to carry on Communist work in them at all costs."[30] Yet the ellipse replaces the modifying phrase "even—if need be—" deleted by Steinberg and the committees, which tones down Lenin's admonition and makes it what it was, a way of emphasizing the necessity of work within imperfect unions at all costs, rather than setting up competing, "pure," leftist trade unions. Moreover, the larger context of Lenin's statement, ironic under the circumstances, was never mentioned: Lenin wrote that Communists might have to resort to such tactics because the "Messrs. 'Gompers' and other 'leaders' of opportunism" would "resort to every trick of bourgeois diplomacy, to the aid of bourgeois governments, the priests, the police and the courts, to prevent Communists joining the trade unions, to force them out by every means, to make their work in the trade unions as unpleasant as possible, to insult, bait and persecute them."[31]

Given the assumption that communism and membership in the CIO were inherently incompatible, all the anti-Communists had to show was that the accused unions had "consistently" followed the party line. Thus, the heart of each hearing was a detailed presentation compiled by CIO Research Director Stanley Ruttenberg that compared the stands, mainly on foreign policy, of the union's newspapers and conventions with those of the *Daily Worker* and the Soviet government. The climax would usually be a chronicling of the support which the union's officers preferred to Wallace's Progressive party. In some cases, for example when Mike Quill and Hedley Stone testified against Bridges, and Homer Wilson and William Eckert testified against Mine, Mill, defectors from the party gave supplemental testimony about meetings between union leaders and CP functionaries. The Mine, Mill testimony was especially damaging because Wilson and Eckert were able to recall a number of times and places in which the party leadership had directly intervened in the running of the union by convincing union leaders, for example, that Reid Robinson should step down and be replaced by Maurice Travis and, subsequently, that Travis should be replaced by John Clark, a non-Communist. In the Mine, Mill case, the committee was able to conclude not only that the union's "policies . . . follow the Communist Party line but also that they follow that line because the Communist Party is in direct control of the Union's leadership and dictates to that leadership the policies it shall adopt."[32]

The testimony of defectors was welcomed by the committees, for it was obvious from the outset that reliance on Charles Ruttenberg's comparisons of the union line with the party line was a dubious proposition. At one of the first of the hearings, the Mine, Mill leadership demonstrated the shallowness of this technique by submitting a memorandum which, by using Ruttenberg's techniques, "proved" that the CIO itself had consistently followed the party line from 1938 to 1947, a charge which the abashed committee called "preposterous" but whose effect was nevertheless telling.[33]

But from the outset there had been little doubt over what the various committees would find and, predictably, during the first six months of 1950, they all issued similarly-worded reports urging the CIO Executive Board to expel the nine miscreant unions, recommendations which the Board dutifully carried out. By mid-1950, unions claiming to represent over one million members had been drummed out of the CIO.

NOTES

1. *National Guardian,* January 16, 1950.

2. CIO, *Daily Proceedings of the Constitutional Conventions,* 1949, 54-56.

3. UE, Press Release, November 1, 1949, copy in Walter Reuther, Papers, Wayne State University Archives of Labor History and Urban Affairs, Detroit, Mich. (hereafter WSUA), Series 3, "CIO-UE" Folder; *The New York Times,* November 2, 1949.

4. Win Booth to Don Bermingham, November 3, 1949, Daniel Bell, Collection of Material on Socialism and Communism in the U.S.A., Tamiment Institute Library, New York University, New York, N.Y., Box 4, "CIO-National" Folder.

5. CIO, *Proceedings,* 1949, 240, 288-89.

6. Blanche Finn to Don Bermingham, November 4, 1949, Bell Collection, Box 4, "CIO-National" Folder.

7. CIO, *Proceedings,* 1949, 239-81.

8. Ibid., 278.

9. Ibid., 274-81.

10. Ibid., 302.

11. Ibid., 325.

12. Ibid., 487. Exactly who terminated the UE-CIO relationship has been a source of some controversy. Matles, Emspak, and the UE leadership always claimed that they left first, that in fact they were not expelled. Carey, Murray, and the anti-Communists, on the other hand, usually described UE as having been expelled as an undesirable from the CIO. There are weaknesses in both cases. In their press conference, the UE leaders did not say with certitude that they were leaving the CIO for good. On the other hand, among the many reasons given for "expelling" them in the resolution was that their October 7, 1949 ultimatum to Murray represented "the final stage" in their plan to withdraw from the CIO and set up a new, Communist-dominated third labor federation. Their press conference, said the resolution, represented the carrying out of that threat. James Matles and James Higgins, *Them and Us* (New York: Prentice-Hall, 1974), 194; Julius Emspak, Oral History Interview, Oral History Collection of Columbia University (hereafter COHC), 28; *NYT,* November 3, 1949; CIO, *Proceedings,* 1949, 308. Moreover, the UE press conference was interpreted as an announcement that UE was leaving the CIO by

Michael Quill, who said shortly afterwards that "the UE has left the CIO . . . they deserted about four hours ago." CIO, *Proceedings*, 1949, 273.

13. Ibid., 344-47.

14. Ibid., 494-505.

15. Finn to Bermingham, November 4, 1949.

16. Ibid.

17. Ibid.

18. *Cleveland Press*, November 1, 1949.

19. CIO, Press Release, "CIO Committees Recommend Expulsion of Four Unions as Communist-dominated," February 14, 1950, copy in CIO, Papers, Catholic University of America Library, Washington, D.C. (hereafter CU), A7-25.

20. *New York Times*, May 9, 1967.

21. *Daily Worker*, December 6, 7, 8, 9, 1949.

22. CIO, "Hearings Before the Committee to Investigate Charges Against the International Union of Mine, Mill, and Smelter Workers, February, 1950" (hereafter referred to as "Mine, Mill Hearings"); CIO, "Report of the Committee to Investigate Charges Against the International Union of Mine, Mill, and Smelter Workers," February 1950 (hereafter cited as "Mine, Mill Report"), copies in CIO, Office of the Secretary-Treasurer, Wayne State University Archives of Labor History and Urban Affairs, Detroit, Michigan (hereafter Carey Papers), Box 111.

23. CIO, "Hearings Before the Committee to Investigate Charges Against the Food, Tobacco, Agricultural and Allied Workers of America" (hereafter referred to as "FTA Hearings"), January 1950, in Carey Papers, Box 109, 234-60.

24. Gold to Carey, February 20, 1950, reprinted in *DW*, February 21, 1950; Fur Section, CPUSA, leaflet, "Ben Gold Awards Nazi Iron Cross Medal to James B. Carey."

25. Fur Section, CPUSA, "Ben Gold Awards Nazi Iron Cross"; CIO, Transcript of Hearings to Investigate Charges Against the International Fur and Leather Workers Union, 1950 (hereafter cited as "Fur Hearings"), copy in Carey Papers, Box 109, "Fur Workers" Folder, 3.

26. CIO, "Transcript of Hearings before the Committee to Investigate Charges against the International Longshoremen's and Warehousemen's Union," May 1950 (hereafter CIO, "ILWU Hearings"), copy in Carey Papers, Box 110.

27. CIO, "FTA Hearings," 1-40.

28. CIO, "FTA Hearings," 257.

29. CIO, "Report of the Committee to Investigate Charges Against the Food, Tobacco, Agricultural and Allied Workers of America," February 1950 (hereafter cited as "FTA Report"), copy in Carey Papers, Box 109.

30. The edition cited was Vladimir I. Lenin, *Left-Wing Communism, An Infantile Disorder* (New York: International Publishers, 1934), 38.

31. Vladimir I. Lenin, *Left-Wing Communism, An Infantile Disorder* (Peking: Foreign Languages Publishing House, 1965), 46-47.

32. CIO, "ILWU Hearings," *passim*, "Mine, Mill Hearings," *passim*; CIO, "Mine, Mill Report.

33. CIO, "Mine, Mill Report." There was nothing unique or original about the "prosecution's" techniques. They had been refined by the House Un-American Activities Committee and its file-amassing general counsel, J. B. Matthews, as well as by the FBI. By 1950, Communists were accustomed to defending themselves against this kind of attack, and the Mine, Mill defense was one of the standard ploys.

17 MOPPING UP

For some months after the purges, there was desultory talk of forming a new left-wing labor federation, but the outbreak of the Korean War, which made the leftist unions even larger targets for government persecution, undermined the idea of creating an organization with that high a profile. Rather, the party leadership, fighting a desperate battle to avoid imprisonment under the Smith Act, emphasized the necessity to take cover in non-Communist organizations. The rationale remained essentially the same as it had been since 1933: to create a "united front from below" by linking bread-and-butter issues with a broad "anti-monopoly, anti-imperialist" platform.[1] By September 1950, while still "greeting" talk of a third labor federation, the party was toying more seriously with the idea of creating something like Foster's old TUEL, a center that would coordinate left-wing activities in both "Left-led" and "Right-led" unions.[2]

But again the party leadership displayed a suicidal inability to leave bad enough alone. Calling for "united action" among left-wing and right-wing union locals on wage negotiations, the party's political leadership tried to press the UE into cooperating with the IUE. It praised UE's (rejected) offer to join with the UAW in negotiations with International Harvester, but bemoaned its failure to extend the hand of cooperation to IUE against General Electric.[3] The result was the final alienation of Matles and large segments of the UE leadership. According to John Gates, in early 1951 Matles broke with the party, telling the leadership he had lost all confidence in their judgment.[4] The loss of influence in the UE, the cornerstone of any new grouping, seems to have put paid to the ideas of a third labor federation and a new TUEL. By early 1953, the party was talking of the inherent weakness of leftist organizations in the prevailing atmosphere. "Every organization established by the Left is branded 'subversive' by the real subversives," wrote Gil Green, and it would be "wishful thinking" to expect a mass influx into them. "Left sectarianism" remained the main danger, he said, and Communists should concentrate on mobilizing the masses from within non-Communist-led organizations.[5] The few remaining unionists who still listened to the party then began searching for ways to reenter the AFL or CIO.

The impulse to take cover was understandable, for all of the traditional forces of anticommunism had now come together in a tremendous barrage on the dwindling Communist positions. The full weight of every kind of governmental institution pressed relentlessly upon them. The Justice Department scrutinized their non-Communist affidavits for signs of perjury; the Internal Revenue Service combed their tax returns; the FBI devoted an immense amount of effort to harassing, infiltrating, sabotaging, and suborning them. The Defense Department and Atomic Energy Commission warned contract holders against dealing with them while the Immigration Department tried to deport them. The Labor Department and NLRB discriminated against them while congressmen and senators drew up ever-more-fiendish legislation to bar them from union activities. The Coast Guard "screened" longshoremen on the West Coast and denied over 700 ILWU members the right to work because of their suspected Communist sympathies. Congressional committees crisscrossed the country in the headline-grabbing race to "expose" them. The House Un-American Activities Committee, the Internal Security Subcommittee of the Senate Judiciary Committee, and assorted other congressional committees investigated "Communist activities" in city after city in 1950, 1951, and 1952, concentrating on locals of those unions expelled from the CIO.[6] Among the shoddier of these sessions were those conducted by Senator Hubert Humphrey's subcommittee of the Senate Labor and Public Welfare Committee in which Humphrey, determined to demonstrate his fervant anticommunism as well as his expertise on the subject, seemed to play the role of chief prosecutor and chief witness as well as the chairman.[7]

The UE, the object of congressional investigations since its creation, remained a favorite target. Even before the 1949 CIO convention, as the forces were marshalled for the 1949 UE convention, UE anti-Communists in the crucial Pittsburgh area were favored with a visit from HUAC just before the vote for convention delegates was held. UE President Albert Fitzgerald charged that the investigation had been arranged by Father Rice, "an ambitious power-hungry priest who makes a career of meddling in labor unions," and his band of "Quislings."[8] Adjectives aside, Fitzgerald was correct. Father Rice had convinced committee member Francis Walter of Easton, Pennsylvania, that this was an opportune moment to investigate Communist infiltration in giant Westinghouse Local 601, the scene of a seesaw battle between Communists and the rank-and-file caucus which Rice backed. Although the committee claimed it was examining the security threat posed by the Communists in Local 601 working in Westinghouse's radar production facilities, western Pennsylvania congressmen told the press that the visit was aimed at influencing the delegate votes for the UE convention.[9]

HUAC pursued the UE relentlessly. In August 1950 the committee sent contempt of Congress citations against the UE and ILWU leaders who had refused to cooperate with the House of Representatives on the grounds of the Fifth and First Amendments. There, only Congressman Vito Marcantonio of New York voted against the citations. Arguing that he did so to uphold the dignity of Congress, even Congressman Emanuel Celler of Brooklyn, who was a consistent opponent of the committee, voted for the citations. Emspak, described by Celler as having shown himself to be "brash, impertinent, and utterly contemptuous of Congress" in his HUAC appearances, was cited by a 373-to-1 vote. As the fifty-five other cases droned on for two days, the votes were equally overwhelming.[10] Now, in addition to battling the preying IUE, the companies, and a host of governmental agencies, Emspak and four other top officials in the UE had to struggle against the United States Congress, intent on throwing them in jail.

The Truman administration did more than supplement congressional pressure on UE. Truman openly favored the "loyal" IUE over the UE, welcoming it as a bargaining agent that would "shun subversive activity" and represent the "hopes and aspirations of loyal American citizens."[11] At the founding convention of the IUE Secretary of the Air Force Stuart Symington hinted strongly that in a national emergency the administration would cancel UE contracts, while Secretary of Labor Tobin, welcoming IUE to the fold, warned that "we don't want any agents of the Kremlin in the American labor movement."[12]

The crucial elections in the giant corporations of the electrical industry, which were to determine the fate of the new union, were held under NLRB supervision from April to June 1950. Thanks to its outside friends, the IUE was able to marshal a formidable array of money and organizational talent. The national CIO made aiding the IUE the top priority for all organizing staff.[13] The CIO gave IUE $100,000 a month from November 1949 to June 1950, a total of over $805,000 by September 30, 1950. The Steelworkers pledged over $200,000 in the first twelve months of the new union's existence.[14] In many of the districts the weight of the Catholic church was thrown on the side of the IUE. In Pittsfield, Massachusetts, the heavily Catholic local voted to join IUE after the Catholic priest in that industrial town told Catholic workers that the election represented a choice between "Christ and Stalin."[15] The media were often helpful as well. Typical of much of the local press handling of the contest was the *Schenectady Gazette*. When, one week before the crucial election at GE in Schenectady, Emspak and Matles were subpoenaed to appear before a New York grand jury investigating subversive activities, the *Gazette* plastered the story over its front page. Just to make certain that no one missed the point, it inserted a box into the story informing its readers that indeed these were the leaders of the very same union that was vying with IUE in next week's election.[16]

The IUE could usually count on the then firmly anti-Communist NLRB when rulings on election disputes were required.[17] It was also helped by the threat of losses of defense contracts should plants vote to remain in UE. In 1949, even before the creation of IUE, the Atomic Energy Commission ordered GE to stop bargaining with UE in any plant working on AEC contracts and began a policy of refusing to give contracts to UE-represented plants.[18] Now, out on the hustings for IUE, Secretary of Labor Tobin, at a rally at the GE plant in Lynn, Massachusetts, warned that the election there was not a local issue. Rather, it was "a question of whether a vital industry will be in the hands of Americans or friends of Soviet Russia."[19] The implications were clear.

The large employers in the industry played an ambivalent game, although they tended to intervene at times in favor of the IUE, saving the IUE a considerable amount of money by themselves filing for certification elections, refusing to continue UE contracts after they expired, and abandoning the checkoff of UE dues. Carey often charged that employers favored the UE because they knew its communism weakened its bargaining position. Yet for the most part the giants, GE and Westinghouse, maintained a stance of neutrality. As they recognized in moments of relative candor, it was clearly in their interests to have representation in their plants divided between two weakened unions at loggerheads with each other.[20]

Each union interpreted the results of the 1950 NLRB elections differently, the UE claiming that it won forty elections to the IUE's fifty,[21] while the IUE, using a different definition of elections and excluding the results of the crucial GE and Westinghouse elections, claimed to have won 135 to the "UE-CP's" 16. By June 15, it claimed that is represented 228,336 workers.[22] Whatever the exact figures, it is likely that by the end of that month the UE had lost 50 percent of its pre-November 1949 membership, the bulk of it to IUE.[23] Over the next ten years its slide lost some momentum and it consolidated itself in a few strongholds, with a membership of below 100,000. The real winners of the protracted struggle over the next decade were the employers. Not only did the number of workers represented by both unions decline to about half of the UE's 1948 membership, but the two weakened unions set off against each other played into employers' hands often enough to allow wage rates and working conditions in the electrical industry to fall far behind those in comparable fields.[24]

There were a number of reasons behind the decline of UE, but the appeal of anticommunism among workers was a relatively minor one. As UE anti-Communist leader Harry Block later recalled, the Carey forces' anti-Communist appeals generally fell upon deaf ears on the shop floor. They were resorted to only because of the lack of anything better to use.[25] Significantly, one of the major factors affecting the decline was the relatively great degree of internal democracy in UE. Contrary to the notion that Communist unionists inevitably fashioned "iron grips" on unions, crushing internal opposition through bureaucratic artifice and administrative purges, the UE leftists had been either unwilling or unable to change its constitution and reduce the substantial extent to which power in the union was decentralized. Thus, throughout the years since UE's founding, many opponents of the administration like Block were able to maintain union posts at the district level and continue their battle against the faction in power from within their union offices.

Another reason for the decline was that although anticommunism may have swayed few members, respect and affection for Phil Murray and the CIO, against whom UE had to run, likely did, especially with the many Catholics in the industry among whom Murray had developed a close following by 1950. Also, the IUE was able to exploit well-grounded fears that the UE would not be able to deliver the goods as well as it could, fears that were given credence by the abundant evidence that the UE leaders had nothing but enemies in Washington, while Carey's union had many friends, very important in an industry so tied up in defense contracts.

The IUE continued to receive aid from Washington even after 1953, when people who were not friends of Carey's took over the White House. Government harassment of the UE leadership continued unabated, with Carey urging on and aiding the various investigations. In 1953 during a contest over representation at the GE company in Massachusetts, he gave the press a list of 200 alleged Communists in UE. Telling the state anti-Communist commission that UE was not a union, but "a Communist organization masquerading as a labor organization," he called on the NLRB to stop scheduling certification elections involving it. He warned that if an election was held at the GE jet engine factory, the UE would win, giving it access to military secrets. He demanded that GE not allow secret work to be done at UE plants and that the government withdraw its contracts from plants represented by UE.[26] This was already being done by the Atomic Energy Commission and was an idea which Carey had repeatedly pressed on his ally, Senator Hubert Humphrey, whose Senate subcommittee held extensive hearings on communism in unions as it considered new anti-Communist legislation.[27]

Carey received help from both GE and Senator Joseph McCarthy on the eve of the crucial Massachusetts elections. When McCarthy's subcommittee arrived in Boston to hold three weeks of hearings on Communist infiltration at GE, the corporation announced that any employees who admitted to being Communists would be fired immediately. Those who refused to testify would be suspended for ninety days with pay and given time either to testify or to conclusively refute the charges against them. If they did neither, they would be fired. Publicly, Carey and the IUE objected to this policy, saying that it would merely get the underlings, the rank-and-file Communists, but leave the real culprits, the top leaders who were not employed at GE, unscathed.[28] Privately, however, he approved. Political freedom was not involved, he told a *Time* reporter confidentially, because "the Communist Party is not a political party but an agency of the Kremlin."[29] The McCarthy committee visit tipped the balance to the IUE and it beat back the UE attempt to regain representation at the GE plants, winning by 5,546 to 4,806.[30]

The most important result of the outside pressure was not that it opened the eyes of so many workers to the nefarious political beliefs of UE leaders but that it inspired in these leaders, hounded as they were both inside and outside the labor movement, a tendency to settle for what they could get from employers rather than risk long strikes during which they would be even more vulnerable to attack. This in turn undermined the workers' confidence in their ability to produce as well as IUE at the bargaining table.[31] This was the major factor, for example, in the UE's loss of its key Schenectady local, whose 20,000 members had been Emspak's original base and had long been a center of leftist influence. When the UE's weakness forced it to accept a poor contract with GE to head off the IUE threat, the local's leadership, many of whom had been close associates of the Communists or party members, took the local into the IUE rather than face almost certain overthrow by a disgruntled membership.[32] The IUE realized that this was its most telling argument against UE. In a pamphlet issued after the defection, it told those who remained in UE that "with so few members, and with the UE spending all of its time trying to defend itself against such disaffiliations, it can't do the job for the people in the plants. UE can't defend you," said the leaflet, "the only way to protect your jobs . . . [is] to unite in the IUE-CIO."[33]

In 1955, the CP decided to give up on independent leftist unions. The Communist Control Act of 1954 had given the government even more power to crush Communist unionism. The attorney general could now have the Subversive Activities Control Board declare a union Communist-controlled, thus depriving it of the protection of the NLRA; as few as 20 percent of a union's members were allowed to call a special election to reorganize the union under new, non-Communist leaders who would be able to maintain their contracts and avail themselves of the NLRA and NLRB. The act in effect exempted unions affiliated with the AFL and CIO, thus solidifying the feeling among the party leadership that independent leftist unions were now simply untenable.[34]

The response of Communist unionists to the party's abandonment of independent unionism was even more ragged than usual. Many of the union leaders were now involved almost full-time in staying out of prison. Their lives had become an endless bout of court cases, their contacts with the party had dwindled compared with their relationship to their lawyers. The entire political leadership of the party had just been convicted of violating the Smith Act and was in no shape to ensure compliance with its orders. Some leaders were already in prison, others were underground, and the rest were desperately battling to stay out of jail. Thus, only some Communists seem to have carried out the order, if indeed it was that explicit, while others, as had always been the wont of many Communist unionists, went their own way.

In the UE, this led to a curious phenomenon. At the very same time that the government tried to prove that it was "Communist-dominated," many Communists left it. Whole Communist-led districts picked up stakes and moved into other unions. Districts 3 and 7 went into the International Association of Machinists. Part of District 8 joined the IAM while the ex-FE locals in the district finally joined the UAW. District 9 dispersed among the IUE, IAM, International Brotherhood of Electrical Workers (AFL), the UAW, and the Allied Industrial Workers. In all they may have led about 50,000 members out of UE.[35] Other Communists, however, stayed. In mid-1955 the UE turned down Carey's terms for a merger of the two unions because he not only insisted on its taking place on a local by local basis, but he refused to have the IUE drop its prohibition against Communist officers.[36]

Communists in other unions were not even as fortunate as those who managed to hang on in the UE. In the UAW, Reuther's 1947 victory had been followed by a purge of impressive proportions. He immediately fired over one hundred UAW staff members, beginning with Maurice Sugar, the union's Communist general counsel. R. J. Thomas fled to the CIO staff in Washington but George Addes and Richard Frankensteen were driven from the labor movement forever, with Addes moving from the ownership of a small night club to a succession of small business ventures.

The days of UAW "frontier democracy," slipping away during the war, now passed rapidly as Reuther built up a well-organized machine based on over 700 well-paid, obedient officials. Dissent of all kinds was punished severely (banishment from office or even the union), and outlets for it were severely restricted, as union conventions became more infrequent and more powerless.[37] The man whom J. Edgar Hoover had suspected so deeply during the war now received aid from FBI agents, who interrogated his opponents and asked why, if they denied being Communists, they did not support Reuther. Immigration Service agents put pressure on those of his opponents over whom they held powers.[38] Many "progressives" saw the handwriting on the wall and joined his side, taking advantage of the fact that he was always ready to accept and reward defectors, no matter how bitter they had been towards him, so long as they submitted to the discipline of his organization.

Finally, with almost 90 percent of the UAW in the hands of his supporters, Reuther ran into one major roadblock: giant Local 600, whose 60,000 members made it the largest union local in the United States. The struggle over Local 600 highlighted a number of factors that were important in Reuther's overall victory in the UAW: the utility of outside help, the absence of the CP's much-touted "discipline," the vulnerability of leftists in the face of the anti-Communist hysteria of the Korean War period, and the leftists' continuing concern for racial equality in a situation where race relations were becoming exacerbated.

Communists had been active in the Rouge River plant since the early 1930s. When Ford finally caved in to the UAW in 1941 and the local was organized, they emerged in control of it. Ford had always hired a larger proportion of black workers than the other companies and by 1950 15,000 of the local's members were black.[39] The Communists, attuned as they were to grievances over racial inequality, developed a substantial following among black workers in the plant. Black unionists assumed prominent positions in the local leadership and many of them joined the party. An influential black minister, the Reverend Charles Hill, was an outspoken defender of the local's leftist leadership.

But Walter Reuther was also a partisan of civil rights. He had made a name for himself as a strong supporter of a national Fair Employment

Practices Commission, had worked to have anti-discriminatory clauses written into UAW agreements, and was a prominent supporter of the National Association for the Advancement of Colored People's postwar assault on segregation. During the war, the Communists had been generally unsuccessful in pinning the "anti-Negro" label on him despite his opposition to their favorite concession to black equality: the demand that one vice-presidency in the UAW be set aside for a Negro.

On this as on so many other issues, Reuther was able to outmaneuver them. By war's end, his commitment to civil rights was public enough and strong enough so that black UAW leaders could change to his side with no qualms of conscience yet not so blatant that it lost him white support. The Communists' aggressive support for racial equality, on the other hand, worked against them. The new postwar generation of white migrants from the South arrived in an auto industry increasingly unsettled by the growing demands of black workers for equality of jobs, especially entry into apprenticeship programs for the coveted tool-and-die jobs and liberation from the disease-breeding, back-breaking foundry jobs where they predominated. Many white local leaders who had previously cooperated with the Communists, including some of their most loyal followers, now deserted them, joining the white backlash in rejecting Negro demands and supporting "lily-white" slates against those of the more militant blacks in union elections. Party discipline within the UAW in Michigan collapsed completely as Communists and fellow travellers alike refused to sacrifice union office on the altar of civil rights.[40]

It was in this unsettled atmosphere that Walter Reuther mounted the final assault on Local 600. In 1951, he managed to insert one of his supporters, Carl Stellato, into the presidency of the local, but after a falling-out Stellato was forced to ally himself with his old enemies, including the Communists.

Reuther's campaign to retake the local received a boost from outside in February 1952, when the House Un-American Activities Committee began hearings in Detroit which concentrated on Communist influence in the UAW and especially Local 600. Many of those hauled up to defend themselves were black, and the link between Communists and the black threat was thereby reinforced in many white unionists' eyes. Anti-Communist, anti-black vigilante groups sprang up in many Detroit auto factories, beating and tormenting suspected black and white Communists in a number of Detroit factories despite the attempts of Reutherite local union leaders to stop them.[41] As usual the star witness at the hearings was a defector, the editor of Local 600's widely-circulated newspaper, who testified that he merely functioned as a messenger boy to the printers for the group of Communists in the local who actually turned out the paper.[42] The UAW Executive Board thereupon put the local under an administratorship, on the grounds that it had violated the union's prohibition against Communists holding union office.[43] "A New 'Ally' for Reuther" was *Business Week*'s headline in reporting the HUAC hearings. He and the committee he had previously denounced as "witch-hunters" were now "working together like a well-rehearsed vaudeville team," gloated the conservative magazine.[44]

Reuther's administrators took control of the local's newspaper, the last remaining anti-Reuther organ in the UAW, and set about establishing control over the local. Nine Communist shop committeemen were expelled from the union as well as the local's PAC director and Stellato's black administrative assistant.[45] The carrot was used as well as the stick. The ex-newspaper editor and another defector who testified before HUAC were rewarded with positions on the UAW staff, despite the latter's reputation for having been one of the most vituperative of Reuther's detractors.[46] At the Executive Board hearings on the situation Stellato and Pat Rice, whose association with the Communists was regarded as essentially opportunistic, were given distinctly more gentle treatment than the two other local leaders, who were more firmly in the Communist camp; the impression was given that Stellato and Rice too would be well rewarded for deserting the Communists.[47] Many months of continuing rule by the Reuther emissaries and the purges finally paid off with the victory in the next elections of a pro-Reuther slate of committeemen to accompany Stellato, who ran unopposed, into office. The last outpost of Communist strength in the UAW had been beaten down mainly through bureaucratic power. An anti-Communist leftist correspondent on the scene lamented the messy business as "a departure from Reuther's one-time method of defeating Stalinism by a superior program and leadership,"[48] but this comment ignored the great difference between the tactics available to those striving for power and those who actually control it.

Meanwhile, Mine, Mill found itself facing overwhelming numbers, wealth, and power. In 1950, the UAW and USW had confidently made arrangements for dividing up the Mine, Mill locals, with the majority to go to USW.[49] With only 90,000-odd members at its peak in 1947, and these spread out from Alabama and the southwest through the dusty open pit mines of Montana and Utah to British Columbia, Northern Ontario, Ohio, and down into the brass plants of Connecticut, its frayed organization was little match for the predators; especially formidable was the smoothly-run, centrally-directed Steelworkers, with well over one million dues-paying members, a professional bureaucracy, a large phalanx of well-paid professional organizers to throw into any battle, and, very frequently, the support of the local authorities in the isolated mining towns where the battles often took place.

The USW was usually most successful when it stayed away from "Red-baiting" and concentrated on "bread-and-butter" issues (or, as in Alabama, allowed the race issue to take its toll). The center of Mine, Mill strength in the United States, the 5,000-member "Mother Local" in Butte, Montana, which had founded the Western Federation of Miners in 1893, was especially impervious to charges of Communist domination. The Senate Internal Security Subcommittee, under the chairmanship of Nevada Senator Pat McCarran, a fellow Westerner, a self-proclaimed friend of labor and the Wagner Act, and an enemy of Taft-Hartley, held special hearings in Butte in 1952 to exhort the miners of Montana to free their union from "Russian control, from Soviet dominance, from Communistic influence," but to no avail.[50]

Two years later, again in Butte, the USW learned the same lesson. The reasons for its defeat there, as outlined at the time by Daniel Bell and the labor department at *Fortune* magazine, are instructive, for the USW seemed to have the local handed to it by the local's own leaders, operating in a part of the country being swept by anti-Communist hysteria. Its leadership had defected and joined the USW after ratifying the decision at a thinly-attended local meeting. "Anti-Communist feeling was probably at its highest pitch in the country and the Steelworkers had made the proven party-line affiliations of the old Mine, Mill, and Smelter Workers a prime issue," they wrote. It was defeated, the *Fortune* staff concluded, primarily because "the Communist issue fell flat, because charges of 'Red' and radicalism had been hurled at miners in Montana for fifty years by the copper companies, and the miners have developed tin ears."

The secondary reasons given for the Steelworkers' defeat are also interesting. Unlike many situations in which the anti-Communist raiders were successful, the powerful employer in the company town, in this case Anaconda Copper, was virtually neutral. As a result, the local authorities stayed out of the conflict and the USW did not have the support of the company-controlled daily newspaper, the only one in Butte. Moreover, because Mine, Mill allowed AFL craft unions to function alongside it in Anaconda installations and the Steelworkers promised no such protection, Mine, Mill had the support of the state AFL. The USW's only hope in Butte, *Fortune* concluded, lay in federal government intervention. If Mine, Mill Secretary Maurice Travis could be convicted of perjury for signing the non-Communist affidavit, the NLRB might rule Mine, Mill off the next ballot and the Steelworkers would have another chance.[51]

Nevertheless, *Fortune* was wrong. Travis was subsequently indicted and convicted of perjury, and so were fourteen other Mine, Mill leaders, nine of whom were convicted and sentenced to prison terms and fines. Yet Mine, Mill stayed alive in its home territory, the Far West, as well as in the Southwest, where its record of promoting racial tolerance earned it the steadfast support of Mexican-American miners.[52]

The weakness of anti-Communist appeals to American workers, even at the height of McCarthyite hysteria, was demonstrated in a number of places. When, in 1955, the Mine, Mill local at the American Brass Company's Torrington, Connecticut plant beat back what had become a virtually annual assault by the USW, UAW, and Teamsters, a local reporter said that the USW's "Red-baiting" had boomeranged. Slogans such as "better to have a lace curtain than an Iron Curtain" fell on deaf ears, he reported, because the workers were convinced, especially after a favorable settlement of a six-week strike, that the union had won the best contracts in the brass industry.[53]

It is perhaps ironic that the smallest of the Communist unions managed to survive the holocaust. The American Communications Association was the *bête noir* of William Steinberg, president of the American Radio Association and the prosecutor at the 1950 CIO expulsion hearings. Steinberg had led a small anti-Communist group out of the ACA in 1948 and had formed the American Radio Association. He confidently expected that expulsion would see the large majority of the ACA's 8,000 members opt to stay in CIO by joining his union. The Communications Workers of America also expected to pick up some members. But nothing of the sort happened. The ACA, the bulk of whose members were telegraphers, retained the allegiance of its members in Western Union and RCA Communications. The center, its 4,000-member local at New York's Western Union offices, held firm.[54]

A larger leftist union also weathered the storm virtually unscathed. In August 1951, a Time, Inc., editor summed up the frustration of Harry Bridges' enemies after watching him endure "more than three years of ceaseless cannonading from all directions." The obituaries for Bridges and the ILWU, he wrote, had been "decidedly premature." The Taft-Hartley Act (which was supposed to mean the end of his hiring hall), expulsion from the CIO, Teamster raids, ILA assaults, government prosecution, the Coast Guard screening program—all had failed, and the ILWU's collective bargaining position was stronger than ever.[55]

Bridges and the ILWU survived because of their decided advantages over their less fortunate leftist brethren in the rest of the country. Their union had a proven record of achievement won over years of often bloody struggle with employers. Because it now bargained with the West Coast employers association as a unit to negotiate the same working conditions for all waterfront employees, regardless of the company they worked for, it was immune from the kind of competition for settlements that weakened the UE. Moreover, because longshoremen were hired in a union hiring hall to work at temporary jobs for various companies, they identified only with the union and not with a particular employer or place of work. These factors made them immune to suggestions that they were falling behind others in the same industry as well as to employer propaganda. The employers had learned that anticommunism had no effect on West Coast waterfront workers in the bitter strike of 1948. Then, it seemed to them, Red-baiting had backfired, uniting the union's right-wing and left-wing against them. "We got our teeth kicked in on the philosophical issue," said an employer in 1953, "and now we realize that it does no good to attack the working man on that basis."[56]

Not only did the employers give up on driving Bridges from the waterfront with Red-baiting, but after the settlement of the 1948 strike they came to regard him more positively. The employers of the Pacific Maritime Association, for example, began to appreciate the peace and orderliness the seven-year contract they signed with the ILWU had brought. Each year, only wages were renegotiated, and Bridges was usually willing to settle for modest gains, enough to keep up with the rise in the cost of living. Moreover, for all his public posturing, Bridges was a cultivated man with whom they could deal reasonably. He was willing to discuss such sensitive matters as mechanization on the docks with an understanding of their position. His AFL rival, Harry Lundeberg, on the other hand, revelled in confrontation rather than discussion. Lundeberg displayed his militancy by refusing to accept arbitration. "The employers," reported a correspondent in 1953, "really prefer to do business with Bridges and [his Communist associate] Bryson rather than Lundeberg. Personally they are more reasonable, more intelligent, and more attractive men. Lundeberg is contentious, arrogant, and insulting at every turn. His pet play these days is to call waterfront employers 'Commie-lovers' because they won't refuse to talk to Bridges and Bryson."[57] It is no surprise, then, that when Bridges faced another one of his trials in 1949, two prominent West Coast waterfront employers appeared as character witnesses for him. It is also no wonder that when, at the 1951 AFL Convention in San Francisco, David Beck of the Teamsters and Lundeberg pledged jointly to "drive these leeches of the Kremlin from our harbors, docks, and warehouses," no waterfront employers rushed to them to be saved.[58]

Nevertheless, in the public eye the loquacious Bridges had become the best-known symbol of Communist unionism. So great was the pressure from outside the government, from the American Legion and a panoply of superpatriotic organizations, and inside, from the

FBI, Immigration Service, and Justice Department, that even had they wanted to, there was little likelihood that either the Democratic or Republican administration in Washington could have accepted defeat in the long-drawn-out struggle against him and pitched camp. In 1949 he was brought up on new charges, this time of having perjured himself in denying previous membership in the CP on his 1945 citizenship application. ("We feel we'll be doing a service to the country if we nail him," the special assistant to the attorney general assigned to handle the important case confided to reporters).[59]

For a while it looked as if Bridges and two ILWU co-defendants had been "nailed," but in 1953 the Supreme Court overturned their convictions on the grounds that the statute of limitations had ran out.[60] Unable to jail Bridges, the government turned again to deportation and assigning its "first legal team" to new deportation hearings in June 1954; confident that it could prove that he had obtained his citizenship by fraud, it was buoyed by the knowledge that deportations of alien subversives were running at an all time high.[61] The Supreme Court, which eventually ruled on the case, was not so impressed by the government's case, and in June 1955 found for Bridges. "The U.S. government has never tried harder to nail a man than it has tried with Bridges in two decades of trials, appeals, and more appeals," wrote an awed *Time* reporter.[62]

In Hawaii, where the ILWU had been successful in organizing plantation workers as well as dockers, the government managed to have the seven top leaders of the ILWU sentenced to long jail terms and fined heavily under the Smith Act,[63] convictions which were eventually overturned. Here too the employers were, if anything, discomfited by the government's harassment of the union's leaders. The ILWU postwar battle to organize dockers and sugar and pineapple plantation workers had been a bitter and bloody one, and Hawaiian employers had developed a kind of grudging respect for the muscular union. When the union responded to the convictions by calling off longshore wage talks near agreement and doubling their wage demands, employers were "filled with apprehension," reported the *Time* stringer in Hawaii. They knew, he wrote, that when the union "talks tough it acts tough."[64] Most employers would likely have been happier had the Department of Justice not bothered the Communists with whom they dealt.

ILWU strength in collective bargaining, its ability to satisfy its membership and satisfy or intimidate the employers, thus helped government harassment backfire. As the liberal writer Paul Jacobs observed in 1956, the employers' attacks, which stopped after 1948, and the continuing government prosecutions "placed him in an almost sacrosanct position within the ILWU." To attack Bridges was "to run the risk of being linked with the employers and government in an effort to smash the union."[65]

Bridges' smaller satellite unions did not have these advantages, and the federal government was consequently more successful in hounding them. The National Union of Marine Cooks and Stewards, led by handsome young Hugh Bryson, had followed Bridges' lead on the West Coast and in the CIO since the late 1930s. When the union was expelled from the CIO in 1950, the CIO gave jurisdiction over West Coast cooks and stewards to Curran's NMU. Harry Lundeberg's AFL Sailors' Union of the Pacific, meanwhile, chartered a special Marine Cooks and Stewards Division.

The NMU had few resources on the West Coast and after a year or so of disappointments it packed its tent and withdrew from the scene. Neither could Lundeberg's union make any inroads, initially, at least. It was severely hampered among the cooks and stewards, over half of whom were black or oriental, because of its reputation for racial discrimination, a reputation apparently well-deserved, in view of SUP's refusal to issue union cards to "colored people." Even the creation of the new AFL Cooks and Stewards Union in 1951, affiliated with the gangster-ridden AFL Seafarers International Union, that took dues-payers of all colors, failed to dampen suspicion. Lundeberg was still West Coast head of the SIU and the new AFL cooks and stewards union was still his baby.

Bryson's union, then, petitioned for a quick NLRB election to settle the representation issue. Lundeberg wanted a delay, and the NLRB went along with him. Indeed, despite Bryson's repeated calls for a certification election, the NLRB delayed calling one for over three years until Lundeberg was ready.

In 1952, Lundeberg got a foot in the door when his sailors struck for two months, demanding an end to the monopoly on the hiring of cooks and stewards held by Bryson's hiring hall and forcing a consent decree which gave Lundeberg's cooks and stewards union a role in the hiring as well. Meanwhile, Department of Justice investigators pursued Bryson. In 1953, he was indicted for perjury in signing the Taft-Hartley non-Communist oath. He and the union leadership now faced endless litigation. The sixty-three-day strike over hiring halls had been an expensive one and the costs of heading off Lundeberg's raids were mounting. The courts were taking to imposing costly fines on the union for "unfair labor practices." The NLRB still refused to call an election. Clearly, the NLRB and Lundeberg were waiting until government persecution gave them legal grounds for keeping the National Union of Marine Cooks and Stewards off the ballot. Into this breach stepped Bridges, whose organizers now began enrolling members of Bryson's union into the ILWU.[66]

The NLRB moved to head off Bridges. In early 1954 it finally called the election, issuing the call before Bridges' ILWU could charter its own cooks and stewards union and get on the ballot. Cooks and stewards were therefore given the choice of voting for Lundeberg's AFL union, the virtually defunct NUMCS, or "neither." The ILWU bade them vote "neither," and that is what 63 percent did, seemingly enabling them to be signed up by the ILWU.[67]

But Lundeberg and the government labor board had not quite run out of resources. In early 1955, another cooks and stewards election was held, this time to decide between the ILWU and Lundeberg's parent Seafarers International Union. Now, the NLRB ruled that instead of being confined to cooks and stewards, the election should comprise all unlicensed sailors and firemen on the West Coast, that is, all the present members of Lundeberg's union as well. It was therefore easy for them to overwhelm the pro-Bridges cooks and stewards in a four-to-one victory.[68] His union destroyed, Bryson was convicted of perjury in 1955 and forced out of the labor movement. While he awaited the outcome of his appeal, he entered the real estate business. Joseph Johnson, an aide, became a subscription salesman for a neighborhood newspaper.[69]

The ILWU was more successful in absorbing the International Union of Fishermen and Allied Workers, but the prize was hardly worth the effort. The union's membership had peaked at about 25,000 in 1947-1948 but declined steadily thereafter, with the decline in the West Coast fishing industry. It merged with the ILWU in July 1949, and managed to fight back raids on its membership. However, the continuing decline of the industry, as well as antitrust decisions which hampered collective bargaining in the industry, led to the virtual extinction of unionism among West Coast fishermen.[70] By 1956, the ILWU reported that membership in its fishermen's locals, which varied greatly according to the season, totalled about 2,000 on-again, off-again people.[71]

At least Joe Jurich, the president of the fishermen's union, and Jeff Kibre, its former secretary, ended up on the payroll of the ILWU.[72] The Communist leaders of the Fur and Leather Workers Union had no such luck. They found themselves facing trials, convictions, and imprisonment. For years, President Ben Gold had been the only union president to openly proclaim his party membership, insulated from attack by the firm support of the large majority of a politically aware union. At the time of its expulsion from the CIO, the IFLWU was still, in the words of David Brody, "A vigorous union with forceful leadership, a loyal membership that numbered 40,000 and a record of achievement in collective bargaining."[73] But first the Taft-Hartley Act, then the Communist Control Act of 1954, caught up with the union leadership and destroyed the union. In August 1950, with raids on his locals by CIO unions mounting, Ben Gold announced his resignation from the party and signed the non-Communist affidavit. The union managed to retain the loyalty of the bulk of its membership in the face of the raids and won most of the NLRB elections into which it was forced. One CIO organizer, describing a 1952 raid on an ILFWU local, said:

Trying to pass out leaflets at the tannery was one of the worst moments of my life. Only one or two people would even accept the leaflet. I never felt so alone before. I was surrounded by a mob of howling, screaming women. I didn't know what would happen. Our mass meeting drew only eight people, while several hundred shouted outside. Our main speaker, a leading minister in the community, cancelled his appearance. We lost the election 10 to 1.[74]

In 1954, however, the federal government pulled the rug from under the union's ability to resist raids. First, it won a perjury conviction against Gold when a grand jury decided that his resignation from the party was a ruse.[75] Then, the new Communist Control Act put the finishing touches on the Communist leadership of the union. If Gold or any other Communists remained in the leadership, the union would almost certainly be deprived of the right to run in NLRB elections.[76]

The union had begun looking for refuge in an AFL or CIO union in 1953, but none would take it with its Communist leadership intact. Now, in October 1954, Gold was replaced as president by Abe Feinglass, a non-Communist, and a merger agreement was reached with the AFL Amalgamated Meatcutters and Butcher Workmen on harsh terms. All union officers, down to the lowest levels, were to sign the non-Communist affidavits. Gold and his Communist aide, Irving Potash, were to quit their posts and never hold union office again.

Even these guarantees against Communist influence were not strong enough for the AFL Executive Council. In order to satisfy it, the terms were made even more severe. Any union local found promoting Communist causes could be expelled and its treasury confiscated. If there were any evidence of Communist activity in the new Fur Division of the Butchers' Union, the offenders could be expelled without trial. Moreover, Feinglass was compelled to conduct a thoroughgoing purge of the union's officials. The union's Executive Board was disbanded and twenty-nine top officials fired. Communist leaders were driven from all the locals.[77] The brutal purge, Feinglass admitted, meant "some sacrifices which might well be described as ruthless," but it did fulfill the demands of George Meany and the Executive Council for a thorough "decommunization" of the union.[78] The merger was approved, and Ben Gold returned to working in a fur factory, his only consolation that a Supreme Court order for a retrial on his perjury charge kept him out of jail.[79]

The small United Public Workers Union did not survive after 1953. Dealing as it did with governments, it was especially vulnerable to the favoritism they showed to anti-Communist raiders. Most of its membership, which may have numbered close to 80,000 on the eve of the expulsions, was snapped up by the newly-created CIO Government and Civil Employees Organizing Committee. By 1952 there were only about 2,500 members left in the UPW, and in February 1953 it disbanded; four of its locals joined the Teamsters and one, the New York Teachers Union, remained unaffiliated.[80]

Government intervention was also important in crushing two and one-half other Communist-led small unions. After their expulsion from the CIO, the FTA and the United Office and Professional Workers had merged with the Distributive Workers Union. The latter was actually New York Local 65 of the Retail and Wholesale Workers Union, whose Communist leadership had pulled it out of the union after years of conflict with the Retail Workers' anti-Communist leadership. The president of the new hybrid union, the Distributive, Processing, and Office Workers Union, was Arthur Osman, the head of Local 65 and former president of the short-lived DWU. Donald Henderson of the FTA was his administrative director and former United Office and Professional Workers head James Durkin, the Catholic so despised as a "front man" for the Reds by Father Rice and Philip Murray, was secretary-treasurer. But even this plethora of administrative experience could not stem the anti-Communist onslaught. One of the major centers of anti-Communist sentiment in Durkin's old union had been, not surprisingly, its insurance agents' locals. The newly-chartered CIO Insurance and Allied Workers Organizing Committee had little difficulty wooing them away from the leftists. Meanwhile, the Retail Workers, Packinghouse Workers, and Brewery Workers nipped off other morsels of the dwindling pie.[81]

They too had help from various agencies of the government. In early 1951, for example, the chairman of the federal government's Displaced Persons Commission, which handed out large sums of money to various immigrant aid groups, announced that he would lift the accreditation of any organization which continued to deal with the leftist union, which represented about 2,000 workers for these agencies.[82] The union's leadership was also hounded by grand juries and congressional committees. In 1951, a secret grand jury was called together in New York to investigate Osman and the union's leadership. The investigation petered out but was revived in 1952 when the union struck a large New York department store. The grand jury heeded the admonitions of the United States attorney and his young assistant, Roy Cohn, that they subpoena the leaders of the union as part of their investigation of Communist attempts to infiltrate strategic war industries. At the time, the union was also trying to organize Woolworth's.[83] In May 1954, Osman threw in the towel. He broke with the Communists and brought the union back into the Retail, Wholesale and Department Store Union.[84]

By the time the purified CIO was ready to merge with the AFL in 1955, the Communists' worst fears during the expulsion crisis of 1949 had been more than borne out. Legal disabilities and government persecution had left them very vulnerable to raiding from other unions, something their ex-compeers in the CIO had joined in with relish. Harassed and on the run, Communists in the unions displayed much of the doggedness that had helped them to power in the first place, but even less of the nationwide discipline and coordination that was reputed to be their hallmark. Indeed, by 1951 party policy in the unions was in a shambles and any hope of real coordination had disappeared. Those Communists who managed to hang on to power in a few unions did so mainly on their own, with little or no help from the party or Communists in other unions.

As for the remaining Communist bastions that were destroyed in the mopping up operation, here again the extraordinary phenomenon was the weakness of the appeal of anticommunism among American unionists. Time and again, at the very crest of the 1950s' wave of anti-Communist hysteria, a sizeable majority proved itself virtually immune to the appeals of anticommunism. Indeed, one could almost say that they were as indifferent to the appeals of anticommunism in the late 1940s and 1950s as they were to the blandishments of communism in the 1930s. The Communists, who had risen to union power through their prowess at achieving bread-and-butter gains, lost it when they seemed to lose the ability to continue doing so.

NOTES

1. William Z. Foster, "Letter to Party Plenum," *Political Affairs*, vol. 29, no. 4 (May 1950), 9; Editorial, *Political Affairs* (May 1950), 5; Alexander Bittleman, "We are the Vanguard Party of Peace," *Political Affairs*, vol. 29, no. 8 (September 1950), 1-14.

2. John Williamson, "Trade Union Tasks in the Struggle for Peace, Jobs, and Negro Rights" (Report to the Plenum of the CPUSA, September 19-20, 1950), *Political Affairs*, vol. 29, no. 10 (November 1950), 37-59.

3. Ibid.

4. Bert Cochran, Interview with John Gates, cited in Cochran, *Labor and Communism* (Princeton: Princeton University Press, 1977), 294.

5. Gil Green [Jonathan Swift], "The Struggle for a Mass Policy," *Political Affairs*, vol. 32, no. 2 (February 1953), 28-33.

6. See David Caute, *The Great Fear* (London: Seeker and Warburg, 1978), ch. 18-21 for the tragic stories of many of the individuals swept away in this wave.

7. U.S. Congress, Senate, Committee on Labor and Public Welfare, *Hearings on Communist Domination of Unions*, 82nd Cong., 2nd sess. (1952), hereafter cited as *Communist Domination of Unions*.

8. UE, Press Release, August 3, 1949, The Rev. Charles Owen Rice, Papers, Pennsylvania State University Archives of Labor History, State College, Pa. (hereafter PSUA), Roll B.

9. Pittsburgh *Post-Gazette*, July 30, 31, 1949.

10. Walter Goodman, *The Committee* (New York: Farrar, Straus and Giroux), 283-85.

11. *The New York Times*, November 29, 1949.

12. IUE, *Proceedings of the First Convention*, 1949, 145, cited in Frank Emspak, "The Break-Up of the Congress of Industrial Organizations (CIO), 1945-1950" (Ph.D. diss., University of Wisconsin, 1972), 346.

13. Emspak, "Break-Up," 340-41.

14. Ibid., 342. Carey asked Walter Reuther to have the UAW contribute an equivalent amount, two cents per month per UAW member, but it is not clear whether Reuther, involved in an unpopular attempt to raise UAW dues, contributed as heavily as the USW. Carey to Reuther, December 23, 1949, CIO, Papers, Office of the Secretary-Treasurer, James Carey, Wayne State University Archives of Labor History and Urban Affairs, Detroit, Michigan (hereafter Carey Papers, WSUA), Box 51.

15. *NYT*, November 22, 1949.

16. *Schenectady Gazette*, September 8, 1951.

17. Emspak, "Break-Up," 348-49.

18. New York *Daily News*, May 2, 1951.

19. *NYT*, May 22, 1950.

20. Emspak, "The Break-Up," 348-50; Robert Ozanne also found no favoritism towards either side. According to him the industry leader in combatting unionism, GE Vice-President Lemuel L. Boulware, called both unions "collectivist" and showed no signs of distinguishing between the two. Robert Ozanne, "The Effects of Communist Leadership on American Trade Unions" (Ph.D. diss., University of Wisconsin, 1954).

21. Emspak, "The Break-Up," 351.

22. IUE-CIO, Organizational Report Covering November, 1949 to June 15, 1950, CIO, Papers, Catholic University of America Library, Washington, D.C., Box A7, Folder 25.

23. Emspak, "The Break-Up," 352.

24. Ibid.; Cochran, *Labor and Communism*, 294.

25. Harry Block, OH, PSUA, 34.

26. Jeff Wylie to Ben Williamson, Time, Inc., December 12, 1953, Daniel Bell, Collection of Material on Socialism and Communism in the U.S.A., Tamiment Institute Library, New York University, New York, N.Y., Box 5.

27. Albert Fitzgerald to Philip Murray, July 18, 1952, Bell Collection, Box 6; Eggleston "Labor and Civil Liberties," *The Nation*, vol. 174 (June 28, 1952), 648.

28. *Business Week*, December 19, 1953; *Union Labor Report*, No. 327, December 18, 1953; GE Press Release, December 9, 1953, in Bell Collection, Box 5, "Subversive" Folder.

29. Darby to Ben Williamson, December 12, 1953, Bell Collection, Box 5, "Subversive" Folder.

30. Ibid., *NYT*, December 10, 1953.

31. Ozanne, "The Effects of Communist Leadership," 94-100.

32. *Labor Action*, September 13, 1954.

33. IUE, "20,000 Members Dump UE, Join in IUE-CIO," leaflet in UE Research File, cited in Emspak, "The Break-Up," 353.

34. Hanniflin to Williamson, July 28, 1955, Bell Collection, Box 6, "Mine, Mill" Folder; "Curtains for the C.P.," *Fortune*, vol. 53, no. 3 (March 1956), 208.

35. James Prickett, "Communists and the Communist Issue in the American Labor Movement, 1920-1950" (Ph.D. diss., University of California at Los Angeles, 1975), 366.

36. Minutes of Meeting of Carey and Harry Block with UE General Executive Board, November 30, 1955, Bell Collection, Box 5.

37. Cochran, *Labor and Communism*, 324-27.

38. John W. Anderson, OH, WSUA, 150.

39. Nat Ganley, "Memo: Negro Workers in the UAW-CIO," Ganley, Papers, WSUA, Box 6, Folder 38.

40. See "Situation in C-Shop," undated [1952 or 1953?], unsigned memorandum, Ganley Papers, Box 6, Folder 36.

41. *Labor Action*, March 10, 1952.

42. Fred Collins to Barron Beshoar, *Time*, March 12, 1952, Bell Collection, Box 7.

43. Collins to Beshoar, March 14, 1952, Bell Collection, Box 7.

44. *Business Week*, March 22, 1952.

45. "Statement of Five Purged Local 600 Officers," undated [March 1952?], Ganley Papers, Box 6, Folder 29. *Daily Worker*, April 1, 1952.

46. *Labor Action*, March 24, 1952.

47. Collins to Beshoar and Saint, March 15, March 17, 1952, Bell Collection, Box 7.

48. *Labor Action*, March 24, 1952.

49. Irving Abella, *Nationalism, Communism and Canadian Labour* (Toronto: University of Toronto Press, 1973), 192.

50. U.S. Congress, Senate, *Hearings on Communist Domination of Union Officials in Vital Defense Industry—International Union of Mine, Mill, and Smelter Workers*, 4-5, 82nd Cong., 2nd sess. (1952).

51. "How the Communists Won a Victory," June 10, 1954, unsigned ms. in Bell Collection, Box 6.

52. F. S. O'Brien, "Communist-Dominated Unions in the U.S since 1950," *Labor History*, vol. 9, no. 2 (spring 1968), 198-200.

53. Berkman, Hartford *Times*, to Mary Johnston, Time, Inc., August 6, 1955, Bell Collection, Box 6.

54. O'Brien, "Communist-Dominated Unions," 197.

55. "Labor Department—November—Seligman (Donovan) October 8, 1951," copy in Bell Collection, Box 7.

56. Al Wright to Ben Williamson, December 5, 1953, Bell Collection, Box 5, "Subversive" Folder.

57. Ibid.

58. "Labor Department—November—Seligman (Donovan) August 8, 1951."

59. Serrel Hillman to Don Bermingham, Time, Inc., May 26, 1949, Bell Collection, Box 7, "Communist Unions—Harry Bridges" Folder.

60. *NYT*, April 2, 1950, June 16, 1953; ILWU *Dispatcher*, June 26, 1953.

61. Hanniflin to Williamson, June 24, 1955, Bell Collection, Box 6.

62. Mohr to Ben Williamson, July 28, 1955, Bell Collection, Box 6, "Communist Unions—Harry Bridges" Folder.

63. ILWU *Dispatcher*, June 26, July 10, 1953.

64. Richard Macmillan to *Time*, June 15, 1953, Bell Collection, Box 7.

65. Paul Jacobs, "The Due Processing of Harry Bridges," *The Reporter*, March 8, 1956.

66. Al Wright to Barron Beshoar, June 24, 1953, Bell Collection, Box 7; Jane C. Record, "The Rise and Fall of a Maritime Union," *Industrial and Labor Relations Review*, 10 (October 1956).

67. Al Wright to Ben Williamson, May 22, 1954, Bell Collection.

68. Record, "The Rise and Fall," 90-91.

69. Mohr to Rosemary Alexander, January 20, 1956, Bell Collection, Box 7.

70. O'Brien, "Communist-Dominated Unions," 195.

71. Mohr to Alexander, January 20, 1956.

72. Ibid. In 1956, Kibre was Washington representative of the ILWU and Jurich was secretary of the union's Seattle fishermen's local.

73. David Brody, *The Butcher Workmen* (Cambridge: Harvard University Press, 1964), 259

74. Robert Ozanne, Confidential Interview with CIO Organizer, 1953, cited in Ozanne, "The Effects of Communist Leadership," 179.

75. Brody, *Butcher Workmen*, 260; O'Brien, "Communist-Dominated Unions," 193.

76. Brody, *Butcher Workmen*, 260.

77. Ibid., 261; O'Brien, "Communist-Dominated Unions," 194.

78. Brody, *Butcher Workmen*, 261.

79. The government was unable to resume the persecution and prosecute a second trial because evidence necessary to prove its case was no longer available. O'Brien, "Communist-Dominated Unions," 193.

80. Ibid., 191.

81. Ibid., 193.

82. New York *Daily Mirror*, May 2, 1951.

83. New York *Daily Mirror*, March 22, 1952.

84. O'Brien, "Communist-Dominated Unions," 193.

18 CONCLUSION: THE EPILOGUE THAT MIGHT HAVE BEEN

As many American Communists came to realize after 1956, the Stalinist utopia which inspired most of them during their years in the mainstream of the American labor movement was indeed a monstrous one. Moreover, there are few indications that, in the extraordinary circumstance of being anywhere close to national political power, the party's political leadership, or at least the group surrounding Foster, would have been any more deeply committed to democracy and human rights than their Stalinist counterparts in the rest of the Communist world at that time. That said, it still remains that the obliteration of Communist unionism had unfortunate consequences, not just for the Communists, but for the CIO, American workers, and the country as a whole.

With the expulsions of its Communist unionists, the CIO lost its organizational momentum. How much this slowdown resulted from the loss of Communist unionists and their willingness to make enormous sacrifices to organize the unorganized will never be known, but certainly the CIO would have benefited from their organizational talents, as well as the redirection of the energy of non-Communist unionists who spent their time and union money raiding Communist unions rather than organizing the unorganized. With its membership rolls stagnating, it was forced into what Victor Reuther has called a "shotgun wedding" with the AFL in 1955.[1] It accepted second-class status as the Industrial Union Department of the AFL, its constituent unions agreeing to pay extra per capita dues to form essentially the same kind of bloc as George Meany's Building Trades Department, albeit with a few more privileges.

Deprived of their organizational momentum, American unions declined steadily until by the late 1970s barely 20 percent of the nation's workers were represented by unions, the lowest percentage of any major industrial country by far. After the merger of the two organizations, the CIO liberals, who would have been right-wingers or middle-of-the-roaders in any major European labor movement, became the left-wing of the new AFL-CIO. Without a socialist grouping of any kind on its left, the American labor movement's mainstream became the most politically conservative of any in the western industrial world. By the early 1960s, democratic socialists in the United States and abroad who had hoped that people like Walter Reuther would lead American labor down their path were becoming dismayed by Reuther and the labor movement. By the late 1960s, disillusion with the movement had spread to liberals as well; even Walter Reuther finally pulled the UAW out of the AFL-CIO he had once aspired to head.

In crushing the Communists, the labor movement also lost unionists who, despite their short run disrepute, in the long run would have helped increase the stature of organized labor in the eyes of the public as well as the workers. In the 1950s and 1960s, continuing revelations of corruption in unionism played a major role in lowering the prestige and influence of organized labor in America. Despite some exceptions, this was not a Communist failing. Public disgust was fueled by the high life style of union officials—the David McDonalds negotiating with steel barons at the Stork Club, the Joe Currans wasting millions on buildings that were monuments to their egos—who awarded themselves salaries, pensions, and other benefits that were nothing short of outrageous. The Communists, in contrast, had nothing but contempt for this kind of lifestyle. Even today, the salary of the top officials of the UE cannot be higher than that of the highest paid worker under a UE contract.

The CIO also crushed many unionists whose dedication and willingness to make great personal sacrifices, as well as their ability to delude themselves about the monstrous nature of Stalinist Russia, stemmed primarily from humanitarian roots which gave them a much wider social vision than most other American unionists of the 1950s. This is not to say that they were the only ones with a social conscience. The victors in the struggle had a social vision too, but it was essentially that of Samuel Gompers: the advancement of the working class would come in the wake of the elevation of the status of its leading sector, organized labor. They thought that by promoting the economic and political power of organized labor, they were contributing to the advancement of the working class as a whole. They went further than the old Gompersians and supported medicare, larger unemployment insurance benefits, and a host of other welfare state measures that would benefit the unorganized as well as organized labor, but few were willing to devote much time, effort, and money to those outside the union movement except when there was the prospect of picking up dues-payers. Had there been a real Left in the labor movement, and had there been a number of wealthy unions committed to socialism, the political history of the 1960s would surely have been altered.

Certainly the role of unions in the racial conflict that marked the 1950s and 1960s would have been different, for in this area the Communists distinguished themselves from many non-Communists through the sacrifices they were willing to make for racial equality. Their record is not unblemished. In their new-found enthusiasm for defense mobilization after the Nazi invasion of the Soviet Union, the Communists did oppose A. Phillip Randolph's proposed March on Washington to demand an end to discrimination in hiring by defense contractors. During the war, they did relegate the fight against racial discrimination to the back seat, along with their even weaker commitment to equal opportunities for women. Nevertheless, in practice, the Communists played very active roles in many unions in combating discrimination in both shop and union affairs. In union after union, Communists challenged the traditional devices built into the rules of unions and work places perpetuating segregation of the races and second-class status for blacks. Their record in unions such as the NMU, Mine, Mill, the TWU, the ILWU, the UAW, and UE was generally exemplary on this score. In some cases, such as in Mine, Mill and the FTA, it played a major role in their demise, yet they stuck with it.

Some of their gestures, such as their recurring demands for a black on the Executive Board of the UAW during and after the war, have been dismissed as window dressing, another aspect of what their opponents often called their eagerness to "use the Negro question for their own purposes." Yet it is difficult to examine the record and behavior of Communists in the unions and agree with this conclusion. Instead, one is struck by the opposite fact that there was no contradiction between Negro rights and "their own purposes." For the vast majority, racial equality was one of the things for which they fought. Although they thought true equality could come only under communism, in practice they fought much more than any other predominantly white group to bring it to American industry.[2] Had the Communists remained a powerful force in the CIO, then, those forces in the labor movement of the 1950s and 1960s attempting to throw the weight of organized labor into the struggle for civil rights in the nation as a whole and for an end to the discriminatory practices of many of their own unions would likely have succeeded to a much greater degree than they did.

Had the Communists in the CIO not been crushed, foreign policy would probably have been affected as well. Once the Communists were obliterated, the country lost what it desperately needed: a politically potent force that could and would challenge and criticize the cold war consensus. Granted that the membership of the leftist unions cared little about the foreign policy stands of their leaders, and few of them were ready to attend mass meetings demanding hands off Albania, the fact is that the leftist labor leaders had the same kind of political clout that the anti-Communists had: money and manpower, the two basics in winning elections. By supporting politicians who were willing to challenge the simplistic assumptions of the bipartisan foreign policy of the 1950s and early 1960s, they could have put forward the alternative views that were so sadly missing. Not only might they have mitigated some of the worst excesses of American policy abroad, but simply by their continued existence they would have prevented the closing in of the almost totalitarian curtain that enveloped the United States in the 1950s, stifling radical criticism in the name of patriotism and a bipartisan foreign policy.

But one can go too far in "might-have-beens," as well as in rosy pictures of leftist unions. The fact is that Communist unions were subjected to most of the same kind of forces that shaped non-Communist unionism. The need to develop a bureaucracy to deal with well-organized management and the necessity to hire "experts" such as lawyers, economists, editors, and accountants affected all unions alike. In the leftist unions as well as the rightist ones, these full-time bureaucrats naturally became part of the leadership's "machine." In Communist as well as non-Communist unions, many of them assumed the political coloration of their bosses in order to survive and rise on the ladder of bureaucratic success. There were, in short, opportunists and "pork-choppers" in Communist ranks as well. The large number of defections of key personnel who felt a postwar change in wind direction in the NMU, TWU, UAW, and UE was not due solely to conscience-stricken leftists finally opening their eyes to what was happening behind the Iron Curtain.

Some authors have portrayed the Communist unions as more "democratic" than those of their opponents, pointing especially to the internal structure of the UE and the decline of democracy in the NMU and UAW after the anti-Communist takeover as proof,[3] but this argument is problematic. Even if one could measure "democracy" in unionism (a proposition made dubious because of the differences between formal democratic structure and the real exercise of rank-and-file rights, a difference which is exaggerated by the generally low rate of political participation which afflicts almost every union), it would be difficult to make this a blanket case. Although Walter Reuther did crush dissent in the UAW and so did Joe Curran in the NMU, it is difficult to prove that, had they been able to, the Communists would not have done the same. The histories of Communist-led unions are almost as full of expulsions for political reasons as are the histories of anti-Communist unions. Were Curran's purges any less democratic after he shifted sides than those in the late 1930s when the Communists helped him tighten his grip on the union? Only the scale and the targets were different. Was the much-vaunted "democracy" of the pre-Reuther UAW really the result of a leftist commitment to democratic trade unionism? Or was it rather, as suggested earlier, the result of the heterogeneous nature of the union? The same applies to UE, whose constitution was shaped by its origins.

The paths followed by two of the leftist unions that survived, the UE and the ILWU, would indicate that there might have been as much variety in the internal government of leftist unions, had they survived, as has existed among the survivors. In all the controversy over the merits of the post-purge path of the ILWU, few people, aside from Bridges and the small cohort who run the union, have suggested that it is a model democratic union.[4] On the other hand, the UE has apparently remained one of the most democratically-run unions.

Bridges' record raises another point at which a revised view of the past can go too far. Walter Reuther and the anti-Communists have been attacked for selling out the interests of the workers at the bargaining table. Most specifically, Reuther has been castigated for signing five-year agreements with GM.[5] More recently, the leadership of the USW was challenged on the same issue. But in 1948, before Reuther's heresy, Bridges signed a *seven-year* agreement with West Coast employers, settling in ensuing years for modest cost of living increases in return for concessions on mechanization and work loads. Moreover, in becoming a model union with regard to helping, rather than impeding, the mechanization of unloading on the West Coast waterfront, Bridges helped create a system which rewarded the full-time, first-class, voting members of his union at the expense of the less fortunate, second-class, non-voting members. From whose vantage point does one judge the ability of this leftist union to "deliver the goods"? From the point of view of those workers who benefited and are happy with their job security, lighter work load and early pensions, or from the point of view of those more casual laborers who lost potential jobs on the waterfront? To engage in speculation regarding the presumed ability of Communists to extract more from management than anti-Communists, then, is futile. There are simply too many other factors involved in labor negotiations. All the indications point to the fact that the politics of neither group played any major role at the bargaining table.

Leftists were routed in a number of unions, though, because their ability to produce at the bargaining table was weakened by the characteristic that made them so vulnerable to repression during the cold war: their Leninism. Their commitment to a vision of socialism that saw the Soviet Union as its bulwark made it extremely difficult not to rush to its aid during the cold war. Their liberal opponents, defending the other bastion, could now call in the entire weight of government, business, and the media to destroy them. Moreover, in acting as if they constituted the kind of small, well-disciplined "vanguard' party that Lenin said led to success in the Bolshevik Revolution, the Communists put their union sympathizers in a strait jacket. Luckily for the unionists of the 1930s, the straps were rarely tied. Communist aspirations for tight discipline were usually modified by the realities of union power and the fact that many leftists had power bases independent of the party. Rarely, then, did their commitment to a Marxist-Leninist party play a role in any major decisions leftist unionists took regarding collective bargaining itself. Only during the war did something like this take place, and even then, their stance differed mainly in style, rather than substance, from that of the non-Communists.

In some internal power struggles submission to party discipline did adversely affect Communists. This was especially true in the UAW, where Browder's intervention in 1939 turned out to be disastrous. But the relationship of Communist union militants to the party's political leadership was never that clear, the lines of authority were never quite untangled. Even in the UAW, it is difficult to say that the Communists were taking orders rather than advice from men whose strategic acumen they respected, and the history of Communists in the auto industry is peppered with occasions when they ignored or defied the party line.

The place where party discipline affected them most adversely was in foreign policy. Here, with few exceptions, Communist unionists took their cues from the political leadership. Normally, their stand on foreign policy hardly affected their status within their own unions, but even before the cold war it had untoward effects on their relationship with other union leaders. Thus, although their policies regarding collective bargaining from 1939 to June 1941 were not only varied but firmly grounded in internal, economic factors, their cacophonous cries that the Yanks were not coming and their apparent abandonment of the fight against fascism alienated a number of key liberals whose cooperation would ultimately be needed to build the kind of "Center-Left" coalition almost everyone agreed was their only hope in the United States. This heightened a deep sense of mistrust and hostility toward them that was never really extinguished even by wartime amicability.

In retrospect this need not have happened. A party leadership less traumatized by the Kremlin's intervention from 1928 to 1931 and less anxious to display its wholehearted commitment to the current line would have made a difference. Even under Stalin, there seemed to have been possibilities for adjusting the international line to local circumstances in ways that would ultimately have strengthened rather than weakened the party, allowing it to move eventually toward the kind of position vis à vis Moscow that the Italian party slowly developed in the postwar years.

Part of the problem lay in style rather than substance, the result of the Communists' having adopted the vituperative, ponderous, alien-sounding slogans of Moscow. When they spoke on union issues, Communist unionists were masters of speaking in a down-to-earth fashion that made sense on the shop floor. When they spoke of foreign policy, they were on less certain ground. Despite their best efforts, they had difficulty avoiding what Joseph Starobin called "the peculiar Esperanto of the Comintern."

The Communists would probably have survived at least as a minority to be reckoned with in the CIO had it not been for that divisive crossroads, the Wallace candidacy. Again, with foreign policy concerns paramount, the party's political leadership made the basic decision and most of the unionists went along, albeit with little enthusiasm. Although made on foreign policy grounds, the decision to support a third-party candidate could not have been more disastrous in terms of its domestic consequences. To CIO liberals, it seemed clear proof that in order to satisfy their foreign masters, the Communists were willing to turn over power in Washington to anti-labor Republicans bent on crushing the labor movement. Given the fact that everyone, including the Communists, agreed that the Wallace candidacy tolled the death knell for the Democrats in Washington, there were ample grounds for this view. Only if one could argue that there was no difference between the Republicans and the Democrats could this suspicion be evaded. Yet, in 1948, there was one crucial difference obvious to all unionists: the Taft-Hartley Act.

Taft-Hartley was especially important because its threat came at the end of a fifteen-year learning process for liberal unionists. The New Deal had caused a revolution in the minds of many unionists who had previously regarded the federal government with suspicion: as an anti-union force to be neutralized, rather than an ally. Now, its intervention, in the form of the Wagner Act, had almost single-handedly created big unionism in the United States. The mutually beneficial relationship carved out during the period of mobilization and war reinforced the message. The creation of CIO-PAC and labor's important role in the 1944 election seemed to seal the new relationship. The CIO liberals, convinced by now of the importance of what the government could give, became obsessed with the threat of Taft-Hartley, by what it could take away. The Communists, by supporting Wallace's divisive campaign, were threatening a relationship with government and the Democratic party that CIO liberals had now come to regard as absolutely critical for the survival and prosperity of their unions.

This time, style meant less than substance. The antics of the leftist in the civil wars that wracked the CIO Councils were no more maniacal than those of their opponents. The only real alternative would have been for Communist unionists to dissuade the party's political leadership from coming out for Wallace. But, when it came to such major strategic decisions, the party's labor "influentials" played a remarkably small role.

But the forces on the other side, the liberals determined to excise communism from the CIO, were also single-minded and intransigent. The cold war and the Wallace candidacy had convinced them that communism, as Walter Reuther often said, was a cancer eating away at the CIO. Cutting it away would weaken the body but save the soul. Thus the Communist unionists and their fellow travellers were caught between inflexible root-and-branchers on both sides. If anything, the liberals were more Stalinist than the Stalinists. At least the party allowed most of its unions to refrain from pushing through official endorsements of Wallace. Murray and the CIO liberals would allow no such flexibility regarding Truman. The decision to support him had been made. Those who refused to go along with it were purged. Even George Meany did not try to deal so harshly with unions who opposed his support of American intervention in Vietnam in the late 1960s.

In the end, then, the Communists were destroyed for reasons that had little to do with their merits as trade unionists, Their destruction also had little to do with the nature of the American working class. They have been criticized, and often criticized themselves, for not "radicalizing" the working class, for not turning the mass of the members of their unions into Communists. Yet this is easier said than done. In the end, as good Marxists know, it takes much more than hard work, organization, the "correct application of Marxist-Leninist theory," and a well-disciplined "vanguard" party to bring about the radicalization of a working class. It takes a confluence of historical circumstances of a kind that were clearly missing in the United States, even the United States of the 1930s.

This does not mean, however, that the United States could not have developed a kind of socialist labor movement, that is, a large number of unions whose leaders supported socialist causes and played a socialist political role, representing union members who approved of them as union leaders but were indifferent to their politics. This was the hope of the Communists in unions: William Z. Foster's original plan was gradually to direct the workers towards socialism by demonstrating that Communists were good unionists who had their interests at heart.

It was not a bad idea. It is difficult to see how socialists could have operated in labor unions on any other basis. In the end, one does not impress millions of workers by haranguing them or handing out leaflets, but by making them feel that one is working in their interests. This is how leftists, rightists, or even gangsters have gained and retained control of unions throughout the world. Although the nature of the membership sets some outer limits on their actions, the leadership is often far from being a reflection of the membership.

This vision of leftist unionism is not one that most socialists would regard as ideal. Indeed, the Communists are often criticized for having had no sympathy for "worker control" of industry. (Their commitment to state control virtually excluded this.) In part, as a consequence, they were not particularly committed to building up strong shop floor organizations in unions, the kind of shop steward power that has played such a great role in British unionism. David Brody has suggested, persuasively, that the absence of this kind of power in the United States helped dissipate working class militancy during the Great Depression and allowed the rise of unions organized from the top down.[6] During the 1930s this cut both ways for the Communists, easing their way into control of some unions, blocking it in others. After the war, when they had to defend themselves against the combined onslaught of the state, business community, and their intra-union opponents, the Communists were weakened by the absence of strong Communist-led shop floor organizations in a number of unions. In the NMU and TWU, the switch of key leaders in crucial positions in the centralized power structure was enough to tilt the balance decisively against the Communists. In the more decentralized UAW, they were not finally eliminated until the Reuther machine was able to neutralize the power of shop stewards and individual locals. Perhaps it is no accident that the Communists survived in the one union that was perhaps the least amenable to coups from the top, the UE.

Yet, granted this weakness on the shop floor, it still remains that, had it not been for a unique set of historical circumstances, a kind of socialist unionism might have survived to play an important role in the United States. Although it would not have met every socialist's standards had it survived, it would most likely have changed. Most of the weaknesses of Communist unionism were attributable to its Leninism and Stalinism. Few of its successes were. Many of its union leaders were aggressive and individualistic and would have been increasingly secure in their own union bases. Had they remained in or allied with the party and had their unions not been destroyed, the internal balance of power in the party would certainly have changed. Increasingly independent, generally less Stalinist than Foster and his allies, they would likely have provided solid support for the group surrounding John Gates in the crucial struggle over the control and direction of the party that followed Stalin's death in 1953. The result may well have been, in 1956, the shift of the CPUSA towards what is now called a Eurocommunist position.[7] Had the shift been accomplished at that time by a party with a base of support in a number of important unions, the impact on American politics and international communism would surely have been great. Certainly the question "Why No Socialism in America?" would have had to be reformulated.

NOTES

1. Victor Reuther, *The Brothers Reuther* (Boston: Houghton Mifflin, 1976), 362.
2. E.g., see Sumner Rosen, "The CIO Era, 1935-1955," in Julius Jacobson, ed., *The Negro and the American Labor Movement* (New York: Anchor, 1968). Donald Critchlow has argued against generalizations regarding Communists and racism in the union movement by pointing out that the UE did not push Negro rights in the electrical industry during the war nearly as hard as did the NMU in the shipping industry. However, his explanation for the differences undermines his general argument, for he says that the root of the differences lay in the fact that the NMU was organized in the South and had a large number of black members, while the UE was practically nonexistent in the South and the proportion of blacks in the electrical maufacturing industry declined from only 5 percent in 1940 to 2.7 percent in 1945. The UE, with a larger female minority in its membership, expended more effort on gaining equality for them in the work place than on blacks, he says. In the light of this, the instances he cites of consistent support by the UE leadership for the FEPC, anti-poll tax, and other integrationist political measures as well as the examples of action by local and district level Communist UE leaders to fight for black employment rights, would seem to support the case that the UE was more active in this sphere than it would have been had it been led by ordinary "business unionists." The real comparison would be with non-Communist unions in similar spheres, perhaps the AFL's International Brotherhood of Electrical Workers. Yet even this is not as simple as it seems, as the case of the NMU illustrates. A comparison of the NMU with its West Coast counterpart, the Sailors Union of the Pacific which was notorious for its opposition to integration, might seem to lend support to the hypothesis that the difference was based solely on the different racial compositions of the unions and the work force, but this would ignore the role of the unions in shaping that composition. The West Coast seamen were almost all white, in part because non-whites could not acquire union cards. The NMU, on the other hand, welcomed and encouraged blacks to join. Moreover, to lump together the NMU's 10 percent black membership and the approximately 25 percent who were Spanish-speaking into a total "minority membership" of 35 percent and assume all to be in favor of black integration, as Critchlow does, is to ignore the historic divisions and antagonisms which often

divided black and Hispanic workers. Donald Critchlow, "Communist Unions and Racism," *Labor History*, vol. 17, no. 2 (spring 1976), 230-44.

3. See especially Len De Caux, *Labor Radical* (Boston: Beacon Press, 1970); James Prickett, "Communists and the Communist Issue in the American Labor Movement, 1920-1950" (Ph.D. diss., University of California at Los Angeles, 1975); and Frank Emspak, "The Break-Up of the Congress of Industrial Organizations (CIO), 1945-1950" (Ph.D. diss., University of Wisconsin, 1972), for this analysis.

4. See Charles Larrowe, *Harry Bridges: The Rise and Fall of Radical Labor in the United States* (N.Y.: Lawrence Hill, 1971).

5. See Prickett, "Communists," for an example of this argument.

6. David Brody, "Radical Labor History and Rank-and-File Militancy," *Labor History*, vol. 16, no. 1 (winter 1976), 117-26.

7. See Joseph Starobin, *American Communism in Crisis, 1943-1957* (Cambridge: Harvard University Press, 1972), and John Gates, *The Story of an American Communist* (New York: Thomas Nelson, 1958), for explorations into this kind of speculation.

BIBLIOGRAPHY

MANUSCRIPT COLLECTIONS

American Federation of Labor. Files of the Office of President. State Historical Society of Wisconsin. Madison, Wisconsin.

Association of Catholic Trade Unionists, Detroit Chapter. Papers. Wayne State University Archives of Labor History and Urban Affairs. Detroit, Michigan.

Bell, Daniel. Collection of Material on Socialism and Communism in the U.S.A. Tamiment Institute Library, New York University. New York, New York.

Blair, Fred. Papers. State Historical Society of Wisconsin. Madison, Wisconsin.

Block, Harry. Papers. Pennsylvania State University Archives of Labor History. State College, Pennsylvania.

Brophy, John. Papers. Catholic University of America Library. Washington, D.C.

Browder, Earl. Papers. George Arents Research Library, Syracuse University. Syracuse, New York.

Clancy, Father Raymond S. Papers. Wayne State University Archives of Labor History and Urban Affairs. Detroit, Michigan.

Congress of Industrial Organizations. Papers. Wayne State University Archives of Labor History and Urban Affairs. Detroit, Michigan.

————. Papers. Files of the Office of Secretary-Treasurer. Wayne State University Archives of Labor History and Urban Affairs. Detroit, Michigan.

————. Papers. Catholic University of America Library. Washington, D.C.

————, Washington Office. Papers. Wayne State University Archives of Labor History and Urban Affairs. Detroit, Michigan.

Frankensteen, Richard T. Papers. Wayne State University Archives of Labor History and Urban Affairs. Detroit, Michigan.

Frey, John P. Papers. Library of Congress. Washington, D.C.

Ganley, Nat. Papers. Wayne State University Archives of Labor History and Urban Affairs. Detroit, Michigan.

Germer, Adolph. Diaries. State Historical Society of Wisconsin. Madison, Wisconsin.

————. Papers. State Historical Society of Wisconsin. Madison, Wisconsin.

Kraus, Henry. Papers. Wayne State University Archives of Labor History and Urban Affairs. Detroit, Michigan.

Murray, Philip. Papers. Catholic University of America Library. Washington, D.C.

Reuther, Walter P. Papers. Wayne State University Archives of Labor History and Urban Affairs. Detroit, Michigan.

Rice, The Reverend Charles Owen. Papers. Pennsylvania State University Archives of Labor History. State College, Pennsylvania.
Roosevelt, Franklin D. Papers. Franklin D. Roosevelt Library. Hyde Park, New York.
Roosevelt, James. Papers. Franklin D. Roosevelt Library. Hyde Park, New York.
Taussig, Charles W. Papers. Franklin D. Roosevelt Library. Hyde Park, New York.
Thomas, Rolland J. Papers. Wayne State University Archives of Labor History and Urban Affairs. Detroit, Michigan.
United Automobile, Aircraft, and Agricultural Implement Workers of America. Records. Wayne State University Archives of Labor History and Urban Affairs. Detroit, Michigan.

ORAL HISTORY MEMOIRS

Addes, George. Wayne State University Archives of Labor History and Urban Affairs. Detroit, Michigan.
Anderson, John W. Wayne State University Archives of Labor History and Urban Affairs. Detroit, Michigan.
Block, Harry. Pennsylvania State University Archives of Labor History. State College, Pennsylvania.
Brophy, John. Oral History Collection of Columbia University. New York, New York.
Browder, Earl. Oral History Collection of Columbia University. New York, New York.
Carey, James. Oral History Collection of Columbia University. New York, New York.
Doll, Tracy. Wayne State University Archives of Labor History and Urban Affairs. Detroit, Michigan.
Edelman, Julius. Oral History Collection of Columbia University. New York, New York.
Emspak, Julius. Oral History Collection of Columbia University. New York, New York.
Fitzgerald, Albert. Pennsylvania University Archives of Labor History. State College, Pennsylvania.
Frey, John P. Oral History Collection of Columbia University. New York, New York.
Ganley, Nat. Wayne State University Archives of Labor History and Urban Affairs. Detroit, Michigan.
Haessler, Carl. Wayne State University Archives of Labor History and Urban Affairs. Detroit, Michigan.
Lahey, Edwin. Oral History Collection of Columbia University. New York, New York.
Leach, Russel. Wayne State University Archives of Labor History and Urban Affairs. Detroit, Michigan.
Leggat, Al. Wayne State University Archives of Labor History and Urban Affairs. Detroit, Michigan.
Matles, James. Pennsylvania State University Archives of Labor History. State College, Pennsylvania.
Perkins, Frances. Oral History Collection of Columbia University. New York, New York.
Potofsky, Jacob. Collection of Oral History of Columbia University. New York, New York.
Powers, Chase. Pennsylvania State University Archives of Labor History. State College, Pennsylvania.
Pressman, Lee. Oral History Collection of Columbia University. New York, New York.
Rice, The Reverend Charles Owen. Pennsylvania State University Archives of Labor History. State College, Pennsylvania.
Robinson, Reid. Pennsylvania State University Archives of Labor History. State College, Pennsylvania.

————; Powers, Chase; and McGuire, Tom, Joint interview. Pennsylvania State University Archives of Labor History. State College, Pennsylvania.

Wallace, Henry. Oral History Collection of Columbia University. New York, New York.

GOVERNMENT AND UNION DOCUMENTS

American Federation of Labor. *Proceedings of the Annual Convention*, 1937.

Association of Catholic Trade Unionists. *Proceedings of the National Convention*, 1956.

Communist International, Executive Committee. *Theses and Decisions of the Thirteenth Plenum*. London, Modern Books, n.d.

Communist International, Seventh Congress. *Abridged Stenographic Report of Proceedings*. Moscow, Foreign Languages Publishing House, 1939.

Congress of Industrial Organizations. *Daily Proceedings of the Constitutional Conventions*.

————. Hearings before the Committee to Investigate Charges against the American Communications Association, unpublished transcript of hearings held in Washington, D.C., commencing April 11, 1950.

————. Hearings before the Committee to Investigate Charges against the Food, Tobacco, Agricultural and Allied Workers of America, unpublished transcript of hearings held in Washington, D.C., commencing January 6, 1950.

————. Hearings before the Committee to Investigate Charges against the International Fishermen and Allied Workers of America, unpublished transcript of hearings held in Washington, D.C., commencing May 25, 1950.

————. Hearings before the Committee to Investigate Charges against the International Fur and Leather Workers Union, unpublished transcript of hearings held in Washington, D.C., commencing June 1, 1950.

————. Hearings before the Committee to Investigate Charges against the International Longshoremen and Warehousemen's Union, unpublished transcript of hearings held in Washington, D.C., commencing May 17, 1950.

————. *Official Reports on the Expulsion of Communist Dominated Organizations from the CIO*, CIO, Washington, D.C., 1954.

United Automobile Workers of America. *Proceedings of the Annual Conventions*, 1935-1941.

U.S., Congress, House, Committee on Education and Labor. *Investigation of Communist Infiltration of UERMWA*. Hearings before a Special Subcommittee, 80th Cong., 2nd sess., 1948.

————. *Jurisdictional Disputes in the Motion Picture Industry*. Hearings before a Special Subcommittee, 80th Cong., 2nd sess., 1948.

U.S., Congress, House, Special Committee on Un-American Activities. *Hearings*. 75th Cong., 2nd sess., 1938.

————. *Investigation of Un-American Propaganda Activities in the United States*. 77th Cong., 1st sess., 1941.

U.S., Congress, House, Committee on Un-American Activities. *Investigation of Un-American Propaganda Activities in the United States*. 77th Cong., 1st sess., 1941.

————. *Hearings Regarding Communism in Labor Unions*. 80th Cong., 1st sess., 1947.

————. *Hearings on Communist Infiltration of Labor Unions*. 81st Cong., 1st sess., 1949-1950.

————. *Hearings Regarding Communism in the United States Government*. 81st Cong., 2nd sess., 1950.

————. *Hearings Regarding Communist Infiltration in Hollywood*. 82nd Cong., 2nd sess., 1952.

————. *Colonization of Basic Industries by the Communist Party of the U.S.A.* Washington, USGPO, 1954.

————. *Hearings on Communist Methods of Infiltration (Entertainment).* 83rd Cong., 2nd sess., 1954.

————. *A Communist in a "Workers' Paradise," John Santo's Own Story.* Washington, USGPO, 1963.

U.S., Congress, Senate, Committee on Education and Labor. *Violations of Free Speech and the Rights of Labor.* Report pursuant to S. Res. 266, 76th Cong., Washington, USGPO, 1942.

U.S., Congress, Senate, Committee on the Judiciary, Subcommittee on Internal Security. *Hearings on Communist Domination of Union Officials in Vital Defense Industry— International Union of Mine, Mill, and Smelter Workers.* 82nd Cong., 2nd sess., 1952.

————. *Hearings on Communism in Labor Unions.* 83rd Cong., 2nd sess., 1954.

————. *Hearings on Communism in Labor Unions.* 85th Cong., 2nd sess., 1958.

U.S., Congress, Senate, Committee on Labor and Public Welfare. *Hearings on Communist Domination of Unions.* 82nd Cong., 2nd sess., 1952.

PERIODICALS

Actist Bulletin
America
American Mercury
Business Week
Catholic Action
Catholic Digest
Christian Social Action
CIO News
Cleveland *News*
Cleveland *Press*
Collier's
Commonweal
Communist
Current History and Forum
Daily Worker
Dispatcher
Fortune
Harper's
International Press Correspondence
Kansas City *Kansan*
Labor Action
Labor Herald
Labor Leader
Michigan Catholic
Milwaukee Sentinel

Nation, The
National Guardian
New Leader
New York *Daily Compass*
New York *Daily Mirror*
New York Herald Tribune
New York *Journal-American*
New York Times, The
Party Organizer
Plain Talk
Political Affairs
Reader's Digest
Rocky Mountain News
Saturday Evening Post
Schenectady Gazette
Time
Transport Bulletin
UE News
Union, The
Union Labor Report
United Auto Worker
U.S. News and World Report
Wage Earner
Washington Post, The

SECONDARY WORKS AND SCHOLARLY ARTICLES

Abella, Irving. *Nationalism, Communism, and Canadian Labour.* Toronto: University of Toronto Press, 1973.

Agee, Philip. *Inside the Company: CIA Diary.* Harmondsworth: Penguin, 1975.

Alinsky, Saul. *John L. Lewis.* New York: Knopf, Vintage Books, 1970.

Auerbach, Jerold S. *Labor and Liberty. The La Follette Committee and the New Deal.* Indianapolis: Bobbs-Merrill, 1966.

Bell, Daniel. "Labor in Post-Industrial Society." *Dissent,* winter 1972.

———. *Marxian Socialism in the United States.* Princeton, N.J.: Princeton University Press, 1967.

Bernstein, Barton. "Walter Reuther and the GM Strike of 1945-46." *Michigan History,* September 1965.

Bernstein, Irving. *The Lean Years.* Boston: Houghton Mifflin, 1960.

———. *Turbulent Years: A History of the American Worker, 1933-1941.* Boston: Houghton Mifflin, 1970.

Biddle, Francis. *In Brief Authority.* New York: Viking Press, 1962.

Boyer, Richard O., and Morais, Herbert M. *Labor's Untold Story.* 3rd ed., New York: United Electrical Workers, 1973.

Bridges-Robertson-Schmidt Defense Committee. *The Law and Harry Bridges.* San Francisco: n.p., 1952.

Brody, David. *The Butcher Workmen.* Cambridge: Harvard University Press, 1964.

———. "Radical Labor History and Rank-and-File Militancy." *Labor History,* vol. 16, no. 1 (winter 1975).

Brophy, John. *A Miner's Life.* Madison: University of Wisconsin Press, 1964.

———. "Twenty Years with CIO." Unpublished manuscript in John Brophy Papers, Box A5-41, Catholic University of America, Washington, D.C.

Browder, Earl. *The Decline of the Left Wing of American Labor.* New York: the author, 1948.

———. *Tehran and America.* New York: International Publishers, 1944.

———. *Victory and After.* New York: International Publishers, 1942.

Bubka, Tony. "The Harlan County Strike of 1931." *Labor History,* 11 (winter 1970).

Cary, Lorin. "Adolph Germer, From Labor Agitator to Labor Professional." Ph.D. dissertation, University of Wisconsin, 1968.

———. "Institutionalized Conservatism in the Early CIO: Adolph Germer, A Case Study." *Labor History,* vol. 13, no. 4 (fall 1972).

Caute, David. *The Great Fear.* London: Secker and Warburg, 1978.

Cayton, Horace R., and Mitchell, George S. *Black Workers and the New Unions.* Durham: University of North Carolina Press, 1939.

Chamber of Commerce of the United States. *Communism: Where Do We Stand Today?* Washington, D.C.: Chamber of Commerce, 1952.

———. *Communist Infiltration in the United States.* Washington, D.C.: Chamber of Commerce, 1946.

Chinoy, Ely. "The Tradition of Opportunity and the Aspirations of Automobile Workers." *American Journal of Sociology,* 57 (March 1952).

Cochran, Bert. *Labor and Communism.* Princeton: Princeton University Press, 1977.

Conlin, Joseph, ed. *The American Radical Press.* 2 vols. Westport, Ct.: Greenwood Press, 1973.

Cormier, Frank, and Eaton, William J. *Reuther.* Englewood Cliffs, N.J.: Prentice-Hall, 1971.

Critchlow, Donald. "Communist Unions and Racism." *Labor History,* vol. 17, no. 2 (Spring 1976).

Dahrendorf, Ralf. *Class and Class Conflict in Industrial Society.* Stanford: Stanford University Press, 1959.

Danish, Max D. *The World of David Dubinsky.* Cleveland: World, 1957.

De Caux, Len. *Labor Radical.* Boston: Beacon, 1970.

Derber, Milton, and Young, Edwin, eds. *Labor and the New Deal.* Madison: University of Wisconsin Press, 1961.

Dimitrov, Georgi. *Working Class Unity—Bulwark Against Fascism*. New York: Workers Library, 1935.

Draper, Theodore. *American Communism and Soviet Russia*. New York: Viking, 1960.

————. "Communists and Miners, 1928-1933," *Dissent*, 19 (spring 1971).

————. *The Roots of American Communism*. New York: Compass Books, 1963.

Dubofsky, Melvin, and Van Tine, Warren. *John L. Lewis*. New York: Quadrangle, 1977.

Emspak, Frank. "The Association of Catholic Trade Unionists and the United Automobile Workers," M.A. thesis, University of Wisconsin, 1968.

————. "The Break-Up of the Congress of Industrial Organizations (CIO), 1945-1950." Ph.D. dissertation, University of Wisconsin, 1972.

Epstein, Melech. *Jewish Labor in the U.S.A.* New York: Ktav Publishing, 1969.

Fine, Sidney. *Automobile Under the Blue Eagle*. Ann Arbor: University of Michigan Press, 1963.

————. *Sit-Down*. Ann Arbor: University of Michigan Press, 1969.

Foner, Philip. *The Fur and Leather Workers Union*. Newark: Nordan Press, 1950.

Form, William H. "Job Unionism vs. Political Unionism in Four Countries." In *The American Working Class in the 1980s*. Edited by Irving Louis Horowitz et al. New Brunswick: Transaction Books, 1979.

Foster, James C. *The Union Politic. The CIO Political Action Committee*. Columbia: University of Missouri Press, 1975.

Foster, William Z. *American Trade Unionism*. New York: International Publishers, 1947.

————. *From Bryan to Stalin*. New York: International Publishers, 1937.

————. *The History of the Communist Party of the United States*. New York: International Publishers, 1952.

Fountain, Clayton. *Union Guy*. New York: Viking, 1949.

Freeland, Richard. *The Truman Doctrine and the Origins of McCarthyism*. New York: Knopf, 1972.

Freeman, James M. *No Friend of Labor*. New York: Pathfinder, 1948.

Friedman, Michael, ed. "Recorded Time: The Story of an American Family. Junius, Gladys, and Barbara Scales, 1920-1973." Unpublished ms. in possession of Mr. Friedman.

Galenson, Walter. *The CIO Challenge to the AFL*. Cambridge: Harvard University Press, 1960.

Gallup, George. *The Gallup Poll: Public Opinion, 1935-1971*. New York: Random House, 1975.

Gates, John. *The Story of an American Communist*. New York: Thomas Nelson, 1958.

Gitlow, Benjamin. *I Confess: The Truth About American Communism*. New York: Dutton, 1939.

Glazer, Nathan. *The Social Basis of American Communism*. New York: Harcourt Brace, 1961.

Goodman, Walter. *The Committee*. New York: Farrar, Straus and Giroux, 1968.

Gould, Jean, and Hickock, Lorena. *Walter Reuther, Labor's Rugged Individualist*. New York: Dodd, Mead, 1973.

Green, James. "Fighting on Two Fronts: Working Class Militancy in the 1940's." *Radical America*, vol. 9, nos. 4-5 (July-August 1975).

————. "Working Class Militancy in the Depression." *Radical America*, vol. 6, no. 6. (November-December 1972).

Grubbs, Donald H. *Cry from the Cotton*. Chapel Hill: University of North Carolina Press, 1971.

Hall, Burton K., ed. *Autocracy and Insurgency in American Labor*. New Brunswick: Transaction Books, 1972.

Hamby, Alonzo L. *Harry Truman and American Liberalism*. New York: Columbia University Press, 1973.

Hamilton, Richard F. "The Behavior and Values of Skilled Workers." In *Blue Collar World*. Edited by Arthur B. Shostak and William Gomberg. Englewood Cliffs, N.J.: Prentice-Hall, 1964.

Harrington, Michael. "Catholics in the Labor Movement." *Labor History*, vol. 1, no. 2 (fall 1960).

Hawes, Elizabeth. *Hurry Up Please, It's Time*. New York: Reynal and Hitchcock, 1946.

Howe, Irving. *The Immigrant Jews of New York*. London: Routledge, Kegan and Paul, 1976. (British edition of *World of Our Fathers*.)

———, and Widick, B. J., *The UAW and Walter Reuther*. New York: Random House, 1949.

Ickes, Harold. *The Secret Diary of Harold Ickes*. 3 vols. New York: Simon and Schuster, 1952-1955.

Jacobs, Paul. *Is Curly Jewish?* New York: Atheneum, 1966.

Jacobson, Julius. *The Negro and the American Labor Movement*. New York: Anchor, 1968.

Jaffe, Philip. *The Rise and Fall of American Communism*. New York: Horizon Press, 1975.

———. "The Rise and Fall of Earl Browder." *Survey*, spring 1972.

Jensen, Vernon. *Lumber and Labor*. New York: Rinehart, 1945.

———. *Nonferrous Metals Industry Unionism, 1932-1952: A Story of Leadership Controversy*. Ithaca: Cornell University Press, 1954.

Johannesen, Edward. *The Hawaiian Labor Movement: A Brief History*. Boston: Bruce Humphries, 1956.

Josephson, Matthew. *Sidney Hillman, Statesman of American Labor*. Garden City, N.Y.: Doubleday, 1952.

Kampelman, Max. *The Communist Party vs. the CIO*. New York: Praeger, 1957.

Keeran, Roger R. "Communists and Auto Workers: The Struggle for a Union, 1919-1941." Ph.D. dissertation, University of Wisconsin, 1974.

Kempton, Murray. *Part of Our Time*. New York: Simon and Schuster, 1955.

Koistinen, Paul. "The Hammer and the Sword: Labor, the Military, and Industrial Mobilization." Ph.D. dissertation, University of California at Berkeley, 1965.

Kraus, Henry. *The Many and the Few: A Chronicle of the Dynamic Auto Workers*. Los Angeles: Plantin Press, 1947.

Larrowe, Charles. *Harry Bridges: The Rise and Fall of Radical Labor in the United States*. New York: Lawrence Hill, 1972.

Lash, Joseph P. *Eleanor and Franklin*. New York: New American Library, 1973.

Lasky, Victor. "Red Wedge in Hawaii." *Plain Talk*, May 1948.

Laslett, John. *Labor and the Left*. New York: Basic Books, 1970.

———, and Lipset, Seymour M., eds. *Failure of a Dream?* New York: Anchor, 1974.

Legget, John. *Class, Race, and Labor, Working-class Consciousness in Detroit*. New York: Oxford University Press, 1968.

———. "Sources and Consequences of Working-class Consciousness." In *Blue-Collar World*. Edited by Arthur Shostak and William Gomberg. Englewood Cliffs: Prentice-Hall, 1964.

Leiter, Robert. "The Fur Workers Union." *Industrial and Labor Relations Review*, June 1950.

Lens, Sidney. *The Labor Wars*. New York: Doubleday, 1973.

———. *Left Right and Center*. Hindsdale: Regnery, 1949.

———. *Radicalism in America*. New York: Crowell, 1969.

Levenstein, Aaron. *Labor, Today and Tomorrow*, New York: Knopf, 1946.

Levenstein, Harvey. *Labor Organizations in the United States and Mexico: A History of Their Relations*. Westport, Ct.: Greenwood Press, 1971.

Levinson, Edward. *Labor on the March*. New York: n.p., 1939.

Lichtenstein, Nelson. "Defending the No-Strike Pledge: CIO Politics During World War II." *Radical America*, vol. 9, nos. 4-5 (July-August 1975).

——. "Industrial Unionism under the No-Strike Pledge: A Study of the CIO during the Second World War." Ph.d. dissertation, University of California at Berkeley, 1974.

Lipset, Seymour Martin. *Revolution and Counter-revolution. Change and Persistence in Social Structures.* Garden City: Doubleday Anchor, 1970.

——. "Why No Socialism in the United States?" In Seweryn Bailer and Sophia Sluzar, eds., *Sources of Contemporary Radicalism.* New York: Westview Pres, 1977.

Lynd, Staughton. "The Possibility of Radicalism in the Early 1930's: The Case of Steel." *Radical America*, vol. 6, no. 6 (November-December 1972).

——, and Lynd, Alice. *Rank and File.* Boston: Beacon, 1973.

McClure, Arthur F. *The Truman Administration and the Problems of Postwar Labor, 1945-1948.* Rutherford: Fairleigh Dickinson University Press, 1969.

MacDougall, Curtis D. *Gideon's Army.* New York: Marzani and Munsell, 1965.

McFarland, Dalton E. "Left-Wing Domination of Labor Unions: A Case Study of Local Union Leadership." *ILR Research*, vol. 1, no. 1 (June 1955).

McWilliams, Carey. *Factories in the Fields.* Philadelphia: Lippincott, 1939.

Madison, Charles. *American Labor Leaders.* New York: Harper, 1950.

Markowitz, Norman. *The Rise and Fall of the People's Century: Henry A. Wallace and American Liberalism.* New York: The Free Press, 1973.

Matles, James, and Higgins, James. *Them and Us.* New York: Prentice-Hall, 1974.

Miller, S. M., and Riessman, Frank. "Are Workers Middle Class?" *Dissent*, autumn 1961.

——. "Working-Class Authoritarianism: A Critique of Lipset." *British Journal of Sociology*, September 1961.

——. "The Working-Class Subculture: A New View." In *Blue Collar World.* Edited by Arthur B. Shostak and William Gomberg. Englewood Cliffs: Prentice-Hall, 1964.

Millis, Walter, ed. *The Forrestal Diaries.* New York: Viking, 1951.

Mills, C. Wright. *The New Men of Power, America's Labor Leaders.* New York: Harcourt, Brace, 1948.

Mitford, Jessica. *A Fine Old Conflict.* London: Michael Joseph, 1977.

Mortimer, Wyndham. *Organize! My Life as a Union Man.* Boston: Beacon Press, 1971.

Mulloy, Sister M. Camilla. "John Brophy, Militant Labor Leader and Reformer: The CIO Years." Ph.D. dissertation, Catholic University of America, 1966.

O'Brien, F. S. "Communist-Dominated Unions in the U.S. Since 1950." *Labor History*, vol. 9, no. 2 (spring 1968).

Ozanne, Robert. "The Effects of Communist Leadership on American Trade Unions." Ph.D. dissertation, University of Wisconsin, 1954.

Preis, Art. *Labor's Giant Step. Twenty Years of the CIO.* New York: Pioneer, 1964.

Prickett, James R. "Communism and Factionalism in the United Automobile Workers, 1939-1947." *Science and Society*, vol. 32 (summer 1968).

——. "Communists and the Communist Issue in the American Labor Movement, 1920-1950." Ph.d. dissertation, University of California at Los Angeles, 1975.

——. "Some Aspects of the Communist Controversy in the CIO." *Science and Society*, vol. 33 (summer-fall, 1969).

Radosh, Ronald. *American Labor and United States Foreign Policy.* New York: Random House, 1969.

Record, Jane C. "The Rise and Fall of a Maritime Union." *Industrial and Labor Relations Review*, 10 (October 1956).

Record, Wilson. *The Negro and the Communist Party.* Chapel Hill: University of North Carolina Press, 1951.

Reisler, Mark. *By the Sweat of Their Brow. Mexican Immigrant Labor in the United States, 1910-1940.* Westport and London: Greenwood, 1976.

Reuther, Victor. *The Brothers Reuther.* Boston: Houghton Mifflin, 1976.

Rice, The Reverend Charles Owen. *How to Decontrol Your Union of Communists*. N.p., 1948.

Richmond, Al. *A Long View from the Left*. Boston: Houghton Mifflin, 1973.

Rosenstone, Robert. *Romantic Revolutionary: A Biography of John Reed*. New York: Knopf, 1975.

Ross, Hugh. "John L. Lewis and the Election of 1940." *Labor History*, vol. 17, no. 2 (spring 1976).

Ross, Murray. *Stars and Strikes. Unionization in Hollywood*. New York: Columbia University Press, 1949.

Saposs, David J. *Communism in American Unions*. New York: McGraw-Hill, 1959.

Seidman, Joel. *Communism in the United States—A Bibliography*. Ithaca: Cornell University Press, 1969.

———. "Labor Policy of the Communist Party during World War II." *Industrial and Labor Relations Review*, vol. 4, no. 10, October 1950.

Shannon, David A. *The Decline of American Communism*. New York: Harcourt, Brace and Co., 1959.

Starobin, Joseph F. *American Communism in Crisis, 1943-1957*. Cambridge: Harvard University Press, 1972.

Stolberg, Benjamin. *The Story of the CIO*. New York: Viking, 1938.

———. *Tailor's Progress*. Garden City: Doubleday, 1944.

Swados, Harvey. *Radical at Large*. London: Rupert Hart-Davis, 1968.

Taft, Philip. *The AFL from the Death of Gompers to the Merger*. New York: Harper, 1959.

———. "The Association of Catholic Trade Unionists." *Industrial and Labor Relations Review*, 11 January 1949.

———. "Some Problems of the New Unionism in the United States." *American Economic Review*, 29 June 1939.

Trumbo, Dalton. *Harry Bridges*. Hollywood: League of American Writers, 1941.

Ward, Estolv E. *Harry Bridges on Trial*. New York: Modern Age, 1940.

Ward, Richard J. "The Role of the Association of Catholic Trade Unionists in the American Labor Movement." Ph.D. dissertation, University of Michigan, 1958.

Wechsler, James A. *Labor Baron: A Portrait of John L. Lewis*. New York: William Morrow, 1944.

Weinberg, Jules. "Priests, Workers, and Communists." *Harper's Magazine*, November 1948.

Weinstein, James. *The Decline of Socialism in America*. New York. New York: Monthly Review Press, 1967.

Weisbord, Vera Buch. *A Radical Life*. Bloomington: Indiana University Press, 1977.

Whittemore, L. H. *The Man Who Ran the Subways: The Story of Mike Quill*. New York: Holt, Rinehart and Winston, 1960.

Whitty, Michael D. "Emil Mazey: Radical as Liberal. The Evolution of Labor Radicalism in the UAW." Ph.D. dissertation, Syracuse University, 1968.

Williamson, John. *Dangerous Scot*. New York: International Publishers, 1969.

INDEX

About the Author

HARVEY LEVENSTEIN is associate professor of history at McMaster University in Hamilton, Ontario. He is the author of *Labor Organizations in the United States and Mexico* (Greenwood Press, 1971), in addition to various articles on labor, politics, and the social history of American food in scholarly journals.